CW00552484

The Convent of the Incarnation (Avila)

Saint
Teresa
of Avila

Marcelle Auclair
TRANSLATED BY KATHLEEN POND

With a Preface by
André Maurois

ST. BEDE'S PUBLICATIONS
Petersham, Massachusetts

Nihil Obstat: Charles Davis, S.T.L.
          Censor Deputatus
Imprimatur: E. Morrogh Bernard
          Vicar General

Westminster
April 5, 1952

Photographs on cover and throughout book by M. Prado Photographers
Salamanca, Spain

LIBRARY OF CONGRESS CATALOGING-IN-PUBLICATION DATA

Auclair, Marcelle, 1899-
  [Vie de sainte Thérèse d'Avila.   English]
  Saint Teresa of Avila / by Marcelle Auclair : with a preface by André
Maurois : translated by Kathleen Pond.
    p. cm.
  Translation of: La vie de sainte Thérèse d'Avila.
  Reprint. Originally published: New York : Pantheon, 1953.
  Bibliography p.
  Includes index.
  ISBN 0-932506-67-4
  1. Teresa, of Avila, Saint. 1515-1582.   2. Christian saints—Spain
—Avila—Biography.   3. Avila (Spain)—Biography.   I. Title.
BX4700.T4A813   1988
282'.092'4—dc 19
[B]   88-18591
                                                              CIP

Published by St. Bede's Publications
          P.O. Box 545
          Petersham, Massachusetts 01366-0545

PREFACE

"OUR thinking, indeed the way we work out our salvation, is by the devoted imitation of moments (in other lives) we know to be sublime. Such is, and always has been, the cult of the dead." For Ignatius of Loyola, to read the *Lives of the Saints* was a preparation for sanctity.

But a well-written life, said Carlyle, is even rarer than a well-spent one. The biographer who attempts to promote the cult of the great dead must be in a state of grace. If he did not feel the greatness of his subject how could the book he writes be great?

I was thinking about what is required for a biography—a literary genre which England justly honours—as I read Marcelle Auclair's excellent, indeed admirable book on *St. Teresa of Ávila*. Here was an occasion for meditating on the rules of the genre and on the attitude of the biographer.

Why did Marcelle Auclair choose St. Teresa for her subject? It was no casual choice that led her to write the book, nor the request of a publisher, nor the discovery of new documents. No, it was a desire conceived in her youth and accomplished in the strength of a maturing talent.

When quite a child she kept the selected works of St. Teresa at her bedside. As a girl she took as her motto this maxim of the saint's: "*Let us risk our life*—he who saves his life will lose it." At the time of the evacuation of Paris in 1940, St. Teresa's *Works* were the only books Marcelle Auclair took away with her and in the tragic circumstances of that time she made a vow to translate the *Fundaciones*.

For—and this is a second important point—by her culture and education Marcelle Auclair is as much Spanish as French. Her father, a French architect, went to work in Chile when she was a child, so that she was brought up in an atmosphere which was that of sixteenth-century Spain. To-day Chile is one of the most modern of South American countries. Then the great colonial families were still living in practically the same way as Teresa de Ahumada y Cepeda had lived in her distinguished home at Ávila.

v

In Chile, Marcelle Auclair came into personal contact with people whose daily lives were permeated with their faith; she saw the enormous crucifixes which hung even in drawing-rooms to recall the sufferings of Christ; in the evenings she attended family prayers with the whole household. That is why, when she studied the saint's youth, she did not feel she entered an alien atmosphere.

A biographer of talent can reconstruct a particular milieu: he will do this still more successfully if he finds the elements of it within himself. If neither Rastignac's ambition nor the bankruptcy of David Séchard had formed part of Balzac's personal experience, would he have been Balzac as we know him?

I am fully aware that certain biographers, Lytton Strachey among them, have maintained that the best biographies have been written by authors who were at daggers drawn with their subjects. It seems at first as if the perfect life of *Queen Victoria* from his own pen proves him right. But, as a great English historian once observed, the most remarkable thing is not that Strachey should have written the life of Queen Victoria, but that Queen Victoria should have conquered Lytton Strachey. He began the book scoffing, he finished it in admiration, and it was to this involuntary respect that he owed the perfection, beauty and poetry of his work.

Marcelle Auclair began by admiring her heroine and ended by loving her. For the charm of St. Teresa is irresistible. In the beginning that charm was merely the ardour and gracious attractiveness of a Spanish girl of good family. "She had always been the most beautiful and the one people loved most: they spoke with pride of her taste, her cleverness, her wit, her gifts as a young writer; they remarked what a graceful dancer she was, how good at chess, how bold a horsewoman. Of a piece of embroidery she made a work of art; and she made the family dinner as exciting as a firework display. In Ávila, people said: 'Teresa de Ahumada? She will marry whomsoever she pleases'."

And then this exacting person, full of the Spanish "point of honour," discovered that human love would not satisfy her. Yet "she seemed so much the less fitted for sanctity as she was very well fitted for worldly success; and in her own view was riddled with faults that were contradictory: proud, but frivolous, domineering but easily influenced; she speaks of her excessive dissimulation and of her horror of a lie, of her love of pleasing people which yet did not restrain her quick temper," and of her wretched self-love. A saint she indeed became, but by force of will.

Will—that is one of her two fundamental characteristics: the second is simplicity. "All is nothing, the world is vanity, life is short; I decided to force myself to enter the convent." Here Teresa pronounced for the first time the word she was to repeat more frequently than any other: *determinación*, decision. "I decided . . . it is tremendously important to begin with great determination. . . . The soul that begins with determination has already travelled a great part of the way. . . ." Here, philosopher and saint meet. "Happiness is by an act of will," said Descartes.

Simplicity—for me, what drew me to her heroine long before I had read Marcelle Auclair, were the wonderful things St. Teresa said about the sanctity of everyday life. "The Lord is to be found among the pots and pans." To be heroic in the face of danger is not the most difficult of achievements; then the greatness of the circumstances temporarily arouses the will. But to be perfect each day, in humble ways, to do well what one does, to treat all those with whom we work with a sense of equality, even with love, there is sanctity indeed. When she was dying, St. Teresa said it once more: "My daughters and ladies, for the love of God I ask you to keep the Rule well; if you keep it in every particular, no further miracle will be needed for your canonisation."

What is so good about this biography is that the writer has succeeded in bringing out the saint without eliminating the woman. And although her book is heavily documented, she does not overwhelm the reader with references. The author has read everything, but she has digested it all and incorporated it into the narrative. Marcelle Auclair has visited all the Carmels founded by her heroine. That, too, was necessary. A house, a countryside, make a living thing of the abstract phantom which rises from the dusty pages. How can George Sand be brought to mind if one has not seen Nohant, or Chateaubriand if we neglect Combourg, or Byron without retracing the steps of Childe Harold's pilgrimage? In the Carmels founded by the saint, life goes on as it did in the sixteenth century. A piece of linen still does duty for window-glass. The chant is the same as it was then and the young nuns gave a friendly reception to her who, like themselves, better perhaps, knew their foundress.

Finally a word must be said of the effect of this biography both on biographer and reader. One cannot live with a saint without coming closer to sanctity. Marcelle Auclair has spared us any exhortation or commentary of her own. It was not a sermon she set out to write but a work of art. Every work of art is a sign; one does not know of what, and in that lies its attraction. Just as, in a beautiful statue of Chartres cathedral each man finds his own truth, I have discovered most precious truths in looking at this portrait of a saint which has been painted by Marcelle Auclair with loving devotion. It is now for the reader to seek his truth there too.

ANDRÉ MAUROIS.

TRANSLATOR'S NOTE

IT has been said, by St. Thomas Aquinas, that the mark of a good translation is that it should faithfully represent the thought of the original, expressing it in the idiom of the language in which the translation is being made. Such has been the principle which has guided this translation of Marcelle Auclair's *La Vie de Sainte Thérèse d'Avila*, though one cannot hope to have succeeded as well as one would have wished to do, and quotations from the Spanish have therefore been re-translated from the original wherever it has been possible to trace the reference.

I should like to thank the friends who have given me advice and help, particularly the Rev. J. D. Crichton for his kindness in reading part of the manuscript and Mr. J. G. B. Gosling for assistance in reading proofs.

KATHLEEN POND.

CONTENTS

List of Illustrations

All photographs by M. Prado, Photographer
Salamanca, Spain
except that facing page 173

LIST OF ABBREVIATIONS
USED IN THE NOTES

CAPITAL letters are used for the writings of St. Teresa herself. For these, I have kept the abbreviations used by P. Luis de San José in his *Concordancias* (Ed. Monte Carmelo, Burgos), an alphabetical index of persons and subjects in the saint's *Works*.

A	Avisos (Counsels)
AB	Ana de San Bartolomé
AJ	Ana de Jesús
AT	Año Teresiano
B	Bollandists
BA	Baruzi
BG	Baltasar Gracián
BL	Bernardino de Laredo
BM	Bremond
BN	Báñez
BR	P. Bruno de Jesús María
BRE	Id., *Espagne Mystique*
BRJ	Id., *Saint Jean de la Croix*
C	CAMINO DE PERFECCIÓN (Way of Perfection)
c	chapter
CAD	CONCEPTOS DEL AMOR DE DIOS (Conceptions of the Love of God)
CC	Canticle of Canticles
CH	*Vie de la vénérable Mère Anne de Saint-Barthélémy*
CONS	CONSTITUCIONES (Constitutions)
CP	Carmelites of Paris
CTA	CARTAS (Letters)
DE	DESAFÍO ESPIRITUAL (Spiritual Challenge)
E	EXCLAMACIONES (Exclamations of the Soul to God)
EM	P. Emeterio de Jesús María, *Ensayo sobre la lírica Carmelitana*
F	FUNDACIONES (Foundations)
FR	Francisco Ribera
GJ	Fr. Gabriel de Jesús
H	Hoornaert
HC	*Historia del Carmel*
IB	Pedro Ibañez
JA	Julian de Ávila
JC	St. John of the Cross
JCC	Id., *Cántico espiritual* (Spiritual Canticle)
JCS	Id., *Subida* (Ascent of Mount Carmel)

JJ	Jerónimo de San José
JG	Jerónimo Gracián de la Madre de Dios
JGC	Id., *Crónica*
JGD	Id., *Dilucidario del verdadero espíritu*
JGM	Id., *Diálogo sobre la muerte*
JGP	Id., *Peregrinaciones de Anastasio*
L	book
LA	La Puente
LL	Fray Luis de León
LO	Llorente
LV	Leo Van Hove
M	LAS MORADAS (The Interior Castle)
MA	Gregorio Marañon
MC	Editions Monte Carmelo, Burgos
MCH	Malón de Chaide
MF	María de San Francisco
MJ	María de San José
MJE	María de San Jerónimo
MJR	Id., *Recreaciones*
MN	Muñoz, *Vida de Fray Luis de Granada*
MP	María Pinel
MVC	MODO DE VISITAR LOS CONVENTOS (Visitation of Convents)
n.	note
O	Osuna, *Abecedario*, Ed. Ribadeneira
p.	page
P	POESÍAS (Poems)
PA	San Pedro de Alcántara
PB	Process of Beatification
PC	Process of Canonization
PP	Pedro de la Purificación
PS	PENSAMIENTOS Y SENTENCIAS (Thoughts and Maxims)
PT	Anon: *Les Parents de Ste. Thérèse*
R	RELACIONES (Relations)
RD	Francisco de Santa María, *Reforma de Descalzos*
RO	F. de Ros, *Osuna*
Sb	Shorter edition of the Works of St. Teresa (P. Silverio de Santa Teresa)
XC	Schneider
SEC	Critical edition of the Works of St. Teresa (P. Silverio de Santa Teresa)
SST	P. Silverio de Santa Teresa, *Vida de Santa Teresa*
TC	Teresa de Cepeda
V	VIDA (Autobiography)
VA	Valbuena Prat

VEJ	VEJAMEN
VH	Vicente B. de Heredia
Y	Diego de Yepes

References without an author's name are quotations from St. Teresa. Footnotes (other than references) are the author's, unless they are marked Tr. (translator).

PART ONE

THE WORLD? OR GOD?

'All the things of God gave me great pleasure,
but I was held captive by those of the world.'

St Teresa of Jesus: *Autobiography*, c. vii

I

GLORY

ON Wednesday, the twenty-eighth day of the month of March of the year 1515, about half an hour after five o'clock in the morning, with the first glimmers of the light of day, Teresa, my daughter, was born,'[1] wrote Don Alonso Sánchez y Cepeda.

The early angelus began to ring out from the church of Santo Domingo; then all the bells of Ávila, San Juan, San Pedro, San Isidro and San Pelayo, San Gil, San Bartolomé, San Vicente, Santa Cruz, San Cebrián, San Nicolás, Santiago, San Román, Mosen Rubí, the cathedral, the convents, from the Benedictines across to the Carmelite fathers, from the Poor Clares over to the Augustinian nuns of Our Lady of Grace, from the Franciscan sisters back again to the Dominican friars of Santo Tomás, from the Cistercians, men and women, at Santa Escolástica, San Millán, Santa Ana, to the Dominican nuns of Santa Catalina, the old stones gave back the echo of the bronze voices of all the saints of the city: for in Ávila there is nothing but saints and stones, 'en Ávila, Santos y cantos.'

On the 4th April, the godfather and godmother of little Teresa asked, in her name, for 'faith and life everlasting' in the parish church of San Juan.

That very day saw the inauguration of the convent of the Incarnation, a house of Carmelite nuns of Mitigated observance: already the door of God's house into which he who was baptizing her 'in the name of the Father, and of the Son, and of the Holy Ghost' was inviting her to enter, was opening.

The child received the Christian name of her maternal grandmother, Doña Teresa de las Cuevas, who, great lady of Castile as she was, could not sign her name. The godfather, Don Francisco Núñez Vela, was a man who thought of nothing but going overseas. It was the dawn of a new era. Scarcely twenty years had passed since Christopher Columbus offered King Ferdinand and Queen Isabella the Catholic, dominion over a continent. Spain was like a caravel dancing on the open seas; Spanish hearts, looking towards the west where these promised lands blazed in splendour, swelled with a feeling of possession.

[1] SEC, vol. II, p. 91.

Don Alonso Sánchez y Cepeda was a man of tradition but also a man of progress. In his library, *Conquest beyond the Seas*, on parchment, had a place beside *The Life of Christ in Pictures*, Guzmán's *Treatise on the Mass*, Boethius' *Consolations of Philosophy*. Having a great respect for books and knowledge himself, he was resolved that his children should know how to spell from their tenderest years and to read before they were seven.

His appearance inspired respect in all who knew him, everything about him gave evidence of his noble birth and dignity of character. He was known as a man of great integrity both in morals and manners, patient and good, very devout, and so compassionate in his ways that although it was considered proper for persons of his rank to have a few slaves, he always refused to do so, and a little Moorish girl whom one of his brothers confided to his care for a certain time was treated by him like one of his own daughters. His conversation was about God, or about the wars in Flanders or in Italy; for him progress in the Indies was measured by the number of souls saved there. He went about, his sword at his side, his rosary within his hand's grasp, administered his Gotarrendura estates himself and saw to it that there was sufficient corn, meat, poultry, vegetables and fruit to provide for the needs of a vast household. Over and above this he had no ambitions and every occasion offered him of increasing his fortune he neglected.

A native of Toledo he bore two great names: Sánchez, illustrious in Castile, Aragón and Navarre; Cepeda, made glorious by Don Vasco Vásquez de Cepeda, lord of that place, who was with Alfonso XI, the Redresser of Wrongs, at the siege of Gibraltar. He was thus an important personage in Ávila, where he passed for a very rich man. On the death of his first wife, Doña Catalina del Peso y Henao, ten years or so before Teresita's birth, he was possessed of 374,000 maravedis, magnificent estates, great flocks and herds, houses and an abundance of jewels. He loved splendour, and his violet damask or crimson satin doublets, shirts embroidered in scarlet and gold, ruffs from Paris, gilt swords with black velvet scabbards and gilded belts, red and yellow saddlecloths from Rouen, the breastplates with his armorial bearings, helmets, gauntlets, steel shoes, all showed that this gentleman-at-arms was not disdainful of fine apparel.

His widowerhood after three years of marriage made him melancholy, but when in 1509—he was nearly thirty—he married Doña Beatriz de Ahumada, as beautiful as she was of high birth and perhaps younger than was altogether fitting—she was fourteen—he strove hard to please her by his display of magnificence. She belonged indeed to that branch of the Dávilas with the thirteen roundels which considered itself the finest flower of the nobility of Castile and looked down upon the other Dávilas whose escutcheon only carried six roundels. The wedding took place at Gotarrendura and with so much magnificence that years afterwards people still talked of its splendour: the bride, 'very richly attired in silk and gold,' was thought to be all the lovelier and more dazzling for her frail appearance.

The Ahumadas owed their name to a feat of arms and to a miracle. Don Fernando, fighting the Moors, had been surrounded and cut off, with his three sons, in a tower which the enemy set on fire: God willed it that the denseness of the smoke should conceal the escape and flight of the besieged. From this day forward, Fernando was named Ahumada from *humo*, smoke; and the king of Castile allowed him to crown his armorial bearings with a tower surrounded by flames.

In her new home Doña Beatriz found a boy and girl.[1] The following year her eldest son, Fernando, named after Don Fernando, was born and in 1511 Rodrigo. At the birth of Teresita this mother of twenty summers thus became responsible for five little ones, a heavy burden for one of frail constitution. Thus, despite her courage, we find her increasingly exhausted as Lorenzo is born in 1519, Antonio in 1520, Pedro in 1521, Jerónimo in 1522. According to custom, some of these children bore their father's name, whilst the others similarly honoured their mother's family. Teresa was called de Ahumada y Cepeda.

The residence of the Cepeda y Ahumada, situated in the Plazuela de Santo Domingo, opposite the church of Santo Domingo de Silos, consisted of two blocks of buildings connected by *patios* and gardens. The house, magnificent and lovely, was no whit inferior in spaciousness or convenience to those of Núñez Vela, of the Águila, of the Polentino, of the Oñate. Above the entrance door, decorated with great studs forged by a first-class craftsman, the knight's escutcheon displayed his quarterings of nobility. The furnishings were handsome without being luxurious, as befitted the rank of the Cepeda and in accordance with the fashion of the day which, without going against the tradition of patriarchal simplicity proper to the great families of Castile, imposed Italian and Burgundian taste. In Don Alonso's house there was no lack of carpets from Flanders, of cushions of rich silk; but there were also the straight-backed armchairs in wood and leather

---

[1] It used to be thought that Don Alonso's first wife had three children; in his *Vida de Santa Teresa*, the distinguished Teresian scholar's most recent work, Padre Silverio de Santa Teresa inclines to the opinion that there were only two: Juan and María. There is no positive trace of the existence of the third and writers are not even agreed on the name: some say Pedro, others Jerónimo.

known as *sillones fraileros* or monastic armchairs, crockery from Talavera and Valencia, the copper pots and wrought-iron chandeliers which lent distinction to the houses of all the rich folk of Ávila and which were at the same time in daily use. The presses and wardrobes of dark carved oak were filled almost beyond capacity with linen and with the skeins of flax or wool which the mistress of the household reserved for her own use for spinning and weaving, as Queen Isabella the Catholic had done: her husband never wore a shirt which she had not spun with her own hands.

In spite of being surrounded by numerous servants, Doña Beatriz was by no means idle. She left to her women the care of getting the children up and putting them to bed, as she did all duties of the kind, but kept for herself the prerogative of a mother's tenderness and anxious solicitude. The slightest hurt, bump or scratch could find relief nowhere but in her arms. It was only when the overflowing boisterousness of the boys and girls found expression in piercing screams and wild scrambles that the noisy crowd was banished to the most distant patio: the favourite game of the boys of Ávila has always been to fight one another with stones.

The garden was the entire world of Juan, María, Fernando, Rodrigo, Teresa, Lorenzo, Antonio, Pedro, and even of little Jerónimo. There a crowd of servants, men and women, was at work on leather or wood for the needs of this large family; here the spinning was done, the sewing, the washing; elsewhere there was the digging, the planting, the horses were groomed and the sheep branded with a red-hot iron. All this meant so much talking, singing, praying, perhaps trembling with fear, according to the news which men come from afar, galloping by on horseback, would hastily fling in passing, or the troops of musketeers of the Tercios,[1] on the road to the wars. And people would repeat to each other with pride that the captains engaged the soldiers of the City of the Knights and Liegemen on the strength of their birthplace alone, so famous were they for their valour. To this renown a couplet with a play on words[2] testified:

> Most skilful in war is Ávila town
> And rightly earns her great renown.

Both the accounts of combats and those of the intrigues fabricated against Castilian liberties by the detested Flemings with whom Charles V

---

[1] *I e.* regiments (Tr.).
[2] The pun, untranslatable, is clearly seen in the Spanish:
> *Se llama Ávila en esta tierra*
> *El que más ávil es para la guerra.*

was surrounded, were handed on from mouth to mouth; the growing audacity of the Lutherans beyond the Pyrenees seemed, to all those in this city guarded by its eighty-two granite towers, a constant menace both to soul and property.

It was not the time to be afraid—what was required was to fight. 'Ávila of the Knights and Liegemen' had always been for the Cross, for the oppressed, had always fought for liberty, given asylum to kings who were minors or suffering persecution. From Ávila Alfonso VIII set out to reconquer his kingdom and, surrounded by men of Ávila, won the famous victory of Las Navas de Tolosa against the Musulman. Again it was the ramparts of this city, chivalrous as it was in no common measure, that protected Alfonso XI when an inconsiderable king of only one year's standing.

But this very city would break out into furious anger against those who wore the crown unworthily. Henry IV of Castile, for instance, whose manhood they suspected, was no sooner crowned than he was so heartily detested by Ávila folk that they accused, judged, condemned and dethroned him in effigy in the process of a ceremony wilfully grotesque.

It was better to avoid arousing the ill-humour of these knights and townsfolk who would spend the time not devoted to punitive expeditions against the Moors in fighting each other: they only gave loyalty where they met it.

The fame of these warriors, often legendary figures even during their lifetime, was sung in *romances* and *coplas*.[1] Among such personages was a woman, Jimena Blásquez. As a child Teresa never tired of hearing the story of how, in the absence of her husband the governor, and of his troops, she defended the ramparts against an attack by the Almorávides. Doña Jimena went up on the towers, leading the women who were disguised as warriors by means of false beards and large hats; there they played such a tumultuous comedy of defence that the Moors took fright and raised the siege. 'She seemed not a woman at all but a strong *caudillo*.' Were great deeds open to everyone, then? The little one dreamed that it was so.

Tales like these began with a kind of incantation:

It came to pass . . .
—Let ill depart,
—Let good draw near.
Ill for the Moors,
Good for ourselves.[2]

[1] Ballads and songs; cf. 'couplets' (Tr.).
[2] *Érase que se era —el mal que se vaya —el bien que se venga —El mal para los Moros —y el bien para nosotros* (quoted Valbuena Prat, *Hist. Lit. Esp.*, p. 179).

There were stories, too, of children being kidnapped and assassinated by the infidels who tore out their hearts to be used in witchcraft. The secret trial of the Holy Child of Guardia who was scourged, crowned with thorns and crucified at some thirty-five leagues from Ávila, had ended up, in 1491, in the marketplace amid the flames kindled by the Grand Inquisitor Torquemada.

Teresita was sorry for these pagans:

'And they'll all be damned, then? For ever?'

Those telling the story did not answer: they preferred to stress the dangers which children who leave their homes to go out alone may meet with.

'But those who die for God go to heaven, for ever?'

Her brothers were amazed that one so young should have such a passionate love for war and glory.

She was five when the *Comuneros'* revolt filled Ávila with secret and solemn deliberations, for the Holy Office met in the very cloister of the cathedral: Castile rose against the Flemish emperor, Charles V, on behalf of the Castilian queen, Doña Juana, daughter of Isabel the Catholic, though she was mentally deranged and a prisoner at Tordesillas.

The City of Saints and Stones had an imperative reason for rising: the Emperor congratulated her on not taking part in the sedition. This was all that was necessary to make Ávila the centre of it and to rally her people at the password, *Comunidad.*

The Cepeda y Ahumada children were fascinated and tremendously excited by the atmosphere of conspiracy and intrigue; the very walls seemed to whisper the names of conspirators, under the seal of secrecy details of the oath ceremony were hinted at: each one present swore on the Cross and the Gospel to defend the liberties of Castile against the abuses of imperial power. The people did not know that they were defending not their own liberties but the privileges of the nobles; not the free exercise of thought and the critical faculty, but the immutable Church. The *Comuneros* went into battle to the shout of 'Long live the Inquisition.'[1] The dean of the cathedral himself presided over the meetings, but it was a sheep-shearer, Pinillos, who, using for the purpose the end of his little switch, gave or withheld permission to address the assembly. Whoever did not side with the *Comuneros* went in dread of them. Don Alonso, often away on his estates at Gotarrendura and, when at Ávila, living increasingly in retirement, succeeded in refraining from taking sides.

[1] Dr. Marañón, in his *Antonio Pérez*, maintains this theory of the people's being the instrument of the nobility in the revolt of the *Comuneros.*

It lasted a year, until the battle of Villalar, where the popular cry of *Santiago y libertad!* was stifled by the imperialists' *Santa María y Carlos!* The leaders were beheaded and those of the youth of Castile who aspired to great things turned their eyes beyond the seas: Mexico, discovered and conquered by Cortés, was named 'New Spain.'

Towards lands beyond the seas, or towards God.

In the home of the Cepedas the stories of warlike exploits were ended: with her brother Rodrigo, four years her senior, Teresita now turned to the *Lives of the Saints*. It was no longer another Jimena Blásquez that she dreamed of becoming but St. Catherine. For it was chiefly the martyrs who excited her enthusiasm, and to her mind the blood shed by St. Andrew, St. Sebastian, St. Ursula and her companions the eleven thousand virgins, was indistinguishable from their aureole of sanctity.

On Sundays, in the parish church of San Juan, she heard preachers thunder against the heretics whose writings were beginning to infiltrate into Spain, but still more perhaps against the lukewarmness of Christians; the picture of the damned writhing in eternal flames haunted her even in her sleep. She would have liked to be able to grasp to the full the meaning and content of this word 'eternal.'

'It means for ever,' Doña Beatriz would answer in reply to her questionings.

In summer under the cool shade of the mulberry trees, in winter in the damp stables, Teresa held long discussions with her brother and both repeated over and over again till their heads reeled:

'For ever, Teresa!'

'For ever, Rodrigo!' [1]

They hid themselves in order to be able to talk about God, conscious of an interest deeper than that considered suitable to children. Teresita considered that martyrdom 'was a bargain price' [2] for the presence of God; not that she loved God overmuch but she wanted to enjoy the heavenly delights of which she had read in the *Lives of the Saints*.

The realistic pictures of religious art showed her quite clearly the tortures of martyrdom in their full horror, but that only excited her imagination the more.

. . . A St Lawrence bound, stretched on the grid, the flames envelop him, the coals seem alive, the fire is so red that just to look at it makes you afraid. . . . This noble flesh seems to be burning

[1] MJR.   [2] Sb, V, c. i-4.

and roasting, the entrails are half showing, the flames curl round the breasts and round the brave heart that will never apostatise, devouring them. . . . In another altarpiece St Bartholomew, bound to a table, is being flayed alive. . . . In the next panel St Stephen is being stoned, the stones crash down one against the other and his bleeding face and cleft skull move all who see them to pray for the brutal fellows who are butchering him. . . . Finally, a crucifix, naked, streaming with blood, the body showing the weals made by the scourging, the entrails pierced. . . .[1]

Suffering which is fierce and keen, but of short duration, in exchange for eternal glory.

'All that is necessary,' she was already telling Rodrigo, 'is a little bit of determination: *una determinacioncilla*. . . .'[2]

Neither Juan, who was fifteen and already thinking of going to the army, nor María, the big sister of thirteen, nor Fernando, still less Lorenzo, were admitted to the conversations in which the children strove to find a way of anticipating eternal happiness by martyrdom. The fact of having relatives seemed to them 'the greatest drawback.'[3] Their age was no obstacle. Ávila had erected her finest basilica to three child martyrs, Vincent and his two sisters, Cristeta and Sabina, who in Roman times refused to sacrifice to false gods. Scourged, broken upon the wheel, they continued to praise Jesus Christ their Lord until someone dashed out their brains on the stones. The pagans had forbidden them burial, but a monstrous serpent, feared all around for the havoc it wrought, constituted itself the guardian of their innocent remains: it frightened away not only birds of prey, but would-be profaners and a Jew who ventured there only escaped by invoking the name of Jesus and promising the monster he would get himself baptized.

Teresita already saw in her imagination another basilica: that of the brother and sister martyrs, Rodrigo and Teresa.

That year the taking of Rhodes by the Turks threw grown-up people into consternation, but filled the mind of a little girl who knew nothing whatever of geography with a longing for sacrifice: she imagined that it would now be easy to go and get beheaded in the land of the Moors, and that by begging one's bread along the roads 'for the love of God,' one could not fail to get there. What is the judgement of a boy of ten worth when confronted by a sister, younger indeed, but already possessed of a keen power of persuasion?

They both slipped away at daybreak, as soon as the gates were

[1] Malón de Chaide.   [2] Sb, C, c. xvi-10.   [3] Sb, V, c. i-4.

opened, crossed the Adaja bridge, and thought that by taking the road to Salamanca they were setting out for the 'lands of the Moors.'

There it was that Don Francisco Álvarez de Cepeda, their uncle, met them: they were walking with firm step, little Teresa's long dress dragging in the dust, both carrying a few crusts of bread tied up in a napkin at the end of a long stick. Rodrigo, whose feet were already beginning to hurt, owned up quickly, whilst his sister angrily clenched her teeth in silence over her secret. They were brought back home where Doña Beatriz, surrounded by her other children in tears and by her servants who loudly accused each other of negligence, was having the well dragged in search of the little truants. When the joy of their return was over, the big brother showed less stoicism when faced with the immediate prospect of a whipping than in his desire for martyrdom.

'It was *la niña* who dragged me into it.'

And *la niña*, the little one, was punished.

The check to her escapade turned Teresa's thoughts towards the life of the cloister, but the hermitages, large enough for a person of her years, which she endeavoured to build by piling up stones in the garden quickly collapsed: would the glory of St Mary of Egypt, whose frightful penances the servants used to sing of in their songs, prove as difficult of attainment as that of St Cecilia or St Agnes? Soon odd bits of stuff lying about the house disappeared: Teresita was founding a religious order; dressed up as a little nun, she obliged her cousins to the observance of a rule drawn up by herself. Naturally she was prioress. Clapping her hands with a hollow sound, she made her sisters, who were amazed at the accuracy for detail of her imagination, kneel down, get up, prostrate themselves, arms in the form of a cross and face to the ground. The children sometimes hid themselves behind the box trees; it was to say the rosary without being disturbed.

At this time Teresa thought she would like to be a nun, but her desire for this was 'less strong than for the earlier things,' less strong than her wish to be a virgin martyr or a desert solitary: the cloistered life would not satisfy her appetite for the romantic.

The children of Don Alonso's two marriages were now, in 1522, eight boys and two girls. Doña Beatriz, still beautiful, was no longer the dazzling vision of her marriage day, attired in silk and gold: the dresses of yellow Chinese silk with their sleeve openings lined with red, the richly embroidered skirts of crimson satin which she formerly wore with a corsage of violet damask striped with black velvet, were for her henceforward merely splashes of bright colour down at the bottom of the chests which Teresita sometimes coaxed her to open.

This woman of barely twenty-seven, whose languid condition made noise and conversation an annoyance to her, chose to dress as a duenna and of set purpose lived as a recluse in her own home. She had so often pleaded her poor health as a pretext for not receiving friends who came to visit her, or even close relatives whose children seemed to her an undesirable example for her own, that the sound of the knocker at the front door seldom disturbed her peace and quiet. She shared in her husband's life of piety but there was a whole world of fantasy in which she wandered alone: that of the tales of chivalry. To say 'alone' is not quite accurate: she had all Spain with her; about the same time a young squire, Ignatius of Loyola, was in raptures over *Amadis de Gaule*.

For Don Alonso, the prevailing fashion was insufficient justification: he was already declaring what Pérez de Moya was to write before long: such tales 'are the bait which the devil dangles before the sentimental feelings of frivolous boys and girls.' [1] Doña Beatriz would not have dared to argue with him, but privately thought that this husband fifteen years her senior exaggerated considerably. Could it be said that such reading was anything more than an agreeable diversion during her long illnesses or after a day entirely devoted to looking after her household and children? Was she any the less devout for it, or less austere in her ways? Did she neglect her duties? Most assuredly not. Moreover, arguments were not lacking to show that such works of the imagination were 'very necessary to excite courage in the pursuit of arms and to stimulate manly hearts to imitate the deeds of their forefathers. Glory and virtue abound in them. . . .' [2] And so she came to encourage a liking for such tales in her children, to save them 'from coming to grief in dangerous pursuits.' [3]

This was particularly so in Teresa's case.

Since the escapade 'into the lands of the Moors,' Doña Beatriz had been watching closely this girl who was wilder than all her brothers put together. On winter evenings the child pushed open her mother's door and found her sitting on cushions flung at random over a great Flemish carpet, reading. Don Alonso had not yet returned from a visit to Gotarrendura, or from a walk with a friend as serious as himself; the boys were taking exercise with a master at arms, María was at the sermon; the house was completely still. Little Teresa would take up her seat around the brasero and throw on the glowing embers a handful of dried lavender whose scent and blue smoke she loved.

Doña Beatriz would speak to her of the love of God and of Our Lady.

[1] Quoted VA, p. 64.   [2] Idem.   [3] Sb, V, c. ii–1.

Avila: One of
the gates lead-
ing into the city

Avila: The so-called "Four Posts" encircling the boundary cross. A famous landmark on the boundary of the city.

'It is she who is your real mother.'

Her continual pregnancies and increasingly painful confinements made her fear she would not live long and Teresita's inventive high spirits made her uneasy: she strove to provide a palliative by keeping both mind and hands constantly occupied: she taught her the art of fine needlework, how to embroider the designs she made with many shades of silk. But this lonely and rather too tender-hearted teacher could not refrain from talking to the child of her favourite heroes equally as much as she did of Our Lady: Oriana, Palmerín, the child Esplandián, and Amadis, the young Lord of the Sea:

King Lisuart's daughter was Oriana, the most beautiful creature men had ever seen. She was so beautiful that she was called the Peerless. The Queen gave her the Lord of the Sea to serve her and said to her:

'Darling, this is a young Lord for your service.'

'He pleases me,' replied Oriana.

This remark was so deeply engraved in the young Lord's heart that it was never more effaced. As the story relates, he was not displeased at serving her and his heart was fixed on her unceasingly. This love lasted as long as they lived, he loving her as she loved him, so that they ceased not to love one another for a single hour.

'They loved each other for ever, and for ever, and for ever?' Teresita would ask her mother.

Doña Beatriz replied:

'For ever and ever.'

'Like Glory, Love has no value, then, unless it is for ever?' This thought sometimes preoccupied Teresa as she was growing up.

The Cepeda y Ahumada spent the summer at Olmedo, at the house of their grandmother, Doña Teresa de las Cuevas, or on their estates at Gotarrendura, three leagues away from Ávila. They went there by carriage, amid a great bustle of boxes and packages, but although the twenty-six little bells which tinkled from the mules' collars had long been Teresa's delight, she now preferred to ride on horseback with her elder brothers: she liked them to admire her fearlessness and the way she bore herself.

She found at Gotarrendura what she most preferred all through her life: a country dwelling house, yet well designed, a lovely enclosed orchard, a dovecot, vineyards, fields, and, what she specially loved, a distant horizon of magnificence. It was there that she learned to love the peasants of her own Castile and to make herself loved by them. Her slender pocket money was used up in alms to tramps and the poor of the neighbourhood. Her father, whose favourite she was, loved her the more because she was both kind and merry.

But Doña Beatriz had just brought into the world a baby girl, Juana, doubtless so named in memory of Juan, Don Alonso's eldest son, who had met death in the war against Francis I. She remained so ill that that year they were unable to return to the town at the beginning of autumn. Even in what hours of warm sunshine there were, she was scarcely able to drag herself as far as the dovecots she loved so much. Though she leant on Teresa for support, the girl felt no alarm that she should be so light a burden.

On the 24th November 1528, she made her will with a calm mind: 'I bequeath my soul to Almighty God who created and redeemed it with his precious blood. I bequeath my body to the earth from which he formed it. ... '[1]

In death her countenance remained so peaceful that her children thought her asleep.

The funeral procession set out for Ávila before dawn; peasants followed the ox-drawn hearse on foot; the servants carried lighted tapers. Teresita, nestling against her elder sister, watched the lights flicker through a mist of tears. She did not realize immediately, however, how great the misfortune was that had befallen her; she was as yet unaware of the void that death means for those who are left.

Soon her consciousness of being weak and alone was so deep that fear took possession of her: rather than put her on her guard against the mistakes of adolescence, Doña Beatriz had preserved her from them. Those who were given the entrée into the Cepeda y Ahumada home were few. But their loss brought visits from relatives and friends and it was in her black mourning dress that Teresa learned for the first time that she was beautiful and was not indifferent to the knowledge. A moment later she wept for shame.

She asked Rodrigo to go back with her along the road they had taken the day of their flight towards martyrdom, but she entered the hermitage of St Lazarus alone. There she knelt before the picture of Our Lady of Charity, the former witness of their childish vow to die in order to win heaven. In tears, her heart still naïve but now no stranger to sorrow, she besought the blessed Virgin Mary to be her mother.

[1] PT, p. 51.

II

LOVE

TERESA DE AHUMADA Y CEPEDA was now fifteen, an age at which her mother was already married; her father was usually worried and preoccupied, her sister absent-minded, while her brothers idolized her; small wonder, then, if she should find herself falling in love.

She was a beautiful girl, though the word beautiful scarcely does her justice: her charm was irresistible. According to Fray Luis de León, a writer not given to exaggeration, people said that anyone who came into close contact with her would 'have his head turned.' 'Her beauty and the care she took of her person, her polished conversation, the sweetness and refinement of her manners made her more attractive still. Saint and sinner, ascetic and worldling, old and young alike came under the influence of her charm, though this in no way detracted from her dignity. Child or growing girl, in the world or as a nun, she attracted all who came in contact with her as the magnet draws steel.' [1]

Was it to be expected that a girl who was maddeningly beautiful, endowed with an 'extraordinary' loveliness of feature, noble, wealthy and surrounded by flattery, could be persuaded that all worldly joys were worthless? A wealth of chestnut hair, naturally curly, set off her high forehead and fluffed around her laughing face which altered so much with her lively and continually changing expression that it was difficult to say if it was round or oval. The straight, round-tipped nose met the arch of the eyebrows in a single curve. It was the full red mouth closing over dazzlingly white teeth which most revealed her personality and the black, rather prominent eyes, round, well-set, as they lit up with a flash of enthusiasm or glowed softly with tenderness as occasion demanded, or again sparkled with mischief or coquettishness. Teresa's complexion was pale but there was colour in her cheeks. Three dimples near the mouth set off her smile. She was well built and of average height. People spoke of the gracefulness of her carriage and of her lovely hands. 'Perfect in every way, she had an indefinable something in addition . . .' [2]—charm, a quality which eludes analysis.

[1] LL, cited SEC, vol. II, p. 475.   [2] María de San José.

How she loved to be told she was beautiful! She simply could not believe there could be anything wrong in that.

With the desire to please came that for dress and finery, unusual in such a young girl: both hair and hands received careful attention; she used cream, rouge and perfume. She now spent more time before her mirror than she did in saying her rosary. She tried different hair styles, piled up her high tresses in imitation of the Empress Isabella, used various oils and juices of plants to make her skin more lovely, plucked her eyebrows, used musk or orange perfume, diluted carmine for her cheeks. She wore amber beads or red or white coral, threaded on ribbon, but she liked best to wear jet for it set off the dark lustre of her eyes.

Her great delight was to get Don Alonso's permission to try on Doña Beatriz's gowns; in this heavy attire she could move as lightly as gossamer and danced about on her small, well-arched feet, with their dainty soft leather slippers, embroidered with flowers worked in silver thread. Needless to say she had openwork stockings.

All this was 'without any wrong intention, for I did not want anyone to offend God through me.' [1]

At sixteen Teresa's frivolity was merely the awakening of normal womanhood. And her taste for novels was shared by most girls of her age.

She always had a passion for tales of chivalry and admits that 'she was only happy when she had new ones.' [2] She hid them from Don Alonso. The sound of her father's footsteps caused her many a heartbeat as she threw a cushion over the open book, snatched up her embroidery and forced herself to speak in a steady voice. It often happened that she had to leave her story at the crucial moment to go to the *estrado* [3] to meet elderly relatives, to play chess with her father or to pore over the household accounts with her sister María. A maddening annoyance.

It was these stirring stories that she talked about with her brother Rodrigo. She called him to listen to passages: the apotheosis of *The Quest of the Holy Grail* delighted them most. The book ended with the entering of Galahad, son of Lancelot of the Lake, into the glory of God: 'The angels attired him in vesture of gold, placed on his head a diadem of precious stones and upon his right hand a ring. It was in this way that the Holy Grail was borne up to heaven. . . .' For a moment this

---

[1] Sb, V, c. ii–2.   [2] Idem, c. ii–1.

[3] The parlour in which visitors were received; sometimes an alcove or balcony at one end of the great hall (Tr.).

made them long to return to the fervour of their childhood and Teresa
would have mused almost endlessly upon the golden robes, the crown,
and the ring of the heavenly nuptials if a book which she was particularly longing to read, the *Olivante de Laura*, had not come her
way.

Teresa lived these adventures as she read them and would sigh with
relief when lover met beloved again after the chapters in which he
had destroyed or triumphed over the greatest possible obstacles and
dangers.

These tales were by no means morally edifying: damsels of high
degree shared their knights' couches unlawfully and unashamedly;
the illegitimate children born of these unions were almost drowned in
tears, but none the less exposed by their mothers to almost certain
death: Palmerín de Oliva, for instance, left on a mountain in a cradle
of water-willow suspended from the branches of an olive tree, or
Amadis, placed by his mother Elisane in a skiff shaped like a coffin and
entrusted to the sea: whence his title, Young Lord of the Sea. Such
love-children miraculously escaped to become valiant if not blameless
knights in their turn. And they too were the fathers of many children.
But in those days no mystery was made of the manner of perpetuating
the human race and the gravest sins were not those of the flesh.

Such stories were calculated to arouse the spirit of chivalry. Teresa
was too sensible to believe that the fantastic exploits really happened,
but the sense of grandeur, of honour, of the love of glory, all these
were real, the very essence of the traditions of her race and lineage.
Juan, her half-brother, had died in battle and even the youngest of
Alonso de Cepeda's sons already regarded themselves as future *conquistadores*. They thrived on stories like these, of course, but they also
knew by heart the discourse pronounced by the bishop, Don Pelayo,
when he knighted Ávila's two heroes, Yague and Mingo Peláez.
They mimed the scene, one of them declaiming:

Noble Squires who are to-day to receive the honour of knight-
hood, learn what Chivalry is. Chivalry is noble behaviour, and a
noble man is one who does no wrong to any creature nor commits
any base deed. In the first place, then, you must swear to love above
all things the God who created you and redeemed you by his passion
and his blood; secondly, to live and die in his holy Law and never to
disown it. Item, to promise to serve the King your Lord loyally.
Item, to swear not to be in the pay of any other king or rich man,
be he Moor or Christian. Item, that in combat you will die rather
than flee. Item, that your tongue shall speak nothing but the truth,

for he who lies is base. Item, always to be the help and succour of the poor. Item, to be the defender of any duenna or damsel who shall summon you to her aid, fighting for her against any mighty man who has wronged her. Item, not to be proud in your speech but humble in your bearing towards all, and, speaking with courteous consideration, to honour and venerate men who are old. And never to provoke without cause any man in this world.

In the Ahumada y Cepeda children a taste for adventures ran parallel with hero-worship.

Teresa was gifted with the type of imagination which immediately transforms thought into action: her idea now was, with Rodrigo—the favourite brother comes into everything—to write a tale of chivalry herself. Wasn't it said that the author of *Palmerín de Oliva* was a woman? Frustrated in her attempt to find glory in martyrdom, she now aspired to literary fame. The two young people, born on the same day though with four years between them, were once more inseparable; after long conversations and discussions Teresa took up her pen.

On the cover of an exercise-book the title: *The Knight of Ávila* by Doña Teresa de Ahumada and Don Rodrigo de Cepeda was imposingly displayed.

Their hero, Muñoz Gil, was famous in the annals of his native city. In this lay the originality of an undertaking in which Teresa already displayed her spirit of initiative, her love of creative work and of reform. Why must the heroes always be English or French, she asked herself? Why all these imaginary great deeds when the real achievements and prowess of the heroes of Castile, and of Ávila in particular, were just as wonderful? In her taste for the marvellous the girl already showed herself a realist; it is her native surroundings she uses as the point of departure for the plunge into her dream-world. 'A fig for the fictitious blows of Amadis, for the terrible attacks of the giants, if only there were a writer in Spain to recount the mighty deeds of the Spaniards!' [1] declared Luis Zapata a little later, after describing the real prowess of a Juan Fernández Galindo, a Ramiro de Cardenas or a Jorge Manrique, who 'with a single stroke of his sword ran his enemy through, the blow passing through the saddle and even wounding his horse.' [2]

Teresa, too, had felt the want and decided to be the writer in question. For months the sheets of paper piled up. Rodrigo often preferred riding, hunting, warlike games or pretty girls to literary

---

[1] Quoted VA, pp. 60-1.　　　　　[2] Idem.

occupation, but his sister continued relentlessly and he left her the glory of the finished work. Relatives and friends said how marvellous it was; they praised the vivacity of her style, its colourfulness, the fascinating way she developed the narrative, and more than one writer of note admitted that the author showed a penetration of mind unusual in one of her years.

But winter, when it is so pleasant to write with one's chair drawn close up to the brasero, came to an end. Spring whispered that when one is fifteen, life is more exhilarating than writing, even when one is writing about the struggle between passion and honour.

Don Alonso, more austere than ever since Doña Beatriz's death, closed the emblazoned door which opened.on to the *plazuela*, to visitors, but in the wall which divided his gardens from those of his brother Don Francisco, there was a private door.

Pedro, Francisco, Diego and Vincent were the. names of Don Francisco Álvarez de Cepeda's sons; his daughters were Beatriz, Ana, Jerónima and Inés. There was also Doña Elvira, daughter of Ruy Sánchez y Cepeda. A fine group of young people in whom must be included Teresa's elder brothers, Fernando and Rodrigo. María was a person apart. She was twenty-four, serious like her father and engaged to a man equally serious, Don Martín de Guzmán y Barriento: their quiet affection as an officially engaged couple brought sunshine into the house.

Don Alonso had scarcely started for Gotarrendura when all this band of youngsters began to dance and sing for joy and talk sweet nothings. What more natural? Teresa loved to be loved, and one of her cousins adored her. Which one was it? Francisco or Pedro? Diego or Vincent? She mentions no one by name. When she mentions these cousins, all she says is: 'They were about my own age, a little older than I. We were always together; they were very fond of me; I used to talk to them of anything that gave them pleasure and I listened to them as they told me of their likes and dislikes and their childish nonsense, and also of certain things that were blameworthy. What was worse was that it was in this way that my soul came in contact with what was the cause of all the harm. . . .'[1] She allowed herself to be influenced because of the feeling of affection she inspired in others: 'As soon as I felt that I pleased somebody, if I found favour with him, I took such a tremendous liking to the person that I would be always thinking of him.'[2] Crystallization could not be defined in fewer words.

She mentions no one by name, keeps silence about whoever it was

[1] Sb, V, c. ii–2.   [2] Sb, V, c. xxxvii–4.

that disturbed her serenity, but there was one cousin whom she would not see again as long as she lived, although she remained in contact with all the others: Pedro. Can we not deduce from this that it was Pedro she loved? What motive could she who was so loyal in the matter of family affection have had for avoiding him? One reason alone: the importance she always gave to the necessity of 'cutting off occasions of sin by the roots.'

We should not take these girlish love affairs (for which Teresa afterwards reproached herself bitterly) more seriously than is warranted by what she says herself. She accuses herself of the pleasure she found in the chatter of a cousin who idled her time away and made her share her taste for frivolities. Had this cousin the reputation of being too much of a flirt? Doña Beatriz had done her best to prevent her children from seeing her, but there was nothing sufficiently definite against her to justify her being forbidden the house. Don Alonso and the prudent elder sister frowned upon the friendship, but without result:

> I had a great leaning towards everything evil [declares Teresa]. My evil inclinations were sufficient in themselves. In addition there were the servants and I found them quite ready to encourage me in anything wrong. If one of them had given me good advice I might perhaps have listened to her, but self-interest blinded them [we can see the lover slipping ducats into their hands] just as my propensity blinded me. I was not wholly bad and everything dishonourable was abhorrent to my nature, but I loved to spend my time in pleasant chatter; that does not alter the fact that the occasion of falling was there, the danger within a hand's grasp, and I was exposing my father and brothers to it. God guarded me so well that he preserved me from falling, even against my will.[1]

In a period in which all passions ran to extremes, custom authorized father and brothers to kill a girl's seducer, and it was not infrequent for a love affair to be responsible for several corpses: it is to such dramas of honour that Teresa was referring. On the other hand the guilty man might be forced to marry his victim. Examples of such laxity of morals were not wanting in the highest ranks of society: the bastards of kings, those of grandees, even those of dignitaries of the Church came in for their share of titles and benefices. The illegitimate child of a girl who could prove her *limpieza de sangre*, that is, that the blood of her ancestors

---

[1] In the attempt to identify this cousin of Teresa's, I have followed the opinion of Fr. Gabriel of Jesus which seems to me the most solidly established of all those put forward on the subject.

was clean from any Moorish or Jewish taint, was more highly esteemed than the legitimate offspring of mixed blood.

Beautiful girls longed for a lover, gallant lovers used no half measures with passion, human life was held cheap; the man or the woman in the upper classes of society who dared to defy a father or duenna in order to enjoy the other's society valued love more than prudence warranted. Honour prohibited a fall but it also forbade too much timidity.

Teresa was not afraid, but she would not have allowed the finger of scorn to be pointed at her, nor was she the kind of girl to get married because honour dictated it. If she had to defend herself from audacious overtures, she did so through a twofold instinct for purity: purity of body in the first place and then care for her reputation. It is too often forgotten that if sexual attraction is a natural instinct, virginity's defence is just as instinctive.

Teresa had an excuse for these secret love affairs: her confessor himself and many other good people of sound judgement saw no sin in her being attracted by a boy whose intention was 'a happy issue by way of marriage.' [1] It was just a love affair in embryo or perhaps a real falling in love, for despite her young years, no diminutive was possible where the sentiments of Teresa de Ahumada were in question. It was so throughout her life. Her own account of it is that one of her cousins was in love with her and that another cousin, a girl like herself, and the servants, were a party to the matter. There may have been a few secret meetings, interchange of notes, an intense uneasiness, demands, tears, repentance, jealousy, all the agitation which a first love-affair unleashes in an impetuous nature. We are not justified in reading more into the affair than Teresa tells us herself.

Yet we can perhaps imagine something of the love affair of a girl who was beautiful, elegant, a trifle coquettish, and who was at the same time closely guarded by her father and sister. An old ballad in the form of a dialogue between two sisters fits the reproaches which María addressed to Teresa so aptly that there is nothing far-fetched in supposing that their discussions would be somewhat as follows:

Miguela scolds her sister Juanilla. She speaks to her words that deeply wound:
'Only yesterday you were quite tiny and wrapped in swaddling clothes; today you bedeck yourself more than other maidens, your joys are sighs, your songs elegies, you rise at dawn and you retire to

[1] Sb, V, c. ii. 4–6, 9.

rest late. In your work I know not on what your thoughts are dwelling, for you look at your pattern and you miss the stitches. They tell me that you are using lovers' signs: if our mother hears of it, things will be altered. She will nail up the windows and shut fast the doors; we shall no longer get leave to dance; she will bid our aunt accompany us to church, so that our friends may not speak to us. When she is absent she will bid the duenna watch the expression of our eyes and scrutinize the passer-by, to see if anyone should stop before the grating and which of us turns our head. . . .'

Juanilla replies:

'Ay! Miguela, sister! How you seek to find evil! You imagine troubles of mine without knowing anything of them. I have a liking for Pedro, son of Juan, who has gone to the wars. His sighs and laments moved me. But absence has made him fickle. . . .'

Thus Teresa who thinks she knows better than persons of experience has to listen to moralizings like those of the austere Miguela from the lips of María de Cepeda.

Your unhappiness will only increase as you grow older. If you doubt it, listen to this proverb: 'You are still a child and think you know what love is; what will it be, then, when you are of an age to love?' [1]

Teresa, it is certain, clung only to that which would last 'for ever and ever': she had not been brought up on the *Lives of the Saints* and the tale of Amadis and Oriana for nothing.

María's marriage brought festivities in which Teresa, now in love, was astonished to find that turning young men's heads still gave her pleasure; but it gave her pain when she saw her lover attentive to the guests.

The wedding took place at Villatoro, where Don Martín Guzmán de Barrientos had distinguished relatives. It was a village half-way between Ávila and Castellanos de la Cañada and here the young couple were to live. The celebrations began with a merry cavalcade and for several days it was nothing but festivities, gay and beautiful clothes, songs, dances to the music of tambourine, flute or rebeck, rustic games, with the whole family there and all their friends and, of course, their first cousins, the inseparable sons and daughters of Teresa's uncle Francisco.

While their house at Castellanos was being got ready for them, María and her husband returned to Ávila to her father's home.

For the City of the Liegemen, 1531 was a glorious year: the Empress

[1] Anonymous ballad (quoted TI, vol. I, p. 141).

Isabella arrived there in May with little Prince Philip; it was there that the ceremonies in the course of which the future Philip II, then four years old, was to exchange his childish dress for his first princely breeches took place. The severe taste of the Portuguese princess had to give way before the official programme. Ávila glistened with gay tapestries and bright-coloured hangings that sparkled against the granite and was completely invaded by the court. Its sombre streets came to life with gay processions, in the squares tourney followed joust and there was a continual but pleasant hubbub intermingled with the sound of music and the clash of bells.

It would not do for one of the prettiest girls of rank in Ávila to be away from these festivities, and Teresa, who could always adapt herself to any set of circumstances, enjoyed them. She was elated by her success but not carried away and there were hours when the longing for Pedro or for worldly pleasure gave way to a feeling of the puzzling emptiness of it all. To one with a nature as straightforward and a character as frank as hers, the dissimulation she was practising towards her father and María could not but cause worry and agony of mind.

For two months she went from one festivity to another. On 26th July, Don Philip was to receive 'his princely liveries.' But—on the 13th Don Alonso sent Teresa to a convent. He put forward a good reason: her elder sister had just left for Castellanos de la Cañada and she could not take part in the celebrations without being chaperoned. Did he feel that the cousins in their smart attire, the velvet doublet knotted with gold tags, the full, goffered ruffles, the short cape which showed the sword beneath, were too irresistibly attractive to allow any really good father to breathe in peace? Teresa answers the question herself: 'My father loved me so much and my dissimulation was such that he did not think me capable of as much evil as was in fact the case: and so I was not sent away under a cloud. There were some slight suspicions about me but nothing definite. I had such a fear of losing my reputation that I took every possible precaution to keep everything secret.'

The goodbyes were secret too, and the servant who was a party to Teresa's love affair with her cousin kept watch while they said farewell. Teresa shed tears. Tears of despair she thought them, but then she wept again when she had to take off her necklace with its fourfold row of gold chain she was so fond of, her rings, bracelets and long earrings which she would no longer be allowed to wear. This confusion between feelings of affection and those of vainglory left her very much disconcerted.

When she was sent to the convent of the Augustinian nuns of Our Lady of Grace, Doña Teresa de Ahumada y Cepeda was sixteen and four months. At a time when there were no establishments of higher education for girls, these nuns received the wealthy daughters of distinguished families. They went there more to deepen the practice of their religion and to strive after the attainment of virtue than for learning: to be familiar with the catechism, to know how to read and write, to have some knowledge of how to keep accounts, to be a skilful embroideress, an accomplished lace-maker, a good spinner, an average musician, this was considered sufficient education: too much mention is made of women who knew Latin and Greek for them not to be the rarest of exceptions. The distinction between intelligence and wit on the one hand and much knowledge on the other was perfectly understood and the affectation of ignorance was considered better form than pedantry. Years later Teresa laughed at a nun who prided herself on her learning: 'I am not so learned as you. Who are the Assyrians? . . .'[1] She no doubt knew perfectly well, but she had too much good taste to neglect to give her daughters a lesson in simplicity.

Such lessons she herself received at Our Lady of Grace. No other convent in Ávila enjoyed such great prestige. The religious were of high birth but they were distinguished not so much for this as for their fervour and austerity. The mistress of the girls sent there for their education, Doña María de Briceño y Contreras, was with them night and day: she shared their dormitory, went with them to chapel and if one of her charges was called to the parlour she accompanied her there. Her devotion to the Blessed Sacrament had been confirmed by a miracle: one day when the celebrant had forgotten to give her Communion she could not repress a slight cry of disappointment and then people saw two hands move towards her bearing the Holy Eucharist. Quite apart from her sanctity the charm of this nun must have been very considerable, for her severity did not prevent her pupils from adoring her.

But even the vigilance of a saint could have little influence on a girl who was angry at being deprived of her liberty. 'At first I was very much upset; but I was already weary of vanity and frivolity, when I offended God I was afraid and I forced myself to confess what I had done as soon as possible. I was so troubled on this account that at the end of a week, perhaps sooner, I was much happier there than in my father's house.'[2]

[1] CTA, ccxxiii.   [2] Sb, V, c. ii–8.

Her new companions loved her, for God had given her the gift of pleasing people wherever she went.

The idea of becoming a nun however did not cross her mind, she was even 'extremely opposed'[1] to doing so, but she was delighted to be living in surroundings where goodness and piety were made attractive.

Teresa accuses the devil, and also 'those from outside,'[2] of having conspired to disturb her peace by messages: notes from the despairing lover found their way through the keyhole, through the parlour grilles or were slipped into her hand by that cousin of her own sex 'of frivolous disposition.' Perhaps there were furtive interviews: brief moments of joy to be followed by prolonged remorse. She has not given us details of the events and feelings which caused her to turn aside from human love even before she was wholly caught up in a love that was divine. But there is one incident of which she has spoken at length and if she has chosen to analyse it, if she comes back to it on more than one occasion, if she showed a particular liking for the central figure of this story, it must surely be because she found there feelings and emotions which were common to her own experience and which she therefore understood and sympathized with all the more: the person in question was Doña Casilda de Padilla, who bore one of the greatest names in Spain and was one of the wealthiest people in the country.

Doña Casilda was twelve when she was married to her uncle.

She began to enjoy the worldly finery necessitated by her rank, finery well calculated to please her girlish years. But she had hardly been married two months when God began to draw her to himself, although she did not then understand that he was doing so. When she had spent a happy day with her husband—they loved each other tenderly despite the difference in age between them, it made her dreadfully sad to find that the day had passed and nothing was left of it and to think that all other days would pass in exactly the same way. . . .[3] At that time her husband had to go away on a journey. She loved him so much that she was greatly upset at this. But soon God made her understand the cause of her suffering: her soul was really longing for that which would never end. . . .[4] As the Lord wanted her for his own, he took this earthly love away from her and gave her the desire to leave everything for him. At the time she was moved only by the desire to save her soul and to find the best means of doing so; it seemed to her that if she were deeply involved in the

[1] Idem.   [2] Idem.
[3] Sb, F, c. x–14.   [4] Sb, F, c. x–15.

things of this world, she would neglect to make the effort to obtain eternity.[1]

Is not this what Teresa de Ahumada was experiencing when she was about sixteen—the passion for finery, the love so ardent that proof of its worthlessness is found in its very excess, the need of loving 'that which has no end,' 'for ever and ever,' the warm but very human love which our Lord stills before he takes possession of a heart smarting under an all too recent disappointment? We can imagine Teresa receiving one of those 'messages from outside,' and her vexation that the joy it gave her vanished so quickly.

'This soon ceased and I again found pleasure in the good I had known as a young child. . . . It seems to me that His Majesty was continually looking for a way to draw me to himself' [2]—as in Doña Casilda's case, without her knowing it.

[1] Sb, F, c. x–16.   [2] Sb, V, c. ii–8.

III

THE FIRST KNOCK [1]

THERE was no doubt that the Ahumada y Cepeda children had been badly brought up: austerity on the father's side and piety on the mother's do not necessarily go hand in hand with the art of governing eight boys and three girls, or provide a healthy outlet for their curiosity or turn their high spirits to the best account. This is shown by the fact that from the moment when Teresa, the spoilt child, the one to whom everyone gave way and to whom nothing was ever refused, found someone to take her in hand, she was a changed being.

María de Briceño was thirty-six; she had been elected by acclamation mistress of the young pupils of Our Lady of Grace, known as the *Señoras Dòncellas de piso*, the 'young ladies of rank.' She proved to be extremely gifted in getting on with her pupils, making them understand what she wanted after she herself had listened to what they had to say. Her illustrious origin carried weight, she was highly intelligent, charmed people by her graciousness and radiated all around her an atmosphere of spiritual things. Perhaps her method varied according to the character of the person concerned? However that may be, far from depriving Teresa de Ahumada of the talks and conversations she so much enjoyed, she turned them to good account: 'I began to find pleasure in this nun's good and holy conversation and was delighted to hear her speak so beautifully of God.' [2]

Teresa de Ahumada had loved to exchange secrets with her rather frivolous cousin, but she found that María de Briceño was willing to take her into her confidence too: 'She told me how it was she became a nun just through reading what the Gospel says, "Many are called but few are chosen," and spoke to me of the reward which Our Lord gives to those who leave all for his sake.' [3]

Did the nun realize how impressionable Teresa was, so impulsive and ready to translate words into action that a mere spark of feeling would kindle the fire needed to bring a project to immediate realization? From early childhood her actions had always been

---

[1] MP quoted SEC, vol. II, p. 102.
[2] Sb, V, c. iii–1. [3] Sb, V, c. iii–1.

prompted by enthusiasm. María de Briceño no doubt understood this, for she turned it to good use: 'Her good companionship gradually rid me of the habits which bad company had given me and awakened in me afresh the desire for what was eternal.'[1] Teresa adds: 'My hostility towards the religious state lessened a little.' Her attitude in the matter was in fact slowly changing and her thoughts gradually turning in the direction of religious life.

But her pride suffered. Up till then everyone had obeyed the self-willed child. By artfulness or wheedling she got everything she wanted. She had always been the most beautiful and beloved of daughters. Her father and mother talked about her outbursts of temper, quoting them as instances of personality; her good taste, cleverness, wit, her gifts as a young writer were boasted of, as were her gracefulness as a dancer, her skill at chess, her daring as a rider; of a piece of embroidery she made a work of art; and she made the family dinner as exciting as a firework display. She could afford to be ambitious. It was said of her in Ávila:

'Teresa de Ahumada? She will marry whom she chooses.'

She had always beaten the cleverest at their own game. But at Our Lady of Grace she was to undergo for the first time the painful experience of realizing that there was something she lacked, a quality, a perfection that was not hers: 'If I saw one of my companions shed tears as she prayed or give proof of some other virtue, I envied her greatly; for my heart was so hard that I could have read the whole Passion through without shedding a tear: and it hurt me to be like that.'[2]

She who did not know what it was to be thwarted, thus came up against forbidden territory. The obstacle was in herself: an incapacity to understand, to feel. She was astonished that joy could be found in humiliation. In her search for adventure she had discovered a limitless world, vaster and richer than any land beyond the seas and one more difficult to conquer: her interior self.

And so it was at the convent of Our Lady of Grace that God gave 'the first knock' on the door which led to the secret recesses of Teresa de Ahumada's soul.

On the advice of María de Briceño she began to pray much aloud: she also asked others to pray for her, that God would show her clearly the state in which she would serve him best: 'I still hoped that it would not be in religious life. . . . Yet I also dreaded marriage.'[3]

In one so hard to please as Teresa, her brief experience of human love had left rather disdain than regrets: as she had known it, it had

[1] Sb, V, c. iii-1.　　　　　[2] Idem.　　　　　[3] Sb, V, c. iii-2.

nothing in common with what she had learnt from the tales of chivalry about love for its own sake. What was a married woman's life in those days? Complete submission to her husband, to his relations as well as hers, to the customs and usages of the time; in spite of strict observance of the practices of religion, the mind scarcely rose above the contingencies of material existence; confinements succeeded each other until she died of exhaustion or in childbirth. Such had been the destiny of Doña Beatriz de Ahumada and such also, in an even briefer space of time, of Doña Catalina del Peso y Henao, Don Alonso de Cepeda's first wife, three years after marriage, after having given birth to her second child.

Teresa de Ahumada later betrayed the fears of her girlhood when as a Carmelite she pointed out to her nuns 'the great grace God had given them in choosing them for himself: he has spared them the being in subjection to a man who is often the cause of their losing their life and God be thanked if he does not make them lose their soul too!' [1]

Fear of an early death would not have deterred from marriage a courageous girl who always adored children, but married life was slavery. The wife had no right to express an opinion before her lord and master, she could only have recourse to subterfuge. What became of the respect and admiration which every woman must feel before she can give submission, when the lord and master turned out to be worthy only of contempt?

Later on Teresa would blame Catalina Godínez for having considered the suitors her father proposed to her unworthy of her, but she added: 'She was not attracted by marriage, it seemed to her a dreadful thing to be in subjection to anyone, and she could not understand why she had so much pride. Our Lord, wanting to save her, knew which chord to strike to awaken her heart's response. Blessed be his mercy.' [2]

It was the same in Teresa de Ahumada's case: she knew that the love of man, love for a man, does not last 'for ever and ever.' It was for this reason she held back from marriage. She was already turning over in her mind the possibility of entering religion, but, if possible, without cutting herself off completely from the world: for instance she would never enter Our Lady of Grace where twelve nuns observed the abstinence, the silence, the practices of mortification so rigorously that the *Señora Doncella de piso* was appalled by it. There were less austere Orders. And Teresa sometimes liked to let her thoughts stray to the convent of the Carmelites of Mitigated observance—the convent

[1] Sb, F, c. xxxi-46.   [2] Sb, F, c. xxii-5.

of the Incarnation—where her great friend Juana Suárez had taken the habit. This convent was large and very pleasant, kept very much alive by its hundred and twenty-four nuns, young and old, among whom were some secular persons. These Carmelites were devout, of course, but they did not carry penance to extremes. In spite of their low ceilings and the grille separating the nuns from the visitors, the parlours of the Incarnation were among the places most frequented by the best society of Ávila.

'I looked more to the satisfaction of sensuality and vanity than to the good of my soul. These good thoughts of becoming a nun sometimes came to me, but soon left me. . . .'[1]

At Our Lady of Grace, Teresa went through a year and a half of interior struggle. 'Spiritually she was attracted to the convent, but the things of sense drew her away from it; sense struggled against spirit and made her heart a battlefield.'[2]

In all this the love of God did not enter into the matter: she weighed the chances of less suffering in this world against paradise in the other: what would be her lot, as a religious, or, on the other hand, as a married woman.

Why was she not a man! She would not have hesitated to follow Fernando, her eldest brother, who came to bid her good-bye: he was leaving for Seville and from there was setting out to join Francisco Pizarro in Peru. Don Alonso Sánchez de Cepeda's sons were crazy about going overseas. Pizarro had been imprisoned for debt almost as soon as he arrived in Spain, but what did it matter? The Emperor had named him *Adelantado* (*i.e.* governor) of the lands he was setting out to conquer, and captain-general. Over there there was so much gold and silver that it was used for the floors of houses, but the future *conquistadores* laid the emphasis on the souls to be saved rather than on the wealth to be gained. The spoils of the conquest were set out in round figures: 21,300,000 gold crowns, the treasures of Montezuma brought back by Cortés; 1,200,000 baptisms between 1524 and 1532. Some, those who said that precious stones rolled about like pebbles under the horses' hoofs, even mentioned 14,000 baptisms a day. After making due allowance for exaggeration, the conclusion was that it was a Christian duty to go off to the Indies.

Teresa was now beginning to suspect that to be baptized was not enough. If she had not had the misfortune to be born a woman, she would not have hesitated to choose the religious state, for she would then have been permitted to go and evangelize these poor people:

[1] Sb, V, c. iii–2.　　　　[2] LL quoted SEC, vol. II, p. 477.

conquerors as well as conquered. What was still worrying her about religious life was the door that was to close 'for ever,' the anguish of feeling that the very fact of dying to self would perhaps cause her to become so bitter that she would lose heaven all the same.

The struggle made her ill, she was only seventeen. At the end of the winter she had to be sent back to her father: the conflict had been so severe, the nervous strain so continual, the alternate depression and excitement so exhausting.

The spoiled child was surprised to feel so little joy over her return home. She loved her family, of course, but she was not sufficiently mature to find pleasure in her father's serious conversation, and the pranks in which her brothers indulged drew from her no more than a tolerant but rather weary smile. Confined to bed, she spent many hours looking at a picture of Jesus and the Samaritan woman which her mother had hung in her room when she was a small child; she could not take her eyes off it and kept on repeating to herself the text beneath: *Domine da mihi aquam.* She had often wanted this living water. Had the Samaritan woman herself wanted it so very much before Jesus came to her? She was a sinner who did not know Our Lord. On the other hand she, Teresa, brought up to believe in him, could not resolve to follow him. Attentive to the heart's movement which should accompany that of the lips, she pronounced the name of Jesus, and did not succeed in awakening a spark of true love. Did not faith imply the power to love God as she loved the absent Fernando, or Rodrigo who was here, or her dead mother, or her father who was still with her? She experienced only one feeling deeply: a kind of jealousy of the Samaritan woman whose indifference Our Lord had shattered so effectively that she set the whole town of Samaria agog with her story.

Teresa's health improved only slowly, to the keen disappointment of her brothers and the crowd of cousins who were in and out and who had hoped to see her take her place again in their little band. Was this the very 'occasion' she wanted to avoid? She asked her father to let her go and join her sister María at Castellanos: the stay in the country would no doubt hasten her recovery. Don Lorenzo and Rodrigo, only too glad to hear her express a wish at all, took her there.

There were not more than ten houses in Castellanos de la Cañada and these were grouped around Don Martín's residence. Here, masters and peasants formed one big family. There was nothing but the fresh clear air, and the silence. The land round about was barren, but there was a fountain and clumps of cork-oak. To the convalescent, the distant sheep-bells as the flocks changed pasture, a sound as crystal-clear as light, seemed heavenly music.

Teresa brightened: she busied herself in the house, played with her tiny baby nephew, and took great pleasure in doing the cooking. Her sister who adored her would have liked to keep her with her always. María was a gentle creature. Her only reaction to her husband's difficult character was perfect submission; she did not rise up in protest when he started a distressing quarrel about the inheritance. Good Christian that she was, she allowed herself to be worn out by cares and worries,[1] of which the couple had many; money was scarce although María's dowry had been three thousand ducats.

If she did not find happiness in spiritual things, Teresa did not find at Castellanos any proof that she would obtain happiness in marriage. On the other hand, was she henceforward to find pleasure nowhere, to see emptiness in everything? She was a little vexed with herself for not being entirely satisfied, surrounded as she was by affection and in the heart of her beloved Castile. Already work seemed to her the only balm for a seared soul.

Work and reading. Not a day passed without her remembering with gratitude the stop they had made on their journey at the village of Hortigosa where her uncle Don Pedro Sánchez de Cepeda lived. His house was known as 'the palace' but the good and serious-minded man who lived in this lovely country residence was far removed from any suggestion of ostentatiousness. He divided his time among his books, prayer, meditation and those works of charity which one no longer dares to call good works since so many 'good' people have confused self-satisfaction with the practice of the love of their neighbour. Despite Teresa's affection for her father, his piety made little impression on her. It is nowhere apparent that he influenced her other than by continual good example and the pious habits she was taught in childhood, whereas Don Pedro's fervour created such a perceptible harmony around him that she could not help being impressed by it. In her turn she delighted her uncle by the quiet way she listened to him and her ready answers.

Don Pedro was a widower and was only waiting till his son's upbringing should be finished to become a monk. In his conversation Teresa found once more the same delight as in her discussions with Doña María de Briceño: 'His most usual subject was God and the vanities of the world.'[2] A cultured man, the only pride he had was in showing his rich library. His finger on a book which he did not take

---

[1] CTA, ii.   [2] Sb. V, c. iii-4.

down from the shelf, for the fantasies of the poets no longer held his preference, he quoted Teresa some lines from one of them.

> Where is the King, Don Juan?
> The Princes of Aragon,
>   Where are they now?
> Where are all the courtiers,
> Where are all the pastimes
>   Which they devised?
> The jousts and tournaments,
> Caparisons and trappings,
>   And helmets plumed?
> Were they nought else but dreams?
> Were they nought else but chaff
>   On threshing floor?
> Where are now the ladies?
> Their kerchiefs and their gowns,
>   Their perfumes rich?
> Where are they now, the flames
> Of passion's fire enkindled
>   By lovers young?

At this time when Spain, enriched by the new world, was moving towards the zenith of her earthly power, her most highly esteemed poet was still old Jorge Manrique, and among all his works the most appreciated were these *coplas* which sang of the transitoriness of things.

> Our lives are the rivers
> Which flow into the sea,
>   The sea of death.

Teresa's lovers, her finery, her pleasures, were fading away into nothingness. The boy who had loved her and whom she herself had loved, what more was he to her now than Palmerín or Amadis? Scarcely a memory. With this difference: that that particular memory was tarnished with a sense of shame; a proud girl like Teresa would never forgive herself. No earthly joy could last for ever, then; the only thing which seemed to be unending was the remorse at having been mistaken.

Touched by the attention his niece showed him, Don Pedro made bold to take down his biggest volumes from the shelves: he asked Teresa to read aloud to him:

'I wasn't very keen to do so, but I made him believe I found pleasure in it. For I was extremely anxious to please people, even if it

meant doing things I disliked; but what would have been virtue in
someone else was a great fault in me, for I often went beyond the
bounds of discretion.' [1]

Don Pedro chose the letters of St. Jerome. 'God,' Teresa says,
'forced me to do violence to myself. I only remained with my uncle
a short time, but the words of God, both those I read and those I
heard, and his good influence made such a deep impression on me that
I understood the truth which I had but dimly sensed as a child: ALL
THINGS ARE NOTHING.' [2]

And so at Castellanos, while she was smoothing little Juan's curls
or stooping to pluck a sprig of rosemary, or thinking of Rodrigo who
was soon coming to fetch her, she repeated to herself again and again:
'All things are nothing.'

For a long time she watched the water from a tiny spring gush
forth among the rocks, spurt upwards and bubble, and she was
surprised to see that 'the sand once disturbed never ceased to rise.'
Perhaps in the same way the love of God would one day cause the
slime of which she was made to rise upwards too?

She pondered over the joy of the thirsty earth when watered and
this made her alarmed at the aridity of her soul, but she remembered
that Christ is 'a good gardener.' [3]

---

[1] Sb, V, c. iii-4.   [2] Sb, V, c. iii-5.   [3] Cf. Sb, V, c. xvii-1.

IV

REASON, NOT LOVE

ALL things are nothing, the world is vanity, life is short: I began to be afraid that if I died I should go to hell, and although I was not yet prepared to become a nun, I saw that it was the best and safest state of life: and so gradually I determined to force myself to enter religion.'[1]

Teresa here pronounces for the first time the word she was to repeat most frequently, the key-word of her spiritual life as it was of her life of action: *determinación*, determination, decision. 'I decided . . .' 'I am deciding . . .' 'It is tremendously important to begin with great determination . . .' 'She who begins with determination . . . has already travelled a great part of the way . . .,'[2] '. . . almost nothing, the smallest of decisions . . .'

When she came back from Castellanos de la Cañada and Hortigosa she was eighteen. At an age when those who are enthusiastic and gifted want to have everything, to find an outlet for all their powers, and when they allow the wild branches to grow side by side in their soul with those that bear fruit, she took the pruning shears and *determined* to cut down those which were weakening the tree and which might prove harmful to the development of perfect fruit.

She had already gradually brought under review the workings of the mind, of her passions, that of the influences to which she was subjected and the movement of the will, all-powerful when we *determine* to rule our conduct, and even tendencies which seem uncontrollable, by it. The astonishing change which had taken place in her since her arrival at Our Lady of Grace was the result of a discipline first imposed from without and then understood and accepted: she had tried out the effects of discipline on herself. She knew for the future that feelings, desires, wishes, attitudes, that which can form our character and yet is nothing but a collection of tendencies which practice and habit can overcome or develop, are under the control of the will. God created man free to choose perfection. 'This act of the will (*determinación*) is what he wants.'[3] He wants nothing more than our willed choice

---

[1] Sb, V, c. iii-5. [2] Sb, V, c. xi-13. [3] Sb, V, c. xi-5.

(*determinación*): then he does the rest himself.'[1] 'The Lord helps those who are determined to serve him for his glory.'[2]

In the sphere of action it could be said of her: 'She thought out thoroughly what she had to do and gave the matter consideration; and after she had made up her mind about it she displayed great firmness and constancy in the execution and fulfilment of her design.'[3] Even when speaking of the highest spirituality she declares: 'All is already as good as done when a soul *determines* to practise mental prayer.' In a short chapter of the *Autobiography* the word *determinación* occurs ten times and is associated with the idea of liberty: 'It is very important to begin with this liberty and this determination. . . .' 'Those who have this determination have nothing to fear. . . .' 'She must be determined not to allow Christ to fall with the Cross even though this dryness should last all her life.'[4]

In 1533 she had not yet found love, but she knew she would not find it in the world; she was *determined* to go in pursuit of it, like the youths of Ávila who were far from possessing the gold they hoped to win, when they took ship for overseas.

The decision to force herself was taken but the interior struggle went on all the same: the end of the journey was decided but the horses were restive and reared up in protest. Teresa argued with herself thus:—

For: The efforts and sufferings which life in the convent would demand of me would not be worse than purgatory, whereas I had truly deserved hell; to live the years I had to live as if in purgatory was only a small thing, since afterwards I should go straight to heaven as I wished.[5]

Against: The devil whispered to me that accustomed to comfort as I was, I could not stand the restrictions of life in a religious Order.[6]

For: Against this I put forward the sufferings of Christ: it was a small thing to bear a few painful things for him; he would help me to bear them.[7]

For and against: I was much tempted during that time. . . . It was servile fear far more than love which urged me to embrace this state.[8]

Temptation was often disguised under the appearance of good. Her father and brothers were glad to welcome her back. She ran the house competently, for her it was a labour of love and they all wondered

[1] Sb, F, c. xxviii–19.   [2] SEC, R, iv, p. 28.
[3] FR.   [4] Sb, V, c. x–6. Idem, 15–12–10.
[5] Sb, V, c. iii–6.   [6] Idem.   [7] Idem.   [8] Idem.

how they had been able to live two years without her. Her talent for organization, her extreme love of order and cleanliness, her intuitive knowledge of character, her need of affection—at that time her need of being loved was greater than her need to love—made of her a woman as attractive as she was accomplished: while she put practical things first, she also gave her attention to what gave people pleasure. Don Alonso had never been so full of joy nor his children better understood or looked after. They crowded around their big sister, so eager for her company that she sometimes had a scruple over it: was not her duty to act as a mother to the two youngest, Agustín whose wildness made her anxious, and the baby Juanilla? As for the others, Jerónimo at eleven was a dare-devil, Pedro, who was twelve, complained of being ragged, Antonio was all submission, Lorenzo at fourteen was already attentive to girls and pious in church; Rodrigo, the eldest of all, busied himself with his love affairs and made his preparations for departure overseas. Teresa was the link that held them to each other and to the old home.

Once more she felt very close to her father, although she did not tell him of the pain it caused her to do violence to herself until she had definitely and irrevocably chosen religious life as her state: she would struggle and suffer alone, now as always. Her worst sufferings she never remembered confiding to anyone; she said one day: 'In that, I am not a woman: I have a hard heart.' [1] Household cares now left her little time for reading, but she was by no means unhappy on this account; she had now come to distrust the tales of chivalry and preferred the *Letters* of St. Jerome. She did not read Erasmus, who in the eyes of such a sober-minded and orthodox person as Don Alonso was a stirrer up of muddy waters, but she could not avoid hearing him spoken about. Spain was then divided into Erasmites and anti-Erasmites, to the extent that the students in Salamanca and Alcalá fought for or against him at the sword's point. Erasmus attacked the vices and abuses of the clergy; all those who allowed no criticism of the Church's representatives, even in the name of the Gospel, rose up so violently against him that his loyal partisan, Manrique, had to take up his defence at the Junta of Valladolid in 1527. The thought and writings of this cosmopolitan—for Rotterdam, Paris, Oxford, Cambridge, Louvain, Basel, Bologna, Padua, Florence, Turin, Venice, Rome were then the entire intellectual world—combined to restore to Spain the traditional sense of austerity which she seemed to have lost in the first twenty years of the reign of Charles V owing to the influence of the

[1] SEC, R, iii, p. 18.

emperor's Burgundian entourage. Erasmus's *Enchiridion*, the manual of the Christian knight, seemed to have been written expressly for devout *caballeros*. It set out to 'lead to salvation a man destined to live in the world. . . . The end of all our works, prayers and devotions must be Jesus Christ alone.'

A wave of mysticism was passing over Spain. To such an extent that the *Alumbrados*, whose name at first had no unsatisfactory associations, went much too far for the liking of the orthodox in the way they handled Scripture; they depended on illumination alone for their interpretation and thus fell under the ban of the Inquisition: the Church sifted to the bottom everything which smacked of Lutheranism however remotely. If prayer alone was sufficient for salvation, what became of the Church's claim to guide and control the faithful? The air of this passion for liberty that was abroad seemed to have something of schism about it.

Teresa was completely untouched by such seductive heresies: she longed for the paradise she had glimpsed in childhood, that of the *Lives of the Saints*, the most orthodox of heavens, and would have been most uncertain of getting there by the devious paths which the *Alumbrados* and *Dejados* [1] used.

She was not one for half measures; she would not have been contented like the *beatas* [2] to save her soul in the world, setting herself up as a living reproach to the frivolous, talking nothing but piety, and dressed with challenging austerity. Except for the reticence with which she now met her cousins' overtures of friendliness, she was in no way outwardly different from the girls of her age whose sole thought in life was to find a husband.

In the spring of 1534 Charles V came to Ávila. Doña Teresa de Ahumada took part in the celebrations. She was there when the youthful Charles, mounted on a black horse and with the imperial crown set on his fair hair, was met at the gates of Ávila by the Marquis of Las Navas, who begged him to swear, before entering the city, that he would respect its privileges, exemptions and liberties, for the knights would set aside nothing of their rights even in the presence of their

---

[1] *Alumbrados* and *Dejados*. Both these terms, and also *iluminados*, were used to describe an heretical sect active in Spain in the sixteenth and early seventeenth centuries. Among other false doctrines, they held that in ecstasy one could not sin, even venially. Seventy-six of their propositions were condemned by Cardinal Pacheco in 1623 (Tr.).

[2] *Beata* is the term used for a woman wearing religious habit, but living in her own house, practising prayer and works of virtue. But the term is applied loosely in Spain to devout ladies given over to prayer and good works of all kinds (Tr.).

sovereign. Charles V took the oath and the Marquis presented him with the keys on a silver paten. He gave them back immediately. Amid the noise of salvoes, acclamations, the cantering of one hundred and fifty of the finest flower of the youth of Ávila's nobility mounted on chestnut steeds, Charles entered Ávila, the city that was always loyal but never in servitude. And Teresa held her proud head high under her curls, as she would do later when she had to hold her own against the great and mighty of this world.

The reception was enthusiastic, but by the royal wish no extraordinary expense was incurred: austerity in spending was the fashion.

The heroic deeds of Ávila's past were recalled and Charles declared: 'This city is the model which all other cities of our realms must imitate,' and Teresa's love of mighty deeds, *hazañas*, which was now moving to the spiritual sphere, grew more ardent in her generous soul: [1] to force herself to follow the only master worthy of her ambitions, self-renunciation, the snapping of the threads of sensible attachment to passing things and to those she loved—that was, she judged, a *hazaña* worthy of the City of the Knights and Liegemen.

She began stern struggles against herself and her health suffered; her fever came back and her frequent fainting attacks frightened her father and her numerous brothers. Rodrigo, although there was so much affection between them, no longer understood her: both the Cepeda and the Ahumada came from fighting stock, they served God by dispatching the greatest possible number of his enemies and Rodrigo was preparing to follow their example in setting out for foreign conquests. The house in which Teresa was fighting her interior battle single-handed re-echoed with Rodrigo's projects. His outfit and equipment cost Don Alonso many ducats and Teresa a great deal of work. But Pedro de Mendoza's expedition to which he was to be attached was the most splendid that ever set sail. Juan Osorio, the master of the camp, was from Ávila and thirty-two noble families of Spain gave him their eldest sons for the war on the Rio de la Plata, whose name of Silver River was given to it because men made their fortunes there. The hopes of the future *conquistador* were so confident that he renounced his inheritance in favour of Teresa, so that a large dowry should help her to make a good match.

For her his departure was one more confirmation of the bitterness of human joys and even of human tenderness, but the irrevocable step was difficult to take; she was resolved, but she must now put her resolution into practice. She often went to seek fresh courage from

[1] Cf. Sb, C, c. vi-4.

María de Briceño or from the Dominicans at the monastery of St
Thomas, but her most frequent objective in her walks was the Incarnation, the convent of Carmelites where Juana Suárez seemed to have
found happiness. Such visits passed unnoticed by Don Alonso: no
well-born girl went out except to Mass and Vespers, to hear a sermon
or for some other devotional purpose. The less devout met their lovers
in church. And so when Teresa went from one end of Ávila to the
other, with her velvet basquine [1] fastened round her waist, swinging
her wide skirt of orange taffetas with its crossbands of black velvet on
which everyone complimented her, and covered in jewels, dignified
but laughing, who would have thought she had made up her mind to
enter a convent?

Finally she grew weary of her own hesitations and *determined* to
bring matters to a head: she would inform her father of her decision
to be a religious: 'This for me was tantamount to taking the habit, for
I so honoured my word that I knew I should not draw back for anything on earth once I had spoken to him.' [2] Thus the *pundonor*, the
point of honour, that form of pride which she, in common with all
Spain, had learnt the meaning of in the tales of chivalry, gave Teresa
de Ahumada the strength which she had not yet found in the love
of God.

The declaration was dramatic: nothing could have led Don Alonso
to foresee that a daughter of whom his only complaint was her excessive love for the world and its pleasures might want to leave him to be
a nun. 'My father lóved me so much that I could not obtain his consent; the most he would concede was that I could do as I wished after
his death.' [3]

She called in friends and relatives to intervene, but no one, not
even Don Pedro de Cepeda, could make Don Alonso give way. He had
been willing enough to enter into a contract to give bushels of wheat to
the poor every year but he persisted in refusing God the daughter he
loved so much; his spirituality did not go as far as complete renuncia-
tion, his generosity only sacrificed what he did not need. Would
Teresa be able to wait and to maintain her inflexible resolve? She
admitted, but to no one but herself, 'I am afraid of myself, of my own
weakness.' [1]

For the world she wanted to flee from still attracted her strongly
at times; she still sought to please people, she still caught herself trusting to the warmth of someone's look and telling herself all of a sudden

---

[1] A sort of outer petticoat—Tr.   [2] Sb, V. c. iii-7.
[3] Idem.   [4] Idem.

that perhaps that particular person would understand loving 'for ever.' But what about heaven? And hell? To turn to God she sometimes had to wrench her attention away from other things as if she were twisting it with her hand. She knew now, after her experience at Our Lady of Grace, that once at the convent she would have no regrets; protected from 'temptations' she would carry out methodically and to the letter, with all the patience the task demanded, the slow work of transformation. Once there, nothing would come to turn her mind away from God. She was simply longing to begin and exaggerated the risks she was running. Her disposition was not one that could brook delay: 'When I want something, I want it for all I'm worth.' [1]

After Rodrigo had gone, she chose the gentlest of her brothers, Antonio, who was only fifteen, as her confidant. She was always talking to him about what she did not yet experience except at intervals, and the more she was tempted by the illusory things of earth, the more ardently and persuasively did she speak to him of eternal life: it was really to herself she was speaking and herself she was persuading. She read St Jerome to him aloud, especially the terrible *Letter to Heliodorus*.

> Your widowed sister will come and hold out her arms to you, the servants will come and the nurse who reared you and her husband who are like a second father and mother to you, and barring your route they will say to you amid their tears: 'Master, to whom are you entrusting our old age? Who will help us to die? Who will bury us?' More than this, your mother, aged and venerable, her forehead worn by wrinkles, her breasts shrunken and drooping, she too barring your way, will give vent to her grief, going over your past life from the day she brought you into the world until now. . . .

Don Alonso, moreover, had recalled Teresa's childhood; he departure, too, would cause both relatives and servants grief. She read on: 'On you alone depends this house now about to totter. . . .' It was true that her father's house depended entirely on her. . . . She turned the page: 'What are you doing beneath your father's roof, weak and cowardly soldier? Even if your mother with dishevelled hair and torn garments, even if your father himself lies across the threshold, step over your father's body. . . . Here filial piety shows itself only by having no pity.'

Antonio was caught up in his sister's fervour and just as *la niña* had persuaded Rodrigo to set out with her in search of martyrdom, so now she persuaded this younger brother of hers to leave their father's house at the same time as she did and to enter with the

[1] SEC, R, iii, p. 18.

Dominicans while she went to join her friend Juana Suárez at the Convent of the Incarnation.

This convent had originally been a community of fourteen *beatas*, fourteen as an act of homage to 'Jesus Christ, our sovereign Good, and his most holy Mother, in the company of the Twelve Apostles.' In short, a group of pious Carmelite women tertiaries, joined together to practise prayer in their own chapel: this particular chapel was a former synagogue which the bishop had set aside for their use. They only took simple vows, but in 1512 their prioress, Doña Beatriz de Higuera, induced them to strive to reach a higher degree of perfection by adopting monastic life and the Rule of the Order of Our Lady of Mount Carmel; this Rule, which was less austere than the primitive one handed down by the prophet Elias and the Fathers of the Desert, was known as the 'Mitigated' rule.

Doña Beatriz began by instituting a lawsuit against her father to obtain possession of her property, and she erected a vast building, outside the walls of Ávila, on the site of a former Jewish cemetery. It was considered a poor place when compared with the carved granite of the palaces of the nobility, but the convent had plenty of fresh air, built as it was in rural style, with arched cloisters opening on to a green patio; the cells were small but well arranged, and some of them formed a small apartment—two rooms and a kitchen with a stove in it. There was a large central staircase and the whole building got the full benefit of the sun. There was a fine view over the city ramparts and a wide background of hills and an abundance of water enabled them to have an extensive orchard. The man-made materials might be poor, but the monastery was rich in natural beauty, the handiwork of the Creator. Teresa liked this contrast and she saw a sign from heaven in the fact that the new convent was inaugurated on the very day of her baptism.

One morning towards the very end of October 1536, when as yet the tops of the trees in the garden were scarcely visible in the grey light of dawn, she came out of her room without allowing herself to give so much as one backward glance, walking on tiptoe and holding her breath as she passed the rooms where her father, her brothers and her young sister Juana were still sleeping. Antonio helped her to move the locks of the heavy entrance door silently, to pull it open and then hold it so that it should shut to noiselessly on all those they were leaving. Teresa recalled her flight with Rodrigo thirteen years before: then she had felt no grief, the fact that she had parents had only been a 'major obstacle' for her and the thought of their grief did not make her suffer. Was she more affectionate now? Or weaker? Had her struggles with herself, the first effects of the awakening of the love of Christ in her soul, softened her hard heart?

On the threshold she hesitated, but Antonio was there, unfaltering because of his very unconsciousness of what was involved. Teresa's code of honour did not allow her to show weakness before one so young. And just as on a former occasion, in the uncertain light of dawn, two thin silhouettes could be distinguished against the grey façade and were soon lost in the crowd of merchants, servants, worshippers who were crossing the Plaza Santo Domingo to go to market or to church. But this time, it was for ever, Teresa knew it by the anguish which she felt.

> I do not believe that I shall suffer more when I come to die than when I left my father's house: it seemed to me that each one of my bones was being torn apart from the others: and as I did not feel anything of that love of God which makes one forget the love of father and relatives, I had to make so great an effort to do it, that if Our Lord had not helped me, my reason would not have sufficed to make me go forward. He gave me courage against myself.[1]

It was in this way that Doña Teresa de Ahumada y Cepeda entered into a bond with her heavenly Bridegroom, but guided by reason, not by love.

[1] Sb, V, c. iv-1.

V

LOVE AND GLORY

TERESA DE AHUMADA was determined to turn her marriage of convenience into a love match. If she had foreseen, as she made her way towards the convent in the coldness of the October dawn, that for twenty years she would be torn between the world and God, she still would not have hesitated in the slightest: she had made Ávila's motto her own, *Antes quebrar que doblar*, to break oneself rather than to yield, to die rather than give up.

She was perfectly well aware that what she would chiefly have to fight was herself. It seemed to her that she was the less fitted for sanctity because she had all the gifts that made for worldly success, and she regarded herself as riddled with faults and inconsistencies: she was proud, but frivolous: domineering, but easily influenced; she talks of herself as being 'terribly given to subterfuge' [1] and yet mentions her horror of lies, or again of her liking to please people which does not, however, bridle a quick temper liable to break out into 'terrible' rages. Then there was the point of honour, this 'wicked self-esteem,' self-esteem regarded from entirely the wrong point of view, which she calls a chain on which no file can make an impression.[2]

Teresa did become a saint by sheer force of willing it and with the grace of God. It is this process of achieving sanctity, the slow and costly transformation, that make her life an unparalleled example for us.

When she had passed the ramparts and crossed the gully which divides the Incarnation from the town, she felt there was now a whole abyss between her and the past. In saving goodbye to Antonio outside the convent, she detached herself from her earthly family; when the enclosure door opened with much screeching of locks and bolts and closed behind her again, convinced now that all things were nothing, she resolutely accepted the fact that God was everything.

Juana Suárez was waiting for her, in the midst of a crowd of young nuns who forthwith proceeded to treat the newcomer both with sisterly love and curiosity. Teresa unbent, smiled and immediately won all hearts. Would it not be easy to tread the path to heaven with companions like these? They had not lost their spontaneity through keep-

---

[1] Sb, V, c. xxxi-23.   [2] Idem, 20.

ing their Rule. Their Constitutions were severe in principle but in practice very accommodating. She had put on her plainest dress but the nuns thought the material lovely. In her eagerness to be at once on the same footing as the others, she begged the prioress, 'the most Reverend and Magnificent Señora Doña Francisca del Águila,' to whom she was related, to give her the Carmelite habit at once. But Doña Francisca had already summoned Don Alonso: nothing would be done without his authorization.

The poor man was at his wits' end: the Dominicans had likewise come to tell him of Antonio's decision to become a Friar Preacher. It meant a hard and bitter struggle between God's service and a father's love. Strongly suspecting that once more it was *la niña* who was responsible for everything, and that if he got her back the boy would follow, he rushed to the Incarnation trembling at the thought that he was really confronting not only his daughter, but God.

With the very first words she spoke in her eager voice, Teresa put his responsibilities so clearly before him that, good Christian as he was, he did not dare to resort either to entreaties or authority, although on his way to the convent he had rehearsed in turn both phrases of tenderness and orders which should brook no refusal. He knew now that even if she were to give way, he could not in the future enjoy the company of the daughter he loved so much without remorse. So he gave way, and all arrangements were made for the dowry and the clothing.

On 31st October 1536, he gave an undertaking before a notary to make over to the convent of the Incarnation every year, twenty-five measures of grain, one half being wheat and one half barley, or, in their default, two hundred gold ducats. Teresa renounced all claims on the family inheritance and made over Rodrigo's eventual legacy to her sister Juana.

Her father also gave the novice a bed, blankets and quilts, six linen sheets, six pillows, two mattresses, two cushions, a carpet, as well as the clothing she would need during the noviciate and after profession: 'the habits, one of fine black cloth and the other of thicker material; three underskirts, one of red wool, another white and the third of fine serge; a sheepskin cloak, her veils, undergarments and shoes; and finally the books which it is customary for nuns to be given.'

Teresa was to take the habit on 2nd November. On the night before, her night of vigil, she did not sleep: all the bells both far and near which had pealed when she was born now tolled to remind her that to-morrow was All Souls' Day. A solemn knell, a discordant clash

of bronze which brought no peace to the soul but rather shook it to
the depths of its self-satisfaction, forcing it to contemplate the effects of
God's anger. Teresa wept; not for the world, but for her sins; not for
what she was leaving behind her, but for what she could not escape
without making expiation: the fear of purgatory and that of hell. A
whole lifetime spent in penance seemed too short. She deserved
damnation. 'For ever and ever, Rodrigo. . . ?' 'Teresa, for ever and
ever. . . .'

The idea she formed of purgatory still resembled the pictures of
which she was so much afraid as a child, pictures which she remembered as patches of vivid red at the back of some dark church, in which
men and women thrust bare arms upwards out of a sea of flame: Our
Lady, the angels leaned down towards them and saved a few. How
many nights had she not aroused the whole house by her screaming as
she awoke from a nightmare in which she had dreamt she was in hell!
When she was quite tiny, she made sacrifices, gave alms, said the
rosary for the *ánimas*, the souls in purgatory. And on her night of vigil
when the bells seemed to be tolling 'for ever' she only found peace in
sacrifice, begging Our Lady of Mount Carmel to accept her as a
hostage that the souls who were most forsaken might be taken out of
the abyss. This practical sympathy for the souls in purgatory was to
remain with her all her life.

When the time for the ceremony came, instead of being pale from
insomnia, the postulant's face was shining with the joy of the first of
her 'heroic acts.' [1]

Teresa kept her name as a novice and thus was still Doña Teresa
de Ahumada to her sisters in religion, but her gift of adaptation made
her immediately conform to nünnish ways: after a few days no one
would have recognized in the young nun who walked with measured
tread and downcast eyes, her hands under her scapular, the girl whose
yellow dress and careless demeanour had caused so much talk. She
seemed to find a kind of pleasure in exercising control over the
expression of her face, and she who never spoke without using 'many
words' [2] to express herself, now gave the briefest replies and forced
herself to silence. Perhaps she realized now to what an extent comport-
ment influences one's interior dispositions. Or was it a sign of the
deep change wrought in her by the taking of the habit? She admitted
that from the very beginning she felt so much joy at having chosen
the religious state, that it lasted all her life through. 'God changed my
soul's aridity into immense tenderness. Everything to do with the

------

[1] SEC, vol. II, p. 244.   [2] Sb, V, xiii-17.

Order was a delight to me; true, I was sometimes busy sweeping at
times when I should formerly have been giving myself up to pleasure
and finery, but when I realized every now and then that for the future
I was free of all that, fresh joy came over me, so intense that I was
astonished and could not understand where it came from.'[1]

She did not realize that it was partly the relief and comfort of having
carried out a decision and so of making the step irrevocable; though
only twenty the girl had brought so much penetration to her understanding of the world, both as regards people and things, that it was
not surprising that she now rejoiced to be free of it all.

In her first contact with religious life, then, Teresa realized the
efficaciousness of what she calls 'the heroic act': 'When I remember
all that, nothing I have to face seems so difficult as to make me hesitate
to undertake it. Experience has shown me that if in the beginning I
force myself to the determination to carry out, for God's sake, something that seems to me terribly hard, the sweetness of the reward will
be in proportion to the greatness of my dread of it.'[2]

More fervent now and already experiencing some small beginnings
of the fire of divine love, she began to exact more from herself. For a
few weeks she perhaps thought she had done everything in leaving the
world and her family, and for the future had no more battles to wage;
then she discovered that the peace she was enjoying was that of a
woman who settles down peacefully in her bed after having bolted
her doors against robbers, but leaves the robbers in the house all the
time: 'There are no worse robbers than those we carry within ourselves.'[3] Everything was effort and humiliation to her:

> I knew few prayers, and nothing about what had to be done in
> choir, I was so careless and taken up with vanity; other novices could
> have shown me what to do, but I committed the fault of not asking
> them so that they shouldn't see how little I knew. My singing was
> bad. . . . Through self-esteem I was troubled about this and so I
> did even less well than I could have done. . . . Finally I forced my-
> self to say so when I didn't know how something went. This cost
> me a good deal at the beginning but afterwards I found pleasure in
> it.[4]

It was bitter pleasure to a proud nature like hers. She resented
annoyances, rebelled when accused without sufficient reason, and in
spite of her decision to accept everything and love everything in
religious life she experienced discouragement, particularly when she

[1] Sb, V, c. iv–2. [2] Idem.
[3] Sb, C, c. x–1. [4] Sb V, c. xxxi–23.

compared herself to some nuns at the Incarnation who were leading lives of penance all the more admirable because they were rare. There was one who rolled herself in nettles like St Benedict, fasted all the year round and did not speak except to God; another was so holy that she worked a miracle while still alive: the candles she lighted on Our Lady's altar burned without being consumed; and there was Doña Teresa de Quezada who, despite her illustrious birth, refused to have a cell to herself and slept in the common dormitory of those who could not afford more.

Teresa had chosen a relative poverty; she liked the two comfortable and well-arranged rooms assigned to her; she gave herself the discipline, using nettles, but did not seem to feel the inequality which in this overcrowded monastery created two standards, one for nuns who were wealthy and another for those who were poor. The perfection of some pricked her self-esteem, but the poverty of the majority seemed to escape her notice. Her distractions in choir and her aridity grieved her, and she was exasperated at not understanding good nuns who talked to each other in her presence of the delights of prayer. Her soul was all disorder and confusion.

Who, then, was it who gave her to understand that there is no progress in the spiritual life so long as we are not loving our neighbour more than ourselves? When they suddenly found her weeping for her sins they made the mistake of supposing that her tears were for the world she had left. This vexed her. Was she thinking only of herself then? She soon put an end to self-centredness.

There was one nun suffering from a disease so loathsome that it was impossible to look after her without shuddering with horror; to do violence to heaven Teresa constituted herself her nurse and when she had to dress the ulcerous stomach which discharged pus, blood and excrement at the same time, her repugnance was changed to compassion. The stench was so appalling that it made her feel sick and she had to rush away quickly, to vomit. But she would come back again, smiling.

The long hours of attendance upon this sick nun, especially at night, coupled with penances so severe that the prioress had to forbid them, undermined what little health she had left; at Office, in the chapel where rain, wind and snow came in through the roof tiles which were not properly laid, she shivered with cold. In the grip of fever and in considerable pain, she asked God for the grace to bear her sufferings for his sake and by them to obtain the mastery over her body which the more fragile it was the more it seemed to require. She repeated to herself again and again: 'We come here to die for Christ and not to coddle ourselves for Christ.'[1] To go on living now seemed to her so hard that she found herself repeating over and over again the argument of her childhood: martyrdom is certainly the cheapest way of winning heaven. Wouldn't it be better to die of some fatal and painful disease as quickly as possible? After her profession, would Our Lord help her even more?

The ceremony took place a year and a day after her clothing, on 3rd November 1537. During the year she had measured the extent of the effort she still had to make. Her face was now just as pale as it had been radiant with colour when she was clothed.

In the chapel, amid the blaze of the candles offered by Don Alonso, the *caballeros* and their lovely ladies, magnificently attired, chattered busily as they were wont to do at weddings, or wept as at a funeral, according to their mood; the present ceremony was, indeed, both wedding and funeral.

Teresa moved forward between two rows of nuns singing the *Veni Creator Spiritus*. She was dressed in the habit only. This was fastened on the chest with a loose knot in order to be able to take the discipline more easily. She carried, neatly folded, her scapular, veil, girdle and a paper on which the *Pater noster* was written, symbol of a life which was henceforward to be vowed to prayer.

She prostrated before the grille, now open on to the sanctuary, touching the ground with her forehead.

The prioress was heard to put the traditional questions:

'What do you ask?'

'I ask God's mercy and the company of my sisters in perpetual enclosure.'

She pronounced her vows in a firm voice after she had listened to the reading of the Constitutions with their severe regulations. And, conscious of her weakness, it was with her whole heart that she identified herself with the prayer: 'May the Lord our God who gives us the desire grant us also to carry it out, *per Christum Dominum nostrum.*

The nuns answered: 'Amen.'[2]

Two sisters conducted her to the parlour. Behind the grille she saw her friends and relatives as in a dream. She had no regrets and was even exultant with a joy shot through with pain. Years afterwards, one day when she was searching for a term of comparison by which to describe a particular suffering, she said: '. . . I do not think that anything in my life hurt so much, not even my profession day. . . .'

[1] Sb, C, c. x-5. [2] Cited SEC, vol. IX, pp. 494-495.

There were festivities at the convent, a collation and dinner offered by Don Alonso who also gave each religious a fine linen coif. There was singing and dancing to the accompaniment of flute and tambourine. Doña Teresa de Ahumada displayed all her charm and high spirits. She who took so much pleasure in pleasing others charmed those present by her gaiety just as she touched them by her devotion. They knew nothing of her interior struggles. People were amazed at her many gifts.

'Doña Teresa de Ahumada is like silk of a golden colour which matches every other shade, for to win us all she suits herself to the character of each. . . .'[1]

All of a sudden there was quite a sensation: an old nun remembered that a *zahorí*, a diviner seeking for gold, who had come to the convent many years ago, had said that one day the Incarnation would have a Teresa who would be a saint. At that time there was no saint of the name and anyone called Teresa kept her feastday on the feast of St. Dorothy.

The newly professed nun hid her feelings under laughter, but she exclaimed:

'God grant it may be I!'

'God grant it may be *I*!' echoed Doña Teresa de Quezada.[2]

From the moment of taking the veil, she redoubled the demands she made on herself, and tightened the grip on her will. When she was tempted to give way a little to softness, telling herself: 'I am no angel . . . I am no saint,'[3] she upbraided herself; she told herself that by continuing to struggle she would doubtless become so. God helps the brave. A moment later she accused herself of vanity.

The fight against vainglory was such hard work for her that, over-excited by the excessive and spectacular penances of certain of her companions, she forgot her sense of proportion and horror of all exaggeration and, trying to crush even ordinary common-sense, she one day came into the refectory walking on all fours, a mule's pack-saddle loaded with stones on her back, dragged along like a beast by a sister who was pulling at the halter which Teresa had put round her neck.

Extravagances of this sort ended in further fainting attacks, in 'pains at the heart'[4] so acute that all who saw her suffer were scared, and in other sufferings too. She frightened the other nuns even more by her refusal of the care that was absolutely necessary than she did

---

[1] Cited SST, vol. I, p. 296.   [2] FR, L. I, c. vi.
[3] Cf. Sb. C, c. xvi–12.   [4] Sb, V, c. iv–5.

by her pallor. Scarcely able to walk, she turned up again in choir, pale
and tottering. To those who implored her to take care of herself she
said:

'What does dying matter? If we don't make up our minds to
swallow both ill-health and death at one draught, we shall never do
anything. It is more important to take this decision than we realize.
In this way we shall gradually conquer this body of ours.' [1]

She endured so much pain that the nuns whispered: 'God must be
dwelling in her. . . .'

When Don Alonso came to see her, she dragged herself painfully
to the grille, except on the occasions when she had to be carried there.
She did not complain, but her father was increasingly dismayed by the
deathly pallor of her face in which the eyes, formerly only slightly
protruding, now seemed to be starting out of their sockets. He sent
round to the Incarnation the best doctors in Ávila and the neighbouring
towns. Matters however grew worse: increasingly frequent and prolonged fainting fits were often responsible for a rumour of consternation in the convent:

'Doña Teresa de Ahumada is dead!'

Medical skill failed. The nuns' prayers seemed of no effect. Was
Christ listening only to those of the patient, who begged him to allow
her to share his sufferings and agony?

In the last resort Don Alonso decided to take Teresa away to
Becedas, a small village where a woman healer famous throughout
Castile was accomplishing wonderful cures. In the Carmelite Rule of
Mitigated observance, enclosure was not of strict obligation; Teresa
was therefore allowed to leave the Incarnation, accompanied by
Juana Suárez, in search of the cure she did not want.

[1] Sb, C, c. xi-45.

VI

NOT QUITE SO MUCH! [1]

THE doctors could not understand the illness of Don Alonso's daughter at all. They hastened to agree with his own explanation of the matter: the different kind of life and different food were at the root of her complex symptoms; their verdict, given in their pedantic jargon, was that if she returned to the family circle where she would have a more abundant and more discriminating diet, it would not take long for this fine young woman of barely twenty-three to regain her health. They saw, of course, no more than she was willing to let them see—a suffering body; the real key to the problem she hid from them. What this was she tells us later when she writes: 'I spent my first year at the Incarnation in very bad health, *although I don't think I offended God much at that time.*'[2] Thus she attributed her illness to a non-physical cause and she was right. She regarded illness as a trial, or else a punishment, and whereas she had not deserved the punishment, she had begged God to give her trials. Because she envied the endurance of the nun whose nauseating wounds she tended, she besought His Majesty to teach *her* patience, too, and to this end to send her 'whatever illness might be necessary.' Soon she was in such a condition that 'although my disease was not the same as hers, I think what I suffered for three whole years was no less painful and hard to bear.'[3]

The violent constraint which Teresa de Ahumada put upon herself to enter the convent had brought on the first crisis; now that she actually was at the Incarnation, all she could see in herself were failures and weakness; certain of her fellow-nuns had attained to the prayer of contemplation—she tried to imitate them and did not even succeed in meditating without distractions; her mind was unable to concentrate on one subject for any length of time; she forced herself, at the cost of extreme nervous tension and although she felt that her 'persistence was injuring her health.'[4] Her fierce anger against herself, her self-imposed penances, her stern persistence in self-conquest, the fits of depression during which 'quite small things caused her intense

[1] Sb, CAD, c. vi-2.   [2] Sb, V, c. iv-5.
[3] Sb, V, c. v-2.   [4] Sb, V, c. iv-8.

suffering,'[1] indiscreet fasting and vigils and finally her earnest prayer for expiatory suffering, precipitated the second crisis: those who really want to suffer seldom fail to get their wish. Teresa was relentless in wearing down her rebellious body, which was too earthly for her soul's flight and brought her spirit to earth with it.

Her tormented mind should have been treated in the same way as we treat hypochondriacs to-day when merely by brooding over their nervous fears they produce in themselves the symptoms of every possible disease. Instead, she was given injections, poultices, was bled, given pills which had to be taken in ones, threes, fives or some other odd number—this gave her devotion because the number of pills reminded her of the seven Gifts of the Holy Ghost or the Five Wounds of Jesus—she was rubbed with scorpion oil, considered to have soothing and stimulating properties and to be good for opening the pores of the skin—or with brick oil refined again and again after a whole process of boiling and grinding of specially chosen bricks, which must be very old and very red in colour. This was supposed to cure diseases of the nerves and joints or those of the bladder and kidneys if the complaint was due to cold. All these were remedies liable to kill a person in good health. Dismayed at the results obtained by such methods, Don Alonso put all his hopes on the *curandera*, the medicine-woman at Becedas. She used simples, a treatment doubtless less brutal than official medical practice.

As the treatment was not to be begun before the spring, it was decided that Teresa and her companion should spend the intervening month of April at Castellanos de la Cañada, with María: Becedas was quite near. The handsome litter which had formerly served frail Doña Beatriz for her journeys was done up for Teresa's use: it had good webbing supports and cost a thousand maravedis at a time when the Cepeda y Ahumada denied themselves nothing. Don Alonso, still in mourning for his wife, as he always would be, and so in black from head to foot and riding a horse with black saddle and breast-strap, accompanied Teresa, as did Juana, her Carmelite friend, who travelled on mule-back, and two or three servants.

The party made a halt at Hortigosa, at Don Pedro de Cepeda's 'palace.' The worthy man was deeply moved at seeing once more the niece whom he regarded as in some degree his spiritual daughter. He had her brought into the library until the meal should be ready. He was solicitous for her comfort and strove not to show the grief he felt at seeing her emaciated condition. Behind the window-panes the

[1] Sb, V, c. v-1.

snow was falling steadily. Warming those lovely hands of hers, almost worn to a shadow now, at the *brasero*, Teresa talked with her uncle and told him the secrets of her interior life, a matter on which she had been reluctant to speak to anyone: was it not he who had opened heaven for her by showing her 'good books' and St. Jerome? What a long way she had travelled since those years!

She told him frankly of her struggles, her hopes, her discouragement, the lukewarmness into which she habitually fell back after transports of love and devotion.

He shook his head.

'It is essential to pray, and to pray much.'

'I do pray.'

'How do you pray?'

She explained that she recited her prayers aloud: some sort of vocal prayer was her only means of keeping her attention fixed. And even then she found herself giving way to distractions during her many *Pater nosters*. But her heart was no longer dry and unresponsive before the crucifix: God had given her 'the gift of tears.'

'The only thing that counts is prayer, by which I mean mental prayer, recollection.'

Mental prayer! Her attempts at it ended in failure. She did not even know how to practise recollection.

Don Pedro went over to the shelves and took down a book which he placed in Teresa's lap. She read: *Tercera parte del libro llamado Abecedario espiritual. Compuesto por el Padre Fray Francisco de Osuna.*[1]

'There's a treatise on recollection for you: the *Third Spiritual Alphabet.*'

Teresa opened the book at random.

. . . Vocal prayer, as thou hast seen, is a petition we make to God to ask him for what is necessary for us.

. . . The second form of prayer, that is without pronouncing the words with the lips, leaves us free so that our heart alone speaks to Our Lord. . . .

. . . The third, which may be termed mental or spiritual, is that in which the highest point of the soul, sustained by love, soars upward to God in the purest and most loving way possible on the wings of desire. . . .[2]

[1] Part III of the book known as the *Spiritual Alphabet*, written by Father Francisco de Osuna. [An English translation of this work, now unfortunately out of print, was published by Burns Oates in 1931—Tr.]

[2] O, pp. 464-7.

That was what she wanted! Why had she not come across this expert in prayer before! And what she liked was that he supported his definition by concrete examples: 'In short, the first is a letter we send our friend. In the second way we send him a person whom we love as our ambassador. By the third method we go ourselves. . . . Or, if you prefer, in the first we kiss his feet, in the second we kiss his hands. In the third we give him a kiss on the lips.'

Recollection consisted primarily in refusing admittance to one's heart to all created things; the writer epitomized his thought in one line:

Desembaraza el corazón y vacía todo lo criado.

'Unburden your heart by emptying it of everything created,' and, he added: 'From everything, extract love.' Love everything, but in God and for God.

Teresa scarcely listened to what Don Pedro was telling her about the author, who had taken part in the battle of Tripoli, became a Franciscan friar and published the *Third Spiritual Alphabet*, his first work, in Toledo in 1527. She dipped into the volume, browsed here and there, fascinated by what she found she could understand of its theory and also by the methodical common sense of the practical applications. One passage arrested her attention:

Look well to the time after Matins, for that sleep is meant rather for the soul than for the body. Do not retire to bed drowsily but rather be fully wakeful in your desire for Our Lord; and like the bride, at night time, seek for God when you retire to rest. . . . Happy are those who give themselves to prayer before they slumber and who promptly return to prayer on waking. Such people, like Elias, feed, sleep, feed again and remain nestled in God's arms as children sleep on their mother's breasts after having drunk her milk, then wake again, feed once more and again fall asleep. With such glorious intervals the time of sleep can be considered more as prayer than sleep. . . . And then, even if they have slept, on waking again they know full well that their soul has slumbered in the arms of the Beloved.[1]

This was Teresa's first experience of that tenderness and intimacy so characteristic of Franciscan ways of talking about divine love. And she discovered that she had, after all, been practising mental prayer without knowing it; it was her habit to fall asleep in the presence of God, as she strove to live in his presence. Perhaps she was not as slow

[1] O, p. 471.

as she feared in climbing the uphill path? She never forgot this abandonment of the babe on his mother's breast and later often used the
comparison herself.

When it was time to go, and the litter was ready and the horses
saddled, she could not tear herself away from the book; with her ready
pen she copied down sentences from it. Her uncle watched her with a
kindly smile, but they came to fetch her. She closed the *Third Spiritual
Alphabet* regretfully.

'Take it,' said Don Pedro, 'it is yours.'

It was in this way that Teresa began her initiation into recollection
and mental prayer: through a book.

Don Alonso left Teresa in María's hands and returned to Ávila.
In the spring the three women set out for Becedas. They stayed in a
comfortably furnished house there, belonging to the Guzmán y
Barrientos. In those days Becedas was a small village with winding
streets; the stream which encircled it left but little room for the low
houses which were huddled against the church. To the sound of the
rippling of water, the rustle of the breeze through the great walnut-
trees, rose the fragrant smoke from the fires kindled with vine-shoots
at the hour when the garlic soup was cooking on every hearth in
Castile. When night fell, the patient closed her book and prayed in
the gathering darkness.

At first the treatment was not too painful; the medicine-woman
kept her patient under observation and merely prescribed a few simples
culled from among the 'holy remedies.' But, since her brief stay at
Hortigosa, Teresa's principal preoccupation was the study and application of Osuna's teaching. Already progress in the spiritual life seemed
to her a matter of laborious detail involving the utmost carefulness; it
meant all the difficulty of progressive abandonment, the rebellion of
her human nature, the slow awakening of a slumbering soul which
little by little begins to make the necessary adjustments and then puts
on the armour of light.

From this time onwards His Majesty showered graces upon her:
'The Lord began to load me with favours to such an extent that I
received the grace of the prayer of quiet; sometimes I even had the
prayer of union, although I did not know what either was. . . . It is
true that it lasted only a very short time, I'm not sure if it was as long
as an *Ave Maria*, but the effects were so tremendous that although I was
barely twenty, I felt as if I had the world under my feet. . . .' [1] Union

[1] Sb, V, c. iv-7.

is the prelude to ecstasy: and Teresa, although only for brief and occasional moments, was already detaching herself from the senses, from images, from the use of the understanding and was being raised to the sphere where God alone is perceived. And she was forcing herself to live in the continual presence of Christ.

For her prayer, however, she needed a book and was afraid to try and recollect herself without its help, 'just as afraid as if I had to fight with many people.' [1] Reading stirred up her ardour for spiritual things and helped her to gather together her scattered thoughts. In this way she managed her soul 'as it were by coaxing.'

The words 'struggle,' 'combat,' 'effort,' 'trouble' recur constantly in her account of her life at this time. Not only was she ill, undergoing severe treatment and suffering acute pain, but at the same time she was fighting for the conquest of the kingdom of the Spirit.

For the *curandera* was now using remedies of a more positive kind, too positive for Teresa's fragile body and frayed nerves.

The young Carmelite let her have her way; she was indifferent to it all. Had she not the universe 'under her feet'? Not that she did not need help. Her keen desire was to find a sure guide who would help her to scale the heights whose steep summits Osuna had shown her. 'And it was there that the demon began to trouble my soul. . . .' [2]

A man. A young man. A priest. But a young priest who was living in sin. He was appointed to the parish of Becedas and had 'great qualities, he was intelligent, he had some education though not too much. . . .' [3] Teresa made him her confessor.

She is frank about it: 'This man I am speaking of grew very fond of me, for I had very little to confess. . . . This affection was not bad, but, because of its very excess it was not a good thing. He understood that I was determined not to offend God gravely for anything in the world, he assured me that it was the same with him and our conversations went on interminably.' [4]

At that time she thought that only mortal sin mattered; when she read in Osuna that it is just as essential to preserve oneself from venial faults, she did not take it in, vigilance to this extent seeming to her impossible. She was not yet aware that in love no offence is trifling.

Thus in the beginning she did not worry about the slight uneasiness she experienced in the presence of this priest—a priest who never forgot he was a man as well. As to his reactions—hitherto women had only inspired him with sinful, physical desires—in the presence of

[1] Sb, V, c. iv-9.   [2] Sb, V, c. v-3.
[3] Idem.   [4] Sb, V, c. v-4.

this girl, beautiful under her Carmelite veil and so pure that when
they met he felt ashamed to be deceiving her as he was, although he
had not the courage to refuse to go on seeing her, he felt new feelings
arising in him. 'I was then so absorbed in God that all my conversation was about him. And as I was such a child, it made the priest
ashamed to see this. . . .' [1]

She spoke of God when the priest would have liked to talk with
her of themselves. Sitting with his back to the light that he might the
better conceal the fact that he was scarcely listening to what she was
saying, he looked into her deeply expressive eyes, shining with
sincerity and with a love not of this world.

To attract this angelic being, to capture her interest, to hold her
down to earth!

Accordingly one evening, the confessor told his penitent that he
was living in sin. Perhaps he hoped that the sinfulness would be contagious: 'For seven years he had been in an extremely dangerous state
on account of his relations with a woman in the village whom he loved,
and yet all the time he had continued to say Mass. The matter was so
public that he had lost both honour and reputation, but no one dared
to take him to task about it. That made me terribly sad, for I was
very fond of him.' [2]

Teresa did not break under the strain; her friendship became
deeper. True, she was very fond of him.

What she said about his affection for her was: ' I never saw any
harm in the great affection he bore me; yet it might have been purer;
there were, too, occasions when we might have sinned gravely if we
had not had a lively remembrance of God's presence.' [3]

How did it happen that María, who could not plead the excuse of
inexperience of life, or Juana Suárez, who was older than Teresa and to
whose care the prioress of the Incarnation had entrusted her, allowed
such an intimacy to form between a girl and a priest whose conduct
was the talk of Becedas? It clearly goes to prove that a woman's only
protector is herself, and also that at that time people shut their eyes to
the faults of the clergy.

Teresa thus went through this sad 'adventure' of sympathy and
affection alone. When, more mature, she saw the danger of it she was
indignant for a second: 'Oh the blindness of the world. . . . The
madness of the world dismays me! . . . Cursed be the law that goes
against the law of God!' [4]

[1] Sb, V, c. v-4.   [2] Idem.
[3] Idem, 6.   [4] Idem, 4.

But at the time she saw only the peril in which the priest who put himself into her hands stood. He had hardly gone when she called María and Juana and begged them to find out all about it, she wanted to know everything 'about the persons with whom he was living.' [1] They told her then about her confessor's mistress, describing her appearance and her ways; she even caught a glimpse of her through the window. Teresa now fathomed the depths of her friend's fall and refrained from judging him: 'The poor man was not so much to blame.' Such deep understanding and mercifulness can only come from unsullied purity.

So she continued to receive 'the poor man' with the same smile and an affection which was now more openly manifest because it was sisterly and full of compassion. Day by day he told her everything:

> The unhappy woman [Teresa does not reproach her either] had put charms in a little brass idol which she begged him to wear round the neck for love of her, and no one had succeeded in persuading him to part with it. Not that I believe in these charms. . . . As soon as I knew all that, I began to show him still more affection. My intention was good, but my conduct bad; for however great the good, one may never do anything wrong however small, to bring it about. I habitually spoke to him of God, but in fact he loved me so much that it was that which counted most with him. [2]

He loved Teresa so much and he had to watch her gradually becoming worse. The cure was turning out to be ruthless indeed. She suffered to such an extent that she sometimes cried out complaining that sharp teeth were lacerating her heart. Fears were entertained for her sanity. She no longer took food, could only swallow liquids and those with repugnance. Was the man who loved her so much going to add to her torments the grief of knowing 'that he was lost for ever'?

One evening he knelt by her, loosened a long cord from his neck and threw at her feet the little brass idol. He wept. So did she. Gently motioning him to go away, she called María who came in immediately; without turning her head, Teresa asked her to go at once and throw the amulet into the nearby stream.

From this moment Teresa watched the priest awake as it were from a heavy torpor; she listened to him as he recounted the story of his years of perdition which he now spoke of with detestation. Finally he told her he had broken off relations with his mistress and could not thank God enough for having opened his eyes. After this the two were

[1] Idem, 5. [2] Sb, V, c. v–5, 6.

united in a friendship that was completely blameless: it was not sin that had proved contagious but white-hot chastity.

Teresa, however, was dying 'of an over-application of medical treatment,'[1] the famous healer had used purges too freely—one a day —her inside felt as if on fire, the fever never left her, she was a martyr to nervous twitching, she was suffering unbearable pain 'and a very deep sadness.'[2]

At the end of July, in this condition, she said goodbye to the 'poor man' whom she had saved and who despaired of ever seeing her alive again. In actual fact it was he who died a year to the very day after entering the house at Becedas for the first time, as confessor to the young Carmelite of whom everyone said in the village: 'She is so ill. She is so beautiful. And she's a saint. . . .'

Don Alonso hastened to bring his daughter back to Ávila where a bevy of doctors again visited her bedside. This time they got out of their predicament by condemning her without hope of reprieve: to their already numerous mistakes they added that of diagnosing tuberculosis.

Teresa was now back in the room which had been hers as a child, near the one in which Doña Beatriz had brought her into the world and had suffered so many years from slow decline. For three months longer she was in such a state that it seemed impossible that anyone could endure such great and manifold sufferings and live: from head to foot there was no part of her that was not in pain. She kept up her courage by saying over to herself the words of St Gregory's version of Job: 'We have received good things from the hands of the Lord: why not evil?' But her poor body could not keep up its resistance.

On 15th August she asked for the last sacraments. Her father dissuaded her, thinking to reassure her.

'You can go to confession later when you are better: for you know you are going to get better!'

That very night she fell into a syncope. The priest who was called to administer Extreme Unction judged her to be dead, not dying. Don Alonso, in despair because he had not allowed her to make her Communion, let his prayers and groans be heard all over the house.

The first day Teresa gave no sign of life.

On the second day her breath did not dull the mirror they held to her lips and the hot wax of the candle which her father held over her

---

[1] Idem, 7.   [2] Idem.

to look at her more closely fell on her eyelids without awakening her to consciousness.

The third day they dug her grave at the Incarnation. She was washed and wrapped in her shroud. Her brother Lorenzo kept vigil during the night. He fell asleep; a candlestick overturned, the bed-curtains caught fire and the seemingly lifeless body was very nearly burnt.

On the fourth day the nuns of the Incarnation came to fetch away the dead body of their sister that it might be buried within the precincts of Carmel. Don Alonso refused to allow her to be taken away, and when he kept on repeating, 'The time is not come for my daughter to be put under the ground,'[1] it was thought he had gone crazy with grief. He claimed to be able to hear the beatings of her pulse and his fingers never left Teresa's wrist.

The nuns stayed on, kneeling upright in prayer around the bed—a couch as tragic on account of the demented father as it was on that of the dead girl.

Suddenly Teresa painfully raised her eyelids which were weighted down by the now cold wax of the funeral tapers. She saw the *capilla ardiente* and other tokens of death around her, with her sisters waiting to carry away the corpse, and she gropingly fingered the shroud.

Her first words were to ask once again for the sacraments. Then she continued speaking: her faint voice seemed to be coming from a long way off; she was alive, but she had not yet completely returned to earth. She said: 'Why did you call me back?' She declared she would have much to do in this world, they had told her so where she had been—in heaven. But she had seen hell, too. In her confused sentences interrupted by sobs—her pillow was wet with tears—they made out the words: 'convents . . . foundations . . . to save souls. . . .'[2] Finally she said:

'Don't think me dead until you see my body covered with cloth of gold. . . .'

The return of her sufferings, now more acute than ever, brought her out of her trance.

Now that his daughter was won back from heaven, or from hell, Don Alonso wanted to clasp her in his arms, but she cried out with pain: the slightest touch caused such agony 'that only Our Lord can know how unbearable these sufferings were.'[3] When the bed had to be made, two persons had to lift her in a sheet. She felt as if she were being torn to pieces, she was delirious. It was impossible for her to lie

[1] FR, L. I, c. vii.   [2] Idem.   [3] Sb, V, c. vi-1.

full length and she lay curled up, her muscles contracted, her knees up to her chin.

The silence and expressions of dismay of those about her frightened her. She wanted to convince them—and herself—that she was not paralysed, but she was unable to move 'either arm, foot, hand or head.'[1] All she could move was one finger of her right hand and with this one more or less normal finger she stroked the sheets. Her throat was contracted, her tongue so parched and swollen with her having bitten it that it felt as if torn into a thousand pieces, and she choked as soon as they tried to pour a drop of water between her lips.

'That went on till Easter Sunday,'[2] nearly nine months; she was shaken to the point of exhaustion with ague, and severe depression impeded her recovery. She now considered herself fortunate, however, for the pain subsided when they left her alone. Each day, on every possible occasion, she begged her father to take her back to the Incarnation. In absolute despair he had her taken there.

Her sisters came forward to receive the body they had been prepared to bury; the soul was still there, but the body itself was worse than dead, reduced to mere bones covered with skin, and frightfully weak.

For three years Doña Teresa de Ahumada remained in the infirmary completely paralysed; it was now her turn to be the great invalid whom her sisters, all eager for an occasion of exercising charity, vied with each other for the honour of looking after.

Her patient endurance amazed the convent and even when she complained, her expressions were those of praise and love:

'Lord, I did not want as much as this!'[3]

And she affirmed that she would not exchange her sufferings for any treasure they could offer her.

At last she recorded a slight improvement in words that are truly terrible: 'When I began to walk on all fours, I thanked God.'[4]

Had she been able to rid herself of her feeling of guilt? Did she now feel pardoned, redeemed? She was conscious of having won a victory, of having the right to receive 'the hidden manna,' 'the white garments,' 'the morning star.'[5] She had never been so free as she was on her wretched pallet. Tried like gold in the fire by the sufferings she had undergone, she had taken her own measure and now that she knew how slight her strength really was, admitted that she had been crushed by the demands of her hard heart—hard not for others but against herself.

---

[1] Idem.   [2] Idem.   [3] Sb, CAD, c. vi-2.
[4] Sb, V, c. vi-2.   [5] Apocalypse ii-17; iii-5; xxii-17.

One morning when the rising signal went and she heard the nuns go to chapel for Prime, a burning desire to follow them came over her and she wished she could be cured: this was tantamount to granting herself absolution for the past. She also wanted to get back to her cell again, for she found it difficult to be recollected in the infirmary where she had other people round her.

She wanted to live to serve God better. In her case, to desire a thing meant to will it.

But earthly doctors had declared her incurable. So she decided to appeal to heavenly ones, and by a refinement of logic she chose St Joseph. 'This glorious saint helps us in every need; Our Lord shows us that he obeys St Joseph in heaven, just as on earth he was under him and called him Father. . . .'[1]

In asking for the cure, she made it emphatically clear that by so doing she was not putting herself into the category of those, 'particularly women, who follow strange devotions which made not the slightest appeal to me, and which have been clearly proved to be nothing but superstition.'[2]

No doubt when in the infirmary she already had the *Subida del Monte Sion* of Bernardino of Laredo to read—the Ascent of Mount Sion—for the book had recently been published. In the appendix were included some exquisite pages on devotion to St Joseph. How Teresa, who clung to life so tenaciously, must have loved the portrait there given of him: 'A youngish man in the prime of life . . . extremely handsome . . . for how could we imagine that our God would have given the Mother of his Son for her companion, to be the one who served them, was with them for twenty years supporting them by the work of his hands—a decrepit old man such as fools described him. It's laughable. . . .'

The 'young' St Joseph 'showed clearly who he was'. One day when Teresa was dragging herself about on all fours, she suddenly felt she could stand erect. She leant her weight on the soles of her feet, found her balance, drew herself up to her full height and walked with as much ease as if she had never been ill. What she called her sins were forgiven her.

The nuns around her declared it was a miracle.

[1] Sb, V, c. vi–6. [2] Idem.

DOÑA TERESA DE AHUMADA

'DOÑA TERESA DE AHUMADA is wanted in the parlour!'
With a step whose regained vivacity she owes to the
'young' St Joseph, the *miraculée* goes to the parlour assigned
to her to see her friends. She appears behind the grille, more beautiful
and charming than ever; the habit and scapular of fine cloth, the white
muslin wimple tastefully folded, the black veil lined with white become
her to perfection and she has too much good taste to attempt to trim up
the religious habit, as many of her sisters do.

The parlours of the Incarnation had always been made use of as
meeting places for worldly society and were frequented with predilec-
tion by its most brilliant members—gentlemen as well as noble señoras.
Doña Teresa now became the principal attraction: her cure brought
her to the front and 'many people of every station in life came to see
her on account of her kindness and graciousness.' [1]

At first she contented herself with answering their questions, with
her eyes cast down, embarrassed at attracting attention, her only
thought to get back to her solitude and her prayers. But the cell from
which one is frequently absent ends by becoming less desirable and the
fusion of Christian charity with the desire to please others cannot be
effected without unfortunate consequences. Was she to let her visitors
go away again without warm words of greeting, and to show no interest in the news they had come to tell her? Teresa had so grateful a heart
that she was later to declare: 'I can be bribed with a sardine.' [2] All her
life she understood the art of making even the smallest gift she received
seem precious by the way she thanked people; she knew how to give,
to congratulate, to sympathize, to give pleasure. Soon all Ávila was
aware of the charms of the young Carmelite's conversation.

People thought it wonderful that a religious of twenty-six should
have retained the charm of the pretty girl whom the world had fêted
so much and that she should have in addition 'something solid' [3]
acquired in the course of her years of solitude due to her illness and also
the fruit of her extensive reading, her meditations and her trials. Her

[1] BN and PB, art. 2.   [2] CTA, ccxlviii.
[3] MJ quoted SST, vol. I, p. 244

soundness of judgement and openness of mind charmed people all the more because at a time when so many good-looking women prided themselves on their Latin and Greek, she laughingly excused herself for not being erudite. This gift of attracting and holding people lasted throughout her lifetime; Don Antonio Aguiar, a licentiate who knew her in later life, at Burgos, said that he spent

> all day long with her without noticing the time, and all night long in the hope of seeing her again next day, for her way of speaking was delightful—and the word *gracioso* in Spanish adds a touch of wit to the delightfulness, and her conversation pleasant and at the same time serious, simple, full of good sense and absolutely sincere: she was so much on fire with the love of God! The warmth radiating from her words was so gently persuasive that it melted the hearts of all who came in contact with her without causing them pain; for among her qualities she possessed *gratia sermonis*, graciousness of speech, and drew to her, as she wanted them and for whatever purpose she wanted them, all who heard her. . . . It might have been said that she held in her hand the helm that steers all hearts. . . .

At the Incarnation Teresa, whom Aguiar himself was to call 'the world's magnet',[1] was already creating a sphere of influence about her.

At the time it was considered very good form to talk of matters of high devotion, more especially in a convent parlour. Could a nun withdraw herself from discussions on mental prayer in which the methods of Osuna were compared with those of Laredo, or in which the merits of the Society recently founded by Ignatius of Loyola were extolled? The way in which Doña Teresa de Ahumada spoke of God was wonderful, but she was listened to all the more readily because she never tired of hearing others speak of him. Any pious nobleman who, during his travels, had had the good fortune to hear Padre Juan de Ávila or Fray Luis de Granada preach was sure to find an appreciative audience at the Incarnation.

'Doña Teresa de Ahumada, in the parlour!'

A circle was formed, Doña Teresa drew up close to the grille—already the visitor was pleased with himself and therefore with her.

'It was on Good Friday. The church was full as could be. Fray Luis got into the pulpit and spoke of the single word "Passion" with so much force, so burning an eloquence and so much feeling that the entire congregation fell to weeping. People sobbed so loudly that the preacher was obliged to interrupt his sermon. . . .'[2]

---

[1] Quoted SST, vol. I, p. 294.   [2] MN, L. I, c. xvi.

Teresa praised the speaker and, from sacred matters, the conversation dropped easily into worldly ones. The frigates which sailed overseas from Seville and returned laden with gold and exotic fruits were always an exciting subject. People brought Teresa news of Fernando, of Rodrigo whom Lorenzo and Pedro had gone to join in 1540. Or perhaps the subject of discussion might be a remedy against fever, one of those recipes of which herbs formed the basis, about which the young nun was curious; or, better still, a well-turned sonnet, or again a battle which had been well and hardly won. To know where and in what manner they were fighting for God and the emperor against Turk, Frenchmen or Indians was to know the fate of the sons and brothers of the well-born families of Ávila.

Everything interested and fascinated Doña Teresa, and there was nothing she said which did not interest, amuse and fascinate her devoted clientèle.

When Don Alonso came to see her now, more and more frequently he found himself interrupting such gatherings. She received him with affectionate deference, but when her friends got up to go she kept them back by vigorously steering the conversation round to general subjects. The poor man was crestfallen and went away broken-hearted. What had become of the time when his Teresa had talked with him at length, just he and she together, with such irresistible eloquence that it was to her he owed his initiation into the art of mental prayer. His daughter had so much persuasive force that she had accomplished one of the most difficult of feats: to raise to the heights of the mystical life one who was merely an everyday Catholic. Could it really be the same Teresa whom he now found laughing and chattering, inattentive to her father and, it seemed, inattentive to God?

One day when he happened to find her alone he reproached her with this. She did not attempt to deny it: she admitted that she no longer practised mental prayer and pleaded ill-health as an excuse.

'For me going to choir is a very considerable effort.' [1]

Don Alonso had now attained the heights of contemplation; he judged his visits to the Incarnation to be 'time wasted' and spaced them out so well that the *habitués* no longer had any need to fear the few minutes of embarrassment which the arrival of the old man dressed in black and with the gentle, sad and penetrating look had caused. 'I was caught up in so many vanities,' said Teresa, 'that I didn't trouble about it.' [2] She had not the courage to tell her father she could no longer recollect herself 'without enclosing within me a multitude of vanities.' [3]

[1] Sb, V, c. vii–12.   [2] Idem, 13.   [3] Idem, 17.

When she recovered from her long and serious illness, or rather from the long crisis, for she remained more or less ill all her life, she very naturally found pleasure in renewed vitality. The delight which friendships and conversation gave her, the distractions which occurred during her spiritual exercises and her long periods of dryness, the fact that she sometimes found herself waiting impatiently for the bell that announced the end of the Office, all these things formed such an utter contrast with her ideal of fervour that she believed herself to be lost, so much so that she no longer dared look God in the face; and she gave up everything the *Third Spiritual Alphabet* had taught her. Disappointed in herself, this 'regal soul' punished herself by mediocrity. What! She had aimed at sanctity? Had dreamed of heroic acts? She had almost died through such pretentiousness and God himself had laughed at her presumption. Is it not possible to save one's soul without extravagant austerities? The convent of the Incarnation seemed expressly created for such a *via media*. Was not that why she had chosen it? How foolish the ambition that had urged her to want to make herself singular by piety and mortifications more severe and intense than those of her sisters! 'The common law seemed to me the best for I was vile and worse than any; to say the prayers of obligation, vocally, would be better than to practise mental prayer and the presence of God for one who merited the company of devils and who was deceiving people; for externally I appeared to be good. . . .' [1]

In choir as in the parlour or at recreation, Doña Teresa de Ahumada had the gift of putting herself at each one's disposal, and, as far as her companions were concerned, made herself 'all things to all, as much by what she was as by what she did, with such a perfection and gift of adaptation that we sometimes even laughed at it',[2] Ana de Jesús wrote afterwards. She imagined she was deceiving those about her, for the standard by which she measured her progress was that of the highest ideals she had set herself; in reality she was living in conformity with the use and custom established in a convent where a multitude of compromises with the Constitutions were 'lawful,' although it was not one of the most relaxed among Spanish convents.

Anything served as pretext, excuse or good reason: tolerance seemed the essential point about the Rule, except for the novices who followed its obligations to the letter; it was on this account that they were only allowed visitors very occasionally. The professed nuns, on the other hand, wore jewellery, chattered unscrupulously during silence time, paid visits in each other's cells and at recreation time

[1] Idem, 1.   [2] Cited SST, vol. I, p. 295.

regaled themselves with worldly music. Did not their devotees bring
them the latest songs? And did they not munch, at all hours of the day,
the sweetmeats they slipped into their hands through the parlour
grilles? One religious, chosen from among the most prudent in the
convent, always formed the third party when visitors came to the
parlour, but hunger was not the prerogative of the frivolous-minded
and even the prudent were not proof against a *pâtisserie*. The convent
was poor and overcrowded, and the starvation diet to which the nuns
were subjected was due more to their extreme poverty than to observance of the rule of abstinence as practised by the Fathers of the Desert
who were the Order's founders; accordingly when a nun found a good
pretext for going back to take meals at home for a time or with devout
people who were only too anxious to have a Carmelite in the house,
the prioress was not slow in giving permission, on condition that the
nun took one of her sisters with her as companion: two mouths less to
feed. This was the reason Teresa herself was often absent; the great
families of Ávila quarrelled as to who should have her with them.

How could unremitting fervour be expected of one hundred and
eighty young women who kept one foot in the world like this, many
of whom had only become nuns in despair of finding a husband? Since
the discovery of what were called the Indies, young men preferred
their visions overseas, even if these should prove to be illusory, to the
sparkling eyes of a Spanish fiancée: in the Cepeda y Ahumada family
alone, the whole seven went off, seven fine young men, any one of
whom would have made a good match, leaving seven girls free 'to
dress the saints,' that is to join the confraternities of pious women who
held sway over the collection of robes used to dress the statues of
Christ or that of the velvet and gold brocade vestments for Our Lady.

With the exception of a few devout nuns, the convent of the Incarnation seemed more like a guest-house for single ladies where each
one, in the measure of her fortune, rank and personal tastes, arranged
for herself a more or less pleasant existence, practising the virtues considered indispensable if one wished to acquire, without too much
trouble, a moderately exalted position in the next world.

In the next world: for in this 'it is impossible to succeed in achieving anything good when there are more than forty women together:
things are nothing but noisy confusion and chaos: they upset each
other.' [1] Teresa found many friends to help her to sink to the lowest
level among the one hundred and eighty nuns of the Incarnation, but
when she wanted to rise above this standard she stood alone.

[1] CTA, xlvi.

It was 'Doña Teresa!' here, 'Doña Teresa de Ahumada' there: there was always a sister to come and distract her when she was trying to practise recollection. They loved her only too well, desirous as she was that people should love her; her gaiety delighted people, her loyalty reassured them; with her you were sure she would not talk about you disparagingly once your back was turned. Those who were of an effusive nature coaxed her; 'My life! My soul! My treasure!' [1] But they soon learnt that the feminine craze for terms of endearment was no more to her taste than tittle-tattle, quarrelling and 'Have you heard . . .' They admired her exquisite thoughtfulness and charity: sometimes when they came to choir for Office in the early hours of the morning, her sisters would be astonished to find their old worn-out cloaks darned: Doña Teresa, feeling that she did not show enough love towards her sisters, had got up in the night to mend them.

Who would have thought, then, of blaming her for the hours she spent in the parlour? She kept within the letter of the law. It would not have occurred to any man of good family, young, handsome, elegant, that a nun of equivalent social standing could dream of refusing to chat with him in the parlour. He was known as her 'devotee,' she was considered to be helping him to save his soul, and if the good-looking nuns were more sought after for such work than the plain ones, this occasioned no surprise. Teresa had too much pride to follow the example of those who continued their apostolate when parlour hours were over 'through the cracks, over the walls, or during the night. . . .' [2]

When Doña Teresa blamed herself for acting as her sisters did, she showed towards herself the severity of the athlete who curses himself when a glass of alcohol endangers his form, whereas those who have already attained the world record drink their bottle without remorse. The nuns of the Incarnation did not know from what heights Teresa had sunk to the level of their routine religion. They sometimes saw her go out of her way to be alone, refrain from speaking evil, abstain from disobedience. They noticed she was punctual and exact at Office, recollected at prayer time. They heard her speak of God with exceptional eloquence. Doña Teresa de Ahumada was always ready to give money to have holy pictures painted on the convent walls, she decorated her own oratory, caused edifying ceremonies to be performed in honour of her favourite saints—particularly St Joseph; at the Incarnation less than this was necessary to pass for a model nun. Her conduct was 'legitimate' for her companions, her superiors, her confessor.

[1] Sb, C, c. vii-8.　　　　　[2] Sb, V, c. vii-2.

To her, that was not the point. What had become of the heroic acts? Of her aspirations to sanctity?

> Oh, what a terrible thing it is when religious . . . do not observe their rule. . . . Their youth and the attraction of things of sense draw them towards the world. . . . The monk or the nun who wants to follow God must fear those of his or her own family more than all the powers of hell. He or she is forced to use more prudence and dissimulation in order to obtain the liberty to live in God's friendship than is required for the particular friendships which the devil brings about in monasteries. . . . If parents took my advice, since they don't seem to think of putting their daughters where they can best save their souls, but rather where there is more danger than there would be in the world, they would look at the matter from the point of view of honour; and they would then prefer to marry them off beneath their station rather than put them in such convents . . . or would keep them at home.[1]

Teresa saw the danger, allowed it to brush past her lightly and escaped it in time thanks to her impregnable sense of honour, but she made no effort to avoid it.

This was not, however, for want of warning.

Among the gentlemen who were devoted to her there was one for whom she declared she had *mucha afición*, which we can translate as 'to whom she was very much attached '—using the expression in the right sense. It appears that this person was Don Francisco de Guzmán; he was young, well endowed with worldly goods and belonged to one of the noblest families of Castile. Was he more dangerous for Teresa than the cousin she had formerly thought of marrying or the 'poor wretched man' of Becedas? God took a hand in the matter—the devil too: 'I had only known him a very short time when Our Lord made me understand that such friendships were not for me. Christ appeared to me with a most severe countenance and showed me clearly that this was not pleasing to him. I was alarmed and troubled and I did not want to see the man again.' [2] But the devil made her believe that this vision was only the effect of her imagination, the visitor persisted, the sisters around her affirmed that the company of so worthy an *hidalgo* not only did no harm to Doña Teresa de Ahumada's reputation, but actually enhanced it: thus it was that she returned to this 'pestilential recreation.' [3] During Office, the thought of this friend became a constant distraction. One day when she was in the parlour 'with the person in question,' an enormous toad appeared to her. Several persons present

[1] Sb, V, c. vii-5, 4.   [2] Sb, V, c. vii-6.   [3] Idem, 7.

saw it 'walk much more quickly than such creatures usually do.'[1] Teresa was very much afraid, but this second warning, too, was neglected.

And when an old religious who was also a relative of hers thought fit to put her on her guard, her only reply was to shrug her shoulders: 'You take scandal over nothing!'[2] and she sulked over it.

The young generation which was contemporaneous with the new world then being born found their elders unprogressive and hidebound with ridiculous prejudices.

All the same: when Doña Teresa was called to the parlour now, her dainty arched feet in the elegant shoes on which 'he' never tired of complimenting her no longer ran there so eagerly. The Bridegroom was keeping watch. His vengeance on such a butterfly bride was to inundate her soul with spiritual delights. He knew her so well; for her it was 'a kind of terrible torture,'[3] to receive graces of which she knew she was unworthy. She pulled herself together but knew all the time that she would fall again.

'From one pastime to another, from vanity to vanity, from temptation to temptation. . . .'[4] 'O Lord of my soul, how shall I ever be able to express my gratitude for your mercies during these years?'[5]

The solicitude with which not only God but the devil surrounded her was truly astonishing. God willed to make her his own, the devil to snatch her away from God. For the thought of spiritual joys weakened the pleasure she found in her eager friendships, and yet when she withdrew to her cell to be alone with God, the memory of such friendships would not leave her.

Thus seven years after she came to the convent 'this soul who has so often worked her own ruin,'[6] was still torn in two directions.

Teresa was to find help at the bedside of her dying father. The year 1543 was drawing to a close. The Carmelite had returned to the house in the Plazuela Santo Domingo to nurse Don Alonso. '. . . There was more sickness in my soul than in his body, taken up as I was by a multitude of vanities, although I do not think I committed mortal sin at this time—a period more wasted than I can say. . . .'[7]

Under her father's roof and surrounded with objects that were familiar to her, she was able to measure the ground covered since the day she had suffered so much at leaving it all and abandoning the old

[1] Idem, 8.   [2] Idem, 9.   [3] Idem, 19.
[4] Idem, 1.   [5] Idem, 19.   [6] CTA, ccclxxxviii.
[7] Sb, V, c, vii–14.

man who now turned his gaze in her direction with eyes already dim. Her departure had meant for him cruel suffering and perhaps financial ruin as well: he was not the sort of man to look after his own interests. Doña Beatriz and then María and Teresa had been the necessary stewards. Left alone, he had become impoverished through his generosity to his sons whose equipment for the army had been on a lavish scale, to María—always in difficulties—to the poor. Don Alonso was considerably in debt, but he was rich in the love of Our Lord.

Teresa, though she thought herself so far away from God, brought deep peace to her dying father. Acute pain in the kidneys was causing him much suffering:

'Father, you have a devotion to Christ carrying his cross. Why don't you imagine that His Majesty is giving you a share of his sufferings while he was carrying it uphill?' [1]

This thought gave him so much consolation that he no longer moaned in his pain. He died fully conscious, reciting the *Credo* and reminding all those of his children who were present that they must remember that everything has an end. 'When dead, he looked like an angel.' [2]

Teresa went to confession to P. Vincent Barrón, who assisted the dying man. He was a man of calm disposition, but exacting and with an eye for detail. She gave him a full account of the state of trouble and confusion in which she was, declaring that for a long time past she had deemed herself unworthy to practise mental prayer.

The Dominican's directives read rather like a doctor's prescription, leaving no room for scruples or hesitations:

(1) Receive Holy Communion every fortnight.

(2) Take up mental prayer again. That cannot but do great good in any circumstances.

With his calm penetration and insight, P. Vincent Barrón gave Doña Teresa de Ahumada the help she needed to become Doña Teresa de Jesús: he charged the patient not to deprive herself of the remedy for her ills any longer, no matter what might happen.

Teresa has summarized the effects of this consultation:

'I returned to prayer without, however, avoiding the occasions of sin; but I never gave up prayer again.' [3]

'My life was full of suffering, for in prayer I saw my faults more clearly.'

This of course was what the experienced director had foreseen.

'On the one hand I felt the call of God; on the other, I continued to

---

[1] Idem, 16. [2] Idem. [3] Sb, V, c. vii-17.

follow the world. All the things of God gave me great pleasure, but I was held captive by those of the world. I might have been said to be trying to reconcile these two extremes, to bring contraries together: the spiritual life on the one hand and worldly satisfactions, pleasures and pastimes on the other.' [1]

'I spent many years in this way. . . .'

To be precise, ten years, dating from her meeting with P. Barrón. But for the future she had 'the strong pillar of mental prayer as her support.' [2]

From God's first insistent call at Our Lady of Grace until the shattering experience of 1553, Teresa de Ahumada continued to live for just over twenty years with her heart divided between the world and God.

[1] Idem.   [2] Sb, V, c. viii–1.

PART TWO

THE ROYAL ROAD

'Lord, he who loves you truly travels in
security along a wide and royal road.'

Autobiography, c. **xxv**

I

THE WOUNDED CHRIST

ONE day in 1553,[1] as she was passing through the oratory, Doña Teresa de Ahumada noticed a bust, an *Ecce Homo*, which someone had left there until some other place could be found for it. 'It represented, and that in a way so well calculated to arouse devotion that from the very first glance I was moved at the thought of his sufferings for us, Christ covered with wounds. My heart was shattered with remorse when I thought of those wounds and my ingratitude. I threw myself on my knees before him, in tears, and begged him to strengthen me once for always, that I might not offend him for the future.' [2]

After Communion she often imagined herself like Mary Magdalene, at the feet of Our Lord, and wept, but such impulsive movements of repentance were soon forgotten: 'Doubtless what was wrong was that I failed to put my whole trust in His Majesty and did not divest myself of my self-confidence.' [3] This *Ecce Homo* with the pallid, death-like flesh showing the wounds, some red and gaping, some congealed, the face streaming with the blood that spurted from beneath the crown of thorns, the heart-rending expression of the glazed eyes, made her understand what she really was: she saw she would find help nowhere but in God, she would not get right again until he answered her heart's appeal.

Such was the first shattering experience. It was Christ penetrating into 'the hard heart' after knocking so often in vain. She was to discover that his love 'is above all the joys of earth, bliss surpassing all other.' [4]

From this day forward she was able to record progress: she avoided the parlour, redoubled both constancy and fervour in the matter of mental prayer and her charity became humbler and more patient. The change did not pass unnoticed among her sisters: they often surprised her at prayer, so absorbed in God that she saw no one, any more than

---

[1] P. Silverio de Santa Teresa assigns to her second conversion the date of 1553. He bases this assumption on the date (1554) of the arrival of St. Francis Borgia in Ávila (SST, vol. I, p. 331).
[2] Sb, V, c. ix-1.   [3] Sb, V, c. viii-12   [4] Sb, M, V, c. i-6.

she read what was in the book open in front of her. For she still needed help to become recollected: 'I find a book useful . . . the country, water, flowers, helped me too. . . .' [1]

At the beginning of 1554 she was given St Augustine's *Confessions*, the Spanish translation of which had just been published. Teresa de Ahumada thought she recognized herself in this man who had loved the world so much and struggled so hard to be detached from it, the reader of worldly books, the sinner for so long impenitent: 'When I got to his conversion, to the point where he hears the voice in the orchard, the feelings I experienced were so intense that it might have been myself Our Lord was calling. For a long time tears streamed down my face.' [2]

This second experience finally delivered Teresa 'out of so mortal a death.' [3] After going the round of temptations and dangers, this was a return to the point of departure, to her early childhood. For in the child Teresa her future development already existed in embryo.

'Teresa is not like herself,' said her companions at the Incarnation, whereas in reality she was at long last like herself, like the child who wanted to be born again in the glory of God 'for ever, and ever, and ever,' even if the price was martyrdom.

'From now onwards a fresh page has been turned for me, I tell you it is a new life.'

'Up till now it has been *my* life. Now God lives in me.'

'God be praised for having delivered me from myself.' [4]

Our Lord was only waiting for Teresa's decision to shower spiritual graces upon her. 'Hardly had I turned my gaze away from the occasions of sin when His Majesty already began to show his love for me again. . . . It seemed to me that I had only just made up my mind to serve him when His Majesty began to spoil me once more. . . .' [5] She was given 'very frequently the prayer of quiet and often that of union which lasted a long time. But at that particular time there had been many women who were the victims of illusion and of the deceits of the devil: so great were the delights and sweetness which I experienced in spite of my resistance, that I was scared.' [6]

To whom did she speak of these fears and favours? The confessors at the Incarnation had never understood her. She dared not speak about them even to the most serious-minded among her sisters. Already, when the first moment of astonishment was over, the change in her

[1] Sb, V, c. ix–5.   [2] Sb, V, c. ix–8   [3] Idem.
[4] Sb, V, c. xxiii–9.   [5] Sb, V, c. ix–9   [6] Sb, V, c. xxiii–2.

caused a certain uneasiness around her: the wise virgins did not yet consider her one of themselves and the foolish virgins were exasperated to find that the very person whose 'frivolities' justified their own was now repenting—such repentance was tantamount to an accusation of them all. When they saw her they began to whisper together; soon many of them pointed the finger of scorn at her, and eventually the whole convent was seething with sarcasm or pity:

'Doña Teresa de Ahumada thinks herself a saint!'

'Doña Teresa thinks she's invented something new!' [1]

The first of her meritorious efforts was the humble willingness to be less acceptable to others; but this was not enough to calm her distress. One day, during the Hours, she heard Our Lord speak for the first time: 'Serve me, and do not concern yourself about all that.' [2] She was more frightened than consoled by the divine words, 'my soul was frightened and upset,' [3] for want of an experienced director.

Fortunately the Cepeda and Ahumada connections were almost unending. The good uncle Don Pedro was connected through his wife Doña Catalina del Águila, with Don Francisco de Salcedo, whom Teresa later termed *el caballero santo*, 'the holy gentleman,' so deep was his piety. And it was enlightened piety: for twenty years he had studied theology at the Dominican college of Santo Tomás and Fray Pedro de Alcántara considered him 'the best bonnet in Ávila'—the most worthy to wear the doctor's cap. Of the many men who practised virtue in the City of Stones and Saints, there was no one equal to him. Best of all: he was kind.

It was to him that Teresa de Ahumada turned. Yet she did not tell him either of her graces or her fears: she merely spoke of the difficulty she had in overcoming self, of her efforts to do better which always ended in disappointment but which she always began again: she was accused of making too many demands upon herself, whereas she reproached herself for her excessive weakness. She needed a director to help her to see clearly and to impose upon her what she had not the courage to impose upon herself: in her own eyes she was not mortified.

Don Francisco brought to her P. Gaspar Daza. All Ávila admired the apostolic zeal of this preacher who did not confine the privileges of hearing the Gospel preached merely to city-dwellers. At a time when the ignorance of country folk was such that in isolated spots the good people did not even know the *Our Father*, he went preaching in remote hamlets, summer and winter alike. Teresa hoped to profit much by his virtue and spirit of refusal to compromise. But Don Gaspar had much

---

[1] Sb, V, c. xix–8.   [2] Sb, V, c. xix–9.   [3] Sb, V, c. xiii–4.

to do in the Lord's service: he felt he had no time to waste on a nun who was not satisfied with the confessors provided by her Order.

He did not even trouble to put her at her ease.

'I was extremely uncomfortable in the presence of such a holy man. I acquainted him with the state of my soul and my manner of mental prayer. He didn't want to hear my confession, saying he was extremely busy.' [1]

Teresa noticed that he regarded what she said to him 'as something which has to be finished with once and for all. . . .' [2] His judgement of her was based on the degree of mental prayer she had attained. He thought her a strong character and ruthlessly cut across her remaining attachments. But she knew how weak she was in spite of the graces Our Lord was showering upon her, still a mere child as far as the practice of the virtues and mortification was concerned and she judged herself incapable of doing what he ordered. 'This was enough to make one lose heart and give up everything,' [3]

Francisco de Salcedo, with somewhat more kindness, came to see her frequently, her confidence in him increased, and one day she told him of the delights of her supernatural prayer: 'That is my expression for what is obtainable neither by skill nor diligence, however much one forces oneself and prepares oneself for it.' [4] She told him about the feeling of the presence of God which took hold of her in so intense a way that she could not but doubt that God was within her and she incorporated [5] in him. She told him, too, of the continual feelings of tenderness, the joy she experienced, 'neither entirely of the senses nor entirely spiritual,' [6] 'sweetness, delight defying all comparison, agony the joys of which surpass all one can say.' [7] 'It is a hard but blissful martyrdom' [8] to 'die to all the pleasures of the world and find one's joy in God.' [9] She admitted to Don Francisco that she was 'as it were beside herself, drunk with this love' [10]: 'pain full of delight,' 'glorious aberration, heavenly folly. . . .' [11]

The good gentleman was completely nonplussed. He summoned Gaspar Daza with all urgency. The latter left all his preaching and came. This nun whom they both thought so imperfect spoke with accents of shattering sincerity of unheard of graces with which Our Lord was favouring her.

'Such things don't go together,' said the one.

[1] Sb, V, c. xxxii–8.   [2] Idem.   [3] Idem, 9.
[4] SEC, R, v, p. 31.   [5] Sb, V, c. x–1.   [6] Idem, 2.
[7] Sb, V, c. xvi–1.   [8] Idem.   [9] Idem, 1.
[10] Idem, 3.   [11] Idem, 1.

'Spiritual graces are only found in those who are very well exercised in virtue and greatly mortified,' said the other still more conclusively.[1]

And their mutual conclusion was:

'Be careful . . . certain factors indicate the work of the devil. . . .'

'They had no sooner spoken,' said Teresa, 'than I was greatly upset and in tears, for I was frightened enough before this.'

And Doña Teresa de Ahumada, the brilliant conversationalist of the Incarnation's parlour, nearly forty and in full possession of her faculties, her genius about to flower to its full perfection, was so much intimidated by these theologians, so terrified at the idea that what she experienced might be a diabolical illusion, that she could not find words with which to give a satisfactory account of the graces God was giving her.

The 'sleep of the faculties' had seemed particularly worrying to these worthy gentlemen. Like a child in desperation at being unable to express itself, she sought in Bernardino de Laredo's *Ascent of Mount Sion* for the phrases which seemed to her to describe what she was experiencing, without stopping to think that the choice of a Franciscan writer was not a particularly happy one: the sons of Ignatius of Loyola, and both Salcedo and Daza were under their influence, accused the Franciscans of too much sentimentality.

> In the place where union with God is spoken of, I found all the signs which I had in myself with regard to the impossibility of reflecting and the 'thinking of nothing' mentioned.[2] I underlined certain passages. . . . 'Let him who has ears to hear, hear, and learn that in this absence of thought is comprised a vast world, which includes perfect contemplation and contains all that is, so much so that when this is present, the rest is nothing: and if it is nothing, one has not to think about it. For truly in the presence of Our Lord and God, all created things are nothing. . . . Of the soul, then, which through the union of love in quiet contemplation is busied with God, one can in truth say that she should think of nothing, for in this absence of thought, she has what is the essence of all thought.'[3]

The two 'holy servants of God,' then, were going to study Teresa de Ahumada's 'case,' documents in hand. Submissively she waited for their decision: 'I was prepared to abandon mental prayer if they considered this necessary. What was the use of running such risks if, after

[1] Sb, V, c. xxiii-11.   [2] Sb, V, c. xxiii-12.
[3] BL, c. xxvii.

twenty years of the practice of recollection, I had gained nothing but to be deceived by the devil? It would be better to give it up. . . .' [1]

For the second time Teresa found P. Gaspar Daza's attitude discouraging; not that she minded being crushed, she had a nature which preferred that to yielding. He was one of those 'people who are only half-learned and easily frightened,' [2] of whom she says that they cost her very dear.

She passed the time of waiting in suffering and prayer.

At length, these half-lettered men, who even taken together were not equal to a single person of ordinary common sense, pronounced their verdict:

'The devil!'

Don Francisco de Salcedo did not desert Teresa. In his opinion the only one who could extricate her from such perilous straits was a Jesuit. He was on excellent terms with the Order, for his brother-in-law had been the principal agent in the erection of their latest house, the hospice of San Gil. The apostolate was what they were founded for, and their methods of spirituality and the austerity of their personal life did not prevent them from understanding human weaknesses. The merits of the Jesuits had often formed the subject of conversation in the Incarnation parlours. It was decided that Teresa should write out a general confession and put it into the hands of whichever of the Fathers might prove willing to deal with her case.

But what a lot of fuss to arrange the visit! And the tittle-tattle that would probably arise from it! Teresa begged the portress not to tell anyone that a Father 'of the Society,' one of those holy men, was coming to see the 'vilest' of the nuns of the Incarnation. As ill-luck would have it, a nun who happened to be about when P. Cetina arrived was one of the gossips. The whole convent talked about it and soon it was all over Ávila.

P. Diego de Cetina was not a great Jesuit. 'Poor health . . . not very intelligent . . . has a liking for the Divine Office and for mental prayer. Likes sermons, Masses and to talk of God.' A confidential report adds: 'Preaches indifferently. Hears confessions. No use for anything else.' [3]

At the time he was twenty-three.

His verdict was:

'God!'

---

[1] Sb, V, c. xxiii-12.   [2] Sb, M, V, c. i-8.
[3] SST, vol. I, p. 339.

As the Dominican, P. Barrón, had done ten years earlier, P. Cetina, her Jesuit adviser, ordered Teresa not to give up mental prayer on any account. In strict compliance with what Ignatius of Loyola laid down, he asked her to focus her meditation each day on one of the Stations of the Cross, and to think of Christ only in his human person. He found her little inclined for penances—her bad health was to some extent the reason for this—and imposed on her mortifications which she found 'little to her taste,' [1] but to which she submitted.

Finally he charged her to resist as far as possible whatever pleasure of the senses she might experience.

'He directed me so well that it seems to me I am no longer the same. What a great thing it is to understand souls!' [2] For twenty years she had been looking for a confessor who would understand her. The 'not very intelligent' P. Cetina was proving his ability for other things besides mediocre preaching: he devoted himself to the exceptional soul who had been confided to his care. When he whom Teresa speaks of as 'the Father Francis who was Duke of Gandia,' *i.e.* Francis Borgia, came to Ávila in the spring of 1544, Diego de Cetina spoke to him about the Carmelite and persuaded him to go and see her.

P. Francisco was famous for having renounced one of the greatest names in Spain for God's sake. The story of his conversion had for long supplied the people of Ávila with a subject of conversation of the sort they loved, grandiose and sinister at the same time.

The event took place in 1539; the Empress Isabella had just died, and her son, Prince Philip II, who was only twelve, was leading the funeral cortège on horseback, as the queen's remains were conveyed across a grief-stricken Spain to her last resting-place in Granada. To Francis Borgia, Marquis of Lombay, son of the Duke of Gandia and of Juana of Aragón and one of the dead empress's favourite servitors, fell the honour of being chosen to identify the corpse.

When the coffin was opened in the mortuary chapel of the Catholic sovereigns, a nauseating stench caused the escort of nobles to draw back. These lords, however, swore—their hands on the hilts of their swords—that this was indeed 'the royal corpse of Doña Isabel de Portugal, empress of Germany, spouse of the magnificent, mighty and Catholic king, Charles our lord.'

The silence of Don Francisco de Borja astonished the archbishop.

'You are not going to swear?'

He looked at the putrefied flesh amid the still glittering gold of the royal robes.

[1] Sb, V, c. xxiv-2. Sb, V. c xxiii-17.

'I can say only one thing; I have seen to it that the body of our noble Lady was under strict guard throughout the voyage from Toledo to Granada. But that I, who ever admired her great beauty, should swear that it is really she—I dare not.'

The archbishop insisted:

'Do you recognize your Lady and your Queen, or not?'

Francis placed his right hand upon his knight's cross of the order of Santiago, a patch of purple on the voluminous white cloak, whilst his left hand let the funeral veils fall back on the royal corpse.

'Yes. But I also swear never more to serve master who is mortal.'

On the death of his wife a short time afterwards the duke renounced honours, fortune and titles and entered the Society of Jesus.

The news came out in 1550 'like a thunderbolt.' There was one man who envied him: the emperor, Charles V, who had already sent emissaries 'to report on the residence, the site, the climate and the general arrangement of the monastery of Yuste.'

In the year 1554, then, P. Francisco came to Ávila from Tordesillas, where he had been staying for a time to be near the queen, Joan the Mad. His sermons drew such vast crowds to the great cathedral that the triumph might have gone to the head of anyone else except this perfect adept of the virtue of humility; in this, as in everything else, he saw only a reason for humbling himself.

Was he perhaps humbler than Prebendary Gaspar Daza—the prelate who had witnessed the dissolution of the spouse of the mightiest of monarchs? P. Francisco did not intimidate Doña Teresa de Ahumada when she had to set out the secrets of her inner life before him. He knew by experience the delights which Christ showers upon those who leave all for his sake.

He confirmed P. Cetina's diagnosis:

'It is truly the spirit of God.'

He added that it would not be right to resist.

'Allow yourself to be delighted by His Majesty, rejoice in him since he wants to give you joy. . . .'

The interview was not without its lighter side: when she was trying to describe the kind of dull stupidity in which she sometimes found herself, though completely absorbed in God, Teresa said:

'It seems to me that my soul is like a little donkey busy grazing. . . .'

Thus Francisco de Salcedo and Gaspar Daza were reassured, the busy tongues of Ávila silenced by the assurances of a Jesuit father 'who was a duke' and Teresa de Ahumada fully justified and encouraged.

But her troubles were not ended.

II

DOÑA GUIOMAR DE ULLOA

DOÑA GUIOMAR DE ULLOA was just over twenty-five. She was the widow of Don Francisco Dávila, lord of Villatoro. In her mourning she was more beautiful than ever and her piety had not yet led her to see the necessity of renouncing a life of luxury and refinement when she made the acquaintance of Doña Teresa de Ahumada, through the Fathers of the Society of Jesus at the church of San Gil. Teresa was charmed by her sympathetic face. Doña Guiomar quickly made friends with her: she soon grasped the fact that Teresa was not getting the solitude and opportunity for recollection she needed at the Incarnation which was indeed a perfect Babylon.

When the Carmelite visited her and Doña Guiomar, with a gracious gesture of welcome, showed her the vast apartments and beautiful patios of her palace, saying: 'My home is yours, too,' she understood that in this instance the usual formula of politeness was meant in all sincerity. And often when her sisters' lack of discretion made life too difficult and prevented her from devoting herself to the task of unremitting vigilance over self which gradual progress in the spiritual life demands—at all events in its initial stages—she took refuge with Doña Guiomar. She was able to give the prioress a sufficient reason: she was escorting one of the young widow's daughters who was a 'secular' at the Incarnation.

Doña Guiomar introduced Teresa to her own confessor when the departure of P. Diego de Cetina for Salamanca left her stranded once more. P. Juan de Prádanos, a young Jesuit who was understanding but severe, added to what his predecessor had required by imposing on his penitent a strict ascetical discipline: God was overwhelming her with his graces and the Jesuit's directive was that henceforward she must no longer neglect even the smallest thing that would please him. Much 'diplomacy and gentle persuasion' [1] were necessary to persuade her to sacrifice what cost her most: 'a few friendships which did not offend God;' [2] such purely human contacts deprived her of silence and solitude and were harmful to the regular life which was so necessary for her.

[1] Sb, V, c. xxiv-5.   [2] Idem.

A nature as affectionate and strong-willed as Doña Teresa de Ahu-mada's contrived to find good excuses: deep affections like these were in no way sinful: was it necessary to be ungrateful to please Our Lord?

P. Prádanos advised her to leave everything to God and to say the *Veni Creator* frequently. One day when she was saying over the words of the hymn, she was suddenly rapt in ecstasy for the first time and heard Our Lord's voice: 'Henceforward it is my will that you no longer converse with men but with angels.' [1]

Teresa was much afraid. When she returned to her normal senses again and saw her astonished sisters all round her, she was still more afraid. All speaking and shouting at once, they deafened her:

'You were like somebody dead!'

'Your limbs were stiff and your body icy cold!'

'Your pulse was scarcely beating at all. . . .'

She hoped they would think it was a fainting fit.

'We've seen you faint more than once. Your face was not ecstatic as it was this time.'

In spite of her efforts she could not yet find the strength to move: her soul seemed to have taken all her strength with it. For two or three days she seemed to have lost the use of her faculties, to be beside her-self, bereft of her senses as it were, lost in God.[2]

She confided to Doña Guiomar:

The poor soul does not realize what is going to happen to it. . . . The being rapt in ecstasy takes the form of a sudden call on the part of His Majesty in the very depths of one's soul, it rushes upon one so swiftly that it seems to raise the soul to its very apex so that it almost leaves the body. Great courage is then necessary to abandon oneself into Our Lord's arms and to allow oneself to be rapt until the moment when His Majesty sets you down in peace, where he wanted to lead you to communicate the highest revelations to you. Certainly when such things first begin to happen, it is essential to have the determination to die for God. Any attempt to resist seemed to me impossible. . . .[3]

When she had eventually recovered the use of her faculties and the turmoil at the Incarnation over the 'novelty' had died down a little, she experienced great joy and felt herself so much strengthened that she broke her worldly attachments without regret. Her only friends now were those who loved God.

Doña Guiomar and Don Francisco de Salcedo were naturally of the number. And P. Prádanos, of course. She loved them tenderly. When

[1] Idem.   [2] Sb, V, c. xx–21.   [3] SEC, R, v, pp. 33–4.

P. Prádanos was seriously ill with heart disease his two penitents took him away to the village of El Palo, where Doña Guiomar had large estates, and there constituted themselves his nurses and servants.[1] Teresa was an expert in cooking and preparing delicacies. The Father was somewhat embarrassed at so much attention and Teresa laughed to herself about it:

'I have always had much affection for those who look after my soul; for me they are God's representatives and I treat them as such. It has happened in the case of some of my confessors that they were afraid I was too much attached to them—although in a holy way—and so I incurred their displeasure. I laughed to myself at their mistake. . . .' [2]

She did not fall under P. Prádanos' displeasure, he was her confessor and director until 1558.

As to Doña Guiomar, she was a different person: one was not the friend of Teresa de Ahumada for nothing; it was impossible to hear her speak of God, of heaven, to hear her affirm in her thrilling voice, 'All is nothing' without a deep and radical change of heart and conduct. It was not that she saw her for long at a time even when she lived with her: just for a few brief moments after meals which the Carmelite took alone, contenting herself with a few herbs when she was not fasting,[3] but her presence permeated the whole house. She was so careful to avoid anything detrimental to progress in perfection, took so many disciplines and such lengthy ones, wore so penitential a hair shirt, that the young widow was soon ashamed to continue to revel in her life of luxury. Her taste for magnificence had been criticized in Ávila, people had even accused her of being so luxurious and extravagant that her thirty thousand *reales* of revenue were insufficient: she was eating into her capital: the evil tongues now took on another tone:

'Doña Guiomar has made a sort of convent of her palace!'

'She no longer deigns to receive anyone except monks, nuns, *beatas* and other servants of God!'

'Have you seen her dressed as a poor person?'

'Have you seen her go to church without attendants, carrying the cushion she uses when she spends hours on her knees, herself?'

All the pride of the *hidalgos* might be discerned in a final reproach:

' She shows as much politeness to all and sundry as if she were a servant instead of a noble lady!' [4]

The widow of the lord of Villatoro! To consider it an honour to lodge in her house Maridíaz, a saint if you like, the greatest saint that

---

[1] SST, vol. I, p. 407.   [2] Sb, V, c. xxxvii–5.
[3] FR, L. IV, c. xviii.   [4] SST, vol. I, pp. 401–9.

Ávila then boasted of, but the daughter of nobody, that is, of poor folk. Doña Guiomar's servants did say she had no chemise.

'They say that the servants, tired of having to serve riff-raff like that, take it out of her by giving her nothing to eat. The fool does not dare complain lest she should be the cause of their dismissal!'[1]

One pious woman assumed a superior air and confided to her listeners:

'That's charity. Maridíaz has given everything to God. She had only one cloak left, she's given that too. God has drawn her to himself from her youth upwards. Before Doña Guiomar arranged a room as a cell for her, she used to spend whole days and nights in a gallery of the church of San Emiliano. She prays unceasingly. She's a real saint.'

Another who claimed acquaintance with the very highest stages of spirituality but said she had returned to lower levels because all that sort of thing smacked of illuminism and smelt of heresy a mile off, wagged her sententious head:

'Mysticism's in the fashion. I've examined it from every angle and I don't trust it. Look at Maridíaz: she's a saint, it's true. But I've none the less heard her complain of the trials which the Lord does not spare her as a recompense for the penances she performs for him: the greater part of the time she lives in a state of terrible aridity.'

'She complains?'

'In a pious way! She says: "Lord, after taking everything in the world away from me, are you leaving me like this?"[2] Isn't it better to confine oneself to honest, every-day prayers, to virtues which put no one in the shade, rather than to make as much commotion as Doña Guiomar's other friend, Teresa de Ahumada?'

One of the duennas assumed her most intelligent air:

'That person isn't a saint. She couldn't be compared with Maridíaz. I knew her as a child. She always liked to attract attention. Poor Doña Beatriz de Ahumada—God rest her soul—didn't know what to do to master her. Didn't she take the idea into her head, when she was five or six years old, to run away from home, taking her elder brother, Rodrigo, with her, to go to the land of the Turks?'

There on the balcony they drew their faces close together when somebody whispered:

'What about her ecstasies?'

For some time past the name of Teresa de Ahumada had been sufficient to cause the speakers to lower their voices in the large, sombre

[1] Idem.   [2] CTA, cdiii.

apartments where the ladies of this very aristocratic town liked to congregate to munch sweets and speak ill of their neighbours. For when the fires of the Inquisition were burning in Valladolid and Toledo the rumours that were bandied about concerning the Carmelite were enough to make one tremble.

'She says that God speaks to her.'

'She has visions!'

A well-informed person added:

'I've seen the friend in whom she confides, Don Francisco de Salcedo. He pretends to be discretion itself, but it's obvious that nobody in the world is more uneasy than he. As to Padre Daza, he can no longer sleep for the business. Both are convinced that it doesn't come from God, but from the . . .'

The *señoras* crossed themselves on forehead, lips and breast and then made one final sweeping sign.

Thus the graces Teresa received were the talk of the worthy town. This time, too, as in the case of the bodily suffering she had asked for, she might have exclaimed: 'Lord, I didn't want so much!' At this time any supernatural manifestation was an object of much suspicion in Spain. The trial of the Poor Clare of Córdoba, Magdalena de la Cruz, had been a great shock to public faith in such matters. As a prophetess she had foretold the battle of Pavia and the captivity of Francis I; her credit was so great that they would have liked to canonize her in her lifetime, had it been possible. Empress Isabella had given her her portrait, that she might be continually in her thoughts and prayers and was granted the very special favour that the nun would make the first robe worn by Prince Philip with her own holy hands. Feminine superstition? Even a serious man like the Inquisitor General, Don Alonso Manrique, went to Seville purposely to recommend himself to the miracle worker. But on 1st January 1544, Magdalena de la Cruz, suddenly seized with remorse, publicly confessed that her holiness was simulated, her ecstasies feigned and her wonder-working the result of a pact with the devil. The Holy Office took up the matter and the story profoundly shocked the whole of Spain.

For there was much confusion throughout Spain—people mistook the marvellous for true religion: extravagant behaviour was found side by side with sincere faith. It was the reading of Osuna which first suggested to Teresa that it was desirable to restrain external signs of devotion. In the *Third Spiritual Alphabet* he collects from his own experience facts which it seemed to him ought to be mistrusted:

. . . A woman who was seized with trembling and convulsions whenever she approached the Holy Table sighed and cried aloud. The priest, having seen other instances of the kind, waited patiently holding the Host until this crazy servant of God had become calm again and could communicate. . . .

. . . A monk confessed his sins in public.

. . . Servants of God ran about in the fields imploring Our Lord with great cries to teach them to do his holy will, or singing hymns of thanksgiving. . . .

. . . Haloes of light surround the forehead of men at prayer. More rarely, they hear a mysterious song within their breast. . . .[1]

In the churches the faithful prayed with arms outstretched in the form of a cross, kissed the ground, dragged themselves to the altar on their knees, struck their breasts violently, cried out loud to Our Lord. For the congregation to be in tears during a sermon was a common occurrence. People were seen in ecstasy before their favourite saint. The humble were not exempt from such hysterical manifestations: 'One morning a day labourer was seized with a rapture and was seen to fall to the ground as if paralysed. When he recovered consciousness and they tried to help him to his feet, he exclaimed: "Leave me alone! You are hurting me by holding me back, just as if you were crushing the wings of a bird ready to fly away!" '[2]

Genuinely pious people, false claimants for the stigmata, sham ecstasies, sincere recollection, orthodox faith, short cuts towards heresy, all this was so interwoven and mixed up together that, after a long period of confusion in which the airs and graces of the *Beata* de Piedrahita as she made way to allow the Blessed Virgin, who, she said, never left her side, to pass, 'edified' all and sundry, the wind suddenly changed and, with the help of the Inquisition, every effect of the love of God perceptible to the senses became suspect: where people thought they had seen Our Lord, they now saw the devil.

If there was a danger of external manifestations being judged as mere pretence, the abandonment of them entirely was no less dangerous: such abstention might be taken as evidence that you were an *Alumbrado*, an *illuminé*. To remain kneeling during the Gospel, to fix one's eyes on the ground during the elevation of the Host, not to fast or mortify oneself to outward eyes, to affect not to amass indulgences, was to invite the Inquisition to concern itself with your affairs; such interventions were all the more dangerous because positions were not

---

[1] RO, pp. 72-101.   [2] Idem.

defined: no case was clear. Francisca Hernández, a Franciscan tertiary, 'who exercises an inexplicable influence, a kind of dictatorship over various associations of spirituality,' venerated by the Friars Minor who regarded a medal touched by her as a pledge of heavenly graces, was treated by some as 'Medusa' whilst others considered her 'a very holy woman.'[1] She cast such a spell over a brilliant young priest and lector in philosophy, P. Ortiz, that some time after Francisca's arrest by the Inquisition, he went into the pulpit at Toledo and exclaimed in the course of an official inquiry, in the presence of the Chapter and all the civic and religious notabilities: '. . . the reason for the present drought is to punish an immense injustice: the imprisonment of a servant of God in this town!' There was no need for him to continue: a three years' stay in prison persuaded him to submit 'unconditionally' to the judgement of the Church.

A word, a gesture, were enough to arouse suspicion and get one arrested; but to clear oneself thousands of arguments in the course of a trial which lasted for years were necessary. Unless the worst happened and the terrible silence of a secret dungeon closed upon the accused.

Since the opening of the Council of Trent the position had been clearer: the Holy Office was less concerned with subtle distinctions between *Alumbrados, Dejados,* followers of Erasmus, reformers and other shades of heretical doctrine, but on the other hand it was no longer satisfied with mild penalties: whoever was suspected of deviating from orthodoxy was accused of Lutheranism. Any work of spirituality written in Spanish was placed on the index, with a very few exceptions, such as the works of Laredo and Osuna. Even the writings of Fray Luis of Granada and John of Ávila did not escape.

To be taxed with Lutheranism meant a request by the Inquisition to clear oneself before its tribunals: those in error were invited to correct their convictions. The obstinate were burned with much ceremony. Those who loved excitement travelled days on end to enjoy the spectacle.

On 21st May and 8th October 1559, the year in which Doña Teresa de Ahumada's visions caused most stir, two typical autos-da-fé were held at Valladolid. Princess Juana, widow of the King of Portugal, sister of the King of Spain and regent of the kingdom, represented the absent Philip II. Thirty heretics on the one occasion, eighty on the second, dressed in the Sambenito, the ignominious yellow tunic, their heads covered with mitres of all sorts on which were painted devils

RO, p. 84.

and flames, and a green candle in their hands, made their way in procession towards the stake or the prisons.

In Ávila there was much talk of such edifying manifestations, particularly at the Incarnation. People spoke of the Princess Regent, in mourning, with black head-dress and gloves and playing with her black and gold fan, of the Prince Don Carlos, the long ranks of monks and penitents carrying lighted torches, followed by the standard of the Holy Inquisition on which the black and white escutcheon of the Order of St Dominic was juxtaposed on crimson damask with the royal arms embroidered in gold. People quoted the sermon of the famous Melchor Cano, the final admonitions to the condemned on the part of the clergy, admonitions which 200,000 spectators gathered from north, south, east and west echoed with their litanies and their groans.

Neither great name nor exalted reputation stayed the arm of the Church. The daughter of the Marquis of Alcañicez, Ana Enríquez, was only restored to her parents on account of her tender years. But Doctor Agustín Cazalla, canon of Salamanca and preacher to the Emperor Charles V? To the stake! Don Cristóbal de Ocampo, Knight of the Order of St John? To the stake! Doña Mencia de Figueroa, maid of honour to the Queen? Condemned! Even the dead did not escape punishment: Doña Leonor de Vibero, who had died before her trial, had been disinterred, her corpse dragged along in the procession, and then she was burned in effigy.

After that people knew what to expect and Teresa had good reason to feel some alarm. Her best friends did not conceal the fact that they were uneasy about her; as to her greatest enemies, one of them voiced the sentiments of all:

'I hope to live long enough to see this nun end up as she deserves, at the stake set up by the Inquisition.'[1]

Unknown persons took the trouble to put her on her guard, or to frighten her.

One day she was asked for in the parlour of the Incarnation. Behind the grille she saw a very distinguished nobleman, richly dressed, in whom she thought she recognized Don Alonso de Quiñones, one of the noblest lords of Ávila. Was it that he wanted to see for himself the nun who was so much talked about in order to form his own opinion of her? When he had greeted her in his grave manner, he stood there in silence. Finally he said:

'Do not forget Magdalena de la Cruz. Spain thought she was a

[1] GJ, vol. III, p. 148.

saint whereas she was the slave of the devil.'[1] Teresa turned pale, bowed her head and answered in the humblest tones: 'I never remember her without trembling.'

Don Alonso was thoughtful as he left the Incarnation and from that day was one of Doña Teresa's defenders. He reasoned: 'So much humility is never found in a tool of Satan.'

[1] FR, L. I, c. ix.

III

HEAVEN AND HELL

AS Teresa was at prayer on St. Peter's day, she felt Christ near her. She saw him neither with the eyes of the body nor with those of the soul but was none the less certain that he was there and was speaking to her. 'Knowing nothing about this kind of vision, I was very much afraid at first and did nothing but weep. A few words from him sufficed to reassure me, and then I was at peace, happy, free from all fear.' [1]

From then onwards she felt Our Lord near her always; instead of being 'full of distractions' she was constantly aware of his presence at her right hand.

One night, coming back from Matins, she said to María de Cepeda, her niece:

'Oh, Sister! If you only knew who our escort was, how delighted you would be!' [2]

Doña Teresa was prouder than Oriana escorted by Amadis, for *her* knight was Our Lord Jesus Christ carrying his cross.

But the enjoyment of such a privilege brought its own difficulties: Teresa had to tell her confessor about it. When she knelt down in the confessional, she was more afraid than if she had had a mortal sin to confess. She managed to get out the stupendous words:

'Father,' she said in a choking voice, 'Our Lord is with me continually, by my side.'

There was silence. She wept. P. Baltasar Alvarez heard the sobs. He was extremely puzzled: yesterday it was divine words she thought she heard, ecstasies—now it was visions. No, she was not lying but, like so many others, she might be the victim of illusion or perhaps trapped in the devil's snares. Unless His Majesty really had manifested himself to this Carmelite. . . .

He questioned her calmly, as if it were a quite ordinary matter:

'How do you see him?'

'Father, I don't see him.'

The priest gave a start:

'Then how do you know it is Christ?'

[1] Sb, V, c. xxvii–2.   [2] MP, quoted SEC, vol. II, p. 113.

'I don't know how I know, Father. But I know it's he.' [1]

She strove to make him understand what must seem unintelligible, sought for comparisons, found none in the world of tangible things and groped hesitatingly for words that would express the divine.

'Perhaps if I put it that he's there in the same way as in the darkness we know that a person is by our side. It's something like that. But not altogether. It's more like a piece of news which is communicated to the soul, an announcement which is clearer than the light of the sun. Not that you see the sun or any brightness, yet a light enlightens the understanding without one realizing it is a light and disposes the soul to the enjoyment of this great good.' [2]

P. Baltasar followed what his penitent said with the utmost difficulty. He grew impatient:

'A light which is not a light? . . .'

'No, for its brightness does not dazzle. It is a soft white glow, so different from earthly light that the sun seems dim in comparison.' [3]

'You say now that it dazzles without dazzling. . . .' The priest's voice became almost curt: 'Who told you that it was Jesus Christ?'

'He tells me so himself. But before he tells me so, my understanding knows it already.' [4]

Teresa who now lived uninterruptedly in Our Lord's presence did not hear the priest say, 'Go in peace,' but 'Watch. . . . Fear. . . . Be on your guard. . . .' Her certainty about the matter was in no way lessened by such admonitions to caution. She was now in a state in which her prayer never ceased, even during sleep. [5]

One day Christ showed her his hands, 'so wondrously beautiful that one couldn't describe them.' [6] This time, too, she was very much afraid; in the beginning, each fresh grace terrified her, but was not this the case with the disciples? The Gospel is full of their fears and terrors.

A little while afterwards she had a vision of Our Lord's countenance and finally, on the feast of St Paul, Christ showed himself to her in his sacred humanity, 'as the risen Christ is depicted in all his beauty and majesty.' [7]

Such gradual advances on the part of the heavenly Bridegroom so completely dissipated her fears that like Psyche she was eager for more: 'I wanted so much to see the colour of his eyes or his stature, in order

---

[1] Sb, V, c. xxvii-3.   [2] Sb, V, c. xxvii-3.   [3] Sb, V, c. xxviii-5.
[4] Sb, V, c. xxvii-5.   [5] See O, p. 114 (Tr.).
[6] Sb, V, c. xxvii-1.   [7] Sb, V, c. xxviii-3.

to be able to speak of them, but this was altogether beyond my deserts and each time I strove to look more closely he vanished altogether. . . .' [1]

Vision followed vision and at the same time the love of God increased in her, burning so intensely that she felt that henceforward she would find life only in death. 'I felt this love with such intensity that I no longer knew what was happening to me, nothing satisfied me any longer, I felt as if I was being swept off my feet, as if my soul was being torn out of me. Oh, what clever tactics Our Lord used! . . . The force of his love crushed me with a dying so sweet that the soul would have wished never to return to life again.' [2]

The final grace was transverberation, which she received many times, both at the convent of the Incarnation and when staying with Doña Guiomar.

One evening Ana Gutiérrez, one of the nuns in the convent, rushed downstairs on hearing cries and groans coming from Doña Teresa de Ahumada's cell. 'How you frightened me!' she exclaimed when she found Teresa quite well. But her countenance was aflame with the glow and radiance of ecstasy; slowly she returned to consciousness of the world around her:

> I frightened you? Daughter, I wish you could have seen what I've seen! [3]
> . . . I saw an angel close to me, on my left, in bodily shape, a thing granted to me but rarely. He was not large, but small, very beautiful, his face radiant. . . . No doubt he was one of those they call cherubim. He did not tell me his name but I see clearly that there is such a difference between one angel in heaven and another, that I could not express it. He held a long golden lance in his hand and I thought its tip was all flames. He seemed to plunge it several times into my heart, right to the very depths of me. When he drew it out, he seemed to pluck my heart out with it, leaving me all on fire with an immense love of God. The pain was so sharp that I moaned but the delight of this tremendous pain is so overwhelming that one cannot wish it to leave one, nor is the soul any longer satisfied with anything less than God. It is a spiritual, not a bodily pain, although the body has some part, even a considerable part, in it. It is an exchange of courtesies between the soul and God . . . so sweet that I beg God to let whoever thinks I'm not telling the truth taste it. . . . [4]

As the love of the creature met the Creator's love a divine spark leaped forth.

[1] Sb, V, c. xxix-2.   [2] Idem, 8.
[3] GJ, vol. III, p. 324.   [4] Sb, V, c. xxix-13.

When she had been thus transpierced and consumed by divine love, she remained 'as it were, stupefied,' 'no longer wishing either to see or to speak, but to be alone with my pain, which was greater glory than any created thing. . . .' [1]

She complained of feeling great heat and asked Ana Gutiérrez to cut her hair, to give her some small relief. Ana was so astonished at the hair's sweet perfume, 'the perfume of heaven,' [2] that she hid a lock of it. Teresa read her thoughts:

'I order you not to think foolish things and to throw that away with the rubbish!'

Henceforward it was impossible for Teresa to resist the supernatural visitations which occurred 'even in public.' [3] 'As a giant lifts a straw,' [4] so the force of ecstasy raised her from the ground and held her suspended in the air. One day after Communion, the congregation who filled the convent chapel saw her raised two or three palms' height above the ground. [5] She strove to prevent this happening, 'with immense fatigue, like someone who is struggling with a strong giant, she held on with both hands to the communion grille, or lay down on the ground.' [6] Nothing was of the slightest use. She felt the force under her feet and it raised her from the ground 'with an impetus so swift and strong that you see and feel the cloud rise—or perhaps I should say this mighty eagle, and he sweeps you upwards with his wings.' [7]

Those who witnessed such divine manifestations gossiped and chattered about them, whereas Teresa was for days in a state of deep intense sadness and her great need was solitude. [8]

Solitude, when one is the laughing-stock of a small town? Peace, when Ávila knew full well that the fires of the Inquisition were blazing for the benefit of lunatics of her sort at Valladolid, Toledo and Seville?

Never had the families of the one hundred and eighty nuns of the Incarnation, their friends or their devotees shown themselves so eager for visits to the parlour. They hastened there 'for news.' Even before she was asked, one sister volunteered breathlessly:

'To-night when she came to Matins, as pale as if she were dying, she began to call out to Our Lord with great cries like someone calling for help, she seemed to be suffering greatly and the contrast between

[1] Sb. V, c. xxix-14.
[2] GJ, vol. III, p. 324.
[3] Sb, V, c. xxix-14.
[4] Sb, V, c. xii-13.
[5] FR, L. IV, c. xii.
[6] Sb, V, c. xx-14.
[7] Idem.
[8] Cf. Sb, V, c. xx-10.

her suffering face and the radiance of her countenance when she presently fell into ecstasy was tremendous!'[1]

There was no need to name the one they were speaking of: 'she' was Doña Teresa de Ahumada, whom some called 'the saint of the Incarnation' but whom the majority of people suspected of imposture or pretended to pity, saying she was possessed.

Things came to such a pass that she would have preferred 'to be buried alive'[2] rather than show herself in public: she thought of escaping to some convent where as a simple lay-sister employed in the most menial tasks she would be forgotten. Her confessor, P. Baltasar Álvarez, would not consent.

P. Álvarez, a Jesuit like PP. Cetina and Prádanos, had been directing her since 1558. He had the open mind of a young man but also youth's lack of experience and timidity allied with a certain intransigence, and he had not yet succeeded in overcoming his natural harshness although he strove to do so by the practice of mortification. When he arrived at San Gil, he chose a cell so small that he could hardly move in it. There was no table: just a plank covered with big books. No chair: a stool. When at Doña Guiomar's, he refused the armchair she respectfully offered him, sitting stiffly and uncomfortably on a seat without a back:

'To suffer in a thousand ways when one has not deserved it is like a mouthful of tender meat in which there are no bones.'[3]

The young father talked of penances as if they were his chief delight. In the choice of the mortifications he imposed on Teresa, he introduced a certain refinement of cruelty:

'You will make your general confession at the College of San Gil (the Jesuit college)—with unveiled face. . . .'[4]

To force Teresa, for whom a general confession was always the most painful of sufferings, for the thought of having offended God was so bitter to her—to make an exhibition of her sins in this way was more than severity: it showed a want of all fine feeling. However she obeyed without a murmur.

He deprived her of Communion for days together: she did not complain.

He ordered her to avoid solitude instead of seeking it: she gave up her own judgement in the matter.

With him there was nothing but 'questions at one time and at another reproaches'[5]; he subjected her to question and criticism as he

---

[1] Cf. SEC, R, i, p. 4.   [2] Sb, V, c. xxxi-12.   [3] LA, c. x.
[4] SST, vol. I, p. 456, n. 1.   [5] Sb, V, c. xxvi-3.

pleased, alleging that she needed all these trials and rebukes because her will was not yet conquered. But, inflexible master though he was, touched by her sweetness he confided to his friends:

'She obeys like a little child. . . .'[1]

The Rector of the Jesuits, P. Dionisio Álvarez, who was choleric in disposition and harsh in character, had given him his instructions: he was never to relax his severity. The pious coterie under Salcedo-Daza leadership wanted to go a step further: Teresa must be crushed and broken to find out what there was at the bottom of the woman. Instead of complaining the victim was moved to pity for them: 'Timid souls, but good ones, those who treated me most harshly were those who loved me most. . . .'[2]

For now more than ever, at the Incarnation, among the clergy and throughout the whole of Ávila, there was only one cry:

'Teresa de Ahumada's visions are diabolical!'

P. Baltasar kept a cool head. He stood by his penitent in his own fashion—which was somewhat grim. When the panic of all those round her was too much for her, she would complain in the confessional:

'Father, I am afraid of deceiving you and deceiving myself at the same time.'

He replied with a tinge of self-conceit but not unkindly:

'Child, don't be afraid. I've got a good enough brain not to allow myself to be duped. . . .'[3]

He gave her some comfort all the same, this terrible man. He went to an infinite amount of trouble over her, his tiny cell was littered up with everything that saintly theologians, including St Thomas, had written on the mystical life and its manifestations, until he ended by declaring despondently:

'I've got to read all these books to understand Doña Teresa de Ahumada.'[4]

He himself had no experience of supernatural graces, but he was convinced of the Carmelite's good faith, and was often awed by the account of her visions. If his treatment of her was harsh it was so that her soul might be strengthened by self-discipline and that she might find resources within herself which would enable her to guide and control her nature. We might accuse him of want of courage, of not having firmly stood out against those who were crying out: 'All that is devilry!' But important people in the city, of whom the Society of

[1] SEC, vol. II, pp. 506–7. [2] Sb, V, c. xxx–6.
[3] Sb, V, c. xxx–13. [4] FR, L. I, c. xi.

Jesus, which was still classed as a new Order, had in its own interests to take account, and other zealous and pious souls, were advising him not to trust the visionary.[1] Perhaps she was possessed? There were many who thought they were being charitable when they suggested that she should be exorcised.[2]

Teresa's outlook on all this was calm and sane. If it is true that she was momentarily tempted to take a less severe confessor—'I am,' she said, 'a person who cannot do my best when led by force'[3]—she did not give way to this transitory weakness and soon admitted that so far she had made more progress under P. Baltasar than under anyone else, even though he constantly mortified her and tried her as much as he could. To him she said, breaking out into her delightful laugh:

'I'm very fond of a certain Father I know, in spite of his bad character. . . .'[4]

The problem was still as perplexing as ever: was it the devil or God?

Teresa sometimes had to master a gesture of impatience: how *could* she mistake one for the other? Who except Our Lord could have brought to her soul so much light, such fulfilment of love and development of new strength in the exercise of every virtue? She argued: '. . . One single word of those I am privileged to hear, one vision, one moment of recollection which does not last as long as an *Ave*, and soul and body are in such peace, the understanding is so enlightened that I am amazed. . . . I know what I was before, on the way to losing my soul, and I no longer recognize myself, I do not understand how I come by these virtues: they are given me, I don't work to win them. . . . God has taken this means not only to win me to his service but to save me from hell. . .'[5]

She knew perfectly well that the devil used no·disguise when he wanted 'to play at ball with her soul';[6] she saw close to her 'a most vile little black creature,'[7] or perhaps a tiny imp sat on her missal making faces at her. She had seen the place allotted to her in hell and declared when she returned to consciousness again: 'There one burns in such a manner that to be burnt here on earth is a trifle in comparison.'[8]

And the 'holy gentleman' with all his pious clique was attempting to identify the God of love, him whom 'one cannot look at any more

[1] Cf. Sb, V, c. xxv-15.   [2] FR, L. I, c. x.
[3] Sb, V, c. xxxii.   [4] FR, L. I, c. xi.
[5] SEC, R, i, p. 4.   [6] Sb, V, c. xxx-11.
[7] Sb, V, c. xxxi-3.   [8] Sb, V, c. xxxii-3.

than one can look at the sun' without falling into ecstasy, with the hellish vermin she was determined to ignore!

For such was her attitude. A daughter of Ávila, the City of the Knights, was not going to allow herself to be intimidated by devils even if they were legion!

'I snap my fingers at devils![1] They frighten me no more than flies![2] It is they who are afraid of me! I don't understand why people are afraid of them. Why should we say: "Devil! Devil!" when we can say "God ! God!" and make them tremble? Come on, all you devils! I am God's servant and I am curious to see what you can do to me!'[3]

She added, referring to her pious persecutors:—'I fear those who are afraid of the devil more than the devil himself. . . .'[4]

She was too exceptional not to puzzle and disturb the small minds which she was not yet of sufficient stature to dominate. And so good, but ordinary, folk entertained doubts for Doña Teresa de Ahumada's sanity. Dangerous and cowardly as they were, they even went so far as to impose on her the most cruel suffering she had yet undergone. The idea was Gonzalo de Aranda's—a fine fellow of a priest who had joined the vigilance committee formed by Salcedo, Daza and their associates. They hurried to the Incarnation:

'Doña Teresa de Ahumada is wanted in the parlour!'

They imparted their idea to her in all its crudeness, gave her their order quite baldly:

'When you see what you think is Our Lord, hold out the cross and make horns at him with your fingers . . .(*las higas*). It's the devil and you'll catch him like that!'[5]

Teresa was completely taken aback. For *them* to talk of making horns at God! She knew something of the gentleness of Christ, but also had experience of his 'terrifying' majesty. 'I say terrifying, for although this presence is more beautiful and delightful than one can imagine . . . his majesty is so great that one is filled with awe.'[6]

There was nothing for it but to submit. The Lord made this trial the occasion of fresh graces when, with humble apologies, she made 'horns' at him:

'Daughter, you do right to obey.'[7]

She offered him the cross as one would offer it to Satan in person. He changed the cross into a jewel sparkling with the precious stones of paradise.

[1] Sb, V, c. xxv-22.   [2] Idem, 20.   [3] Idem, 19-20-22.
[4] Idem, 22.   [5] Sb, V, c. xxix-5.
[6] Sb, M, VI, c. ix-5.   [7] Sb, V, c. xxix-6.

But when her mentors enjoined upon her not to practise mental prayer any more, Christ was angry:

'Tell them from me that that is tyranny.' [1]

God—or the devil? God—or the devil?

'It was enough to send one out of one's mind.' [2]

She did not go out of her mind. Imperturbable common sense together with her fondness for household tasks fortunately provided her strong nature with an outlet which had a soothing effect upon her 'interior troubles.' When her sisters maliciously endeavoured to catch the saint—or the possessed nun—by surprise, they found her busy arranging flowers or decorating an altar; even more often, broom in hand, they found her making war on the dust in every nook and cranny.

And the woman who spends her time cleaning and polishing keeps her wits about her.

[1] Idem. [2] Sb, V, c. xxviii–18.

IV

FRAY PEDRO DE ALCÁNTARA

THE sun beats fiercely down in Castile in August and at siesta time every road is deserted: not a man, not even a dog. I am wrong, however. In the distance a dark blob shows up against the light which is so brilliant that every speck of dust is separately visible. A friar. A pilgrim perhaps? His brown habit which is all in rags sweeps the dust, the Franciscan hood is well down over his eyes. Not that he is afraid of being blinded by the dazzling light—the brilliance of his interior vision is more intense than any sunlight—but he despises the world which he treads beneath his bare feet. Vagabond that he is, he has never consented to travel otherwise than as the very poor do, begging his bread; he has been all over Spain and Italy with his regular, measured tread. Moreover, he asks for alms but seldom: with a hunch of bread every three days, he has as much as he wants. 'It's a matter of habit,' he says. Witnesses affirm that he has sometimes remained a whole week forgetting to take any earthly nourishment.

He goes on his way towards Ávila, his eyes cast down all the time, and does not see the battlements and bell-towers silhouetted in the distance. But the sun has been travelling too, sleepers yawn, life seems to reawaken from its torpor, its resurrection being immediately expressed by the cheerful trot of a donkey, or a song interspersed with words of encouragement addressed by the donkey-boy, a bright lad who is not content to be quiet for long, to his beast. He calls out to the friar as he passes:

'Hey now, friar! You're on foot but I have a donkey to ride!'

The friar trudges on his way without raising his eyes, his 'peace be with thee' is uttered from under his hood. His cheeks are hollow, his beard white. And the swarthy, wrinkled body hidden under his Franciscan rags is twisted and knurled like the roots of trees.[1]

' Fray Pedro!'

The friar does not so much as move an eyelid. His silence betrays his identity and the lad spurs on the donkey with his bare feet, forcing it to trot more quickly, and hurries off to the town where he cries out to all and sundry:

[1] SB, V, c. xxvii–18.

'Fray Pedro's along the road! He's coming to Ávila! Fray Pedro de Alcántara! The saintly Fray Pedro!'

The saint: the man who imposed on himself the severest of penances, and spent all his time standing or kneeling in order to conquer sleep. For forty years he allowed himself only one hour of sleep in the twenty-four and that in a sitting posture 'his head resting against a block of wood.' [1] Moreover it was impossible for him to lie down in his cell, which was only four and a half feet long. He never wore any other garment but his drab-coloured habit and had no cloak, however bitter the cold or drenching the rain. Even in the snow he never went otherwise than barefoot.

All Ávila knew his story: he was born in wild Estremadura of a distinguished family connected with Hernán Cortés, the famous conqueror of Mexico. He became a Franciscan at nineteen and, with the habit, acquired something which was of greater value, St Francis' burning love of God, his love for his brethren and for 'Lady Poverty.' Even in those days he had dreams of reforming the Order, of bringing it back to its original Gospel severity, but he decided to begin by reforming himself. It was known that when quite a young man he remained three years in one monastery without distinguishing his brethren otherwise than by the sound of their voices, for he had imposed on himself the mortification never to raise his eyes; 'and so he didn't know the way to the place of necessity, but merely followed the friars.' [2] For years he had not so much as looked at any woman. Now, it was indifferent to him whether he saw one or not. As he walked people would try and catch the sound of the chinking of his penance—made out of pieces of tin. [3]

'Fray Pedro de Alcántara!'

All the pious folk flocked to meet him. 'The blessed man' had many friends in Ávila and often went there. Juan Velázquez de Ávila, lord of Loriana, offered him his house which was not far from Doña Guiomar's palace.

'It's God who has sent him to us.'

And Doña Guiomar ran off to the Incarnation to drag permission out of the prioress to keep Doña Teresa with her for a week: she *must* have the opportunity of seeing Fray Pedro de Alcántara. At last! A saint would study her 'case' and the authority of Fray Pedro was such that his verdict would certainly be the accepted one. For Doña Guiomar had never had any doubt: her friend's visions 'were from God.'

---

[1] Sb, V, c. xxvii–17, 18.   [2] Idem.
[3] Sb, V, c. xxx–2.

Soon all Ávila was aware that Fray Pedro was treating the Carmelite with marked kindness, nay, even more: that he found joy in her visits.

'He says that her presence is a comfort to him, his greatest consolation being to meet those on whom God lavishes great graces. . . .'[1]

The tribe of loud-voiced critics lowered its tones when he declared publicly that he was very sorry for her because she had suffered the most severe trial possible: that of opposition from good people. . . . He added that no one in Ávila was capable of understanding her.[2]

He understood her, not through theology or because he had studied mysticism, but from personal experience: he knew all about this invisible presence of God, the mind taking flight, the complete overthrow of the senses which occurred in adoration, the divine words, their effects, the joy they gave the soul.

'Don't be troubled any longer, child; thank God and rest assured that all this is *his* spirit. There is nothing more certain, nothing in which you can more safely believe, except the truths of faith themselves. . . .'[3]

He offered to speak to P. Baltasar Álvarez, to the Daza-Aranda following, and the 'holy gentleman' heard someone who was holier than he solemnly affirm: 'After the Holy Scriptures and all the Church orders us to believe, there is nothing more certain than the divine origin of what this woman sees. . . .'[4]

All were convinced except poor Salcedo: he did not dare to protest, but all the same he secretly retained a certain amount of misgiving. It could well have been argued against him:

'If Teresa were not holy, she would not put up with such an obstinate blockhead as you. The very fact of her never having said a bitter word against you, of having shown so much affection for you, of being entirely without spite, the delightful letters she has written you. . . . "Don't say so much about your being old, for to think of it makes my head hurt all over . . ." [5]—that alone deserves a halo. . .'

In Fray Pedro de Alcántara Teresa had won a lifelong friend, more than lifelong even, for he appeared to her more than once after his death, 'in very great glory.'

Not only did this good man extricate her from a difficult position, but she found him charming. What a contrast between his gracious kindness and the hard rigidity of the 'learned' and pious! 'With all his sanctity he was very courteous and easy of approach; a man of few words, except to answer the questions put to him, but what he said

---

[1] Sb, V, c. xxx-5. [2] Idem, 6. [3] Idem, 5.
[4] PA, quoted SEC, vol. II, p. 307. [5] CTA, x.

was very much to the point and showed that he had a sense of humour.' [1]

Teresa breathed again and came to life, now she had every joy, even that of intelligent and delightful conversation. 'God preserve us from gloomy saints!'

Teresa and Fray Pedro did not part without promising to correspond and to recommend each other to God. 'His humility was so great that he set some store by the prayers of this wretched creature, to my great embarrassment. He left me greatly strengthened, reassured and happy. . . .' [2]

Francis Borgia's approval had protected Teresa only for a short time. Would that of Peter of Alcántara prove more effective? In the end Teresa succeeded in winning Ávila to her side, but this was due more to her own humility and obedience than to the influence of distinguished 'servants of God.' Like her first master, Osuna, she never failed to recognize that 'weak women' may be the victims of illusion and so she left herself entirely in the hands of the learned Doctors. But one does not cease to be a human being because one is an expert in theology, and such pious persons, conceited as they were in their own fashion, finally ceased to doubt the genuineness of the graces received by a woman who treated them with all the submission and veneration they considered their due.

It had become a sort of habit with them to insist upon her 'giving an account of her soul' to experts of their choice: after P. Francis Borgia, Fray Pedro de Alcántara, after Fray Pedro de Alcántara, P. de Salazar, after P. de Salazar, Master Juan de Ávila, after Master Juan de Ávila, P. Pedro de Ibáñez, not to mention all those for whom she had been asked to write out a general confession. They all approved her; P. Ibáñez even wrote: ' I cannot do otherwise than consider her a saint.' [3]

Although the fact did not occur to them, these frequent accounts of her spiritual life and mystical experiences were actually a remarkable intellectual training and a valuable exercise in literary expression. Forced as she was to analyse her feelings, examine her conscience, deepen her self-knowledge, and constrained to comprehend what she would have been content to feel, to define the indefinable, to describe the indescribable, her reasoning faculty became more developed and acute, while her spirit cleaved to God. Salcedo, Daza, Aranda, with

---

[1] Sb, V, c. xxvii–18.　　　　　[2] Sb, V, c. xxx–7.
[3] IB quoted SEC, vol. II, p. 149.

their punctilious demands, were thus partly responsible for building up in Teresa a realist mind so clear and virile, and for her forming a style so precise, persuasive and expressive. The memory of these various worthies survives only because she recorded their names.

The first of these *Relations* is dated 1560. It is addressed to P. Pedro Ibáñez, a learned Dominican whom Teresa often went to consult at the monastery of Santo Tomás. It introduces us to a woman of forty-five who is emerging from her trials and the flood of graces she has received unscathed and unspoiled—a woman with a wonderfully clear mind and so well balanced that she seems able henceforward to stand up against anything. The progress since the time when she gave herself over to spectacular penances is evident. The desire for perfection can be seen manifesting itself in small things—which, after all, are the most important—forgetfulness of self, detachment, obedience, poverty, kindness, the determination never to offend God again, even by venial sin. This admirable ascending curve shows only one deviation: the conviction that 'all is nothing' is over-emphasized to the extent that the beautiful things she has loved so much, 'water, the country, perfumes, music,' seem to her as nothing 'but rubbish.' [1] But the time will come when she will learn to praise the Creator in his creatures.

Fears, tears even, still persist but from a fresh and different cause: 'The desire of serving God which comes to me is so intense that I should like to shout out and tell everybody how important it is not to be satisfied with giving only a little. . . . This desire is so keen that the very notion of my weakness crushes me interiorly. This body of mine fetters me. If it were not for that I should do great things. My helplessness in serving God causes me unbearable grief. . . .' [2]

This was the first manifestation of Doña Teresa de Ahumada's great need to express herself in activity although she had only just won the right to live in peace.

Daughter of Don Alonso and Doña Beatriz, sister of seven young men gone off overseas, would she be able to remain quietly in her convent? She had a fighting nature, certainly, but at the same time she was practised in every form of self-discipline and *ascesis*: without this discipline her impetuous nature would doubtless have only stirred up turbulence and disorder. But in her prayer she 'gathers up' her forces, binding them into a bundle of which her will to serve is the cord.

Doña Teresa was to prove to the world that contemplation is the most powerful lever for action.

[1] Cf. SEC, R, p. 4.   [2] Cf. Idem.

V

THE TROUBLES OF THE KINGDOM OF FRANCE

TERESA DE AHUMADA'S desire was to plunge into action the moment she was ready to do so: she would never be found letting opportunity slip by until it was too late. In her, joy was uppermost, for love is joy and Teresa was now wholly possessed by love. What one does through love, with love, never hurts.

The gateway which leads to God for her was not a narrow one; on two occasions, in almost identical terms, she for whom Our Lord 'is not a dead man, but the living Christ,' [1] and who owned her preference for the risen Christ 'without suffering and full of glory,' [2] affirmed: 'Lord, I do not see in what way the road which leads to you is narrow: it is not a footpath but a royal highway.' [3] And again, 'Lord, he who truly loves you moves in security along a wide and royal highway.' [4]

The characteristics of the woman of action could be clearly discerned in her: 'God endowed her with an amazing courage. She who was formerly so timid now put the devils to flight. She knew nothing of the affected ways and foibles peculiar to women. Scrupulosity was foreign to her nature; she was extremely frank and straightforward. The clarity of her mind, her understanding of spiritual things, were remarkable.' [5]

Teresa had regained her equilibrium. Or, to put it more correctly, they at last allowed her to show that she had never lost it: if the worthy folk by whom she was surrounded had not driven her nearly distracted with all their talk and fuss about the devil, she would doubtless have quickly overcome her initial fears, and from earthly things would have turned to move in the sphere of heavenly ones with perfect ease, radiating heaven upon earth.

Obliged as she was at this period of her life to give some care to temporal matters, she acquitted herself well. Through her father's death and the absence abroad of her elder brothers, she had now become

---

[1] Sb, V, c. xxviii–8.
[2] Sb, V, c. xxxv–13.
[3] Cf. Sb, V, c. xxii–6.
[4] Idem, 14.
[5] Cf. IB quoted SEC, vol. II, p. 132.

the head of the family. There was the business of getting the damages reduced in a lawsuit instigated by a crochety heir, Martín Guzmán, María's husband. She had to face it alone, as she did the departure for overseas in their turn of Antonio, Pedro and Agustín, who removed the furniture and belongings from the family home, let it out at 30 ducats and left her with the responsibility of bringing up her young sister, Juana. Teresa brought her to the Incarnation where she shared her own cell, and in 1553 married her to Don Juan de Ovalle, a distinguished gentleman of Ávila. Amid her visions and all they involved, she had to see to it that the father-in-law, 'Juan de Ovalle the elder,' gave the young couple a sufficient allowance.

At the end of the year 1560, in spite of wretched health to which she paid no attention, Teresa was at the height of her powers; in addition, she also had the precious advantage of tried and henceforth unshakable friendships. All of them, Francisco de Salcedo, Gaspar Daza, Gonzalo de Aranda, P. Pedro Ibáñez, were now not only convinced, but completely won over to her: even should she ask them to go through the eye of a needle, she would not lose their friendship. The veneration of the 'holy gentleman' for her would soon be as remarkable as his doubts had been:

'If they were to tell me that St John the Baptist was at the gates of Avila and Mother Teresa in some other part of the town, I would throw away the opportunity of seeing St John the Baptist to cast myself at Mother Teresa's feet and ask her blessing.'

Fray Pedro de Alcántara was her friend, P. Francisco de Borja sang her praises, 'those in the Society' respected her, the Dominicans revered her, the Franciscans loved her; and Doña Guiomar de Ulloa, who never ceased to stand up for her, was always there.

At the Incarnation hostility died down, the sceptical apologized; more than forty nuns followed her example in the ways of prayer and imitated her virtues. Her virtues and not her ecstasies: she strove to persuade her sisters that heaven was more easily to be won by obedience and forgetfulness of self than by the desire for supernatural graces: raptures and ecstasies proved God's loving kindness; they were no guarantee of perfection.

In this convent Teresa could gently pursue her progress heavenward. Along a royal highway? The convent was more like a main street or a fair in the market-place. The number of nuns, to which must be added that of the secular persons in the convent, was always excessive and those who troubled to observe the Constitutions in the minority. The noise and bustle of the world penetrated everywhere and Doña Teresa de Ahumada was called to the parlour too frequently for her liking.

All these conversations were a waste of time, a source of distractions in prayer leading to coldness in divine love. Henceforward for Teresa relatives and friends were merely the enemies of the interior life: she had proved by experience the dissipating effect of useless talk, the corrosive action of criticism which it was not always easy to put down.

On the other hand, solitude would mean silence; silence, concentration; and concentration, strength. Strength for love. Strength for happiness. Not in her own interests, but for the world. The awakening in her of the need for action manifested itself under the form of desire for the apostolate.

Teresa, being a Castilian, was a realist. In her obedience to the divine law she found such joys, so concrete an increase of happiness, that human ways seemed to her only 'rubbish'; she was seized with compassion for those who persisted in not understanding this.

> *Come to me, all ye that labour and are heavily burdened, and I will refresh you.* . . . What more do we want, Lord? What are we asking for? What are men running after if not rest and refreshment? Help us, my God, help us! What does this mean, Lord? What a pity it is, what blindness to be seeking where it is impossible to find! Have pity on your creatures, O Creator. Consider that we do not understand ourselves, that we do not know what we desire and have no idea what we are asking for. Give us light, O Lord . . . . What a hard thing I am asking of you, my true God: to love one who loves you not, to open to one who doesn't knock, to give health to one who enjoys being ill and looks for diseases! . . .[1] Have pity on those who have no pity on themselves![2]

Teresa was well aware that God had created man for happiness in the accomplishment of successive resurrections in him [3]; in the Gospels he taught the art of living happily. By breaking the divine law, man made his own unhappiness, just as anyone who infringed the natural law by refusing to breathe would cause his own death. But this was what the creature persisted in refusing to see: 'God wills that we seek truth and we choose a lie; he wants us to seek what is eternal and we love passing things; he wants us to aspire to great and high things, but we love what is dust, and earthy; he would wish us to love only

---

[1] Sb, E, c. xviii-2, 3.   [2] Sb, E, c. ix-1.
[3] *I.e.* in the spiritual life, every degree of surrender to God brings its own 'resurrection' or new and deeper life in him (Tr.).

The Troubles of the Kingdom of France   111

certainty, but all we love here on earth are things that are uncertain. . . .'[1]

Teresa now experienced a new feeling: that of compassion for mankind and in particular for the kingdom of France. At that time France was Spain's most formidable enemy, but Teresa's love goes beyond the concept of patriotism. 'At that time I understood the calamities and miseries of France and the harm the Lutherans had done there. That hurt me, and, knowing that this was the only way I could do something to help, I wept before Our Lord and begged him to remedy the condition of affairs. I would have given my life a thousand times over to save a single one of the souls that were being lost there. . . .'[2]

The passing moment in which she spoke in this way was one whose influence would endure unto eternity. The combat which she was ready to wage was not a war of hatred: Teresa was against no one, all she wanted was the unrestricted penetration of love. She did not judge, she loved; she did not condemn, she did not castigate, she only wanted to give and to give herself. 'The world is burning!'[3]

Like Loyola's legionaries, she had the gift of infusing love wherever it was necessary. But the human voice is not so far-reaching in its influence as a soul grafted in God by prayer; silence which is gathered up in him is more powerful than vociferations.

From the negative conception of unity expressed in the phrase 'all is nothing,' Teresa passed to that of constructive and positive unity: 'God is all.' She was fully aware of the strength of two or three gathered in his name. She pondered over what Our Lady's Order had been like before Pope Eugenius IV, on account of the extreme wretchedness of the times, mitigated the rigours of the primitive Rule, thus turning Carmels which were formerly strongholds of penance and prayer into sanctimonious houses of refuge for lonely bachelors and spinsters.

Such thoughts worried Teresa. At this time they formed her principal subject of conversation.

Doña Teresa de Ahumada's cell was attractive; it was detached from the main convent and consisted of two rooms built one above the other. On the ground floor was an oratory, very well kept, and having a recess adorned with pictures; above them was a Latin inscription: *Enter not into judgement with thy servant, O Lord.* She slept on the first floor and this she also used during the day; here she had a room

[1] Sb, C, c. xlii-4.   [2] Sb, C, c. i-2.   [3] Sb, C, c. i-5.

whose windows looked on to the garden. Here also she received many visitors, for visits from cell to cell were one of the pleasures of life at the Incarnation.

One day Doña Teresa de Ahumada, sitting on a cushion on the floor, as was quite usual since so many Moorish customs had crept into daily life, was working at her embroidery; her closest friends were there with her: Ana and Inés de Tapia, her cousins, and the faithful Juana Suárez. Leonora and María de Ocampo, her special favourites, loved to hear her talk, for their aunt Teresa spoke of Our Lord with such charm and eagerness that they never tired of hearing her. As she narrated them, the lives of the holy Fathers of the Desert in the far-off times when the Order of Carmel first began were so full of colour that they reminded one of an illuminated manuscript. Not that one could really hope to be fed by an angel like the holy prophet Elias any more than plaited palm would now be a suitable material for nuns' habits— but what grandeur there was in their silence and what strength in their solitude!

'The Eternal was not in the strong and mighty wind, he was not in the earthquake, he was not in the fire, but he was in the still, small voice, and he spoke to Elias. . . .'

From the patio used for recreation rose the sound of flutes and tambourines through which could be heard someone singing one of the latest *romances*.[1]

'Who indeed among us here would be able to hear the still, small voice? Life in this convent is difficult, there are too many of us. . . .'

'Superiors themselves make a complete withdrawal from the world impossible.'

Did they not frequently oblige Teresa to go and make a long stay in the house of some noble family of Ávila 'who enjoyed her company?'—People so important that they dare not refuse them. . . .

And the parlours . . .

It was María de Ocampo who spoke first:

'Let's go away then, all of us here! And let's organize a solitary life for ourselves "like the hermits did." '[2]

Teresa gave her young niece a searching glance and lowered her eyes again over her embroidery. She thought to herself: 'At last!' and thanked God.

María was seventeen. She was a lay boarder at the Incarnation as her aunt had been thirty years before at Our Lady of Grace. When Teresa saw the grandchild of her uncle Francisco for the first time at

---

[1] *I.e.* ballads (Tr.).   [2] FR. L. I, c. xiii.

La Puebla de Montalbán, on the occasion of a pilgrimage to Our Lady of Guadalupe, she was so taken with the child's bright face that she asked to have her with her: she would bring her up in her cell instead and in the place of her sister Juana. She loved children so much.

María de Ocampo, however, did not come until ten years later and even then put off her arrival: she could not come without renewing her wardrobe, for 'she was then very grand and elegant and to keep up this appearance she had to display much ingenuity and use extraordinary contrivances.'[1] She took so much pleasure in these contrivances that the idea of becoming a nun which she had entertained for a short time was completely stifled. Teresa did not receive her young guest any the less affectionately for that. Nor did she reproach her for thinking of marriage:

'Juana lived here for ten years, she left to marry Juan de Ovalle.'

She did not blame her for liking tales of chivalry and never thought of forbidding her to read them:

'You get a taste for reading that way. I used to like them, too. You'll perhaps come one day, as I did, to want more serious reading....'

That was why this sudden desire for the solitary life made her both smile and give thanks to God.

The idea was launched, 'in jest.' But those who were present found it so attractive that 'one word led to another and the evening was spent in devising ways and means of setting up a small convent and in discussing what it would cost. . . .' For earthly wealth is necessary to found a miniature paradise.

What of it! María was determined to have her hermitage and appealed to her aunt:

'Found one! Like the one we've been talking of! I'll help you with my fortune!'[2]—her share, that was, of the family inheritance.

Such enthusiasm amused Teresa very much. The next day, still laughing about it, she said to Doña Guiomar:

'These young people were in high spirits yesterday. They amused themselves with working out a plan for us to found a small convent after the style of the Discalced Franciscans.'

Doña Guiomar did not treat the project as a joke.

A great movement for the reform of the religious Orders, the lax condition of which was openly admitted, was sweeping over Spain. New Orders were founded, the Rule of old ones put into force again where necessary. The Society of Jesus was a new Order: the reform of the Order of St Dominic, intensified in Spain by Hurtado and his

---

[1] Idem.   [2] Idem.

followers, represented a return to primitive austerity. In short, in a Europe rent asunder with the struggles between Catholics and Lutherans—to use Teresa's terms, for she did not so much as mention the name of Calvin—Philip II was going to make the maintenance of religious unity in his realms his primary aim.

The girl who thus suggested the idea of reforming Carmel 'in fun' was impregnated with the thoughts and dreams of the woman with whom she lived; it also happened that she was thinking along the same lines as her sovereign who was then preparing to build the Escorial, the place where kings would crumble to dust, that he might dwell there amid the continual vision of the hollowness of this world.

That was why Doña Guiomar treated the matter with all seriousness. She said to Teresa:

'Found. I will help you.'

This was to respond to the Carmelite's secret wish by a call for immediate action. But she alone had considered the project deeply enough to realize the difficulties of carrying it out; she alone, because she had experience of such things, knew how sharp the uprooting would be. She alone knew, moreover, that from the moment when she 'decided' no amount of opposition would make her draw back.

We admire Teresa de Ahumada for many things, but we love her for having told us her very feminine reason for a momentary hesitation: 'I liked being in the house where I was very much, for I had my cell arranged exactly to my taste. . . .' [1]

She gave a quick look round; she felt regret leaving such pleasant surroundings.

But it was not for her to choose: 'We decided quite firmly to leave all that in God's hands.' [2]

---

[1] Sb, V, c. xxxii–10.   [2] Idem.

VI

THE PLOT OVER ST. JOSEPH'S

TERESA DE AHUMADA received from God the command to do her utmost to found the new convent.

From that moment, 'shoulder to the wheel,' her life became active as well as contemplative and henceforward she was no longer her own mistress. He whom she called 'His Majesty' was an insistent director of operations. His orders were clear from the start: she was first to lay the plan before her confessor, telling him not to oppose it.

Her feminine instincts made her recoil for a moment: she wanted to gain time, owned that she had loved to dream 'of a poor house where she would live with a few sisters of the same mind as herself, and where they would all give themselves solely to prayer, with no parlours and no grilles, detached from all earthly things, their hearts consecrated to the Bridegroom alone,' [1] without really believing that she would one day be obliged to turn the dream into reality. So many obvious difficulties could be foreseen that she might have complained once more: 'Lord, not quite so much!'

His Majesty insisted. Teresa argued:

'Lord, are there not others, particularly theologians, men who, if you spoke to them, would do what you ask much better than a worthless person like myself can?' [2]

Our Lord replied 'in a tone which showed his heart's pain':

'It is because men and theologians will not listen to me that, despised by them, I come like a beggar to talk of what I want with poor, humble women, and to find rest in their company. . . .'

The divine compassion sought to win her by appealing to her imagination:

'This convent will be dedicated to St Joseph. He will guard one door, Our Lady the other. . . .' [3] He reasoned with her: 'What would become of the world if it were not for religious?'

Her Master had spoken. She was beside herself with joy, but so scared at the idea of conveying the message to P. Baltasar Álvarez that

[1] Y, L. I, c. i.   Cf. IB quoted SEC, vol. II, p. 150.
[3] Sb, V, c. xxxii–11

she could not make up her mind to do so by word of mouth; her skill
as a letter-writer was already so persuasive that the formidable man,
although he did present objections 'in conformity with right reason,'
advised her to put her request before the Carmelite Provincial, P.
Gregorio Fernández.

Doña Guiomar undertook to transmit the request: a rich widow
was more likely to obtain a favourable hearing than an obscure unknown nun. The Father Provincial seemed very pleased, entered into
the details of the plan, declared himself glad to learn there would not
be more than thirteen nuns and promised his authorization.

The news so far was good, too good: it exploded on Ávila as if it
were a bomb. Doña Teresa de Ahumada was beginning to get herself
talked about again! This Carmelite, so much the subject of discussion
and hesitation that it had taken the evidence of several holy men
to get the genuineness of her visions attested, was now presuming
to want to revolutionize her Order and to found a convent where
mere weak women would be setting themselves up as rivals in austerity
with the Desert Fathers! Some ridiculed the idea, others were indignant, all said:

'She's mad!'

The most charitable found it difficult to defend her.

'Why doesn't she try to let people forget her and stay quietly at the
Incarnation?' [1]

Doña Guiomar was not spared :

'If she wants an outlet for her zeal, she has one ready to hand: it's
time she looked after her children!'

Ávila was in an uproar and took sides for or against. And every
man or woman thought he or she had the right to throw ridicule on
the plan for this convent.

At the Incarnation itself matters were much worse: as might be
expected, convents where the laxity permitted by the Mitigation was
enjoyed took a poor view of a return to the primitive Rule. The
calmest were sentimental about it:

'We thought Doña Teresa loved us. But not only does she show
she has no love for the house in which she's been living for more than
twenty years, she's trying to found another. If she's in a position to get
hold of money and revenues, why doesn't she give them to us, her
sisters, for we haven't the money to buy enough to eat?' [2]

Those who even in the service of God did not divest themselves of
their pride felt themselves injured:

[1] SST, vol. II, p. 22.   [2] Cf. Sb, V, c. xxxiii-2.

'Her pretensions are against all reason, they're an insult to us! Haven't holier people than she adapted themselves to the Mitigated Rule?' [1]

And those who were most incensed over the matter:

'The prison cell's for rebels of her sort!'

Teresa was unperturbed. The time had gone by when 'the opposition of good people' was pain to her. 'She cared nothing for what people said, for honour or dishonour, for the exhausting labours she would have to undergo, for the money—though it was so necessary and she had nothing. She went forward in the boldness of the Holy Spirit, for her courage exceeded that of ordinary men and women.' [2]

She did, however, put up some pretence of being sensitive to the general feeling of anger 'in order not to seem to be showing contempt for what was said to her' [3] . . . A truly angelic ruse; unless you love men and forgive the injuries they have done you, you will not resist the pleasure of showing them that you do not feel what they do to you. Only on one occasion did she burst out laughing in her opponents' faces: when certain well-intentioned persons who had heard a rumour that she was going to launch out upon 'this venture' because of a revelation, tried to frighten her with the threat of the Inquisition. In the parlour she had found some very terrified people who said to her in hushed tones:

'Beware! Times are terrible! They're talking of denouncing you to the Inquisition!'

Teresa could not prevent her laugh from breaking out:

'You amuse me! I've never been afraid of it. For all matters of faith, for the very least of the Church's ceremonies, for any truth of Holy Scripture you like to name, I would die a thousand deaths. Reassure yourselves: my soul would be in a very bad way if there were anything in all that to make me fear the Inquisitors. If I really thought there was any reason, I would go straight to them myself; but if anyone does delate me falsely, Our Lord will save me, and it will be of great benefit to me.' [4]

The clergy, however, and other religious Orders attacked her violently: every priest and friar felt himself threatened for his daily bread, in these times of famine and growing poverty. Were there not too many convents already in Ávila to share the insufficient alms? In the church of Santo Tomás a preacher even took her to task in the course of a sermon, thundering against 'religious who go away from their

[1] Cf. Idem. [2] JA, L. II, c. i.
[3] Sb, V, c. xxxvi-13. [4] Cf. Sb, V, c. xxxiii-5.

monasteries; under the pretext of founding new Orders they only seek their own liberty—with other references so pointed that her sister Juana who was with her blushed at the insult and wanted to make her escape.' [1] Teresa, calm and smiling, did not seem to understand that it was levelled at her. Out of the corner of her eye she glanced at her Book of Hours opened at a series of short ejaculations of peaceful self-conquest which she had composed and liked to repeat:

> Let nothing disturb thee,
> Nothing affright thee.
> All things are passing,
> God never changeth.
> Patience gains all things.
> Who hath God wanteth nothing.
> Alone God sufficeth.[2]

The campaign against the poor little convent of St. Joseph's proved efficacious, for it was well organized.

Influenced by people of rank and importance and upset by so much scandal, the Provincial withdrew his authorization.

At the instigation of his rector, P. Dionisio Vázquez, P. Baltasar Álvarez ordered Teresa to give up having anything to do with the foundation. 'One day you will come to see that all this was only a dream,' [3] he wrote to her.

To crown everything, on Christmas night a priest refused Doña Guiomar absolution unless she stopped aiding and abetting the scandal.

Our Lord, who was Director of operations, ordered Teresa to obey her confessor and keep quiet for the moment.

'. . . And we had just bought the house, small but well situated! I wasn't upset over it: Our Lord had told me to do my best and that I should see what His Majesty would do. I *have seen!*' [4]

Teresa had one very powerful ally: P. Pedro Ibáñez. From the very beginning Doña Guiomar laid the project before him. He had asked the two women for concrete details as to their aims and the means they had to achieve them, the house, María de Ocampo's promises, what the young widow was able to offer; and all this was explained to him with a clearness which augured well for the future Foundress's gifts of organization. Teresa had said nothing about visions, she had given 'human reasons.'

---

[1] TC quoted SEC, vol. II, p. 333.
[2] *Nada te turbe —nada te espante —Todo se pasa —Dios no se muda —La paciencia —todo lo alcanza —quien a Dios tiene —nada le falta —Sólo Dios basta.*
[3] Sb, V, c. xxxiii-3.   [4] Sb, V, c. xxxii-18.

He asked for a week to think the matter over. They were already taking their departure and crossing the courtyard in front of the convent of Santo Tomás when he called them back:

'Are you quite determined to follow my advice?'[1]

The assent was unanimous. A week later he sent them his reply:

'Get on with this foundation with all possible speed. You have very little money? Then you must put yourselves into God's hands. . . . If anyone raises difficulties let him come and talk to me.'

The result of this unqualified approval was to win Teresa the whole-hearted adhesion and collaboration of P. Daza, Salcedo and a few other worthy men.

They were not going to be deterred on account of a prohibition. Our Lord inspired them with the wits to defeat their opponents. Teresa could not disobey her confessor. What of that! Urged on by P. Ibáñez, Doña Guiomar, in her own name and in the greatest possible secrecy, asked Rome for authorization to found a convent in accordance with the primitive Rule of Carmel. It would be under the jurisdiction of the Bishop of Ávila instead of depending on the Provincial of the Order, and would be none the worse for that.

There was a change for the better: the Jesuit rector who was so hostile was replaced by P. Gaspar de Salazar, who had only to meet Teresa to be instantly won over both to her and her project. He authorized Baltasar Álvarez to allow his penitent to go on 'courageously' with her plans as Foundress. There was only one condition: to act with the greatest secrecy.

But to go and found a convent in Ávila without people knowing about it!

Teresa complained: 'Lord, why do you command me to do impossible things? If I were only free, it would not matter so much being a woman! But I am bound on every side, without a farthing, and, what's more, without the means of getting any money, without the brief, without anything, what can I do, Lord?'[2]

In her convent she was closely watched and in the town enmeshed in the net of espionage formed by all the other Orders and their friends. To go to the site where the new convent was to be, she had to cross the whole town, or else take the route right round the walls. To allay suspicion she used to make as if she were going to the convent of Santo Tomás which was not far away from the future foundation. It was really essential to find a solution.

In August 1561 it transpired that Doña Teresa de Ahumada's

[1] Cf. Sb, V, c. xxxii-16, 17.   [2] Sb, V, c. xxxiii-11.

sister and her husband Don Juan de Ovalle were leaving Alba de Tormes and coming back to live in their native town. What could be better? The prioress of the Incarnation did not dream of refusing to allow her subject to spend some time with her beloved Juana, to help her to settle in.

The ruse succeeded. The little house purchased in the name of Teresa's brother-in-law was to become the cornerstone in the reform of the Order of Carmel, the glorious convent of St Joseph of Ávila.

The Ovalle house was adapted as follows. On the ground floor was the future chapel and on the first floor thirteen cells and the necessary offices. All this was built round a patio and looked out on to a tiny cloister: Teresa wondered—though she still had not a farthing—if it would not be better to buy something bigger.

The Director of operations was displeased:

'Did I not tell you to begin as you could? Oh, the greed of the human race, always afraid that the earth will not be large enough for it! How many times did I not sleep in the open, amid the night dew, for want of a place to lay my head?'[1]

And so Teresa was satisfied with her small house. Situated in the northern part of Ávila, in the populous district of San Roque, had it not indeed what she loved best in the world, 'a most beautiful horizon and the country'?

Teresa stayed some months with the Ovalles who obligingly played up to the pretence of setting up house. 'Doña Juana is an honest woman, courageous, and with the soul of an angel.'[2] Don Juan's character was far from easy and Teresa often pitied her sister: her distinguished husband was both suspicious and fickle, jealous to the extent of being hurt over his sister-in-law's friendship for Doña Guiomar, but completely devoted to the foundation.

The work progressed slowly as St Joseph's 'conspirators' managed to find a few maravedis. María de Ocampo was not yet free to dispose of her inheritance. Doña Guiomar took what she could from her revenues, ready, when she had no more money at her disposal, to sell a scarlet quilt or a cross embroidered in silk.

Teresa made her plans, gave orders to the workmen, provided for a double grille between the chapel and the choir, made of bars extremely close together, so that the nuns could follow the Offices without being seen. The walls would not even be rough-cast and everything would be very poor, but very clean. Teresa had such good taste that all the proportions were harmonious.

[1] Sb, V, c. xxxiii–12.   [2] CTA, ii.

The difficulties were so great that the courage of some of the little group faltered, but that of the Foundress never failed; she was 'determined' to go through with it. She had already become the woman who 'will not hesitate to undertake great and extraordinary things and will make it her delight and pleasure to go through with them to the end, for things that were easy gave her no satisfaction.' [1]

A wall collapsed when in process of construction. Doña Guiomar, in spite of all the persistence she had shown, lost her head:

'It's the devils who've knocked it down! God isn't pleased with this convent.'

Teresa could no longer be frightened with the prospect of the devil's tricks, she was unperturbed.

'The wall is down? Let them put it up again then!' [2] and her authority overcame all reluctance.

The brief asked for from Rome was late in arriving. Once more, Doña Guiomar got anxious. Teresa's only reply was to ask her to get missals and a bell for the future convent. The Foundress gave herself to prayer and then acted. She wrote late into the night.

In obedience to P. Pedro Ibáñez, she began the account of her life and of the graces Our Lord had given her. Was this writing a pleasure to her? Her only allusion to the work thus imposed on her was that it was an additional burden, added to all her other labours. But one cannot be gifted with such liveliness of expression, describe people's characters with so colourful a pen, exercise the gift of the balanced phrase, of the striking realistic image, one is not a born writer as she was, without finding some pleasure in writing. With an expansive nature like Teresa's, constrained as she was to keep silence about her activities for the time being, it was a relief to let herself go and say all there was to be said about the past. Her only regret was that her confessors had forbidden her to speak 'in detail and clearly' about what she called 'my great sins and vileness'; were not the wonders God wrought in her so much the more marvellous in proportion to her unworthiness? She asked her readers not to forget that she had been 'so vile,' [3] that she had not been able to find a single example as bad as herself among those saints who had returned to Our Lord after having been sinners. 'After the call of God they did not offend him any more, whereas not only did I become worse than before, but it could have been said of me with truth that I set my mind to resisting the graces His Majesty favoured me with. . . . May he be blessed for ever, he who waited for me so long. . . .'

[1] FR, L. XVI, c. i.   [2] SEC, vol. II, p. 320.   [3] Sb, V, JHS-1.

She called this autobiography 'my great book,' 'the book of
the mercies of God,' and when she sent it to Doña Luisa de la
Cerda, it was with the words: 'It is my soul I am entrusting you
with.'[1]

It was an account of her life, certainly, but also the clearest and most
accurate route-map ever drawn up for men and women who want to
use the path of mental prayer, to mount step by step from earthly
illusion to spiritual reality.

Teresa de Ahumada's first analysis of the greatest experiences
which it is given to a human being to undergo, was made when she
was beginning her life of activity. The uninterrupted presence of God
was the connecting-link between these two poles.

One day P. Pedro Ibáñez asked her:

'How do you spend your time?'

'I thought,' he said, 'that she devoted some hours to mental prayer
and the remainder to other exercises.'

He saw Teresa's beautiful face light up with love:

'Imagine a person so much taken up with another that she cannot
spend a moment out of the presence of the one she loves. . . .'[2]

'That was the way,' the Dominican added, 'that she lived with Our
Lord, speaking only of him or with him . . . all her actions for him
alone, writing only of his marvels.'

Wherever she was, she brought God with her. She diffused divine
love in her sister's home. The effects of such love were wonderful, but
its demands were such as to make one afraid.

Teresa seemed to have power over life and death. The Ovalles had
only just arrived at Ávila when Juan 'one day found his son, little Don
Gonzalo, lying across the doorway giving no signs of life and quite
stiff. He took him in his arms and called him, but the child did not
answer.' Was he dead? They did not know. Juan de Ovalle carried
him to Teresa.

Doña Juana was in the other room, heard the noise and was upset; Doña Guiomar calmed her, pretending that everything was all
right, for it was the ninth month of Juana's pregnancy. All the same
she came out in great anguish to see what it was and called loudly for
her son. Teresa was silent, as they all were; they waited in suspense
to see what would happen. Teresa lowered her veil; they saw her
crouch down with her face close to the child, but inwardly she was
calling on God. She remained like this for a good space of time, until
the child showed signs of life again, putting his hands on her face as

[1] CTA, viii.   [2] IB, quoted SEC, vol. II, p. 148.

if to caress her and play with her; and as if nothing out of the ordinary had occurred, as if he were merely awaking from an ordinary sleep, she gave him back to his mother saying:

'Oh, dear Lord! What a state she was in about her son! Take him. . . .'

The child at first showed some weakness and could not stand; afterwards he ran about in the room, coming back to his aunt and kissing her from time to time.[1]

When later Doña Teresa was asked how she had given back life to little Gonzalo she was displeased and asked them not to say foolish things.[2]

But there was an occasion when she brought death.

The child whom Juana was carrying was born in September; she called him Joseph after the protector of the future monastery of the reform. He was given her dearest friends as god-parents: Doña Guiomar de Ulloa and Don Francisco de Salcedo. There was a feast for the baptism and Gonzalo, the child whom Teresa had raised to life, was there round the cradle.

Teresa loved the fine, healthy babe—but her affection had no trace of earthly feeling in it. Doña Juana was frightened when she saw her press the infant in her arms as she murmured a strange lullaby: 'If you are not to grow up a good man, I pray God, my son, to take you as you are, you little angel, before you offend him. . . .'

Three weeks later the babe was dying. Teresa took him on her knees, covered him with her veil—the sign of her consecration to Our Lord and separation from the world—and, her face aflame, fell into ecstasy. A very long silence ensued. Doña Juana durst not move and yet she felt sure the child was dead. When Teresa came out of her rapture she got up, slowly, without saying a word, and bearing the tiny body in her arms, went out of the room.

'Where are you going?' called Juana. 'Why don't you tell me my child is dead?'

Teresa turned towards her with a countenance of joy and wonder

'Let us go and thank God together. For we should praise him when we've seen the soul of one of these little ones go up to heaven, and the host of angels come to fetch it. . . .'[3]

It was never told whether Doña Juana would not have preferred to keep her son, not very good, perhaps, but alive.

At that time Teresa made long stays at Doña Guiomar's 'in order to

---

[1] FR, L. I, c. xv.　　　　　　　[2] SEC, vol. II, p. 507.
[3] TC quoted SEC, vol. II, pp. 339–40.

be quieter.' The Ovalles themselves were perhaps 'quieter' in their
daily routine.

The building progressed as money came in. Certain things were of
urgent necessity, but Teresa durst not order them to be done for want
of funds. The good master carpenter St Joseph appeared to her and
ordered her to get in the workmen *sin ninguna blanca*, without having
even a farthing: the Lord would provide for it.

And on 23rd December, she wrote to her brother, Lorenzo de
Cepeda, the *conquistador* of the family who had been most successful
and who had made a rich marriage in Quito:

Señor,
It is, I think, by an inspiration of God that you have sent me so
much money. For, for a nun like myself who considers it an honour,
thanks be to God, to wear a darned habit, I've had all I needed up
to now.

But for reasons which I could not gainsay, for they came from
God, certain holy and learned persons will have it that I must not be
slothful, but must do all I can to found a convent of thirteen nuns
living in very strict enclosure in that they will never go out, and never
go to the parlour without covering the face with a veil, the life being
based on prayer and mortification.

. . . I didn't know how to construct certain things. Relying on
God alone, I sent for the workmen. This seemed sheer madness, but
His Majesty has intervened and inspired you to provide for it. What
amazes me most is the 40 piastres which you have added and of
which I was in most urgent need. . . .[1]

All was well.

Was all well?

On Christmas night a messenger from the prioress of the Incarnation came to Doña Guiomar's to warn Teresa de Ahumada; she was to
be ready to start for Toledo, where the daughter of the Duke of
Medinaceli, Doña Luisa de la Cerda, was demanding her presence
at the earliest possible moment.

This was indeed the sort of enforced distraction which she hoped
that absolute enclosure would set her free from in the future. What was
she to do when she was with these grand people? Would her absence
be long? It was impossible to say. Several months, no doubt.

> Let nothing disturb thee,
> Let nothing affright thee,
> Alone God sufficeth. . . .

[1] CTA, ii.

VII

DOÑA LUISA DE LA CERDA

DON ARIAS PARDO DE SAAVEDRA, Marshal of Castile and one of the richest men in Spain, had died a year before, but the grief of his widow, Doña Luisa de la Cerda, daughter of the second Duke of Medinaceli, grew more intense instead of diminishing; it amounted almost to delirium and those about her feared for her reason. That was why Doña Teresa de Ahumada was asked to come to her. Obsessed as she was with grief, only a saint could turn her thoughts away from herself and give new meaning to the words: 'I believe in the resurrection of the body,' which although she had lost hope she kept on repeating. But it had to be a saint possessed of the necessary tact for dealing with a great lady who took it ill that God should have taken away from her what she loved.

Up to that time no one had succeeded in consoling her, neither her seven children nor the princes of the Church, nor the princes of this world: this woman who had so much, took their attentions for granted. Only the God of the humble could perhaps save her through the intermediary of one of his servants who, in the poor convent of the Incarnation, was dreaming of still greater poverty and the most austere penances.

Doña Luisa heard a good deal of talk about Teresa on the balcony of the Moorish apartment where the portrait of her uncle, Cardinal Tavera, held the place of honour. The widow spent all her days there, lying on cushions embroidered with her coat of arms and surrounded by her maids who chattered over their sewing. She did not want to forget, but she was so worn out with her sleepless nights and her tears that she began to hope for some consolation.

And so she listened to those who sang the praises of a Carmelite of Ávila, Doña Teresa de Ahumada. One of her close friends, P. García de Toledo, son of the Count of Oropesa and a near relative of the Duke of Alba, had a very high opinion of Teresa who had occasionally been his penitent at Santo Tomás; he praised not only her spirituality but her intelligence, the wit with which she seasoned her conversation, and her lovable character; she would be a helpful and pleasant companion for any disconsolate woman.

The youngest of her attendants, María de Salazar, so pretty at fourteen that it almost made one overlook her wit, yet so witty that it would not have mattered had she been plain, never tired of hearing this nun spoken of. When her mistress was beside herself with grief, she would say to her with childlike faith:

'Your Ladyship will see . . . when the saint from Ávila comes. . . .'

Was Teresa's reputation, then, so great outside her native city? The Carmelite Provincial, a great friend of Doña Luisa, was partly responsible; he was by no means displeased that there should be this opportunity to take his subject's thoughts away, by a change of scene, from her tiresome idea of reforming the Order. It looked as though she was not thinking about it any more? Sly tongues affirmed the contrary: it had very naturally been impossible to go on with the work at St Joseph's without a certain amount of help, discreet or otherwise.

The idea that people should think her a person of great merit caused Teresa an 'interior upset' which could only be calmed by His Majesty.

' . . . I who am so vile! . . .'[1]

'Go there,' Our Lord said to her. 'As to the convent, it is essential that you should be elsewhere until the brief comes. Fear nothing, I will help you there.'

In the beginning of January 1562, the journey across the Castilian plains under the icy breath from the Guadarrama, so faint that it would not put out a candle, though it would cause a man's death, was long, uncomfortable and bitterly cold. Teresa was escorted by her brother-in-law, Juan de Ovalle, and Juana Suárez. Juana Suárez had been her constant companion for years; little is known of her except that she was constant in her loyalties, that is, opposed to any change, for she would not leave the Incarnation for any of the new foundations. Thus accompanied, Teresa at last entered Toledo by the Bisagra gate.

It was the first time she had seen such a large city, its streets always noisy with much traffic, with the merchants and their business or the pageantry of some great noble passing by with his retinue. Ávila was only like that on high days and holidays. There was the continual click of the thousands of looms on which thousands of weavers wove for the whole of Europe velvet, satin, taffeta, cloth and brocade. At Toledo shoes were made, wax candles, iron was forged, the steel of the famous Toledan swords was tempered in the waters of the Tagus, there was smelting, engraving, niello-work, and the songs learned from the Moors mingled with the sound of men's voices, with the clang of hammer on anvil, with the rumble of carriages and the neighing of horses.

[1] Sb, V, c. xxxiv-2.

Philip II had just made Madrid the capital of the realm, but Toledo kept her title of crowned imperial city. The nobility had not yet deserted this ancient stronghold of Castile against enemies from the east—in a still more distant age the bastion of the Moor towards the west—the promontory on which the flashing blades of two civilizations and two religions had been shattered in turn. The Moorish style of art had infused itself into the decoration of church and palace; this mozarabic style which she scarcely knew astonished Teresa, and in the heart of the narrow streets, behind austere Castilian façades, the half-open doors provided glimpses of patios adorned with the arabesques of Islam. Her slightly protruding eyes, keen and accustomed to take in every detail, scrutinized this new world. Her gaze passed from people's faces to the wrought iron gates, from the paving stones to carved doorways, from the belfries to the sky, silvered by a light clearer than any other in the world.

Toledo, the very cradle of the Sánchez y Cepeda: at Ávila Don Alonso had been surnamed 'the Toledan.' Teresa always loved the city with a special love: 'I feel better there than I do elsewhere.' [1] She never referred to these ancestral ties, but her gaiety sparkled the more brilliantly for being set in a framework of Toledan charm—that 'school of polished conversation,' and perhaps she owed the sharpness of her wit to the race which had given its name to the steel of which the finest blades in the world were made.

The travellers dismounted in front of the Master of Calatrava's palace: there it was that Arias Pardo's widow was living in royal state, dying of grief.

At the entrance, squires, valets, footmen, pages, duennas, maids, a gaily-coloured, motley, bustling, curious, yet solemn crowd, welcomed Our Lord's delegate with every mark of deep respect. The staff of ceremony of the major-domos resounded on the steps of the great staircase of marble with its agate banister which led to the apartments where Doña Luisa was waiting for them.

With lowered gaze, her eyes looking down on the rose pattern of a great Flanders carpet, the Carmelite passed through an archway elaborately adorned with foliage arabesques. The huge, rock-crystal lustres, gleaming with lighted candles, lit up her darned habit and her faded veil almost yellow with age. And the richest woman in Castile stepped down from the *estrado* to clasp in her arms the nun for whom God alone sufficed.

Doña Luisa had prepared a sumptuous apartment for Teresa and

[1] CTA, xii.

her companion—everything in this palace was sumptuous. Here she
had to practise a new form of mortification: that of accepting, through
politeness, the comfortable, wealthy surroundings which to her were
irksome. Along with the bundle of which her entire luggage consisted
she had brought, her discipline, and certain fixed ideas about the great
and wealthy, inspired by tales of chivalry in which these exalted personages are of superhuman calibre; she was considerably surprised to
find that the higher the rank the more cares they had: ceremonial
'does not allow them so much as to breathe' [1]; the nun was sorry for
the woman who was the daughter of dukes. To restore this woman
whose nerves were overstrained to sound health of mind and body,
some change in and simplification of her diet would have been
advisable, whereas she was forced 'to eat at irregular hours dishes considered appropriate to her rank, but which suited neither her temperament nor her taste. . . .' [2] No relaxation, never the smallest degree of
liberty: Doña Luisa had to watch her every word, restrain any expression of enthusiasm, for the quarrels over precedence between duennas
and attendants were such 'that one could not be spoken to more than
another, under pain of causing the rest to turn their back on whoever
appeared to be favoured.' [3] Teresa herself had to suffer on account of
these jealousies and was accused of 'mercenary and selfish pretensions.' [4]
It gave her the opportunity of discovering 'that from then onwards
backbiting did not hurt her any more than it would if she were someone deprived of reason.' [5]

Poor Doña Luisa! 'For persons of her condition everything is bondage and one of the world's great lies is to call lords those who are
merely the slaves of a thousand and one things. . . . I derived great
benefit from observing all this and I told her so.' [6]

Teresa had the art—or perhaps it was kindliness—of persuading
Doña Luisa that she had not come either to teach or to preach, but that
she too had a lot to learn and if she discovered that the great lady 'was
a woman and subject to weakness and passion like herself,' [7] the great
lady learned from Teresa that nuns had their passions and weaknesses
too. This exchange of confidences formed a lasting bond between
them. Doña Luisa showed Teresa every possible delicate consideration:
as, for instance, the day she tried to cure her of an attack of fever by
showing her the sparkle of the only substance in the world in which
fire and water are mingled: her diamonds [8]; Teresa even ventured

---

[1] SB, V, c. xxxiv-4.   [2] Idem.   [3] Idem.
[4] Idem.   [5] SEC, R, ii, p. 14.   [6] Sb, V, c. xxxiv-4.
[7] Idem.   [8] Sb, V, c. xxxviii-4.

to offer the wealthy woman tiny gifts: 'A mere trifle gives her pleasure.'[1]

Doña Luisa de la Cerda had a distinguished face, she carried her head like one accustomed to the weight of jewels, and in her mourning attire she was truly majestic; for all this, she was none the less humble of heart, a true Christian, a devoted friend and as simple as the solemnity of her rank allowed. She could not bear, now, to be far away from Teresa de Ahumada who spent long hours in her room, at prayer, or writing her autobiography, and she clutched at any excuse to bring her out on to the *estrado*, where Doña Luisa spent her time when there was no sermon at San Ramón, no procession at San Clemente or benediction at Santo Domingo el Antiguo: for at Toledo one seemed to be 'in a perpetual Holy Week.'

Doña Luisa worked at her embroidery while she listened to one of her attendants reading a few pages from the *Lives of the Saints* in which new beauties were discovered: Doña Teresa made the reading more interesting by comments which were all the more delightful for the gracious tones in which they were uttered, without the smallest display of learning. Soon all the wits of the town flocked to the palace: they all wanted to meet this nun who was said to speak of God more eloquently than the Doctors and to have saved the widow of the Marshal of Castile from despair.

Yet Toledo was the most exacting town in Spain in the matter of fine talk: 'The Toledans are distinguished for cleverness not of the hands, as in other places, but of speech.' [2] Teresa soon learned to adapt her way of speaking to court circles without departing from her extremely tactful reserve. Here, it was her business to please people and if she attracted them without meaning to do so, when she did try to please she enraptured her listeners. She was in need of friends for God, for her reform, and she made friends, and influential ones: the Duchess of Escalona, the Duchess of Maqueda, the Marchioness of Villena, Princess Juana, the Duchess of Medinaceli, the Duchess of Alba, and they helped her all her life.

It was there, too, that she made a less fortunate acquaintance in the person of Doña Luisa's niece, Ana de la Cerda, Princess of Éboli, who had not yet begun to be talked about, but who, at twenty-one, was already famous for her piquant beauty and her no less sharp character. Ana was by no means willing to pass unnoticed, and to attract the attention of this Carmelite who seemed to be in the fashion, by turns made witty sallies and affected devotion. A close friend of Queen

[1] CTA, xii.   [2] BG.

Isabel of Valois, the gentle French princess whose marriage with Philip II awakened so many hopes that she was called 'Isabel of Peace,' she flattered herself on being able to obtain whatever she wanted from Teresa and to give her just what she chose. To such offers, which were accompanied by a great jingling of bracelets in the cool breeze of her fluttering fan, the Carmelite replied:

'I thank your Highness, but a daughter of God needs nothing other than God,' for it did not take her long to sum anyone up.

She learned, too, how to distinguish those who should be called Your Highness from those whom it was sufficient to address as Your Grace, and was no longer obliged to conceal her ignorance of etiquette under a peal of laughter.

Nothing of all this troubled her interior recollection: that was firmly established now and Teresa de Ahumada would not let herself be caught up again in the entanglement of worldly vanities. From Toledo she wrote to P. Pedro Ibáñez, anticipating Calderón de la Barca: 'I go forward as in a dream, and I know that when I wake up it will all be nothing. . . .'[1] As often as possible, when the conversation in the drawing-room veered round towards the theatre, of which Toledans are passionately fond, or towards games of one sort or another, bullfights or running at the ring, slipping quietly from the room and through one gallery after another, she made her escape from the visitors. Sometimes at the rustle of a silk skirt her face betrayed her secret feelings: Doña María de Salazar, the child already mentioned, was still there watching her, drawing back the tapestry hangings quickly or hiding behind a door which seemed to open of its own accord. María endeavoured to convince the saint, both in prose and in verse, of her desire to enter religion. One day she slipped a poem into her hand in which she made a great parade of her love of God:

> . . . If aught of good you owe to me,
> Mine eyes, you'll not refuse a tear.
> For tears alone can solace be.
> Much more than grief, I pleasure fear. . . .

> . . . How should I seek mine own content—
> To set my soul from bondage free,
> My King from sufferings dire is spent
> And scourging cruel—and all for me.[2]

Teresa took in at a single glance the exquisite profile, the beribboned hair, the gay silk dress stiff with its silver embroidery.

[1] SEC, R, ii, p. 14.   [2] MJ, quoted EM, pp. 41–2.

'Child, you're preparing for convent life by many frivolities!'—
and avoiding such naïve demonstrations as she avoided the rest, she
took refuge in prayer.

She did not suspect that the women of the household took turns
at the keyhole of her door. A rapture which had come upon her 'in
public' [1] had caused a lot of talk, and nobody believed what she said
about heart attacks and fainting: they were on the watch for her to
have an ecstasy. The fiery radiance of her countenance seemed to
penetrate the very walls, the breath of God breathed over the palace:
'All made progress in the service of the Lord.' [2] She converted Ham-
mete, the Turk, which caused a great sensation, and P. García de
Toledo, whom she now met again, was so much impressed by the
earnestness with which she begged him, good though he was, to
become still holier, that he gave himself up entirely to a life of prayer.

She was adored by the servants below stairs as much as she was
admired by the court above, and it is said that when after communing
with God she again turned her attention to earthly things, she liked to
talk with the maids.

It was during this stay with the rich and mighty that Teresa's 'hard
heart' melted with compassion. Perhaps it was the contrast, the
inequality of circumstances, so much luxury for some, so much
wretchedness for others. In bending over sordid rags to dress a dis-
charging wound, she now felt more tenderness than repugnance. Doña
Luisa had 'her poor'—which gave her an excuse for not bothering
about the verminous, half-starved, repugnant rabble that swarmed in
this city of eighty thousand inhabitants. In Ávila charity called the
poor each by his own name; in Toledo this seething, nameless wretchedness appalled and sickened Teresa. It was on one of the tables of
precious wood in the Master of Calatrava's palace that she wrote: 'It
seems to me that I have more compassion for the poor than formerly,
I pity them greatly, my desire to help them is such that if I let my
heart speak I should give them the habit off my back. I feel no repugnance at all even though I am close to them and touch them: I see
that this, too, is the gift of God, for I used to give alms for the love
of him without feeling any natural pity.' [3]

The footmen were accustomed to strange tatterdemalions coming
to ask for Teresa. One day they came to call her: a woman in the habit
of a Carmelite *beata* but in rags, the pilgrim's staff in her hand, wanted
to see her. Teresa hastened to her, kissed her, and, a few minutes later,
in her forceful way of expressing herself, she explained to Doña Luisa

[1] SEC, R, ii, p. 13.   [2] Sb, V, c. xxxiv-5.   [3] SEC, R, ii, p. 14.

that this woman, María de Jesús, had tramped sixty leagues on foot to come and talk over with her a project for the reform of Carmel: she too wanted to found a convent where the primitive Rule would be observed: and she had the brief of authorization!

The great lady gave orders that the visitor was to be shown into a room where a canopied bed was prepared for her.

María de Jesús' energy was prodigious. Born at Granada and left a widow when she was still very young, she had consecrated herself to God in a Carmel of Mitigated observance. She left before being professed: Our Lord had commanded her in the same month and on the same day as Teresa, to found a convent which should conform to the primitive tradition of enclosure, austerity and penance. Unlike Teresa, María de Jesús was free. She sold her possessions and, dressed in sackcloth, with a little money sewn in a tight-fitting bodice padded and secured, she set out, barefooted, for Rome.

Pius IV saw coming slowly towards him an emaciated creature, worn out by her journey, and whose every step left a trace of blood. But what valour in her countenance! He listened paternally to what she had to say:

'Courageous woman! Let all she asks for be done!'

The papacy encouraged the reform of the religious Orders on the lines laid down by the Counter-Reformation. María was allowed to enter the enclosure of the Carmel of Mantua, where the primitive austerities were so rigidly observed that the religious were known as 'the immured.' María de Jesús was able to investigate all that was still observed of the ancient traditions as regards clothing, manner of life, the arrangement of the Rules and Constitutions. And Doña Leonor de Mascarenhas, the king's former governess, gave her a house at Alcalá de Henares to found the monastery of La Imagen there.[1]

For a fortnight María de Jesús talked and Teresa de Ahumada made notes. The *beata*, who was gifted with the excellent memory of those who cannot read, could remember the Rule by heart; Teresa reconstructed it. This penitent was so austere in her ways that the palace began to take *her* for a true saint: Teresa herself felt unworthy in her presence: 'She is so much more fervent than I am in the Lord's service!'[2] María de Jesús also had a good head: she initiated Teresa into the details of Vatican procedure with all its red tape through which she had threaded her way admirably.

When they parted the opinion of both on an essential point disputed up till then was strengthened by each other's support: in the

---

[1] SST, vol. II, pp. 93–4.   [2] Sb, V, c. xxxv–2.

reformed convents the nuns were to live by the work of their hands
and to have no revenues. On that point it was essential not to yield
either to bishops, the city 'juntas' or to anyone at all: the primitive
Rule was explicit. Teresa had not known this, but the discovery was
an 'immense joy' for her.[1]

She was none the less anxious about it for she knew that those who
were supporting her most effectively would consider such complete
dependence on Providence madness. From this moment she never
ceased to 'argue with theologians.' She wrote to P. Ibáñez on the
subject and he countered her idea with two pages of theological arguments. Confessors and doctors of divinity hurled such a multiplicity
of arguments at her that she knew not which way to turn. For she
was the last person ever to think it possible to dispense with advice:
throughout her life, one of her most absorbing occupations was to win
round divergent opinions to her own way of thinking after having
listened to everyone, for win them round she did.

In the spring of 1562 the matter had still got no further than lively
discussion when that supreme arbiter, Fray Pedro de Alcántara,
arrived in Toledo. Doña Luisa, who was enthusiastic over the idea of
thirteen women living together in absolute poverty for the love of
Our Lord, had invited the holy man.

This grand old man, wasted away by austerities, spoke of renuncia-
tion beneath the panelled ceilings, with their immense stars, of the
Master of Calatrava's palace; there he was, treading on marble with
those feet which had grown hard from contact with the stones by the
wayside; there he was, seated on a chair of Córdoba leather, his emaciated hand resting on a table of ebony inlaid with silver and mother of
pearl; his ascetic profile showed up against the background of the new
tapestries from Flanders.

It was in this luxurious setting that he discussed with Teresa de
Ahumada the bases of the Rule of absolute poverty in her convents.

She showed him the letter she had received from P. Ibáñez. Fray
Pedro smiled and with a good-humoured air threw a few stones into
the doctor's garden:

> I am surprised that Your Reverence should submit to theologians
> points which they are incapable of understanding. . . . It is only
> those who are living the perfect life who can speak of it. Can it even
> be questioned whether it is essential to follow the evangelical coun-
> sels or not? . . . If Your Reverence wishes to follow Christ along
> the perfect road of poverty, you should know that it is open to

[1] Sb, V. c. xxxv–2.

women just as much as to men. . . . But if you want to take the
advice of theologians destitute of spirituality, look for great revenues,
and see if all that is worth more to you than renouncement in obedience to the words of Jesus.[1]

Teresa admitted that His Majesty had given her the grace to desire
poverty:

As to myself, there are days when I could wish to possess nothing,
not even a roof over my head, and to beg my bread for the love of
God. But I'm afraid that those who are not yet ready to go so far as
that may be dissatisfied and that our penury may be a cause of distractions to them. . . . I know poor convents where there is little or no
recollection.[2]

Teresa was thinking of the convent of the Incarnation. Fray Pedro
insisted:

Because such religious are poor against their will, and not out of
obedience to the will of Christ. I am not extolling wretchedness: I
am praising poverty patiently borne for the love of Christ Our Lord,
and, still more, poverty which is desired and embraced through love.
I shouldn't consider myself a man of sure faith if I felt otherwise. In
this as in all things I trust Our Lord; I believe firmly that his counsels are very good, I believe that he who follows them is much more
perfect than he would otherwise be. As His Majesty promised us, I
consider the poor in spirit, those who do not seek their own will,
blessed. I trust God more than my own experience, but all the same
I can say that I have always seen those who are poor through the love
of that condition live a happy life, by God's grace, a life such as
those who love God, abandon themselves to him and hope in him
have here below.

Don't for a single instant believe those who affirm the contrary,
because they haven't tasted how sweet the Lord is to those who renounce all goods which do not help to increase their love.[3]

After this interview Teresa replied to P. Ibáñez that she had decided
to keep the vow of poverty faithfully; she would follow the counsels
of Christ in their perfection without taking advantage of the opportunity theology offered her of dispensing with their observation. . . .[4]
At the same time she informed him that she had finished writing her
autobiography.

The convents of the reformed Order of Our Lady of Carmel were
then to live in the same way as St. Joseph's was founded: *sin blanca.*

This was the reason His Majesty had sent Doña Teresa de Ahumada to
Toledo. The stay need not be prolonged now. It had lasted six months.

[1] PA quoted SEC, vol. II, p. 125.   [2] Sb, V, c. xxxv-2.
[3] PA quoted SEC, vol. II, p. 125.   [4] Sb, V, c. xxxv-4.

VIII

24TH AUGUST 1562

DOÑA LUISA'S patio was an oasis of flowers and greenery. Teresa was happy for she was surrounded by good friends. When her Provincial, P. Ángel de Salazar, left her the choice of returning to Ávila for the election of the new prioress or of remaining in Toledo, she decided to remain where she was: 'Very glad not to be arriving there in the midst of all the bustle,'[1] she said in her letter to the convent of the Incarnation, as she begged her sisters not to vote for her as they wished to do.

When she had recovered her equilibrium a little, her gift of adaptability came to the fore again; at Doña Luisa's, she found 'quiet and consolation, and was free to give long hours to prayer.'[2]

But there was to be no rest for her. The Master of the work gave orders for departure.

'You wanted the cross: I have an excellent one in readiness for you.'[3]

Had she so far forgotten the little convent of St Joseph's that she thought for a moment that the cross would be that she would be elected prioress at the Incarnation? She wept at first, but after a few tears immediately accepted the idea of the journey: 'I saw clearly that I was about to fling myself into the midst of a fire, for Our Lord had told me so . . . and yet, in spite of all this, I was even then so full of joy that I couldn't contain my impatience to begin the fight. . . .'[4]

Her confessor was afraid of the journey for her in the great heat and imposed a delay: but she entreated him: 'If I am to die through this, I must die!'[5] and he allowed her to go.

Her belongings were quickly packed, she tore herself from the arms of her friends who wept as they bade her goodbye, and pushed away María de Salazar who clung to her habit; all this affection touched her, she felt she ought to have shared their grief, but in her joy was uppermost: 'I am blessed with so grateful a nature that at any other time all this would have been enough to upset me very much, but at this moment I found it impossible to feel any grief. . . .'[6]

---

[1] Sb, V, c. xxxv–8. [2] Idem, 10. [3] Cf. Idem, 8.
[4] Idem, 10. [5] Idem, 8. [6] Sb, V, c. xxxv–11.

After a brief moment of weakness, she was once more wholly resolute and ready for action.

The courtiers who watched her as she gradually disappeared from sight were of opinion that the Carmelite would have made a fine Amazon. They did not realize how correct their judgement was.

She arrived at Ávila in good time. 'It was so imperative for the business of this blessed house of St Joseph's that I shouldn't be away one day more, that I don't know how matters could have been brought to a conclusion if I had not returned then. Oh, how great God is! I often marvel when I consider how His Majesty helped me to found this little hidden house of God.' [1]

The brief, so long desired, which authorized Doña Guiomar de Ulloa to found a convent of reformed Carmelites under the jurisdiction of the Bishop of Ávila, arrived that very day.

Doña Juana and her husband, weary of waiting so long, had left for Alba de Tormes. One might wonder how the building of the convent could be carried on with the requisite discretion, but 'God's help effects more than rising betimes. . . .' [2] By a decree of Providence, Juan de Ovalle, who had come over to Ávila on business, as he got off his horse was seized with 'terrible' fits of shivering, followed by a severe attack of double tertian fever. Nobody pitied the poor man for never was an illness better timed: there he was, back in the house he had left, and his sister-in-law installed there to look after him, while she speeded up the building operations. The conspirators of St Joseph's had no need to do any more scheming for a long time. 'Truth suffers but does not perish.' Teresa liked to embellish her conversation with proverbs.

They still had to obtain the Bishop's permission for the convent to be founded 'without revenues.' Don Álvaro de Mendoza, son of Don Juan Hurtado de Mendoza, brother-in-law of secretary Cobos, one of the most mighty personages in the kingdom, was a great lord indeed. Poverty? This was an aspect of life according to the Gospel that seemed to him out of date: did not the sons of St Francis and St Dominic possess rich convents, were they not now rich Orders, well provided with everything? It was true that not one of these friars possessed anything of his own, everything was common to all. To refuse revenues was just like a woman who was said to have visions. . . . This convent would either have revenues or not be founded!

The timely intervention of Fray Pedro de Alcántara saved the situation. Prevented by illness from visiting his Illustrious Lordship, he

---

[1] Idem, 12.   [2] CTA, xxviii.

wrote to him begging his consent that the convent 'should be most fervent and in every respect perfect, conformable in all things to the primitive Rule of the Order of Our Lady of Mount Carmel.' He also mentioned the Foundress: 'I think the spirit of Our Lord is in her.' [1]

His Illustrious Lordship left for his country house without replying to one of the most revered men in Spain. Was this a tacit refusal, or displeasure, or perhaps annoyance?

With no more thought for his dignity than he had for his old bones, Fray Pedro had a mule saddled and covered twelve leagues in order to take Don Álvaro by surprise in his retreat at El Tiemblo. The only thing he minded was that he was obliged to travel in such great state, for he always went on foot.

The Bishop was impressed with the importance which the great Franciscan attached to this insignificant convent of thirteen women devoted to penance, but all the same he let him go away again with a refusal: it took more than this to make a Mendoza yield. He repeated, obstinately:

'I won't have poor nuns!'

Perhaps when he was alone he suddenly realized how strange his persistent repetition of this prejudice sounded upon the lips of a representative of Jesus Christ on earth. Perhaps the eulogies of Lady Poverty, expounded so lovingly by Fray Pedro despite his weary voice, found the way, beneath the purple, to a Christian heart. However this may be, that very evening the Bishop sent the Franciscan a double message: (1) The convent of St Joseph might be in conformity with the law of evangelical poverty; (2) Doña Teresa de Ahumada was to prepare to receive a visit from him: he was returning to Ávila on purpose to make her acquaintance. The very next day, his Illustrious Lordship, Don Álvaro de Mendoza, asked for her in the parlour.

It was all very well for Teresa to say that in future it did not matter to her 'that people were fond of her' [2]; she did more than persuade the Bishop; he was completely won over, charmed, all resistance gone. It was the end of the good man's whims and caprices: whether he knew what he wanted or not, he would always know quite definitely what Teresa wanted and he would always be entreated, with all the graciousness in the world, to do his very utmost on behalf of the reformed Carmels. Teresa was to find in him her most constant and efficacious support and she gave him her affection till he died, as she alone knew how to give it—an affection that was the most reverent, most tender and most exacting in the world.

[1] PA quoted SEC, vol. II, p. 127.   [2] SEC, R, iii, p. 17.

The game was won. Fray Pedro could go back again. Their farewells cast a cloud over Teresa's joy: both knew they would never see
each other again on earth. She begged him, if he had any affection for
her, to come and take his last meal in Ávila in one of the Incarnation
parlours, and, like the fine cook she was, she devised exquisite dishes
for this poor friar who was accustomed to eat only bread. A snow-
white tablecloth, simple crockery spotlessly clean, Teresa, who stood
behind Fray Pedro, serving with lowered eyes, a few prying sisters
who must poke their noses round the door: but they saw Christ himself feed the friar with his own hands and the whole town knew that
the meal had been 'an angels' banquet.' [1] Great friendship, like great
love, is written in heaven.

Pedro de Alcántara left with Teresa one of his spiritual daughters,
Antonia de Henao. At St Joseph's she took the name of Antonia del
Espíritu Santo and was one of the 'four poor orphans' [2] who were to
become the cornerstone of the Reform.

Gaspar Daza gave Teresa Úrsula de Revilla y Álvarez—Úrsula de
los Santos. Doña Guiomar's gift to Carmel was her favourite attendant,
María de la Paz, who became María de la Cruz, while the future
chaplain, Julian de Ávila, made a Carmelite of his own sister, María de
Ávila—María de San José.

Julian de Ávila was an excellent priest and a charming man. He had
a good heart and a ready tongue and he amused Teresa with his keen
and ingenious wit. His courage was all the more meritorious since it
meant the overcoming of a natural cowardice, at which he laughed
himself. This brother and sister came of good stock. Their father, a
humble weaver, left, in what is one of the most delightful documents
of the time, a testimony to his love of God:

I, Cristóbal de Ávila, this day, the feast of St. Mary Magdalene in
the year 1536, have decided to reform my life in order to serve God
and his holy Mother, Saint Mary, better, if the Holy Spirit consents
to give me his grace, his help and the necessary fervour for this
service.

Of the twenty-four hours of the day and night, I will take six
to sleep; one to hear Mass, another to read in the book of the Gospels
the Gospel of the day, or the *Lives of the Saints*; another for my
prayers, another for walking. I shall have fourteen hours left in
which to work and earn my living.

May all be for the greatest service of God and of his blessed
Mother, Saint Mary, and may she graciously be with me in all
things.[3]

[1] SST, vol. II, p. 131.   [2] Cf. Sb, V, c. xxxvi-6.   [3] SST, vol. I, p. 317.

The first Discalced Carmelite nuns were evidently the fine flower of the race of Castile.

Essentials were now ready and the final preparations for the opening of the convent moved very quickly. Teresa found it difficult to hide her joy. Happiness brought out all her charm and made her so gay, so humanly beautiful that a gentleman could not refrain from complimenting her on the dainty foot peeping out from beneath her nun's habit. She burst out laughing.

'Look at it well, for soon you won't see it any more!' [1]

She was in a hurry to get behind walls and grilles where she would be alone with her sisters in poverty; not to prevent herself from going back to the world but to erect an obstacle between the world's importunities and a solitude filled to overflowing with God. With her faithful friends, working night and day, she herself cut out and sewed the habits of frieze, hemmed the back veils, cut out the coifs in the rough crash. She wanted these last to be close-fitting, to hide the roots of the hair, in order that the nuns might save time over doing their hair, a solicitude which in no way implied negligence, for she saw to it that the coif was always carefully adjusted. She found a delightful expression with which to reprove someone whose coif was put on awry:

'A nun badly coifed is like a woman badly married. . . .' [2]

The convent's protectors were installed, one on each side of the chapel doors—a gilt wood statue of Mary bearing 'her precious Son' in her arms, and a statue of St Joseph, their patron, sumptuously attired in a tunic embroidered by Teresa herself and a silk mantle; he held his lily in one hand and a hat in the other. . . .

The church was so tiny that there were not more than ten paces between the entrance porch and the choir. The bell which summoned the people around to Mass and the sisters to work or prayer weighed scarcely three pounds.

There was much noise of saw and hammer, things were hung in place here or hooked to the wall there. It was Teresa's heart's delight to polish, to wash and iron the altar cloths or to decorate the chapel with flowers or sweep out a corner. It seemed difficult to believe that such a woman had ever been so ill that they thought her dead. Yet even now she vomited every morning, suffered from continual headache and frequently from fever, but her vitality was such that, despite the cost to herself, she displayed as much energy as those in perfect health.

At long last it was dawn on the 24th August 1562: for Don Alonso's

[1] Quoted H, p. 55.   [2] SST, vol. II, p. 588.

daughter, all the great events of her life began, as that life itself had begun, 'at the first streak of dawn.'

That morning the district of San Roque awakened to the tinkling of a bell, cracked, for it had been bought second-hand. Sleepy, but curious, the people of the neighbourhood were at their doors, the sound of the bell guided them to a chapel which seemed to have sprung up in the night,[1] the first ever dedicated to the great St Joseph. It was poor like the stable in Bethlehem, but 'the very walls sufficed to touch people's hearts,'[2] and the atmosphere of prayer was so palpable that they held their breath.

Master Gaspar Daza said Mass on an altar which was spotlessly clean: this was the only sign of luxury. A nun from the convent of the Incarnation, Doña Teresa de Ahumada, very much beloved by the humble folk of the district, gave the habit to four girls whom nobody knew. It was a habit that was strange to people, of stuff so rough that it reminded them of the camel hair in pictures of hermits.

There were three other Carmelites there: Doña Juana Suárez, Doña Inés de Tapia and her sister Ana; also Don Juan de Ovalle and his wife Doña Juana, as well as some people who were often known to stay with them : Don Francisco de Salcedo, whom everybody called the 'holy gentleman,' Don Gonzalo de Aranda, Julian de Ávila, who always had a witty remark to make as he passed you, and the rich widow who was dressed like a poor person, Doña Guiomar de Ulloa.

The people round about St Joseph's asked about the convent and thought it all wonderful. They commented:

'They're going to live enclosed. . . . The fast. . . . The discipline. . . . To pray for you and me. Saints in our part of the town—what a grace from God!'

Everyone tried to get out more quickly than her neighbour to spread the amazing news.

At long last Doña Teresa was to know the glorious achievement of a work which had been one of long preparation and waiting, a work she had so much desired. 'It was like heaven for me to see the Blessed Sacrament exposed, to know that four poor orphans . . . great servants of God, were now safe and free to serve him. My happiness . . . at having accomplished what Our Lord had commanded me . . . was so great that I was as it were beside myself and deep prayer came upon me.'[3]

---

[1] SST, vol. II, p. 148, n. 1.   [2] TC quoted SEC, vol. II, p. 321.
[3] Sb, V, c. xxxvi-6.

IX

GRAVÍSIMA CULPA

THE news of the foundation of the new convent soon spread all round the town. The joy which broke out was so vociferous in its acclamations that one was forcibly reminded of the entry of Jesus of Nazareth into Jerusalem; it only needed the crowd assembled in front of St Joseph's to cry out: 'Blessed is he that cometh in the name of the Lord!' [1] for the resemblance to be complete.

But on that fine Sunday, the Passion was not far off: God, whose ways are hidden, allowed a change to come over the opinion of the notables of Ávila. They took offence; in less than two hours enthusiasm gave way to fear, and, consequently, to hostile opposition. Anyone would have thought that this poor humble house was a danger to the city.

'Down, down with the convent! Let's save our children's bread!'

The principal argument was that the town could not feed these few nuns who, moreover, asked for nothing.

Stones were thrown, people hammered on the door, there was a threat to break in and destroy everything. It was a veritable riot and merchants shut their shops to join the band of brawlers. Fire, or the French at the city gates, could not have produced a greater mob of people, more feverish activity or swifter decisions.

The hubbub brought Teresa out of her ecstasy.

At the convent of the Incarnation the fury was no less. Every one of the 'Calced' Carmelites felt herself insulted by this return to the strict observance of the primitive Rule, the essential points of which were absolute enclosure, silence, fasting, bare feet, penance, and they were all seized with panic: might it not be that one day someone would take it into his head to 'reform' them too and to force them to practise these austerities? On this 24th August 1562, Doña Teresa de Ahumada had no longer any friends among the Mitigated Carmelites.

They sneered:

'She's never been capable of following even our Rule, which she says is lax, in every detail. How then will she set about observing the Rule a Pope found too severe?'

[1] JA quoted SEC, vol. II, p. 191.

'Through her pride she's made trouble in the community,' ran their accusations.

Already the most senior among them, those who knew the Constitutions, were predicting the punishment that would fall upon her. They weighed up facts, gauged the circumstances, and worked them out in the ratio of 'grave fault' (*culpa grave*), 'graver fault' (*culpa más grave*), 'very grave fault' (*gravísima culpa*), the last implying life imprisonment and sometimes even the refusal of Christian burial.

They wrangled over it in the Lord's name.

'She lied: and so there's *culpa grave*. She'll be given the discipline twice in chapter and put on bread and water for two days. . . .'

An old nun threw up her arms and interrupted this verdict with indignant exclamations:

'What! *Culpa grave*! Are you thinking what you're saying, sister? Hasn't she sown discord here? Hasn't she fabricated intrigues with secular persons, stirred up scandal, thrown discredit on the Order? Isn't she rebellious and contumacious? It's *culpa más grave* we must call it! And even *gravísima culpa*! Since Father Provincial refused his authorization, she's clung to her error obstinately. *Gravísima culpa!* Life imprisonment! Ah, she wants austerities, does she? Fasting and abstinence all her life long, here, at the Incarnation, in the name of the Mitigated Rule!'

The punishment seemed adequate, but by no means spectacular. More than one hoped that Teresa, guilty of having by her attitude brought the convent and its prioress into ill repute, would do public penance in the refectory, wearing a habit on which tongues had been sewn 'in order that the great wickedness of her tongue might be punished.' [1] She would eat her hunch of bread on the floor and would finally be taken away to the prison cell.

While the fate of those they looked on as her accomplices—the two Tapia sisters, Juana Suárez, María de Ocampo—was being decided, they treated them as if they had the plague.

The whole convent was up in arms: yet thirty of these same nuns were later to follow her whom they would call 'Mother Teresa of Jesus,' 'the Mother Foundress,' 'the Holy Mother,' and were to be pioneers of her Reform.

These poor nuns of the Incarnation were blinded and driven on to fury by the devil; he attacked Teresa herself and plunged her into the midst of a great 'spiritual conflict.' [2]

[1] SEC, CONS, pp. 20-5.   [2] Sb, V, c. xxxvi-7.

After the ceremony of inauguration, when she heard the noise of this great surging mob of people all ready to attack the poor little convent, she went to seek for strength before the altar: what she experienced there was fear in every shape and form.

Fear of having failed in the obedience due to the Provincial, although she had not acted without the consent of her confessor; fear of being unable to feed those who joined her, since she had no revenues; fear of being unable to stand so much austerity herself, with her illnesses. Fear, too, that she might regret the great dismantled, but spacious and delightful convent of the Incarnation and of not finding the same friendly understanding with her new companions. Kneeling there, within the space of a few moments she went through 'the pains of the agony of death.' [1]

'Our Lord's commands, the approval expressed, the unceasing prayers, I had forgotten all this. . . . Faith and every other virtue seemed temporarily in suspense. . . .' [2] 'This was one of the severest trials I've ever suffered in this life.' [3]

But she then felt the presence of Christ who reasoned with her as if she were a small child.

What was she afraid of, he asked? Why should her strength fail in his service? 'The more difficulties one has to overcome, the greater the reward.' [4] Remember, Teresa: 'Thou art mine, I am thine. . . .' [5]

He flooded her soul with light and she was comforted, 'although very weary after this battle with the devil; I came out of it laughing at him, for I saw clearly that it was all his work.'

It was time for the mid-day meal and for a siesta: she had worked all through the night and the past few days had been exhausting.

At last! The table in the little refectory, the five places laid, the frugal meal, seasoned with the joy of this solitude in God which was theirs at last. The noise in the street had died down, all Ávila was taking its siesta, it might have been thought that all Ávila had grown calm again.

It was at that very moment that a messenger from the prioress of the Incarnation, Doña María Cimbrón, arrived to intimate to Doña Teresa de Ahumada that she must return to the convent which she was not authorized to leave.

She met this occurrence as she met all great disappointments, calmly, joyfully, determined not to give way. Her grief at leaving the four girls who had just been clothed, her fear of seeing what she had

---

[1] Idem, 8. [2] Idem, 7. [3] Idem, 8.
[4] Cf. Idem, 9. [5] Sb, V, c. xxxix-21.

built up destroyed, can well be imagined. But God so strengthened her that in spite of the many reasons she had for distress and despondency, she was completely happy: the convent had been founded, and was she not now being offered a precious opportunity of suffering for Christ? She was already prepared to be thrown into the prison cell: that would be welcome when it came, at last she would have some sleep and innumerable hours for prayer; she felt 'battered all over for having been among so many people.' [1]

After committing the new Carmelites to the care of their father, St. Joseph, she gave them Ursula de los Santos as prioress, and set off to confront Doña María Cimbrón.

Julian de Ávila offered to accompany her:

'I will be your squire and your chaplain. I mean it, if you will have me.' [2]

Doña María was expecting to find a rebellious nun: she saw a humble subject come into the choir, abjectly prostrating before her and fully conscious of her faults. [3]

Teresa could now no longer hide anything, so she freely spoke of Our Lord's command to found the convent of St Joseph and of her confessor's approval in consultation with the rector of the Jesuits; she mentioned the encouragement of P. Pedro Ibáñez and finally, besides the brief from Rome and the authorization of His Lordship the Bishop of Ávila, she produced the letters of Fray Pedro de Alcántara who had so constantly counselled, encouraged and upheld her during this year of struggle.

The prioress's anger died down so considerably that those who were awaiting the result of the investigation learnt to their amazement that Doña Teresa de Ahumada was not being sent to prison: she was merely enjoined to keep her cell; she was not made to fast on bread and water: they even brought her the wherewithal 'to make a very good dinner.' [4]

From then onwards a few courageous nuns took her part against the over-excited who accused the prioress of partiality.

'Doña María Cimbrón is related to the Ahumada. But Doña Teresa's got to go before the Provincial. *He* won't be weak!'

Ángel de Salazar. Excellent Father Provincial. To suppose him capable of resisting Teresa was to expect a good deal of his powers of indignation; for she was not fighting alone; her humility and her con-

[1] Sb, V, c. xxxvi–11.   [2] JA quoted SEC, vol. II, p. 192.
[3] Sb, V, c. xxxvi–12.   [4] Quoted SEC, vol. I, p. 309, n. 2.

sciousness that in herself she was nothing were the source of her supreme assurance: God acted for and triumphed through her because she abandoned herself to him.

The Provincial summoned her to appear before a tribunal at which all the senior nuns sat in judgement. He reprimanded her very sharply. She made the prostration without seeking to excuse herself, waiting to speak until he ordered her to do so.

She began by begging him to punish her, but not to refuse to pardon her. She explained her actions in such a way 'that neither the Provincial nor the others who were there found any reason to condemn me.' [1]

This was already a considerable argument in her favour, but Padre Salazar was to have the full benefit of her powers of persuasion: 'Afterwards, when I was alone with him, I spoke to him still more plainly. He was very satisfied; he even promised to authorize me to return to St Joseph's when the town should be quiet again: for the uproar there had been very considerable. . . .' [2]

The four newly discalced Carmelites who remained all alone in the little convent knew all about the uproar.

On 25th August, the consistory which met to deal with this grave matter with all the seriousness it demanded, decided to disband the nuns. The *Corregidor* [3] in person, 'The Most Magnificent Lord Garcí Suárez de Carvajal,' presented himself at the door of St Joseph's, accompanied by constables. His violent knockings roused the neighbourhood, which was only waiting for an excuse.

The nuns did not open.

What, 'a few poor girls' were not to be frightened by intimidation?

'Our Lady who guarded one of the entrances and St Joseph who guarded the other gave the four poor girls such strength and courage that they answered the *Corregidor's* demands by a categorical refusal to leave the premises:

' "We shall only leave here at the orders of the one who brought us here."

' "If you do not open of your own accord, we shall force the door." '[4]

While one of these 'lambs in the midst of wolves' argued in this way, the other three pushed heavy beams against the double-sided door.

---

[1] Sb, V, c. xxxvi-14.   [2] Idem.
[3] *I.e.* mayor or governor—Tr.
[4] JA quoted SEC, vol. II, p. 193.

The blows redoubled but were not so loud as to drown a gentle but very determined voice:

'Force the door and much good may it do you! But just think of the consequences. For not only are you going against the will of God, but against the Holy Father's brief and against His Illustrious Lordship, our Bishop.'

Feeling that they had now spent enough time in talking, all four betook themselves to prayer, leaving the Magnificent Lord *Corregidor*, the constables and the crowd to storm and shout.

The door held, the nuns were not dispersed, the convent was not destroyed: the authorities returned crestfallen.

Four girls could not be allowed to hold public authority at defiance with impunity; it was accordingly decided to convene a *junta* 'of the utmost solemnity possible' consisting of the authorities and notables of Ávila, with all urgency.[1]

When it opened on 30th August 'punctually to the minute,' it comprised an impressive number of 'magnificent lords' and of eminent representatives of the religious Orders and the clergy: doctors, heads of religious houses, canons, the 'Prior of the monastery and illustrious house of our master, Saint Thomas Aquinas the Royal,' 'the Abbot of the house and monastery of our Lord the Holy Ghost,' 'the Guardian of the monastery of our lord Saint Francis,' and other great lords temporal and spiritual.

The Bishop was invited to be so good as to consider 'the serious harm which the existence of this convent may cause both to the city and to the monasteries of Orders already confirmed in sanctity, religion and good example, which will certainly be gravely injured by the alms given to the above-mentioned convent.'

Against the Bishop himself they brought a charge of irregularity: the brief had not been presented 'to the Royal and Catholic Majesty of the King our Lord, or to the Lords of his Royal Council.'[2]

During this time Teresa was talking with a no less exalted Majesty:

'O God, this house is not mine, it was founded for you; since there is no one to plead for it, may Your Majesty deign to take it under your charge.'[3]

The divine voice replied, 'very softly, speaking as it were in a whisper'[4]:

'Do you not know that I am almighty? What do you fear?'[5] And he assured her that the convent would not be dissolved.

[1] Idem, p. 194.   [2] Quoted SEC, vol. II, pp. 170–1.
[3] Sb, V, c. xxxvi–17.   [4] Sb, V, c. xxxix–3.   [5] Sb, V, c. xxxvi–16.

After this, how could she be otherwise than 'as calm as if the whole world had been negotiating on her side'? [1]

Only one person, but a distinguished one, rose to speak for the defence; P. Domingo Báñez, one of the most renowned and revered theologians of the Dominican Order. He was opposed to the immediate suppression of the convent which all present were unanimous in demanding, with the exception of Brizuela, the Vicar-General.

The Dominican was enthusiastic for a return to traditional practices, as well as for the twofold ideal of a life which should be both contemplative and active, such as Hurtado and his followers had introduced into the Order of Preachers in Spain. The Vicar-General spoke on behalf of the Bishop.[2] Their combined efforts resulted in a decision to go to law: it was so much time gained.

'The commotion lasted for the half of a year.'[3] The matter was brought before the Royal Council, Don Álvaro de Mendoza did not yield, Gonzalo de Aranda went to court to defend the convent at his own expense, powerful friends whom Teresa had made at Doña Luisa de la Cerda's used their influence, and whilst all this 'busy-ness' was going on the people of Ávila found other subjects of conversation. Not only did Ávila grow calm, Ávila forgot.

The moment had come to remind the Provincial of his promise. Teresa begged him to allow her to go back and join her abandoned 'lambs' at St Joseph's. He still hesitated but she had the courage to insist:

'Father, have you considered that we're resisting the Holy Spirit?'

Her tone was such that he saw clearly that she was speaking under the impulse of the Spirit, and he was won over.[4]

At the beginning of the spring of 1563, Doña Teresa de Ahumada was authorized to leave the Incarnation and even to take four nuns who wanted to go with her to St Joseph's: Ana de los Ángeles, María Isabel, her cousin Isabel de San Pablo and the Marchioness of Velada's daughter, Ana de San Juan.

She bade her companions a tender farewell, as she did the house in which she had lived twenty-seven years, suffered greatly and experienced joys unknown to mortals.

Along the road which was to take her to perpetual enclosure, her heart was as light as the small package consisting of a few items of

[1] Idem, 17.   [2] VH.
[3] Sb, V, c. xxxvi–18.
[4] HC quoted SEC, vol. I, p. 515, n. 3.

immediate necessity which she borrowed from the prioress and gave a written undertaking to return:

> One straw mat.
> One penance, of metal links.
> One discipline.
> One old habit, very much darned.[1]

As she passed the basilica of San Vicente, she went in, going down into the crypt and taking off her shoes before the Virgin of the Soterraña: Doña Teresa de Ahumada was henceforth dead to the world. From her ashes Teresa de Jesús was born.

[1] Idem.

X

THE WAY OF PERFECTION

IN the convent of St Joseph's the few nuns and their prioress were, so to speak, gathered up by Our Lady of Carmel in her great white mantle. Teresa of Jesus installed herself in active peace; she felt she had the time to train the nuns gradually. It was not as if she had to pull them after her 'with a drag-net'; she won them 'by sweetness and it was for their great good.' [1]

When she begged her daughters to let what she said to them speak to their 'inmost heart,' [2] she did so because 'a single person truly on fire with the love of God is more useful than many souls if they are tepid.' [3] Her purpose was efficacious achievement: 'The world is on fire! Christ is being condemned over again and a thousand false witnesses are being raised up against him. O my Redeemer! What is happening to us Christians? Must it always be so, that it is those who owe you most who cause you the most suffering? Those you have chosen as your friends, who have you near to them, to whom you give yourself in the sacraments, are they not ashamed that you have endured such torments for them?' [4]

Each Carmelite must substitute herself for those who had no love for God, or very little, for those who did not pray or prayed badly, and must give herself completely for the salvation of the world and of souls, for the Church and its priests.

'Sisters,' said Teresa, 'that is what you are called to; that is why you are here together; that is what your business is, that is what your desire must be and the object of your tears and supplications.' [5]

A few women, then, had made a vow to follow 'the evangelical counsels with the utmost perfection possible.' [6] The first of these counsels was: 'Pray without ceasing.' That might be expressed as to work without ceasing, build convents without ceasing, but the work would be worth no more—and no less—than the workman.

Mother Teresa guided her daughters along the way of perfection as her own experience had taught her. She spoke to them in practical

[1] Sb, V, c. xi–16. [2] Sb, C, c. vi–4. [3] REC, iii, 18.
[4] Sb, C, c. i–3. [5] Sb, C, c. i–5. [6] Idem, 2.

terms and her purpose was a very concrete one: the discovery and
conquest of God's kingdom and its spread among mankind. Not for
their own glory, but as the vanguard of the Church militant and to
help a suffering world which had lost its bearings.

Enclosure, silence, recollection—all were necessary for the satisfactory accomplishment of the 'precision work' they had undertaken
—to grind in well the cogs of the essential virtues—as the earth needs
to be hardened by frost and pressed well down if the seeds beneath it are
to germinate.

The virtues in question are three:

'The first is to love each other; the second, detachment from all
created things; but the most important, although I have mentioned it
last, is true humility which includes all the others. . . .'[1]

And the Mother added:

'Those who, without possessing these virtues, think themselves
very contemplative, are much mistaken.'[2] 'Right thinking helps a
good deal towards the accomplishment of noble deeds.'[3]

Love—Like the Gospel, the Epistles and all the saints, Teresa spoke
of the love of one's neighbour and, in her tireless search for perfection
even in the minutest detail, she found new terms in which to express it.
She was talking to women and she had a bad opinion of women: she
could not have expressed herself with more conviction: ' Anything
can be harmful to weak women like ourselves. . . .'[4] 'It is enough for
me to be a woman for my wings to drop off. . . .'[5]

She knew how the common life lived in an enclosed convent
sharpened both the need for affection and one's susceptibilities:

> It would be a terrible thing, very hard to bear, to be only a few
> in number and to get on badly together. May God's goodness never
> permit such a thing![6] Sisters, the time for childish games—'you
> love me . . . you love me not'—has gone by.[7] I am older . . . I
> have worked a longer time . . . someone else is better treated than
> I am. . . . To dwell on such thoughts or make them the subject of
> conversation is a pest.[8]

On the occasion of even the slightest word that may cause enmity,
one must hasten to apologize, pray much, not turn one's grudge into
a point of honour. Ah! 'these little points of honour' (*puntillos de honra*)
which for so long had been Doña Teresa de Ahumada's stumbling

[1] Sb, C, c. iv-4.   [2] Idem, 3.   [3] Idem, 1.
[4] Sb, C, prologue, 3.   [5] Idem, c. x-8.   [6] Sb, C, c. vii-9.
[7] Idem, c. xx-4.   [8] Idem, c. xii-4.

block! Teresa of Jesus exclaimed: 'My blood freezes when I think of it! If it were like that with you, you could consider yourselves as good as lost and that you had driven the Bridegroom away from his house—in that case cry to His Majesty for help and remedy the matter.' [1] And she uttered the first of her terrible anathemas:

> Let the prioress watch; if she sees a nun upsetting the house, let her endeavour to send her to another convent. God will provide the dowry. Cast out the plague-bearer, cut down the branches as far as possible; if that does not suffice, tear up the roots; and if that should prove impossible, the one who is causing the trouble must be kept in the prison cell and not come out : that is better than exposing the rest to the danger of infection. For it is a great evil! I would rather see our houses on fire and for us all to be burned! [2]

To help one another, to be compassionate, 'not only to show good-will but tenderness with it,' [3] to be merry with the sisters during recreation 'even if you don't feel like it,'[4] to look after the sick, to serve in the lowliest tasks—Mother Teresa put all this on just as high a level as contemplation of Our Lord, or mental prayer. 'What does it matter whether we are serving him in the one way or in the other?' [5] Divine love is inseparable from the love of one's sisters. True affection, which has nothing in common with earthly attachments, helps us to make progress. Perfect love does not hesitate to warn those who are following the wrong path of their mistake, it avoids flattery as much as it does secret blame, and submits to criticism without bearing a grudge. One cannot hide anything from true friends: 'They see the little faults,' and Teresa who, even though she was prioress, did not cease to be a woman talking to women, used an expression which was especially applicable to defects in textiles: *Las motitas ven. . . .* Tiniest blemishes are seen. . . . [6]

Throughout her life Teresa implored her nuns to reprove her when she deserved it and she accepted criticism humbly.[7] All her life long she showed each Carmelite how she must 'preach by deeds, since the Apostle and our lack of knowledge prevent us from preaching by word of mouth.' [8]

But how was one to achieve, in love and detachment, this combination of firmness and gentleness, this doing away with the 'black point of honour'? By one supreme virtue on which all the others depended: the knowledge of self.

[1] Sb, C. c. vii–10.   [2] Idem, 11.   [3] Idem, 7.   [4] Idem, 7.
[5] Idem, c. xvii–6.   [6] Idem, c. vii–4.   [7] FR, L. IV, c. vii.
[8] Sb, C, c. xv–6.

The knowledge of self—'Self-knowledge is the bread which must be eaten with every dish, even the daintiest . . . there's no nourishment without that bread.' [1] The Mother never ceased to insist on the extreme importance of clear self-knowledge. Hers was a strong character, progressively released by prayer and divine grace from the weight of what a psychoanalyst would call her self-punishing complexes. When she took as her motto the three words: 'To act, to suffer, to love,' [2] the quest for suffering did not signify a morbid tendency: 'Try us, O Lord, you who know the truth, in order that we may know ourselves!' [3] Suffering alone shows our true strength, or, on the other hand, what an illusion our self-complacency is. For Teresa of Jesus to suffer was to learn to know oneself.

But her prudence and good sense were such, she had known so many people—herself included—whom the shame of finding nothing good in themselves had driven away from the Lord of all mercies instead of bringing them close to him in childlike abandonment, that she immediately added a rider that would comfort the scrupulous: 'This bread must be eaten with moderation; once the soul is submissive, when she has seen clearly how little she gives in exchange for the gifts given to her by so great a King,' what need is there for her to spend further time over this? 'Let us go on towards something else, towards whatever the Lord places before us. . . .' [4]

For 'the understanding must be ennobled in order that self-knowledge does not rob us altogether of our courage.' [5]

Humility—For Teresa, the depths of humility lay very close to the highest of honours, of which for a long time she herself had had no experience: 'If I had understood, as I do now, that my soul's tiny palace contained so great a King, I shouldn't have left him there so often alone, I should have stayed with him from time to time and, moreover, I should have made an effort to keep his house in less dirt and disorder. . . .' [6] It was in this way that the Mother who wielded the broom so energetically and compared sin to spiders' webs—she was a good housewife and a courteous hostess—referred to the presence of God in man.

'Humility is to keep within the bounds of truth,' [7] she said. 'The truth is magnificent: we are nothing, but God dwells in us and God is everything.' 'Worse than the beasts as we are, we don't understand our

---

[1] Sb, V, c. xiii–15.
[2] SEC, R, xxxvi, p. 64.
[3] Sb, M, III, c. i–9.
[4] Sb, C, c. xiii–5.
[5] Sb, M, c. ii–8.
[6] Sb, C, c. xxviii–11.
[7] Sb, M, VI, c. x–7

soul's great dignity and we insult it by bringing it down to the level of the vile things of this world. . . .'[1] 'Let us beware of the false humility which refuses to recognize the gifts which God has so generously bestowed upon us: Let us understand clearly, absolutely clearly, about this: God grants them to us without any merit on our part and therefore we should thank His Majesty. . . . The richer we find ourselves, knowing all the time that we are really poor, the more progress we make in true humility.'[2]

The effects of this union of the humble soul with God are wonderful. Teresa returns to her liking for tales of chivalry and draws upon that source to explain these effects to her nuns more clearly: 'If an insignificant peasant girl married the King would not their children be of royal blood? When Our Lord gives a soul the great grace of uniting himself to it so intimately, what fruit, what heroic acts will not be the result.'[3] But for Teresa of Jesus a heroic act is no longer what it was for Teresa de Ahumada, a sacrifice quickly over, the 'cheap' way of gaining heaven, but the perfect accomplishment of every single action, even the most ordinary.

'It is the humblest among you who are the most perfect,' she said, 'not those who are favoured in prayer or with ecstasies.'

And it was to mortify herself that she added: 'I am glad to give this advice, but it is counsel which contemplatives will find humiliating.'[4]

This slow transformation of women far from perfect into the brides of Christ, into the servants of all in the world who suffer, this training of the character, of heart and soul, to live on the mountain tops of spirituality, this ' precision work' in which the adaptation of body and mind to the spiritual life consists, was part and parcel of the primitive Rule of Carmel.

The anchorites of Mount Carmel claimed to be the direct heirs of the prophet Elias; for long centuries these Fathers of the Desert had worn garments of plaited palm fibre. It was they whom Teresa wanted to imitate when she had to resign herself to not dying a martyr's death. About the year 1200, Albert, Patriarch of Jerusalem, had given them a Rule and Constitutions, and from the end of that century onwards, protected by the crusaders, they continued to found numerous monasteries in Europe, frightening in their austerity but nurseries of saints, until the great plague of 1348: the few friars who survived, feeling a little sorry for themselves, relaxed the observance. It was thought that

[1] CTA, xix.
[2] Sb, V, c. x-4.
[3] Sb, CAD, c. iii-9.
[4] Sb, C, c. xviiii-9.

now humanity had grown weaker it could not bear the rigours imposed by its ancestors without danger and, in 1482, Pope Eugenius IV attenuated and mitigated the primitive Rule.

The fasts, which had lasted from the feast of the Exaltation of the Cross until Easter, *i.e.* seven months, were reduced to three days a week, except during Advent and Lent.

Perpetual abstinence from meat was likewise reduced to three days a week.

The coarse habit was replaced by one of fine cloth; they no longer went barefoot. Formerly obliged to seclusion and perpetual silence, the friars were now authorized to talk to each other freely in the cloisters.

As to the nuns, not only did they visit each other's cells, but visitors, both pious and worldly, thronged the parlours, and the sisters were allowed to absent themselves from their convent.

Teresa adopted the primitive Rule in every single one of its requirements. What was called her Reform was in reality a return to the observance of the ancient Order of Carmel. She restored in her convents the character of laboratories of spiritual culture in the strict sense of the term. She would not even allow her daughters—bound as they were by vow to live by the work of their hands—to have common workrooms: this would be a pretext for chattering and thus for dissipation. A Carmelite must work alone, in her cell, seated on the ground. She might speak only at recreation and even there a little rattle was frequently shaken to remind one of the presence of God. The enclosure door shut on her for ever. For her rare visitors she remained invisible behind the barrier of grilles, curtains, veils.

To be solitary, silent, despising the body and its needs, but gay as children; humble, but conscious of their soul's dignity; submissive, but to spiritual things; in love, but with Christ; deprived of everything, but queens of the world, 'for those who trouble about no worldly thing are rulers over all;'[1] that was was the pattern Teresa of Jesus set for Our Lady's daughters.

'This house is a heaven if there is one upon earth.'[2] The Mother who initiated her daughters into mental prayer by first of all teaching them to say 'Our Father, who art in heaven . . .' well, commented on the beginning of the *Pater* with her magnificent logic: 'You know that God is everywhere, it is clear that where the King is there is his court; in short, where God is, is heaven. You will allow that where His Majesty is, there is all glory. St Augustine says that he sought him everywhere and found him in himself. Do you think it a matter of

[1] Sb, C, c. ii–5.   [2] Idem, xiii–7.

small importance for a soul who wants to open her heart to understand this truth, to see that she has no need to go to heaven to speak to her eternal Father and enjoy his presence, that it isn't even necessary for her to raise her voice? She has no need of wings to go and seek him: all she needs is to be alone and contemplate him in herself. . . .' [1]

Not only was the house a paradise on earth, but each Carmelite carried her paradise within herself.

[1] Idem, xxviii-2.

XI

A WRETCH AMONG ANGELS

IT was still dark when the little bell rang, giving out its cracked sound: five o'clock in the morning. The Mother Prioress of the convent of St Joseph of Carmel made the sign of the cross and got up; she listened and heard sounds of her convent awakening.

A voice cut the silence: 'Praised be Jesus Christ, praised be the Virgin Mary, his Mother! To prayer, Sisters! Let us praise the Lo–o–o–rd!'

The vibration of the young, high-pitched voice was prolonged on a single note, with one sheer intake of breath: it was Isabel de Santo Domingo. . . .

A brief pause, then another voice: 'Praised be Jesus. . . .' The more solemn, slightly husky timbre of a woman of mature years: Úrsula de los Santos.

Two voices rang out at the same time from the far end of the cloister, vibrating in harmony: '. . . To prayer, Sisters! . . .'

In imagination Teresa of Jesus could see the cell doors opening in the light of dawn and her daughters on their knees as the day came into being. At the beginning of each day it was her delight to hear these chants rising to God from Carmel, as from a tree full of nests, nests which were full of song-birds. That was why she always came out last. The sky above the patio was tinged with a blue still milky-pale when the Discalced Carmelites and their Mother Prioress made their way to the chapel, to the accompaniment of a heavy swish of moving frieze.

Mental prayer and the little Hours: Prime, Terce, Sext, None. Then Mass.

After breakfast, which was about nine o'clock, each nun went to the work assigned to her.

The cell was quickly swept and put in order. The straw pallet, which the planks scarcely raised above the level of the red-brick floor, was shaken and the thick frieze which did duty for bed-linen put back in place. The warm brown colour looked well against the white-washed wall whose only decoration was a large cross. The rough wood door formed a brown mass, the window a patch of blue. In a corner stood the blue and white earthenware pitcher and basin in use everywhere for one's ablutions at that time. On a narrow piece of board stood a few books. On the floor was a cork mat which did duty as a seat. That was all. Nothing more. But the 'nothing' was so clean that it positively shone.

It was there that any Carmelite who had no particular office assigned to her worked at her spinning in silence, to earn her bread and that of her sisters.

But 'with your eyes on your Bridegroom. It is to him you must look for your food. If he is pleased with you, even those who love you least will give you something to eat. Even if you were to die of hunger, blessed the nuns of St Joseph's! . . . Leave all anxiety about food on one side, then, otherwise everything is lost. Abandon this care to him who is Lord both of revenues and those who possess them: we are here at his command, his word is truth, and heaven and earth will fail before that fails us. . . .' [1] 'He never fails those who are in need. Either you believe this or you don't believe it; if you believe it, why kill yourselves with worry?' [2] 'There was a time when I trusted the world's aid; I see clearly now that all that is worth no more than a few sprigs of dried rosemary. . . .' [3]

Before the bell rang for dinner a short time was spent in the deepening of self-knowledge: the examination of conscience.

The refectory was rectangular, with narrow tables arranged round the sides. Along the white walls the Carmelites sat on wooden benches, each one with a spotless serviette, stiff because perfectly ironed, in front of her. The earthenware drinking-bowl which was lifted with both hands formed a splash of blue, the wooden utensils, the bread, provided patches of light colour. The huge black cross hung over all. Vegetables, eggs or fish were eaten in silence. From a pulpit constructed in the recess in the wall formed by one of the windows, a sister read aloud, her black veil standing out against the blue of the Ávila sky.

White: walls and coifs. Brown: the habits, the wood-work. Red: the tiles of floor and roof. Blue: a few pieces of earthenware, the sky. Such are the only colours found in these Carmels. And over all that, the sun of Spain.

When there was only one egg, it was kept for the most delicate among them, they vied with each other as to who was strongest, each refusing to eat it.

When there was nothing in the turn and the purse was empty, Prioress Teresa of Jesus made her daughters come to table all the same

[1] Sb, C, c. ii-1, 2.   [2] Idem, c. xxix-2.   [3] R, iii, p. 17.

and she spoke to them of God in such wonderful words that they forgot their hunger.

At that time at St Joseph's there were none of those lay-sisters whom the Mother was later to call so delightfully 'those with the white veil'; the choir nuns shared all the household tasks. Teresa used her privileges as prioress only to take upon herself the hardest tasks. Her 'week in the kitchen' was a red-letter week for them all. 'She did all she could to give them a treat' [1] and Our Lord sent her the where-withal to do it. In her opinion, to make the best possible use of what God gives was one way of praising him.

'Daughters, don't let's give way to disappointment when through obedience we are occupied in external things. If your job is in the kitchen, don't forget that Our Lord is there in the midst of the pots and pans!' [2]

So much was this the case at St Joseph's that one day Isabel de Santo Domingo found Teresa in front of the kitchen stove in ecstasy:

'Dear God! Our Mother will upset the little oil that's left to us on the fire!'

But, although she was rapt to heaven, her feet were firmly planted on the ground. Teresa did not loosen her grip of the handle of the frying-pan one whit and the eggs went on sizzling. . . .[3]

She was Martha and Mary in one.

Úrsula de los Santos was over forty: it was late to begin to mould oneself to obedience, especially for one who had been mistress of a household and responsible for the upbringing of a family. Teresa accordingly watched her closely and saw to it that the ordinary trials of religious life were multiplied in her regard: Ursula came off with flying colours.

Did the prioress feel that this nun was not entirely free from mental reservations? However this may be, she decided one day to put her through an extraordinary test and was fully determined to deprive her of the habit if she showed a want of docility.

She stopped her abruptly in the cloister:

'Oh dear, Sister, I *am* sorry for you. Go and get into bed: it's essential.'

She felt her pulse, behaving as though she found her very ill. Úrsula de los Santos went to bed. When they came to ask her how she was, she replied:

[1] SEC, F, p. 7.   [2] Sb, F, c. v–8.   [3] SST, vol. III, pp. 78–9.

Saint Teresa's
kitchen at her
first founda-
tion, Saint
Joseph's in
Avila

St. Teresa's drum, whistles, and tambourine

Mule chair used by St. Teresa in her travels on horseback

'I am very ill.'

'What is the matter? Where are you in pain?'

Ursula did not hesitate.

'Sisters, I know nothing about it, but Mother Prioress says so.'

Teresa was not yet completely satisfied. She went to see the patient herself and took her pulse again.

'Oh, dear me! Sisters, send for a barber quickly! She will have to be bled.'

The barber came and bled her; Úrsula de los Santos' only response was complete and perfect obedience.

After this, the Mother loved her with an especial love 'so much did the bleeding of this good nun contribute to the extraction of self-will from these convents. . . .'[1] 'Any one wanting in obedience shall not be a nun here, . . .'[2] said Teresa. 'The way of obedience is the way which leads most quickly to absolute perfection.'[3] The logic of this was obvious. 'Obedience is the true means of submitting one's will to reason.'[4]

In short: it is essential to know how to obey if one wants to command and particularly if one wants to command oneself. A daughter of God must show obedience, just as a soldier must. Teresa did not forget that she came of a warrior race; she used to give her nuns examples from military life: 'Soldiers must always be prepared for their captain to send them where he will. . . .'[5] And her summons to spiritual exercises rings out like a trumpet blast: 'Mental prayer, Sisters, or if that is impossible, vocal prayer: holy reading, colloquies with God.'[6]

And what about María de Ocampo who had promised 'her inheritance' to help in the foundation of St Joseph's convent? She came to join the others on St John's day 1563. She had been 'the most elegant and the best-dressed among those with whom she associated. Her fine dresses went to make altar frontals, chasubles and other things needed for the chapel. . . .'[7] Her famous 'inheritance' settled one of the convent's debts and paid for the erection of a few hermitages in the orchard 'where one could give oneself to prayer'. The paintings on their walls inspired devotion. The Mother Prioress would not allow María de Ocampo's father to give more.

María de Ocampo now ceased to be: Sister María Bautista had so completely overcome vainglory and her own will that when Teresa

[1] SEC, vol. V, p. 94, n. 1. [2] Sb, C, c. xviii-8.
[3] Sb, F, c. v-10. [4] Idem, 11. [5] Sb, C, c. xviii-3.
[6] Idem, 4. [7] JA quoted SEC, vol. V, p. 9, n. 3.

ordered her to go and plant a rotten cucumber, she merely asked:

'Vertically or horizontally?'

'Horizontally. . . .'[1]

That was the way obedience was practised. But María Bautista's obedience in no way diminished her common-sense, as she showed when the prioress asked her to give her opinion: the well-sinkers alleged that to dig the well more deeply in the hope of finding drinking water would be 'a waste of money.'

'Let them try. Our Lord will certainly have to send us someone to provide us with water, and the food for whoever he sends: it will be easier for His Majesty to let us have water here and he will not fail to do so. . . .'[2] As it turned out, good fresh water was found and the well was named María Bautista. . . .

His Illustrious Lordship Don Álvaro de Mendoza, Bishop of Ávila, became very fond of St Joseph's. Someone had just given him a life-sized crucifix and he had this taken to the convent to show the Discalced nuns, for he was sure they would find it moving. He returned later to fetch it and as he was talking to Mother Teresa at the parlour grille, the sound of the chanting of litanies reached their ears, although it was not the customary hour for this exercise:

'Lord, Lord!'

'Stay with us!'

'Jesus crucified!'

'Stay with us!'

The sound of the voices came nearer and the nuns came into the parlour in procession, headed by two sisters carrying the large crucifix with much difficulty:

'Jesus crowned with thorns!'

'Stay with us!'

They were chanting in all seriousness and their pageantry was without the slightest tinge of impertinence. Teresa blushed with embarrassment and, begging Don Álvaro to excuse the nuns, she began to scold them forthwith. The Bishop, however, laughed heartily:

'Good! Let them keep it then!'[3]

Miracles are the due reward of innocence. When the most naïve among them—for María de San José was noted for her childlike simplicity—asked the crucifix:

[1] Sb, F, c. i–3.   [2] Sb, C, c. i–4.   [3] SST, vol. I, p. 83.

'Lord, what is your name? You are sometimes called "Christ of the Agony" or "Christ, our Saviour," but what name are we to give you for this crucifix?'—she was in no way surprised when Christ, the friend of the childlike and simple, answered: 'Call me the holy Christ of love. . . .'[1]

When money ran very short the nuns contented themselves with dry bread, but there was never any lack of wax candles for the altar and everything connected with divine worship was as exquisitely perfect as possible. A visiting priest was scandalized:

'What! A scented towel to wipe one's hands before saying Mass?'

Teresa, her fine face lighting up with fervour, took the blame on herself:

'It is from me my daughters get this imperfection. But when I remember the way Our Lord reproached the pharisee for not receiving him with sufficient honour, I could wish that everything here in the church, from even its very threshold, were perfumed with sweet waters. . . .'[2]

The construction of a larger church was clearly indispensable. Teresa called the depositrix:

'How much money have we?'

'Mother, *un cuarto*, a farthing.'[3]

'That will please him greatly,'[4] and she put the work in hand. For in the absence of even a sprig of dried rosemary, God would provide.

María Álvarez Dávila y Salazar was one of Mother Teresa's nieces: of the highest ranks of nobility and as beautiful as one could wish. One September day she invited her friends to go out with her: the ladies went in litters, the gentlemen on horseback. She was a very splendid figure, María Dávila, 'attired in much silk and gold and all the magnificence one could desire.'

She led the cavalcade in the direction of St. Joseph's and there stepped down from her litter; the enclosure door opened and Teresa, who was waiting for her, appeared carrying a crucifix. María kneeling 'kissed the feet of the crucifix fervently, then without turning round to acknowledge her friends' farewell, she allowed Teresa to close the door behind her and divested herself forthwith of her fine apparel. . . .'[5]

María Dávila thus afforded much astonishment to all the nobility and gentry of the town.

[1] Idem.   [2] Y quoted SEC, vol. II, p. 499.
[3] MJE quoted SEC, vol. II, p. 292.   [4] Idem.
[5] FR, L. II, c. 5, and B.

But María Dávila had ceased to be: all there was in her stead was a young Discalced Carmelite, Sister María de San Jerónimo.

One night after Matins when Teresa had stayed behind to pray, she saw the five Marías, the two Isabels, Ursula, Antonia, Ana and Petronilla come into choir in procession, carrying lighted candles and preceded by a crucifix carried by the youngest. They were singing hymns, followed by this strange couplet:

> You clothe us with apparel new,
> > Heavenly King!
> Should creatures vile infest our frieze,
> > Delivrance bring![1]

As a very special favour, they had just obtained permission to wear the roughest frieze even next to the skin, with a view to greater mortification. In future they would wear no more linen and even the handkerchief would be of coarse material. 'But fearing lest such coarse wool should be infested with lice, with the image of the Crucified at their head and in deep recollection they came to pray God to spare them such an unclean pest!'

Touched—and amused, Teresa answered their *coplas* by improvising a reply. And in the chapel of St Joseph's could be heard a curious concert, 'against impertinent little creatures':

> *Teresa:*
> These tiresome creatures much disturb
> > in time of prayer
> Minds which are ill establishèd
> > in things of God.

> *All*
> Should creatures vile infest our frieze,
> Delivrance bring!

> *Teresa*
> You who've come here prepared for death,
> > Yield not one whit,
> And such vile creatures great or small,
> > Fear not at all.

> *All*
> You've clothed us now in livery new,
> > Heavenly King.
> Should creatures vile infest our frieze,
> > Delivrance bring!

[1] SEC, vol. VI, pp. 117–19.

'From that day onwards not even one such creature was ever seen either in the habits or in the gauze veils.'[1] And they called the Christ who worked the miracle the Christ of the lice.

Stories like this were told with every freedom to the hum of the spinning-wheel at recreation—unless in their great joy the nuns broke out into songs and dances or the playing of the flute and tambourine. These 'hermits' were by no means gloomy; at St Joseph's the atmosphere was enlivened by the poetry and music which entered into everything; as Teresa said, 'all that is most necessary to render our life bearable.' She took part in it all but never left off her spinning. One day, a sister who had finished her work took up a spool and wound the thread on to another empty spool.

'What are you doing, Sister?'

The child had to admit that she wanted to spare herself the shame of being idle in the prioress's presence.[2]

For the Mother never allowed herself any rest, but was always spinning, weaving, sewing or darning. She found the curtains drawn behind the parlour grilles a convenience, for she was thus able to work with her hands while discussing convent business.

Don Francisco de Salcedo, 'holy gentleman' as he was, was slightly irritated by this.

'Mother, you don't listen to what I say. It's impossible to listen when you're spinning so fast.'

'Am I not obliged to do so? Isn't it my duty to do everything in my power to feed my daughters?'

He proposed a bargain: when he came to see her he would pay her the equivalent of an hour's work on condition that she did not inflict on him the sound of the spinning-wheel humming behind the black curtain. After this, when he went away, he deposited the amount of his debt in the turn, with the parlour key. . . .

It was with distaste that Teresa obeyed the order P. Báñez gave her to set down in writing, as her daughters wished, the day-to-day counsels she gave them. Why must she always be forced to spend her time writing? She had only just finished the second version of her autobiography which she had revised at the request of P. García de Toledo. Were they always going 'to prevent her from spinning'?[3] So in the matter of what she called 'the little book' (*el librillo* . . .) on the *Pater noster*, later to be known as the *Way of Perfection*, she placed obedience before every other virtue.

[1] SST, vol. III, p. 82.   [2] B.
[3] Sb, V, c. x–7.

About 11 o'clock at night, when Matins and Lauds were chanted, the nuns of St Joseph's retired to their cells. They knelt down on the threshold, as they had done in the morning. The youngest sister gave three knocks and on two notes chanted a *saetilla* [1] composed of a few lines providing a theme of meditation for the night:

> Sister!
> You will die only once,
> If you go astray . . . woe betide you!
> Sister!
> No man can escape death,
> Neither poor man, king nor pope. . . .
> Sister!
> In a deep dark tomb
> Endeth the joy of this world! [2]

The prioress went round the cloister, stopping to bless each nun as she passed. One after another the doors closed. Teresa, last of all, did not close hers until the portress handed her the bunch of great keys which locked up the convent.

The browns, blues, the russet red, the white even, all the colours of Carmel became indistinguishable in the darkness.

In the little convent all was darkness and silence except for the light of a smoky oil lamp coming from the prioress's cell.

For she was not going to let writing prevent her from spinning any longer: she would take the hours from her sleep. Seated on the ground in front of the stone block which served her as table she wrote the *Way of Perfection* for her daughters.

The 'little book' included, in addition to the counsels on asceticism contained in the first fifteen chapters, a treatise on mental prayer in ten chapters—although the word 'treatise' is very pedantic in the case of a woman who all her life long sought to avoid any display of learning— and finally a commentary on the *Pater* showed how vocal prayer could lead souls to supernatural prayer.

Teresa wanted to cure her Carmelites of an evil of the day, the mechanical repetition 'of many vocal prayers said very rapidly as if one were dispatching a duty; they are convinced they have got to recite them every day, so much so that when the Lord puts his kingdom into their hands, they do not accept it.' [3] 'You do more by saying a single word of the *Pater noster* from time to time. . . .' [4] 'The Lord attaches

---

[1] The *saeta* (lit. 'arrow') is a cry pronounced in a long modulation something like an Arab chant.
[2] EM, p. 157. [3] Sb, C, c. xxxi-12. [4] Idem, 13.

The cell of St. Teresa at the convent of St. Joseph in Avila

The corner of St. Teresa's cell at St. Joseph's
where she wrote her *Way of Perfection*

no importance to our hurting our heads with a multiplicity of words when we speak to him. . . ."[1] You must understand what you say . . .'[2] 'and understand to whom you are speaking. . . .' [3] 'When I say the word *Credo*, it seems to me reasonable to understand and know in what I believe; and when I say 'Our Father,' to understand who this Father is and the Master who has taught us this prayer is a work of love. . . .'[4]

She does not preach or become excited, the tone is natural, affectionate and yet firm, the plan is absolutely clear. To this framework of the interior life she brings the same accuracy as she does to the organization of the material life of the convent, down to the last detail. Her sentences have the ring of her conversation about them and have caught something of the sound of her voice. On paper she questions those who are asleep not far away from her, proving that they are always in her thoughts: 'What are we to do in that case, Sisters?' 'Sisters, have you ever noticed? . . .' [5]

When she wanted to show that a thing was blameworthy, she did not hesitate to quote her own example: 'I sometimes imagine I am quite detached from the world . . . but at another time I find myself so attached to things which I should have despised the day before that I don't recognize myself. . . . Sometimes I think I have a lot of courage and would not refuse anything in God's service; but then comes another day when I could not kill an ant for God if you tried ever so little to prevent me. . . .' [6]

The acknowledgement of her mistakes could not harm a prioress who made herself not only mother to the nuns but their sister and who gave the example of trying to acquire self-knowledge. They were so near to her heart, her Discalced Carmelites, and she expected so much from the four young ones, María Bautista, María de San Jerónimo, Isabel de Santo Domingo—these three scarcely twenty—and Isabel de San Pablo, not eighteen. The Lord was already endowing them with so much perfection, overwhelming them with such high graces that she felt 'covered with confusion' [7] in their presence. For Teresa of Jesus remembered how many years it had taken Doña Teresa de Ahumada to reach, as they had, the stage of 'finding her consolation in solitude and of looking upon visits as something painful. . . . If one of them has permission to live apart in a hermitage, she considers herself the most favoured. God has his purpose when he gives his daughters a courage in his service far beyond the courage of women. . . .' [8]

[1] Idem, xxix–6.   [2] Idem, xxiv–2.   [3] Idem, 6.
[4] Idem, 2.   [5] Idem, xxxviii–4.   [6] Sb, C, c. xxxviii–6.
[7] Sb, F, c. 1–6.   [8] Idem, 6.

What was his purpose? What was so much courage for? Were they not contemplatives? Did not the world consider women who did nothing but pray, useless? It was this that made Mother Teresa stress the significance of their vocation: 'Although the ensign does not fight in the war, he is none the less in the thick of the danger, he holds the standard and cannot defend himself. He will not let go of it even if they hack him to pieces. Contemplatives are like that. Their rôle is to suffer like Christ and to raise the standard of the cross on high. If they loose hold of the flag, the battle is lost!' [1]

'Completely humble and considering obedience a joy, these hand-maids of the active virtues are truly blessed. . . .'[2] 'As to the joys of prayer, raptures and visions, we must wait until we get to the other world to know what all that means. . . .' [3]

For a moment the flow of the pen was interrupted. Teresa was now reflecting, as she was always inclined to do, on her own miseries: '. . . miserable sinner that I am in the midst of these angels. . . .' [4]

[1] Sb, C, c. xviii–5.   [2] Idem.
[3] Idem, 7.   [4] Sb, F, c. 1–6.

PART THREE

GOD'S KNIGHT ERRANT

'Our Lord will never abandon those who love him when their venturing into the unknown is for him alone.'

PASCAL: *Pensées*, ch. iii

'To have courage for whatever comes in life, everything lies in that.'

Autobiography, ch. iv

'Let us risk our life, for he who will lose his life shall best find it.'

Poems, xix

I

THE BIRTH OF THE FOUNDATIONS

'OUR Mother is going away!'
When they learnt at St Joseph's that Mother Teresa was thinking of leaving Ávila to go and found other convents, her nuns were filled with dismay.

She did not try to console them: instead she fired them with enthusiasm for her work.

'Can the Order of Our Lady of Mount Carmel be limited to one poor convent? Is each of us to save herself alone? Even for thirteen Discalced Carmelites, is it enough for us to give ourselves to prayer and penance, considering ourselves worthy of the bread we eat only if we have earned it by the work of our hands, and saving just ourselves? No. The world is still burning!'

The prioress reminded them of P. Alonso de Maldonado, the Franciscan who, on his return from the Indies, his face weather-beaten from wind and spray, had made the whole of their tiny church re-echo with his cry of alarm.

'Millions of souls are being lost in these conquered lands where the sword does not always clear away the obstacles in the path of the cross!'

Over the mighty empire of all the Spains the sun never set but it did not dissolve the darkness of violence, of greed, of everlasting death. From Flanders too there came tales of churches pillaged and desecrated, of profanations of the sacred Host. Whereas the daughters of Our Lady of Mount Carmel were at rest in the lap of their father St Joseph, busy spinning the cocoon of their new life.

'I say to all of you who are fighting under this standard, do not sleep, do not sleep, there is no peace upon the earth!'

'And since like a mighty captain our God willed to die, let us follow him, we who have slain him. . . . Do not sleep, do not sleep, for God is no longer upon earth!'

'Oh, what blessed warfare! Let no one desert! Let us risk our life, for he who will lose his life will find it best!'

'Let us follow this standard, Christ is marching before us!'

'Be fearless! Do not sleep! There is no peace upon earth!' [1]

Teresa already saw herself at the head of legions of fighting angels.

And then she wept. For whole days and nights she wept in the hermitage of Christ at the column, beside herself with grief and helplessness. 'A poor weak woman like myself could do nothing.' [2] Nothing, nothing but weep? 'Don't let's think that everything is done by much weeping, but let us put our shoulders to the wheel.' [3]

Prayer in the first place. Prayer can be warfare, silence a fortress, and mortification, strategy; a soul centred in God is as mighty as armies on the march, and women who are silent and still under their black veil can fight for the peace of the world by making every single thought, every single sacrifice 'an heroic act.'

Teresa of Jesus could be said truly to love God only from this moment when her heart, grown larger now, embraced the whole world; now she loved all mankind and would have given her life to save the least among them. 'He who loves not his neighbour loves not you, O Lord!' [4]

Alas! Only a poor insignificant woman and her sisters! So much fervour, so much austerity already: was it possible to increase it? Teresa mingled her blood with her tears.

This continued until one evening Our Lord appeared to her with a most tender expression as if he wished to console her, and said:

'Wait a little, daughter, and you will see great things. . . .' [5]

At this time Philip II was so desirous of reforming monastic life in his dominions that he invited the General of the Order of Our Lady of Mount Carmel, P. Juan Bautista Rubeo, of Ravenna, to come and investigate the means of carrying this out. He was received with very great honour. The 'Most Reverend Master General' visited Castile. At Ávila, the Bishop, Don Álvaro de Mendoza, did not fail to bring to his notice the example of a return to the primitive Rule afforded by the convent of St Joseph, which he took him to see. He was amazed to find these 'nuns so different from all the others, clad in frieze, wholly unostentatious, wearing sandals, humble, mortified.' [6]

During his stay in Ávila, he frequently returned to this oasis of pure and austere life. And this great prelate, whose face had, as well as a slight puffiness about the cheeks, something of the nobility of feature of the ancient Romans, called Teresa of Jesus *la mia figlia*, 'daughter mine.'

[1] P, xxix.　　　　[2] Sb, F, c. ii–4.　　　　[3] Sb, M, VI, c. vi–9.
[4] Sb, E, ii–2.　　　[5] Sb, F, c. i–3.　　　　[6] JA, p. 238.

On his departure he left her a letter patent:

We, Fray Juan Bautista Rubeo of Ravenna, Prior and Master General . . . to the Reverend Mother Teresa of Jesus:

There is no good merchant, labourer, soldier or man of culture who does not take care of, look after, employ all solicitude over and go to much trouble to enlarge, his house, his honour and all his possessions.

How much greater should be the efforts made by the servants of God to extend their work to other places, to build churches and religious houses and do all that is necessary to serve souls and for the glory of the Divine Majesty!

To the Reverend Mother Teresa of Jesus we grant the faculty and power to set up everywhere in the kingdom of Castile convents of our holy Order, where the nuns will live in accordance with the primitive Rule, the habit and other holy customs being those in use at St Joseph's. . . . Let them wear brown frieze. . . . If frieze cannot be found, let some other coarse stuff be used. And we shall give them vicars or commissioners to govern them.[1]

Then a second letter patent:

'It is understood that our authorization is for the whole of Castile, Old and New. . . .'[2]

Finally, a third letter patent from P. Rubeo marked one of Teresa's greatest triumphs: she was authorized to found houses of friars under the primitive Rule, to the number of two to begin with. Here the principle of penance, together with that of deep prayer, would not be allowed to fall into disuse.

Only men could preach and spread these principles; only men could undertake the spiritual direction of the Discalced Carmelite nuns. In that matter, too, Teresa had experience to guide her. She knew only too well the damage which 'the half-educated and timorous'[3] could do and how much she herself had suffered from want of understanding on the part of her confessors. 'What a lot of time I've lost through not knowing what to do! I am terribly sorry for those who, when they reach this state, are alone, without help. . . .'[4] She had known so many who, with God's grace, were soaring upwards in the spiritual life like eagles until they were constrained by some timid director to walk 'like chickens with their feet fastened together!'[5]

For the spiritual direction of the daughters of Carmel, she wanted priests who were both intelligent and experienced. 'If they are learned

---

[1] SEC, vol. V, pp. 333-4.   [2] Idem.   [3] Sb, V, c. xx-21.
[4] Sb, V, c. xiv-7.   [5] Sb, V, c. xxxix-12.

as well, so much the better.' [1] But she considered the first two qualities the most important: 'It is no light cross to submit our intelligence to someone who hasn't very much himself. Personally, I've never succeeded and I don't believe one ought to do it.' [2] 'God preserve us from foolish devotions!' [3]

In his letter patent P. Rubeo gave a perfect résumé of Carmelite prayer:

> We desire that all religious who are sons of this Order be transparent mirrors, burning lamps, flaming torches, and shining stars to enlighten and help those in the world who go astray. We therefore particularly desire that they should devote themselves entirely to continual and familiar converse with God and that, consecrated as they are to prayer, contemplation and holy meditation, they should strive to be so closely united with him that their spirit, though still fettered by the body, already dwells in heaven. . . . Forgetful of themselves, wholly absorbed in those frequent and sublime flights of the spirit in prayer, which it is impossible to define for they are extraordinary, their light travels quickly, whether, since it is inherent in the soul it is indistinguishable from it, whether it withdraws to its inmost centre, or whether it moves, rises, descends, in such a way that the understanding cannot grasp it: it leaves tears in the eyes, but in the heart the most refreshing and profitable dew.
>
> Urged, then, by the desire of extending our Order, it seems to us our duty to grant the petition we have received that we should authorize the foundation of certain houses of friars; they will celebrate Mass, pray, chant the Divine Office; will devote the requisite number of hours to mental prayer, meditation and other spiritual exercises, and will accordingly be known as houses or monasteries of contemplative Carmelite fathers; they will also be a help to the others and will live in conformity with the primitive Constitutions. [4]

It was indeed given to Teresa of Jesus to see 'great things': without money, without support, without houses, without friars, she was given the mission of peopling Old and New Castile with Carmelite houses. From now onwards there would be no rest for Mother or daughters.

In agreement with P. Baltasar Álvarez, Medina del Campo was chosen for the first foundation. Teresa took six nuns with her, two from St Joseph's and four from the Incarnation; among them were Isabel Arias and Teresa de Quezada who embarked on the adventure despite the opposition of all their relatives.

---

[1] Sb, V, c. xiii–16.   [2] Idem, 19.
[3] Idem, 16.   [4] SEC, vol. V, p. 336.

Avila: On a
cloudy day

Avila: The fortifications

The time came to say goodbye. The Mother would not show her feelings except to Our Lord. She retired to the hermitage of Christ at the column, the place where she had received his great promises. She begged him that on her return she might find the house holy and recollected, as she was now leaving it.

On the occasion of every departure she was to experience a heart-ache which she always succeeded in concealing. This time the pain of parting was severe. Ávila said that Mother Teresa was madder than ever; even the kindly Bishop had no encouragement to offer. But what were obstacles, however great, to such a fervent will, such wonder-fully forthright energy as hers? Her enthusiasm and tenacity in action found expression in a strength that was almost unbelievable: '. . . A firm and very determined act of the will not to relax until the end was attained, come what might, whatever happened, whatever hardship there might be, whosoever grumbled, even if one were to die *en route* or one felt the trials were beyond one's courage, or even if the world should fall to pieces!' [1]

She put considerations prompted by human reason on one side and decided once for all that it was no use being guided merely by natural wisdom: 'it's a hindrance. . . .' [2] For her the difficulty dis-appeared from the moment she took the decision to conquer it: 'at the beginning the effort it costs is only small.' [3] What this woman, who was always in poor health, called 'a small effort' were enormous labours in which she would cheerfully take her share. Hesitation was not part of her character: she knew at once what she wanted and she set to work straightway. When circumstances obliged her to mark time, she held on without allowing her determination to weaken by one iota.

Neither the talk in her native city nor the apparent coolness of her bishop in any way diminished her courage. She commissioned the prior of the convent of friars of Mitigated observance in Medina, P. Antonio de Heredia, to find a house for her, hoping that Our Lord would take in hand the business of paying for it, for on the day of departure she had to say:

'I've scarcely a *blanca* in my pocket; and who'd give credit to a gadabout like me?' [4]

Don Quixote also was to travel *sin blanca*, for he had never read in tales of chivalry of a knight errant carrying money with him. Teresa of Jesus had had too close an acquaintance with Amadis of Gaul

---

[1] Sb, C, c. xxi-2.
[2] Sb, V, c. xv-6.
[3] Sb, F, c. xiv-5.
[4] Sb, F, c. iii-2.

and Esplandián in the days when she was Doña Teresa de Ahumada to be troubled because she had not a well-filled purse.

Teresa was a great Castilian: in the course of her journeys where she is continually plunging into fresh adventures, she often reminds one of that other Castilian, Miguel de Cervantes, who a generation later would write the work in which the soul of his country was to become incarnate: its ideal of heroism in the person of a great madman attacking windmills, its practical realism in a good honest peasant.

Says Don Quixote:

'Don't you see coming towards us on a roan horse this knight in a golden helmet?'

'I see only,' answers Sancho Panza, 'a man mounted on a reddish-brown donkey like mine; he wears something shining on his head. . . .' A village barber using his shaving dish as a hat.

But Teresa, who prided herself on being 'not only poor in spirit, but completely mad' [1] for the love of Christ, also said: 'I am much more worried about what men can take from us than about what the devils can take from us . . .' [2]; she said that nuns whose prayer gave rise to peculiar manifestations should be made to eat meat: 'let us mind that her sanctity does not arise from melancholy. . . .' [3]

Whilst Miguel de Cervantes was to immortalize in two characters as different as possible from each other, the manifestation of the soul of Spain at its two most extreme human tendencies, Teresa of Jesus condensed in her single person by a miracle of tension, and for all future time, Spain's ideals and Spanish realism.

At the time when she began her great foundations Teresa was fifty-two. Religious life had in no way stifled that which had made her life in the world such a brilliant success: she was still beautiful, gay, lively, more eloquent than ever and endowed with a charm which it was useless to try and resist. In her, one experience did not efface a previous one, each merely added something to her amazing personality without taking away or destroying anything of it.

Teresa was determined not to allow the maladies of every sort from which she suffered continually and of which the daily vomiting was the least painful of consequences, to be an obstacle. During the five years of enclosure at St. Joseph's she had matured; without her even being aware of it, her very high state of prayer had equipped her for action. She was free now, in full liberty of spirit, mistress of herself

---

[1] Sb, C, c. ii–5.   [2] CTA, cxxxiv.

[3] CTA, lxxxvii. Cervantes was born in 1547—Tr.

because she was detached from all egoism, pride or self-interest: brave with the courage of her race, bold 'with the boldness God gives to the ant.' [1]

At break of day the streets of Ávila awoke to the sound of the screeching and jolting of three heavy carts; they contained the few essential household articles for the installation of the future convent of Medina del Campo, and a few nuns, proud of 'their leader.' [2] Servants and Julian de Ávila, the chaplain, followed on muleback. It was the 13th August 1567. The bells of every church rang out the angelus, as they had done for the birth of the babe Teresa, for her flight to martyrdom with her brother Rodrigo, and for the departure of Doña Teresa de Ahumada, accompanied by her brother Antonio, for the convent of the Incarnation. She was not alone this time, any more than she had been on the previous occasions: she was taking with her in the grey light of dawn souls who were on fire with love and fervour.

[1] Sb, F, cii–7.   [2] FR, L. II, c.v.

II

A FRIAR AND A HALF

THE same day at nightfall the little group, worn out by the jolting of the rickety carts along the bad roads, arrived at Arévalo, where they were to halt.

One of Teresa's friends was waiting for her: he whispered in her ear that everything was going as badly as possible, there was now no house for her, the one which Antonio de Heredia had rented for her was next door to a monastery of Augustinian friars who refused to have a convent so close to them, lest the good people round about should divide their alms into two portions.

Teresa begged him to keep the matter secret.

Her daughters from St Joseph's, María Bautista and Ana de los Ángeles, would go through fire and water for her, as would her cousins Ana and Inés de Tapia, but the others who had come from the Incarnation, Teresa de Quezada and Isabel Arias, were not imbued with the fighting spirit of the daughters of the house of Cepeda y Ahumada. Teresa was beginning even then to prefer to keep the difficulties for herself alone; she felt it was quite enough to have to face them without having to brace up the fainting courage of others in addition. But the idea of giving way in the face of difficulty never so much as crossed her mind: they would install themselves at whatever cost and would end by coming to an understanding with these Augustinians.

What they had to do now was to get in secrecy into the house to which they had been denied entrance, but Mother Teresa was handicapped by all the paraphernalia of her carts, her mules and her nuns. In order to eliminate noise, the little band was reduced to two nuns only, with P. Antonio de Heredia who had come to meet the foundresses and Julian de Ávila who would have died of grief had he missed such an expedition. A man as much devoted to the cause of the foundation as he was to gossip, he was itching to have adventures to recount:

The Medina del Campo foundation! What a business! We arrived at Medina at midnight; at the entrance to the town we had to get down and walk, for our only remaining cart made a din in the night calculated to awaken the entire population. There we were in the streets, friars and nuns, laden with the sacred vessels and vestments necessary for saying the first Mass and fitting up the chapel: we looked like gipsies who had been robbing churches; if we had run into a police patrol we should have spent the rest of the night in jail. Luckily the only people who saw us were the sort of rogues who prowl about in the dark because they have good cause to prefer night to day. They were ready with a few pleasantries of the usual sort. We didn't utter a word but stepped out briskly.

We had to wake up the caretaker and summon him with all urgency to open the house and clear it for us. O Lord! We had scarcely got in when we thanked God with all our hearts: he saved us in the nick of time from six bulls for the next day's *corrida* which were dashing madly across the town to the arena.

It was nearly dawn. You should just have seen the prioress, the sisters, all of us, some with brooms, others on ladders busy putting up hangings or fixing the bell in place. We had no nails and it wasn't the moment to go and buy any. Mother Teresa made good use of those she found in the walls; somehow or other the place was cleared and the porch began to look more or less presentable.

All that now remained was to get the Vicar-General to come and give his confirmation that the convent was being founded in accordance with the Bishop's authorization: they got him out of bed.

The altar was dressed, the chapel well decorated, but all the light we had was one poor candle and in the darkness we might well wonder if the installation of the chapel really had been made inside the walls and not in the middle of the street. . . .

As soon as it was daylight, we joyfully pealed the bell for Mass, one stroke after another. Those who heard the peal came in to find a convent sprung up during the night. They were left speechless with astonishment. Soon there were so many people that our little porch was filled to overflowing.

The nuns had to make way for the crowd but where were they to go? Fortunately one staircase had not been pulled down, and they took refuge there, hiding behind the door. The chinks in the woodwork served them as choir to follow the Office, parlour to receive visitors, confessional to confess their sins and prison to weep in. . . .[1]

Such was the account of these memorable events given many times over by Julian de Ávila. Daylight revealed that the house consisted only of a few half-crumbling walls. The Blessed Sacrament would be exposed right in the open in a town where the fair attracted merchants from all over Europe, many heretics among them, at a time when the

[1] JA quoted SEC, vol. V, pp. 352-3.

Lutherans were asking for nothing better than the opportunity to commit sacrilege.

They had never seen Mother Teresa of Jesus happier—or in greater distress. She was happy because once Mass was said, the Convent of St Joseph of Medina del Campo was well and truly founded, whether the Augustinians liked it or not: the Vicar-General's approval anticipated any attempt at expulsion on their part. But all the same His Majesty was in great danger. Teresa did not sleep and through a fan-light kept vigil by the Blessed Sacrament.

It was going to take no end of time to reconstruct the dilapidated house. Where were they to lodge in the meantime? Medina, on the high tide of prosperity, was full to overflowing with travellers and visitors. There was nothing to let, then, and they had no money at all.

The Lord touched the heart of a merchant, Blas de Medina, and he offered the 'wanderers' a storey in his house and a room 'large and gilded,' for use as a chapel, until their convent should be ready.

The Lord also raised up benefactors for them.

And all the little group managed to live and the work of reconstruction went forward satisfactorily. The Tapias and their two companions from the Incarnation rejoined the infant community. Teresa made their beds, cleaned and swept their cells, saying to María Bautista who was helping her:

'Daughter, it is only right that we should wait on these ladies who have been good enough to come and help us. . . .' [1]

Teresa had already made some friends at Medina del Campo. The Carmelite friars of St Anne's monastery of Mitigated observance frequently came to see her, in particular the prior. P. Antonio de Heredia had legitimate reason to hope that he would eventually attain the very highest rank in the Order of Our Lady of Mount Carmel and people saw in him a future provincial. He was by no means displeased at this and his complete self-satisfaction was expressed on his countenance. He was tall, with a handsome face and fine carriage, as careful of his person as was possible for one who, while he never forgot he was of gentle birth, was also a friar; at the same time this former student of Salamanca was a good religious, 'studious and fond of his cell.' [2]

His meeting with Mother Teresa made a deep impression on him: the Carmelite's black and very much worn veil, her habit of coarse frieze—she insisted on wearing a darned one—her cheap, common rope-soled sandals, her joy in sacrificing every comfort and convenience, to which she had been as much accustomed as he, reminded

[1] CP, vol. III, p. 292.   [2] Sb, F, c. iii–16.

him that he too had wanted to gain heaven by an austere life. She who
was already known as the *Madre Fundadora*, the Mother Foundress, received him in the gilded room of Blas the merchant which did duty
as parlour in addition to its other use, unless sometimes he chose to go
with her to the scene of the work on the dilapidated house: she super-
intended the work of reconstruction with an energy that was astound-
ing in a woman. The convent began to take shape. It was something
like a country cottage, it was so rustic—some compared it to a golden-
brown loaf or a honeycomb—but solidly built around its patio with
good, light cells and vaulted refectory. Each time Antonio de Heredia
was increasingly sorry to leave Mother Teresa and in his monastery of
well-fed, well-housed friars, the permitted comforts of the Mitigation
seemed to him a heavy burden. The Mother spoke of Our Lord with
so much love and a fervour that was so contagious that he burned to
do more in God's service. Theologian as he was, he marvelled to hear
her say things about prayer that were so sublime and yet in perfect
conformity with reason. He experienced a joy that was unusual for
him and was convinced that the Carmelite was enlightened by the
Holy Spirit. 'She expressed herself with a force that was more than
human without departing from her infinite sweetness and charity.'[1]
And so the day when, with the sole idea of asking his advice, she spoke
to him of P. Rubeo's letters, authorizing her to found two monasteries
of men in conformity with the primitive Rule and of the difficulty in
which she found herself for want of friars, Antonio de Heredia
exclaimed:

'I will be the first.'[2]

Teresa thought that the brilliant prior was joking, and laughed
heartily: could he seriously be considering a change that would be so
hard for him, especially after fifty-seven years of comfortable existence? But he insisted, thus displaying more humility and spirit of
penance than might have been expected of a friar so nice in his ways
and dress and noted for the artistic taste with which he decorated his
cell.[3] The Mother did not fail to tell him that she did not think him
made for this heroic undertaking:

'Each one has his own way, Father, and you are following the one
which suits you. No doubt you do aspire to austerities. . . . But there
is a "but" . . .'[4]

The prior was obstinate. He announced his intention of entering
with the Carthusians: he even had the Provincial's authorization. No

[1] SEC, vol. I, p. 87, n. 1.   [2] Sb, F, c. iii-16.
[3] SEC, vol. V, p. 406.   [4] Idem.

austerity frightened him, he was ready to take his oath on it. Teresa, who was not to be satisfied with words alone, asked Antonio de Heredia to try to keep to what he was promising for a whole year, during which he would practise the most severe penances. Her satisfaction at having one friar at least to count on was not unmixed with anxiety.

One day, however, there arrived a young Carmelite friar who 'pleased her much'[1] from their first meeting. Juan de San Matías had just said his first Mass at St Anne's monastery. Since then he had felt such a strong call to the solitary life of a hermit that he, too, had decided to enter the Charterhouse of Paular where the cenobitical life was carried out with the utmost possible austerity.

Teresa knew that Juan de San Matías was the son of a *hidalgo*, Gonzalo de Yepes, who had been cast off and 'abhorred' by his family for having married a girl as beautiful and virtuous as she was poor, so poor that she earned her livelihood by weaving silk. And this grandson of one of the men-at-arms of John II, this nephew of an Inquisitor at Toledo, with three of his relatives canons at the cathedral, had likewise become an artisan. He died young and Catalina was left alone to bring up her children with the utmost difficulty on the earnings from her weaving, at which she worked day and night.

Juan, the fervent and emaciated young friar who stood before Teresa, was the youngest of Catalina Yepes' sons. 'Fathers whose name carried weight' had spoken highly of his learning and piety and one of his companions had even added 'wonderful things about his kind of life.' Teresa, however, was surprised to find him so small—his height was less than five feet—as she was at the breadth of his forehead and the fire in his dark eyes. She who was such a good talker also knew how to listen: she let Fray Juan de San Matías talk freely and she praised God for what she heard. For himself, although he belonged to the Mitigated observance, he kept the primitive Rule of the Order. Not only was he unafraid of its rigours, but he was not prepared to live a life that was not austere.

The eager spontaneity of Teresa's character would not allow her to wait for a second interview to tell him about the great project of the Reform; it was not necessary for him to ask her to allow him to be one of the first Discalced: her face flushed with joy, she 'begged him earnestly'[2] to be patient a little longer before entering Paular; Our Lord could not fail to give them a house in which to found this monastery of Carmelite friars soon. Would it not be an additional perfection for him to be able to serve God as he wished without doffing the habit of

[1] Sb, F, c. iii–17.   [2] Idem.

a son of Our Lady, Mother of God, whom since childhood he had called 'the Morning Star'?

He gave her his word that he would wait, but with an impetuosity not unworthy of Teresa herself this boy of twenty-four added:

'On condition that I haven't to wait too long. . . .'[1]

That evening Mother Teresa was full of joy and as always when she was particularly happy, the salt of her Castilian wit broke out into a quaint phrase:

'Daughters, I have a friar and a half.'[2]

But the half friar was not tiny Fray Juan. If he alone had been in question, with God's help, without a *blanca*, without a house, she would have set out that very day to found her monastery of Discalced Carmelite friars. She only delayed a little because she was 'less satisfied with the prior. . . .'[3]

She saw Juan de San Matías again. The better she knew him the more she liked him. 'Although he is small, he is great in the eyes of God. . . . He is full of good sense, well fitted for our kind of life and so I think Our Lord had predestined him to it. There isn't a friar who doesn't speak well of him for he has lived in a great spirit of penance. It seems as if Our Lord is leading him by the hand and in spite of a few differences in the course of this business—I alone was the cause for I have allowed myself to get irritated with him—I've never come across any imperfection in him. And he's courageous.'[4]

Such is, in brief, the picture of the relations of the Mother Foundress with him whom she afterwards called 'my little Seneca' and whose logic and stoical independence 'irritated her' more than once. But years slipped by and she still had not discovered any imperfections in Juan de San Matías, now become John of the Cross. His courage continued to make her marvel and in the end she saw him 'reach to the greatest height of sanctity a human creature can attain to in this life.'[5]

Good Julian de Ávila summed up the matter: 'In this town of Medina del Campo, a sort of fair where you find everything, the Mother found the cornerstone of her monasteries of Discalced friars.'[6]

[1] Idem. [2] SEC, vol. V, p. 30. [3] Idem.
[4] CTA, x. [5] Quoted BRJ, p. 316. [6] SEC, vol. V, p. 406.

THE WORLD'S GREAT ONES

DOÑA LUISA DE LA CERDA had been 'very fond' of Teresa of Jesus ever since the time she had been her guest on the eve of the foundation of St Joseph's at Ávila; she offered her hospitality whenever she had business in Toledo. In her house Teresa went about so cheerfully and simply, taking such good care not to betray the secrets of her inner life by any outward show of feeling, that when the daughter of the Duke of Medinaceli began to think of gaining a little merit by founding a convent on her property at Malagón, she said:

'It must be a convent of Carmelites of the Reform. I did think of María de Jesús, but I don't want to have such a great saint to found my house. . . .'

An opportunity of humility for Teresa! No, indeed, she was not such a great saint! The penances imposed by María de Jesús at the convent of La Imagen seemed to her so little calculated to advance spiritual progress that she agreed to spend three months at Alcalá de Henares, in the hope of moderating her excesses.

'Exact much in the way of the practice of virtue but not in that of penance,' such was the principle she enjoined. She added: 'This perhaps proves that I am only a mediocre penitent.' What it proved was her intelligence: to sublimate one's instincts instead of ruthlessly crushing them calls for as much lucidity as it does strength of soul. Formerly, when at the Incarnation, Teresa had practised corporal macerations with an ardour that was truly terrible; the walls of her cell were bespattered with her blood. But in every excess the devil can find a foothold and she now saw that to submit one's will absolutely to all the prescriptions of the Rule was a better thing than to ill-treat the body. In the hierarchy of perfections she placed obedience above austerity.

Her high state of prayer and the signs of heaven's favour would have remained her secret alone, if the raptures which came on her in public had not betrayed her and if her fear of being the victim of illusion or deceived by the devil had not brought her to give an account of her visions to her confessors. She strove to compensate a reputation which made too much stir for her liking by an attitude that was very simple and even gay.

She liked to disappoint the hopes of those who came to see her moved solely by curiosity. When she was in Madrid, staying with Doña Leonor de Mascarenhas, former lady-in-waiting to the Empress Isabel and governess to Philip II, a Portuguese, all the pious people at court—for piety was in the fashion—flocked to meet 'the saint of Ávila.' They hoped at least to see her work a miracle, fall into ecstasy or be lifted off her feet and carried up to the ceiling. But all Teresa of Jesus let them see was her modest and courteous graciousness with perhaps a touch of studied simplicity. Those who expected to hear sublime phrases from her lips were very much surprised to hear her exclaim: 'What fine streets there are in Madrid!'—or talk only of the rain or the fine weather.[1]

But the Descalzas Reales, where Teresa went to visit Princess Juana, the King's sister, were delighted beyond words:

'God be praised! He has granted us to see a saint whom we can all imitate. She talks like us, sleeps and eats as we do, and her conversation is unpretentious. . . .'[2]

If Doña Luisa fell into the error of thinking that a pleasing manner was incompatible with being a 'great saint,' María de Salazar made no such mistake.

The little maid of honour who on the Mother's previous visit had slipped pious verses into her hand was now twenty; she was still charming, just a tiny bit over-keen about literature and Latin, but most gifted. It was when Teresa visited Toledo to discuss the Malagón foundation with Doña Luisa that she accepted as a novice the girl who was to become María de San José, the best loved of all her daughters and one of her most remarkable prioresses. 'Her tact and sweetness always attracted me to her,' said María. 'Her wonderful life and the way she spoke would have moved the heart of a stone. . . .'[3]

Teresa was firmly opposed to Doña Luisa de la Cerda's wish: a convent could not find sufficient to live on at Malagón. Who would buy the sisters' work there? Doña Luisa offered revenues which Teresa firmly refused: Carmelites were to depend for their daily bread, as they did for their spiritual sustenance, on no one but their Father in heaven. P. Domingo Báñez had to intervene. He blamed Teresa for obstinacy in refusing to found a house in a place where Our Lord would be well served merely to avoid breaking a law about work which she herself had laid down. The holy Council authorized her to accept revenues on condition that the nuns possessed nothing as

---

[1] SEC, vol. V, p. 72, n. 2.   [2] Idem, p. 133, n. 4.
[3] MJ quoted SEC, vol. V, p. 218, n. 3.

individuals: was not her attitude as much an attachment as any other, an attachment to her own idea of poverty?

She was obliged to yield. Thus at the outset of her work of foundation she was often forced to accept patrons, benefactors or benefactresses. She strove to do without them as much as possible, preferring that her houses should have to struggle with difficulties rather than be enslaved to the caprices of the great.

In exchange for the revenues they gave or the houses they bought, the patrons of a convent would reserve the right of entry there for subjects of their own choosing and wanted to impose other hampering restrictions. When such patrons were reasonable and sincere, like Doña Luisa de la Cerda or the Bishop of Ávila's sister, Doña María de Mendoza, the Foundress's tact could smooth away the difficulties, but with the Princess of Éboli, benefactress of Pastrana, events took a dramatic turn.

For Teresa of Jesus did not give in to the great ones of this world. The solicitude of which she was the object on the part of her noble protectresses 'was enough to kill' her, and to her 'if it is not with God and for God, all rest is wearisome.' [1] She always spoke her mind; the Bishop himself, Don Álvaro de Mendoza, did not come off scot free when he thought it best to remain neutral in the fierce quarrel with the relatives of Doña Casilda de Padilla who, at the age of twelve, had run away from her husband to enter Carmel: 'It seems to me that Our Lord defends his daughters better than Your Lordship defends your subjects.' [2]

As to Teresa, no one in the world would force her to take a subject with whom she was not completely satisfied. She proved her greatness as foundress and organizer by her determination only to accept as novices those who were first-class from every point of view.

> . . . If Your Ladyship commands me, there's nothing more to be said, I shall obey. But I do ask Your Ladyship to reflect seriously and to want nothing but the best for your house. Where the nuns are few in number, the quality must be proportionately higher. I can find subjects everywhere, but I haven't dared to take one—for Valladolid—for I want them perfect. On my own account I shall not accept either of the two of whom you speak to me. I find in them neither sanctity, courage nor talents sufficient to be an advantage for the house. And if the house is to lose by them, why does Your Ladyship want us to take them? If it's simply to extricate them from a difficult situation, there's no lack of convents. . . . For

[1] Sb, V, c. xxvi–1.   [2] Cf. CTA, liii.

the love of God, I beg Your Ladyship to consider all these points and not to forget that the good of all must always be preferred to the interests of one person alone. If Your Ladyship commands this thing, your orders will be obeyed, but, should matters not turn out well, the entire responsibility will be yours. May Our Lord arrange the matter for his greater glory and may he enlighten Your Ladyship.[1]

An unmistakable refusal nicely sandwiched in between two compliments. The benefactress, this time Doña María de Mendoza, did not insist. One of the candidates had only one eye which caused Teresa to declare:

'I don't want any one-eyed nuns!'[2]

There are cases where charity consists in putting the good of all before the interests of one person alone. Too many convents were simply a refuge for poor girls who were no use in the world—this was one of the causes of their laxity: in the reformed Carmels Teresa wanted there to be room for nothing but the love of God. At the beginning there were thirteen nuns in each, later twenty-one, but no more: there was no room for mediocrity or for concessions; the brides of Christ must at least have the qualities which any ordinary man has a right to expect in his wife, and fervour in addition. On this point Teresa never yielded in the slightest degree.

'The Lord showed me such great favours while I was there and that in turn gave me so much liberty of spirit and made me so despise what I saw, that in my dealings with these great ladies whom I might have considered it an honour to serve, I kept as much liberty as if I had been their equal.'[3]

'She spoke to them with a "natural majesty," '[4] just as if she had indeed been one of them.

She never put aside this natural majesty, even in her relations with the King.

The Princess Doña Juana undertook to transmit to Philip II a message which Our Lord had given Teresa for him. It concluded thus: 'Remember, Sire, that Saul, too, was anointed, and yet he was rejected!'[5]

In her *Autobiography* she addressed sovereigns as if she too were a queen:

Blessed is the soul to whom Our Lord gives an understanding of his truth! What a realm that would be for kings! They would do far

[1] CTA, xxxiv.
[2] SEC, vol. VII, p. 85, n. 2.
[3] Sb, V, c. xxxiv-3.
[4] FR. L. IV, c. i.
[5] Quoted LV, p. 433.

better to strive to acquire that, rather than to seek great power. What righteousness there would then be in their kingdom! How many evils would be averted! . . . In those conditions no one would fear to lose life or honour for the love of God. . . . To increase faith in souls or to enlighten heretics, such a king would willingly lose a thousand kingdoms. For to gain a kingdom of which there shall be no end is a more advantageous thing. . . .[1]

The King, Don Felipe, received the Carmelite's message 'respectfully.' This king was only too ready to lose 'a thousand kingdoms' to gain one, and the saint's words did but echo a dispatch which he charged his ambassador in Rome to communicate secretly to the Pope:

. . . I would lose all my realms and give my own life a hundred times over rather than suffer the least schism in religion or in the service of God; I have not the least intention of reigning over heretics. I intend to try to smoothe out the religious difficulties in the Low Countries without recourse to arms, if it is still possible, for I see clearly that a war would involve the country in total devastation; but if matters cannot be put right without armed intervention, I am resolved to take up arms and take part in the battles myself; nothing shall hinder me, neither the ruin of this country nor that of the lands I possess elsewhere.[2]

Teresa of Jesus used love to bring about God's triumph, the King thought he could bring it about by bloodshed; Teresa passed her life in penance and prayer for the redemption of the heretics whom the King was causing to be massacred; Teresa hoped that the King would make Spain a beacon light, but he made it a stake. Saint and king used the same words but with different meanings for they lived on different planes.[3] Had Teresa been able to form some idea of the world's intrigues, she would have hesitated and trembled to advise the mighty and would have shuddered to learn of the veneration the Duke of Alba, who had shed so much blood, had for her; she would have begun to wonder to what cruelties the reading of such a work of love as the account of her life, which he was so eager to learn about, might move him.

The political unity of the vast kingdom which was now about to break up was too closely linked with its unity of belief for the work of spreading the Gospel not to take advantage of the opportunity of using

---

[1] Sb, V, c. xxi–1.   [2] Quoted SH, p. 229.
[3] For a different view of Philip II, see Gachard: *Lettres de Philippe II à ses Filles* (Paris, 1884)—Tr.

military methods: people could only fight with the weapons they were
familiar with. The intermingling of the spiritual and temporal in
government has always had the most disastrous consequences and
Philip II made a further mistake when he replied to the proposal to
abandon the Philippine Isles, which were ruinous to colonize, more as
if he were a monk than a king: 'To win a single soul to God, I would
sacrifice all the treasures of the Indies and if that were not sufficient I
would throw in Spain, too. . . . For to me and my descendants the
Holy See has transmitted the mission of the apostles, which is to preach
the Gospel; so that it may triumph to the ends of the world and
beyond . . . without the intervention of any hope of gain.' [1]

Philip II ruined Spain without succeeding in making the spirit of
the Gospel triumphant in the world, for it was not without reason
that Christ commanded Peter to put back his sword into its sheath.
An army of mercenaries even if Friars Preachers walk before it will
never open men's hearts to the word of Christ. In their convents
Mother Teresa and her daughters fought more effectively.

Teresa of Jesus made use of the great and powerful but never ceded
one inch of her independence or judgement. 'What it was necessary
to say was said and their faults were pointed out to them with no small
courage.' [2] Only the fear of hurting others restrained her, but when
the good of souls was in question she turned such fear aside. There is
no doubt that of all the devout ladies of high degree who, because they
revered her, imagined they had the right to give her orders, Doña
María de Mendoza was nearest to her heart, and yet she was the one
whom she most liked to take up sharply: 'I hope to find Your Ladyship more mistress of herself: you have the strength of character. . . .
Your Ladyship would gain from being with me, just as I gain from
the presence of the Father Visitor. As my religious superior, he tells
me the truth about myself, and I'm willing to do the same for Your
Ladyship, for I don't lack courage and am accustomed to your not
minding my frankness. Ah! If Your Ladyship had as much nobility of
soul as of bearing, how lightly you would esteem what are called
trials!' [3]

She sugared the pill with a dusting of compliments, for God himself had taught her how little case should be made of creatures however
good they may be, and how it is sometimes necessary to use a grain of
diplomacy.[4] Great ladies and powerful lords gave large sums to her
convents. She was grateful to them for doing so, but did not fail to

[1] Quoted SH, p. 153.   [2] FR, L. IV, c. i.
[3] Cf. CTA, xxxv.   [4] CTA, cclxx.

tell them that 'to give *reales* is nothing: you scarcely feel what you give. . . .'[1]

Doña María de Mendoza and her brother the Bishop of Ávila gave her *reales* but they also gave her constant proof of deep friendship. Don Álvaro was so kind to the reformed Carmel that Teresa was afraid he would get into debt through helping them. Her letters telling him of the affairs of the Order are a mixture of respect and fun, of piety and of intelligent instinct for business:

'Your Lordship is surrounded by holy people, you should then recognize those who are not holy and you forget about me. But in heaven I think Your Lordship will see that you had a duty to this miserable sinner. . . .'

The good Bishop's brother, Don Bernardino de Mendoza, had offered the Mother Foundress a fine house in Valladolid to set up a convent there, but Doña Luisa de la Cerda insisted so strongly on her beginning the Malagón foundation that she agreed to do so. Doña Luisa gave them adequate revenues and a house which enabled the nuns to live decently and with some convenience.

Accordingly Teresa left Toledo and set out for Malagón along the road which passes over the high rocky hills, sloping down again to the bottom of the valleys where the vine and olive grow in the drab ochre-coloured or reddish earth. It is the road to the south along which, village by village, the granite-built houses of Castile give place increasingly to façades limewashed in white or blue with geraniums climbing up the balconies.

Teresa took with her in her completely closed cart two of her nuns from St Joseph's and four from the Incarnation.

After a few days in Doña Luisa's mansion—absolutely necessary to allow time for the Mother Foundress to superintend the final preparations herself—the convent of St Joseph of Malagón was inaugurated on 11th April 1568.

Inaugurated, but not altogether to Teresa's liking. Too close to the square where the markets and fairs with all their din were held, it afforded insufficient possibility of silence and recollection. . . .

The whole village took part in the opening celebrations, particularly as the Carmelite, distressed at the ignorance of the village girls there, had sent for a woman who was 'a good Theatine,' that is to say, well acquainted with the methods of the Society of Jesus, to teach them to sew and other useful hand-work: 'under this pretext she was

[1] CTA, xiv.

also able to teach them Christian doctrine and how to serve God well, all things very profitable to them.'[1] Teresa thus showed that in this case she considered work as important as prayer; at that time this was tantamount to a revolution.

But Don Bernardino de Mendoza died suddenly very shortly after having partially redeemed a frivolous existence by his gift of the Valladolid convent. Teresa would have stayed on at Malagón but Our Lord called her to order: she was leaving a soul to linger suffering in purgatory. So she set off with all possible speed, although nothing was ready for the new foundation.

All the haste in the world could not shorten the length of the journey and Teresa was forced to make certain détours: she went back towards Toledo, passed through Ávila where she collected María de la Cruz, Antonia del Espíritu Santo—of the 'shock troops' of St Joseph's—and Isabel de la Cruz, a future prioress, and stopped at Medina where His Majesty's injunction became even more pressing. 'This soul is suffering greatly. . . .'[2] She finally arrived at Valladolid at the beginning of August.

It was a fine house standing in the midst of vineyards and lovely orchards, but situated outside the town itself, at Río de Olmos, on the banks of the river and surrounded by unhealthy swamps.

Ought she to hesitate? There was no time, Our Lord urged her forward: Don Bernardino would not go to heaven until the day the first Mass was said. Tertian or quartan fevers notwithstanding! The authorization of the Ordinary was slow in arriving; Teresa decided to do without it and hastened to have a Mass said, not expecting, however, that the promise of heavenly glory for Don Bernardino would be fulfilled before the day of the official foundation. Doubtless Our Lord intended to do without official authorizations: at the Communion, behind Julian de Ávila who was holding the sacred Host, Teresa saw 'Don Bernardino, his face resplendent with joy.'[3] He thanked her for what she had done to release him from purgatory and went up to heaven. Teresa, in ecstasy, was caught up to heaven with him.

It would have been bliss to stay there. When she came to her senses again after such raptures, which she endeavoured to disguise from those around by asking for a glass of water or some remedy for her heart trouble whereas the radiant expression of her face deceived no one, she resumed the routine of daily life, but sorrowfully: it was for God's sake alone that she took up the heavy burden again.

[1] CTA, vi. [2] Sb, F, c. x–3. [3] Sb, F, c. x–5.

The house at Río de Olmos was delightful, but the Carmelites caught marsh fever there. It was essential to move elsewhere. What did it matter if the installation was already finished? They would begin over again.

Doña María de Mendoza gave them another house in Valladolid itself: grilles, enclosure, chapel, cells, offices, were set up anew. Teresa took special care that in each new convent founded the practice of perfect recollection and exact observance of the Rule should be established.

One day the bell failed to ring at the appointed hour; she was angry:

'If things are like that while I am alive, and when I am present, what will they be when I'm dead?' [1]

It was necessary that she should learn to desire to live, in order that the Reform should be established on unshakable foundations.

[1] SEC, vol. V, p. 79, n. 2.

IV

SO MANY CROSSES!
SO MANY SKULLS!

WHILE she was talking things over with Doña María de Mendoza at Valladolid, or while at Alba de Tormes the Duchess, Doña María Enríquez, invited her into what might be called the holy of holies of earthly riches, one name, 'Duruelo,' was refreshment and joy to Teresa of Jesus.

At Alba de Tormes the Carmelite could not suppress a slight shudder as she entered the small room where the treasures of the Dukes of Alba were displayed. Everything around her shone, glittered, sparkled; there was nothing but the fiery gleam of jewels with their lustre and brilliance: 'What good can this heap of objects be?' And then she praised the Creator for the variety of the 'things' his creatures had made. The Duchess drew her attention to the gold chasing, the magnificent diamonds, the purity of the. emeralds, expecting that Teresa would admire them, and was very much astonished when she said shortly afterwards:

'There was so much to see that I've forgotten everything, I've retained no more impressions of these jewels and precious stones than if I had never seen them and I couldn't tell you what they were like." [1]

But as long as she lived she never forgot the poorest thing she had seen in the world: the little village of Duruelo, scarcely twenty hearths, situated in the depths of a valley of Old Castile and, in this hamlet, a *casita*, whose ceiling was so low that one had to stoop to go into the lean-to which served as choir, so poverty-stricken a place that it reminded one of the stable at Bethlehem. But Our Lord poured forth his spirit and his grace there in overflowing abundance and the first two subjects of the Order, Fray John of the Cross and Fray Antonio de Jesús lived there 'in great joy.' [2]

For at Duruelo the first monastery of Discalced Carmelite friars had just been founded.

A nobleman had offered Teresa a tumbledown old place in this isolated village, so far off the beaten track that when she went to visit

---

[1] Sb, M, VI, c. iv-8.   [2] Sb, F, c. xiv-3.

it accompanied by Antonia del Espíritu Santo and Julian de Ávila, the two Carmelites and their chaplain wandered about all day, jolted by their mules under the August sun which beat fiercely down on man and beast. 'When we thought we had arrived, we had still as far to go as we had already travelled. . . . I shall never forget how tired we were nor what confusion we were in. . . .' [1]

At nightfall they came to an oasis—green chestnut trees and running water, but they did not find the peaceful rest they had hoped for: songs and shouts, the thrumming of tambourines and the shrill sound of the flute came from the house where shepherds, tillers of the fields, farm labourers and gleaners were celebrating the harvest. When the Mother appeared at the door with her black veils, very erect in her darned habit, the din ceased but only for a few minutes: and it was in this din that she visited the dirtiest and most cluttered-up place she had seen in her life: later on, she would see many others.

A brief glance sufficed. When Teresa had made up her mind, no disappointment could damp her enthusiasm. Her talent for organization immediately began to work:

> The house consisted of an entrance porch of reasonable size, a room with a lean-to and a small kitchen: that was the whole of our monastery. I calculated that it was possible to make the chapel in the porch, the choir in the lean-to and a dormitory in the room. My companion, although a much better person than myself and one who had a real love of penance, would not allow me to think of founding a monastery in such conditions. She said to me: 'You can take it for granted, Mother, that not even the most fervent would be able to put up with it. Give it up.' [2]

But in the church where she spent the night to escape from the noise and dirt, the Foundress could see with her imagination the Carmel rising from the wretched hovel where peasants drunk with 'the wine of the earth' were dancing with the girls.

She hastened to Medina del Campo with all possible speed. The prior, Antonio de Heredia, had shown an admirable constancy in the year of trial, Teresa was beginning to change her opinion of him; and Juan de San Matías, who had indeed been practising mortification by controlling his impatience, would not have to wait much longer.

Immediately upon her arrival Teresa sent for her friar and her half-friar and kept back nothing of the deplorable state of the little house. It was the prior who first exclaimed:

---

[1] Sb, F, c. xiii-3.   [2] Idem.

'Not only am I willing to live there, but in a pigsty if it should be necessary.' [1]

Teresa's heart almost burst with love for the poverty of the thing, the stuff of which saints are made.

Dear God! How small a thing are buildings and exterior comforts in our inner life! Fathers and Sisters, I ask you for the love of God to be always very modest and not to want vast and sumptuous houses. . . .[2] Great houses are ill suited to poor, insignificant people like ourselves. . . . Remember that everything will crumble to pieces on Judgement Day and it isn't right that the house of thirteen poor women should make a lot of noise when it falls. . . . I have seen more spirituality and exterior joy when the body has scarcely the bare necessities of life than when it has all it wants in a great house. We only live in a cell. What does it matter to us whether it's spacious and well built or not? We don't spend our time there looking at the walls. We shall not always live in it, our time there will be no longer than our life on earth. . . . To live poorly, like our good Jesus, requires only a small effort and that a pleasant one. . . :[3]

Fray John said nothing, but he offered to set out immediately.

That day, Teresa gave her nuns the rough brown frieze, and the habits of the Discalced friars were cut out and made up.

The following day, the Mother Foundress, behind the parlour grilles, in the presence of the nuns in their long white mantles as, lighted candle in hand, they sang the *Veni Creator Spiritus*, herself gave the habit to Juan de San Matías. He solemnly renounced the Mitigation, promising to live according to the Rule of Our Lady of Carmel, in obedience, chastity and poverty.

And, barefooted, at long last slave only of his vows, at last free from the fetters of the world and material things, he who would in future be known as John of the Cross, wended his way to the *casita* of Duruelo.

The prior Antonio de Heredia who was now Antonio de Jesús joined him there soon afterwards.

It was Fray John of the Cross who was 'the first.' Fray Antonio was not too well pleased at this and John in his charity allowed him the pleasure of boasting that he was Discalced before anyone else. He was also quite willing for him to be prior of the Duruelo house, but quietly stood out against the twists and turns given to the primitive Rule by a man who had lived more than thirty years in the Mitigation. That was why Mother Teresa put all her energies into obtaining Constitutions for

[1] Sb, F, c. xiii-4.   [2] Sb, F, c. xiv-5.   [3] Idem.

the friars, 'for some were of one opinion and others of another,' and
the Foundress was often ' considerably troubled by their differences.' [1]

All this did not prevent Antonio de Jesús from chaffing Fray John
because he had received the habit at the hands of a woman, the very
same who, at Valladolid, when she was superintending the completion
of the construction of the enclosure, instructed the young friar on the
manner of life in monasteries of this sort, and on everything else, 'our
mortifications, as well as our fraternal friendship and the recreations
which we took together.' [2] In these directives as in those Teresa of
Jesus gave her nuns, the keyword was 'moderation.'

Afterwards when Fray John of the Cross, now Padre John, was
away in distant Andalusia (it was only in the beginning that all the
Discalced Carmelite friars were called Fray), she remembered the rapt
attention with which he had listened to her words. 'He was so perfect
that I could have learnt more from him than he from me; however,
I did not take the opportunity, for I was busy explaining to him the
manner of life of the sisters.' [3] There is a note of regret in these reminiscences: it would have been delightful to listen to him who at that time
called himself her disciple but who was already imbued with the spirit
that would make him the 'Father of her soul'; but it was urgent to get
on with the work of construction.

A few months later, taking advantage of a journey to Toledo, the
Mother Foundress went a little out of her way and arrived one fine
morning at Duruelo. They did not expect her, but she found the prior,
Antonio de Jesús, in front of the monastery busy sweeping, like a simple
lay-brother, his face lit up with the joy that comes from casting aside
vainglory. He led Teresa towards the chapel:

> I was amazed at the spirit which God had infused into the place.
> Two merchants who had travelled with me did nothing but weep.
> There were so many crosses! So many skulls!
> I shall never forget a little wooden cross above the holy-water
> stoup. The picture representing Christ which was glued to it,
> though only of paper, inspired one with more devotion than if it
> had been an exquisite carving. . . . On either side of the chapel
> Fray Antonio and Fray John had erected two hermitages so small
> that they could only sit or lie prostrate there; they had filled the
> hermitages with hay, for it was very cold and the roof was almost
> touching their heads; through two garret windows they could see
> the altar; they had a stone for pillow, their crosses and their skulls.

---

[1] Sb, F, c. xxiii–12.   [2] Sb, F, c. xiii–5.   [3] Idem.

I learned that after Matins until Prime, instead of going to rest they remained there so absorbed in prayer that they sometimes came into chapel for Prime with their habits covered with snow, without noticing it. . . .[1]

In 'this little stable of Bethlehem,'[2] Teresa found once more the spirit of the Fathers of the Desert, with their austerity and love.

This house, which was now spotless, whitewashed, the dust laid and the floors polished, to conform with the Foundress's ideas of cleanliness, had already become an object of reverence to the good folk of the neighbourhood. These friars who went out preaching the Gospel for ten leagues around, always barefoot whether in puddles of water or in the snow, made themselves so much loved that 'it was wonderful to see the peasants bringing baskets with bread and all they required to eat.'[3] And Teresa thought herself in paradise, as did Julian de Ávila who was privileged to spend several days there.

Each of the brethren praised the austerity and perfections of the others. It was well known that Fray John took more pleasure in eating dry bread than if he had been eating pheasants. And he surpassed the requirements of the primitive Rule in austerity. One day when, ill and almost exhausted with fatigue, he had begged Fray Antonio de Jesús to allow him to take his collation a little sooner than usual, he was so remorseful at having thus yielded to the demands of his wretched body that he was not satisfied with accusing himself of it in Chapter; at supper-time his brethren saw him come into the refectory with bare shoulders and discipline in hand; he threw himself on his knees on some broken tiles which he had scattered over the floor and scourged himself until he collapsed with weakness and pain on the ground, which was red with his blood.

Antonio de Jesús sent him to his cell to pray God to forgive men their wretchedness.

This story and others like it frightened Teresa: 'Weak and vile as I am, I begged them not to give themselves up to penance with so much rigour. . . . I was afraid the devil might take this means to make an end of them before what I hoped for from these Fathers had been effected. . . .'[4] It was not the first time she attributed excessive mortification to the inspiration of the devil. 'He sees the harm they can do him so long as they are alive and leads them into the temptation of giving themselves up to crazy penances to destroy their health. . . .'[5]

[1] Sb, F, c. xiv–6, 7.
[2] Idem, 6.
[3] Quoted SEC, vol. V, p. 111, n. 1.
[4] Sb, F, c. xiv–12.
[5] Cf. Sb, F, c. xiv–12.

The idea of having to live reasonably because one was living for God was already taking root in her. But neither her entreaties nor her reiteration of the word 'moderation' were listened to. Perhaps she was mistaken? She was always ready to believe she was wrong when her opinion did not coincide with that of 'wise and learned' men. Was she not 'so wretched, so base, so weak and miserable, of so little worth,' [1] a woman in short? What met her eyes at Duruelo was like a scene from the Bible and all she heard there, the converse of seraphim. She left 'in a state of immense interior joy.' [2]

Her steed jogged along the road to Toledo. The Mother Foundress's silence was one long interior thanksgiving.

The merchants who were her travelling companions talked indeed but found no other subject of conversation than their edifying visit:

'I would not exchange what I've seen there for all the goods in the world,' said the one who had hesitated to make this détour along the bad, rough roads.

The other declared that so much virtue and poverty seemed to him more enviable than all his riches.[3]

But neither the one nor the other turned his bridle, renouncing his ducats in order to be happy rather than rich.

Teresa heard them vaguely and refrained from smiling. For she reflected that in this world there must be saints but there must be merchants too, and that it is already no small thing when a merchant amid his satiating riches experiences from time to time a longing for extreme poverty.

[1] Sb, V, c. xviii–4.   [2] Sb, F, c. xiv–11.   [3] Idem.

V

THE MERCHANTS OF TOLEDO

EVERY merchant who had become rich by honest means, trading in Córdoba leather or in Toledan swords and cloth, intended to enjoy the goods which his prudence and his flair for business had earned him in reasonable measure, but, no less reasonably, in the evening of life, before giving up his soul to God and rendering him a strict account, he divested himself of his heaviest ingots in order to mount up to heaven as lightly as a poor man.

It was this that decided the pious and wealthy Martín Ramírez, merchant of the city of Toledo, to found after his death a church, with several ecclesiastical benefices: without doing his heirs any great injustice, he would thus be well provided for and favourably regarded as far as eternity was concerned, just as he had been prosperous and honoured in this world.

When Martín Ramírez was 'struck down by a fatal illness,' P. Pablo Hernández, a Jesuit and a great friend of Mother Teresa, explained to him that the foundation at Toledo of a convent of reformed Carmelites would be a more novel and at the same time more efficacious means of appealing to the Judge before whom he must appear. The merchant died before he had had time to take the necessary legal steps, but he charged his brother, Alonso Álvarez, 'a godfearing and prudent man,'[1] to open negotiations with the Mother Foundress.

Teresa arrived at Toledo on 24th March 1569. She brought with her only two of the 'young ones' of Ávila, Isabel de San Pablo, and Isabel de Santo Domingo who was to become one of the most energetic prioresses of the Reform. Julian de Ávila had caught fever at Valladolid and so had to forgo the joy of adding to his series of travel diaries. Gonzalo de Aranda replaced him: he was a silent man and left no reminiscences.

Doña Luisa de la Cerda received Teresa most warmly and put two rooms at her disposal, thus providing a cell of recollection in her wealthy mansion. Teresa had a great deal to do: Alonso Álvarez conducted the negotiations with her through his son-in-law, Diego Ortiz,

---

[1] Sb, F, c. xv-2.

known as 'the Theologian,' who had as much talent for legal quibbles as he had for discussions on thorny points of doctrine. He wore out the Foundress's inexhaustible patience, though she never refused to listen to his wearisome arguments when he brought his little boy of four with him. She told the porter:

'Always call me when Martinico comes with his father: I like that child, he is virtuous already.' [1]

She adored children, and, strict as she was when it was a matter of observance of the Rule, she would go against the letter of her own Constitutions to receive in her convents girls of nine, twelve or fourteen, destined eventually for the religious life, whose naïve sayings, charm and piety she never wearied of talking of. When Diego Ortiz announced once more that his search for a site for the convent had failed, Teresa consoled herself with Martinico.

The authorization, too, was slow in arriving. These authorizations caused the Mother Foundress endless worry. Besides the brief which the Master General of the Order had given her, she had to have authorization from both the town and the Ordinary, not to mention the goodwill of the other Orders in the city which it was necessary to strive to acquire; for if the Augustinians, Franciscans or Mercedarians could not prevent her from founding a convent, through the influence they exerted they could make things difficult for her.

That was why Teresa decided that in future she would take possession of the buildings of her future convents like a thief in the night, as it were: once the first Mass was said, both neighbours and reluctant authorities would yield to a *fait accompli*, with sometimes perhaps more fuss and threats and sometimes less. In the course of the negotiations, her diplomacy generally won over in the end even the most ill-disposed. 'The Foundress had a horror of lies and her diplomacy was beyond reproach. I have never seen anyone more skilled in the art of disclosing nothing she wished to hide, yet without lying. . . .' [2]

The situation at Toledo was complicated by the absence of the Archbishop: Bishop Bartolomé Carranza was awaiting the result of his trial in the secret dungeons of the Inquisition: in his *Commentary on the Catechism* numerous propositions had been instanced in which strict censors thought they could perceive a flavour of Lutheranism: he concerned himself in popularizing the words of Christ himself and the theologian Melchor Cano found in him 'a taint of illuminism' because he affirmed that there were people of good sense and measured judgement, so good, so devout, that one could put the entire Scriptures

[1] SEC, vol. V p. 117, n. 3.   [2] JG quoted SEC, vol. V, p. 94, n. 1.

into their hands as safely as one could into those of many learned men knowing Latin; 'not that I claim that learning has not its place in Scripture, but because the Holy Spirit has his disciples whom he helps and enlightens.'[1]

It was then that the Grand Inquisitor Fernando Valdés published his *Index* which prohibited the translation into Spanish and the reading of the majority of works on mysticism: 'illuminations' of the spirit were to remain the prerogative of the clergy or of privileged souls who had the advantage of being directed by a learned confessor. It seemed impossible to allow the ordinary faithful to practise mental prayer. There was a solid prejudice of caste. Ten years after these events, Teresa of Jesus' troubles were a consequence of this prejudice.

So a man who was neither illustrious nor of noble birth had the audacity to want to be the patron of a convent! That was no more possible than to allow a carpenter's wife to practise a high degree of mental prayer.

In the Archbishop's absence, the head of the Council of government of the archbishopric of Toledo, Don Gómez Tello Girón, was all powerful. He it was who was informed of the incredible pretension of the deceased Martín Ramírez and his heirs. Unkind comments ran about like wildfire and Teresa knocked on closed doors: Doña Luisa de la Cerda herself became reticent and cool.

But Rubeo, the Master General, had enjoined on the Mother Foundress not to discourage the benefactor: the fact of having bought things to sell them again did not make an honest man unworthy of acquiring a good place in heaven. He wrote to her:

. . . Avarice, cause of innumerable crimes, devours one's neighbour's work, grasps everything for oneself and is never weary of coveting. Nations eaten up by this vice are in peril, and souls too fond of earthly riches, those who spend on pleasure what they acquired without toil, are put in the centre of the earth and justly punished after being sentenced by the Most Just Judge.

That is why men who fear God, afraid of being caught in the snare of riches, give the greatest part of their gains to the Church.

You, Reverend Mother Teresa, must not be surprised that the noble and devout *caballero* Martín Ramírez, wanting to be united with Jesus Christ and his holy Mother in paradise, has given away a part of his goods to this end. . . .[2]

The Master General did not hesitate to class as ' noble and a

[1] Quoted BA, p. 132, n. 2.   [2] Quoted SEC, vol. V, p. 424.

gentleman' a merchant who belonged to the only aristocracy which counts: that of a generous heart.

Mother Teresa rated work too highly to despise those who had not acquired their riches 'without toil'; she esteemed merit above birth, 'for, before God, titles and functions will not count.' Diego Ortiz, ill at ease in his rôle as benefactor, was more intransigent than he would otherwise have been because more than one *hidalgo* took it upon himself to humiliate him; there were points on which the Foundress could not give way and it was not her fault if all negotiations between her and the merchants were finally broken off. And the promised 12,000 ducats took wing.

There she was, then, in Toledo, without patrons, without any to give security for her, without a house, without money, esteemed of little account by the mighty men of this world, but determined not to admit defeat. To the two Isabels she said:

'Now that the idol of money has crashed to the ground, I consider this foundation more certain than ever. . . .'

Once more, human help had proved itself to be worth no more than a few sprigs of dried rosemary: but once more His Majesty would show his power.

Teresa began to look for a house on her own account. Without anyone's support she endeavoured to approach the Governor, who obstinately refused to receive her. Fortunately for the business in hand, the churches were at that time a kind of forum or fair-ground; business less innocent than the foundation of a new convent was transacted there. Teresa waylaid the Governor near the altar where he was accustomed to hear Mass and begged him to come and speak to her in the chapel where she had withdrawn to avoid prying eyes. 'Our Lord gave her a great spirit of determination.' [1]

Although he was a very serious man and conscious of his exalted dignity, she infused so much charm and sweetness into what she said and spoke to him with 'such a great and holy liberty' [2] that, first of all surprised and then won over to her, he listened to all she had to say:

'It is hard that women whose only desire is to live in austerity, perfection and enclosure, should be prevented from serving Our Lord by those who are not caused the least inconvenience by all that and who think of nothing but living out their days comfortably. . . .' [3]

She added 'many other things besides,' and, finally, this:

'If this foundation fails merely because of Your Lordship, do you

[1] Sb, F, c. xv-5.   [2] FR, L. II, c. iii.   [3] Sb, F, c. xv-5.

think you can justify yourself over the matter when you have to appear before Our Lord?'[1]

Teresa was so 'gentle and charming,'[2] even when she was threatening an ecclesiastical Governor with the thunders of the Most High, and made such a deep impression on Don Gómez Tello Girón that he granted her the authorization she asked for forthwith, on one condition: the convent was to have neither revenues nor benefactors. In this way he hoped to prevent her from raising merchants to the rank of patrons of Carmel.

She went away delighted, 'as though she had everything, although she had nothing.'[3] She had only three or four ducats left. 'Teresa of Jesus and three ducats are nothing, but Teresa of Jesus, three ducats and God are everything.'[4]

She eagerly spent her last ducats: two pallets, a blanket, and two pictures for the future chapel, one of which showed Jesus falling under the weight of the Cross, the other Our Lord in prayer, seated on a rock. This was the bare minimum for three poor little nuns: the wherewithal to pray and to sleep.

But 'as to a house, there was no sign of one at all.'[5] As was her wont, Teresa toiled, laboured, acted to the utmost in the measure of her resources and even beyond and then, imperturbable, she waited for the accomplishment of the promise: 'Knock and it shall be opened unto you.' Knock, that meant work.

Did she see in a youth who came up to her one day in a church the chosen instrument of the promise's fulfilment? In both appearance and dress he was more like a *pícaro* than an honest man. When the two Isabels saw him come up, they stood round their prioress ready to defend her: these Toledan churches were frequented by people whose devotion must be accepted with a certain reserve and Teresa had already been the subject of attack by a woman who used her fists and who accused her of having stolen one of her clogs. What with crooks on the look-out for an easy prey and thieves who were satisfied with a purse, there was every need to take care: but what danger of this kind could a poor woman who had nothing and who when she was attacked gave praise to God, incur? She got a lot of fun out of the incident of the clog.

The poor fellow greeted her politely, said that his name was Andrada and that he came on behalf of Fray Martín de la Cruz, a Franciscan and a friend of the Mother Foundress.

[1] FR, L. II, c. iii. [2] Idem. [3] Sb, F, c. xv–6.
[4] Quoted BRJ, p. 71. [5] Sb, F, c. xv–6.

'Fray Martín told me: Go and find Mother Teresa of Jesus, put yourself at her disposal, help her all you can and even more than you can.' [1] Having no money, living rather in poverty and wretchedness, he could only give what he had, his person, his obedience, his knowledge of even the most remote corners of Toledo and agile legs to take him all over the city with rapidity. Finally, no small measure of the gift of the gab with which to make inquiries of all and sundry.

Teresa listened to what he had to say with a kindly smile and asked her nuns not to forget any of the directions through the labyrinth of narrow streets to the place where she could find the youth who said he was 'her servitor' when needed.

The honesty both of what he said and of his face pleased Teresa greatly: she loved ordinary folk and persons of low degree so much that she did not forget Andrada's offer, but when she wanted to send for him to ask him to look for a house, Isabel de Santo Domingo and Isabel de San Pablo, after having had a good laugh over it, looked at each other with dismay:

'Mother! You're not going to get that man here? What will the porter say? What will Doña Luisa say? And her attendants and the servants! You've got a strange messenger, just the sort for Discalced Carmelites! What hope is there that a man in rags and tatters can find a house when rich merchants, a canon of the cathedral who was the son of a Governor of Castile, and so many other important persons have sought one in vain?'

'Don't talk like that,' said Teresa. 'What harm could people think of poor pilgrims like ourselves? Fray Martín is a saint: he has sent me this youth Andrada, he had his reasons and they were good ones. I will see him.' [2]

Nobody ever dared answer the Mother's 'Don't talk like that.' Andrada came. When he replied: 'A house? Nothing easier. I will find that for you,' Isabel de San Pablo shrugged her shoulders to convey to Mother Teresa that the poor fellow certainly had not all his wits about him. But a few days later, when the three Carmelites were hearing Mass in the Jesuit church, he came up to them:

'The house is found.'

He had brought the keys with him; they set off eagerly to look at the house and found it exactly what they wanted.

Teresa was never gentler than when she had good cause to triumph:

'His Majesty is proving to us that we must take care not to consider

<hr>

[1] Idem.   [2] FR, L. II, c. xiii.

it an honour to rub shoulders with the great ones of this world, but with those who are poor like the apostles were! . . .' [1]

But she laughed to herself when her daughters begged her not to let Andrada see that their entire household possessions consisted of only two pictures, two pallets and a single blanket: they were afraid the poor fellow might lose interest when he found they were even poorer than he was. . . .

The little convoy which was to see to the removal and make the foundation formed as soon as night fell: it consisted of the two Isabels, Andrada and a Calced Carmelite friar who carried the vestments and sacred vessels which the monastery of Mitigated observance lent them. All the money Teresa had was one hundred reales borrowed from the wife of Doña Luisa de la Cerda's butler. [2]

They spent the night sweeping, cleaning and arranging the house, making primitive attempts at decorating the wretched place. There was no room for a chapel: the altar was erected in a room to which the faithful could only have access through the house next door, which likewise formed part of the buildings of the future convent. But the two women who were living in it had not been told for fear of gossip. They were awakened by great bangs on the wall: Andrada and the Calced friar were breaking through their partition. When they saw them appear they thought they were in hell and broke into loud complaints. Teresa succeeded in calming them down by a well-balanced combination of soft words and ducats.

At dawn all was ready. Doña Luisa de la Cerda and her ladies took their places in the chapel as the little hand-bell used for the elevation was ringing to announce the first Mass: there was no proper bell. But a small child who was passing by in the street, when he saw the altar lighted up, the palms [3] and the pictures, exclaimed:

'Blessed be God. How lovely it all is!'

'For this exclamation of praise alone coming from the lips of such a little angel, I consider myself well repaid for all the trouble this foundation has given me,' said Teresa to her companions. 'It was God's will that the agreement with Alonso Alvarez should come to nothing in order that this foundation should be built solely on work and poverty.' [4] 'Andrada, a poor boy, found the house for us, the humble wife of a servant of a great house has given the necessary money; finally, upon all these poor people comes the blessing of a little child.'

[1] CTA, ccclxxx.
[3] It was Palm Sunday—Tr.
[2] FR, L. II, c. 13.
[4] Sb, F, c. xv-8.

She was thinking of the stable at Duruelo, of Fray John of the Cross, of Fray Antonio de Jesús, and gave thanks to God.

At last the three Carmelites were alone in the convent of the Glorious St Joseph of the city of Toledo and were now well and properly enclosed. The menu for this day of rejoicing consisted in a few sardines which they were slightly regretting being unable to grill for want of a little wood, when providentially they found a faggot in the chapel. They cooked their meal on a borrowed stove. A paper with a stone on top lest a breath of air should blow the salt away served them as salt cellar.

Teresa was delighted: up till then had not her love of poverty been that of a person who had never lacked what was necessary? Toledo was the means of her initiation into absolute poverty—'the arms on her standard.' [1]

One night—the nights in May are still fresh at this altitude—she was cold and asked the nuns to cover her up. They laughed heartily:

'Mother, you already have all the coverlets there are in the house, that is to say, our cloaks. . . .' [2]

Teresa was touched and amused at the same time. She laughed with them.

Teresa of Jesus had wanted to negotiate with merchants. What she now said, was:

> Such great poverty when the lady who was so fond of me was at hand in her own house may seem incredible. I don't know what the cause of it was except that God doubtless wanted to show us the benefits of this virtue. I asked Doña Luisa de la Cerda for nothing, for I don't like to bother people and fortunately she did not notice our extreme lack of everything. I owe her a great deal more than she could have given us. . . . [3]

Our inward joy was so great that I often remind myself of all Our Lord told us was involved in this virtue. Our poverty was the means which brought us to blessed contemplation. This did not last long for people soon began to give us what we needed. This made me as sad as if a lot of gold and jewels had been taken away from me. I saw that the nuns were sad and asked them why:

'Mother, what could the reason be except that we are no longer poor?'

From then onwards my desire for poverty increased and I felt all the richer for not caring about temporal goods. When they are lacking, interior riches increase and they indeed satisfy us more fully and bring us a much greater peace. [4]

[1] Sb, C, c. ii–7.   [2] FR, L. II, c. 13.   [3] Sb, F, c. xv–13.   [4] Idem, 14.

In the midst of all this difficulties arose with the owner who did not want her premises turned into a convent. The wife of an eldest son, *i.e.* an heir, a powerful woman and given to intriguing, she stirred up the ecclesiastical Council. The Governor, Tello Girón, was away and so could not confirm his verbal authorization, the whole of Toledo was indignant 'at the audacity of an insignificant little woman,' [1] in founding a convent against the will of the notables of the town. She was threatened with excommunication if she continued to have Mass said.

In her, bad news or any other blow merely aroused fresh fervour. The blood coursed more quickly through her veins and her maladies disappeared. Toledo, all its annoyance notwithstanding, found a woman whom nothing could move despite her meekness; to threats she gently replied that she would obey although she was not obliged to do so. But whether she was holding her own or, as the case might be, putting up undaunted passive resistance, whether she was suffering from cold, or hunger, she worked with might and main for the completion of what had to be done to the house, so that those of her daughters who were to form the community might come soon; whenever she was free from the necessity of defending her cause in the parlour, she worked with her hands, not even allowing herself respite for prayer and contemplation: to serve is also to pray.

On Pentecost eve the ecclesiastical Governor Tello Girón returned and the Council calmed down. The work on the buildings was finished, the owner appeased and the nuns arrived and installed themselves. Teresa took her place in the refectory 'so glad to think that at last she could rejoice in the Lord for these wonderful happenings, that she could not eat, she was so overwhelmed with joy.'

At that moment they came to call her: a messenger from Ana de Mendoza y la Cerda, Princess of Éboli, was asking for her urgently in the parlour.

[1] Idem, 11.

VI

ANA DE MENDOZA Y LA CERDA, PRINCESS OF ÉBOLI

THE whims of Ana de Mendoza y la Cerda, Princess of Éboli, were commands: she had known Teresa of Jesus at Toledo when the latter was staying with her aunt, Doña Luisa de la Cerda, and her immediate caprice was to have in her duchy of Pastrana a convent which she herself had founded, just as she would have demanded a farthingale overnight from a fashionable dressmaker.

She sent a carriage which was not to leave without bringing back the Mother Foundress.

Teresa gave the princess's suite a meal and, leaving the refectory, hurried to the chapel. She fell on her knees:

'O my delight,' she prayed, 'Lord of all creation, my God! How long must I wait to enjoy your presence? What relief do you offer those who find no rest in this world but in you? Oh how long life is! And how painful! O life which is no life at all! Oh for solitude alone! Oh where does the remedy lie? How long, O Lord, how long, how long? My only good, what am I to do? Must I desire not to desire you? O my God, my Creator, you hurt without anointing the wound!' [1]

She could bear no more. For what was she asking for, this daughter of Our Lady of Carmel? Simply to live enclosed, cloistered by God himself. The number of those who were enjoying silence and peace in her convents increased every day—Ávila, Medina del Campo, Valladolid, Toledo, besides the friars at Duruelo. But Teresa herself? Each time she was just beginning to hope to enjoy it, she had to leave.

And yet nothing equalled the joy of them all when, as each foundation was made, the sisters at last found themselves separated from the world by thick walls and a whole host of grilles, bolts and locks, Constitutions and prohibitions. There no earthly noise, no human being could touch them, there, 'trampling the world beneath their feet,' they were free, queens and mistresses of the kingdom of the spirit. How could they breathe elsewhere? 'A fish thrown on the bank cannot live: similarly souls made for the living waters given by the Bridegroom die

[1] Sb, E, vi-1.

when caught in the meshes of the world, if they are not thrown back into the living water. . . .' [1]

Perhaps she had not deserved to enjoy the solitude she preferred to all else? For when scarcely on the fringe of her oasis, she had to turn back to what she 'abhorred,' [2] all the bustle of people and business and money. She would have made light of all the work of the foundations if it had not been for having to see all these men and women of whom she had to form an opinion, whom it was necessary to solicit or get rid of, to charm or to win over, to circumvent or to dominate: this meant an adjustment of oneself to the sphere of the infinitely small, whereas her soul was attuned to the infinitely great.

'Pity on me, pity on me, Lord! This exile is very long and in it the heavy penalty of unsatisfied desire for God is exacted. O sweet refreshment of the lovers of God! O suffering! Pity on me, Lord!' [3]

She begged Our Lord, who was her Counsellor, to dictate to her a letter of refusal which would not offend the Princess: for the sake of the Order, she could not displease Doña Ana nor her husband, Prince Ruy Gómez, the most powerful man in Spain after the King.

A friend of Philip II in childhood, the Portuguese Ruy Gómez da Silva had remained his intimate counsellor throughout the years. The King, who wished to honour him, had, however, not made him an attractive present in giving him Ana de Mendoza y la Cerda, one of the greatest names and fortunes of all Spain, for wife. She was the great-grandchild of Don Pedro González de Mendoza, Cardinal Archbishop of Toledo, himself the son of the illustrious Marquis of Santillana, the famous warrior and one of the best poets of the fifteenth century.

'The mighty power of Pedro González de Mendoza was such that he was surnamed "the third king of Spain" at a time when the other two were no less than Ferdinand and Isabella the Catholic, and his vitality was so superabundant that after making the kingdom resound with his political, social and military exploits, he left several natural children.' [4]

The Princess of Éboli had inherited the turbulence of her distinguished ancestor. She was famous for her beauty although she had only one eye, which flatterers expressed by saying that she 'had only one sun'; that one was sufficient to enlighten the court of Spain and the world. She was no less famous for her quarrelsome, haughty and unscrupulous nature. She was now thirty. The King had no illusions about her: 'She wants everything that comes into her head and sticks

---

[1] Sb, F, c. xxi–46. [2] CTA, xxx.
[3] Sb, E, xv–1, 2, 3. [4] MA, vol. I, p. 167.

at nothing to gain her end; her rages and ill words are unparalleled for
one of her rank.' The court feared the sting of her tongue and her
husband had made up his mind once and for all not to contradict her.
To alienate Doña Ana was to alienate Ruy Gómez; to alienate Ruy
Gómez was to alienate Philip II.

Our Lord dictated no letter to Mother Teresa: he ordered her to
leave for Pastrana, for the journey was more important than she
thought it was. He added that she was not to fail to take the Rule and
Constitutions with her.

Teresa of Jesus' joy in obeying was so great that it cut short all regret.
When in accordance with the divine plan she went back into the world
she did not leave God. Rather, he went with her.

On the way she was obliged to pay her respects at the court: the
King's support was essential to her, especially for the monasteries of
friars. At that time the sight of Teresa in the streets of Madrid, soliciting
the help of lords and princes, was not uncommon.

Her reputation was already so great that Doña Leonor de Mascaren-
has herself had gone to the trouble of trying to recruit subjects for the
Discalced Carmelite friars and held Mariano Azaro and Giovanni
Narducci in reserve for her.

If little Fray Giovanni, going straight from the studio of the painter
Sánchez Coello to the 'desert,' showed 'a great simplicity in worldly
matters,' [1] Mariano Azaro looked down on the world from the
height of great birth and privileged intelligence. A Neapolitan, Knight
of the Order of St John of Jerusalem, formerly Master of the Palace to
the Queen of Poland, he was in addition a great geometer, a great
mathematician and one of the best engineers of the day.

Mariano and Giovanni were living as hermits in the 'desert' of
Tardón, from which the engineer was called away somewhat too
frequently for his liking by Philip II. After the victory of St Quentin
which was partly due to his work, the King summoned him to construct a canal connecting the Tagus with the Guadalquivir. When the
work was finished he returned to his solitude.

At present he was preparing to leave for Rome. Since the Council
of Trent, hermits had to be incorporated in some already existing
Order and Mariano wanted to persuade the Pope to permit him to remain in the 'desert' with his companion.

When Teresa learnt from Doña Leonor that, not content with
observing silence and solitude, they were practising penance, abstinence, fasting and mortification and living by the work of their hands

[1] Sb, F, c. xvii–6.

and not by begging, she was delighted: was not this the essence of the primitive Rule of Carmel?

She showed Mariano Azaro the Rule and Constitutions which Our Lord had told her to bring: he could save himself the trouble of asking for exceptional treatment—a step which did not go hand in hand with perfect obedience—and, as a Discalced Carmelite, live far away from a world 'lost by reason of its cupidity.' [1]

Averse as he was to the company of men, Mariano Azaro avoided that of women still more: was he to exchange his hermit's robe for a Carmelite habit at the first bidding of a person belonging to this crafty sex? He said he would like to sleep over it but God disturbed his sleep and, before dawn, he had made up his mind and 'was very much astonished that he had changed his opinion so quickly, particularly under the influence of a woman.' [2] Our Lord's command was wonderfully clear. He had just received from Prince Ruy Gómez a very good hermitage situated in Pastrana itself. Did not Teresa of Jesus' invitation, coming as it did at this identical moment, prove that this hermitage was destined to become the second monastery of Discalced Carmelite friars?

When the Mother Foundress left Madrid, she took with her two more friars, and the 'Rose of Lebanon,' Beatriz Brances, a friend of Doña Leonor de Mascarenhas, who was to take the Carmelite habit at Pastrana under the name of Beatriz del Sacramento.

At Pastrana there was a fuss about authorization as usual; but a warm welcome from the Prince and Princess.

Delays, as usual: the Princess had had the house demolished all except the walls and was setting herself enthusiastically to the task of getting it rebuilt. But Teresa and her nuns were lodged in the palace and their rooms were shut off from the noise of the world and the chatter of attendants and valets by thickness after thickness of heavy curtains of magnificent splendour.

Much work, as always. But quarrels, as never before: the Princess was punctilious about her rights and the ceremony she considered her due. Teresa found the necessity of concealing what she really thought and of not always having direct access to the Princess, trying. The King of Kings had treated her with less formality: 'With him I can speak as with a friend, although he is the Lord God, because he is not like those whom we have here who display their power even when it is based upon a sham authority. . . .' [3] Ana de Mendoza insisted on presenting

[1] Idem, 9.   [2] Idem.
[3] Sb, V, c. xxxvii-5.

as a subject a certain Sister Agustina, but the Mother Foundress did not want nuns already formed to the observance of another, and different, Rule. The Princess now haggled over the amount of revenue she had offered the day before, the next day quibbled over the regularity of the allowance, finding a hundred and one points for discussion which she tried to turn into points of dispute. It would have been like founding a convent on a volcano if the Prince had not used the wonderful and kindly forbearance acquired during his married life to persuade the haughty Princess to yield to the requirements of holiness.

Having a freer hand for the monastery of friars, the Prince was so generous that the skill of Mariano Azaro and four hundred ducats were employed to bring water to the top of the hill where the hermitages were grouped; in this way it was possible to make delightful kitchen gardens and orchards, gay with the songs of birds. Taking advantage of this generous zeal, the Discalced friars gave themselves the luxury of cells that were more like tombs than dwelling-places for the living. Everything was so rough, so austere, decorated with crosses and skulls as at Duruelo, 'that even the most sluggish devotion came to life there and the hardest hearts softened.' [1]

The Prince paid secretly for all the work done, 'so that the village should not cease giving the friars alms,' and also that Doña Ana should not get too touchy about his generosity.

The Princess's nuns sewed the habits the Prince's friars were to wear: Mariano Azaro became Fray Ambrosio Mariano de San Benito, and Giovanni Narducci, Fray Juan de la Miseria. Neither of them wanted to be ordained priest, because they wished to be employed only in the lowliest tasks.

P. Antonio de Jesús came to Pastrana to establish perpetual adoration there: night and day, two friars would remain in prayer before the Blessed Sacrament. 'He implanted this holy exercise so well there that it is still practised as fervently as it was at the beginning . . . And all the friars there live in the enjoyment of abundant heavenly consolation. . . .' [2]

The foundation of the convent of nuns took place on 28th June 1569. The Princess provided the chapel with gold and silver vestments, together with an amazing abundance of relics.

With a great pealing of bells, in solemn procession, amid shouts of enthusiasm, with singing and dancing, amid the rhythm of litanies of which the responses were taken up by the crowd, Teresa of Jesus, the prioress Isabel de Santo Domingo, the sub-prioress Isabel de San Pablo

[1] SEC, vol. VI, p. 126.   [2] Idem, p. 127.

—always the two Isabels—followed by their sisters in white mantle and black veil, entered their convent.

The crowd of religious, noble lords and ladies, and villagers was immense; the demeanour of the Prince was recollected; the Princess in her splendour was more than ever like 'a precious stone set in the enamel of nature and fortune,' as the madrigal of Antonio Pérez, the King's secretary and her admirer, would have it.

The ceremony was as edifying as it was gorgeous. The court and the town talked for a long time to come of the opening of this convent which had been constructed, financed and equipped by Ana de Mendoza y la Cerda, Princess of Éboli, who had now no further cause to envy her relatives, Doña María de Mendoza and Doña Luisa de la Cerda: she, too, had her Carmelites now. . . .

Mother Teresa of Jesus was so weary of courts and courtiers that she refused to found a convent at Madrid: eager to get back to the poor again and her merchants, she set out with all speed for Toledo.

Up to the last the Princess was to prove no friend to her. She had insisted on her taking her carriage and a priest saw the Carmelite getting out of the luxurious equipage in front of the convent. He asked for her in the parlour and insulted her:

'So you're the saint who is deceiving everybody and going about in a carriage?'

This priest was mad and he went on to add all the words of abuse which came into his head.

Teresa, thinking he was in his right mind, listened to him humbly, without seeking to excuse herself: 'You are the only one courageous enough to point out my faults.' [1]

From that day she travelled only in the poorest and most uncomfortable carts.

[1] FR, L. IV, c. xvii.

VII

MOTHER TERESA AND HER DAUGHTERS

THE Mother Foundress was not to remain idle long at Toledo. With more pleasure than she had obeyed the orders of the Princess of Éboli, she answered the appeal of the Rector of the Jesuits at Salamanca and set off to found a convent in the great university city. She took the prioress, María del Sacramento, away from Malagón but took no one else with her: experience had taught her that two women, if already accustomed to hardships, could deal with the difficulties much more easily when they had not to bolster up the courage of timid young sisters. But even when Teresa of Jesus set out on her travels in secret, priests or laymen—the latter perhaps *caballeros* or merchants—who considered it an honour to escort her, would join themselves to her company. All these people formed a gay and motley cortège around her closely covered cart: there were *hidalgos* in doublets with their short, brightly coloured capes; commoners enriched by trading and no less gaily attired, who adjusted the steady trot of their hacks or the ambling step of their palfreys to the pace of the mules of the churchmen; ecclesiastics all in black, each wearing the monumental hat known as the *teja*, and on his nose the enormously large spectacles which travellers used to protect their eyes against the sun and dust. As to the friars, Our Lord was their support throughout the many miles they covered on foot or on donkey-back.

Such were the knights serving this 'dame errant'[1] who enlivened all of them by her conversation and who was more charming to the humble folk, serving boys and muleteers, than to churchmen or nobles. 'She was full of gaiety,' but the merry conversation was always interspersed with remarks which turned one's thoughts to heaven.

Among the travellers affectionate familiarity was the rule and Teresa showed so much gratitude towards anyone who rendered her some slight service that all were delighted to help. And yet, if this unusual company 'edified' some people, many otherwise good Christians—especially pious women—assumed a strait-laced air or openly blamed the Carmelite, whose passage disturbed the towns and

[1] SEC, vol. V, p. 6.

villages of Old Castile too frequently, brought the evil talkers out on to their doorsteps and too often furnished idle tongues with subjects for gossip.

But God's service was more important than the fear of chatter:

'So long as God is praised and a little better understood the whole world can cry after me!' [1]

Teresa of Jesus did not hesitate to go considerably out of her way to visit the Carmelite houses which were within reach. *Hidalgos*, merchants, priests, friars, servants followed her: the gossips too.

To reach Salamanca she went through Ávila. Each time she came back to St Joseph's, the first of her foundations, she was deeply moved:

'I come back to my mother. . . .'

This time, the prioress, María de San Jerónimo, formerly the lively María Dávila, presented two novices to her.

One, Ana García, was the daughter of peasant folk. As a child she had lived on such intimate terms with Our Lord that she would apologise to him when the other children asked her to join in their amusements: 'I am going to play and I'll come back straightway. . . .' Later she deliberately frightened off her first admirer by appearing with a towel on her head instead of an elegant head-dress. When she was twenty she had a vision which resulted in her entering Carmel. In a dream she saw herself in a small convent remarkable for its poverty but where the silence was permeated through and through with the love of God. She asked for something to drink: nuns dressed in a habit made of heavy, coarse brown stuff held out an earthenware pitcher to her; never had her thirst been slaked by fresher or cooler water. From this description the priest in her village recognized the convent of St Joseph of Ávila and spoke to the prioress about Ana. It had just been decided to add two lay-sisters to the community and the young peasant girl was sent for. She recognized the house down to the last detail, even the earthenware pitcher. That was how Ana de San Bartolomé became the first Carmelite lay-sister.

The Foundress loved this simple, timid girl as soon as she saw her. Ana had so much good sense that later on she made her her secretary; and she was so gentle and loving that Teresa chose her as her infirmarian and inseparable companion.

The other novice was as brilliant as Ana de San Bartolomé was humble. Born at Medina del Campo, Ana de Lobera was now twenty-five: her passage through the world had been so striking and her reputation for beauty such that she was surnamed 'the queen of

[1] Sb, M, VII, c. 2.

women.'[1] And queen she remained even in the cloister, on account of her talents, energy and the high degree of spirituality she attained. Her entering St Joseph's was also marked by a miraculous sign: in a picture of Our Lord in the Hermitage of Christ at the pillar, she recognized the face and eyes of a beggar who had asked her for help one day. She had given him an alms and went her way, but moved by his look of sorrow and at the same time of love, she turned her head to look at him again. He had disappeared. It was from this moment that she detached herself from everything which had hitherto constituted her pleasure. Teresa, like a water-diviner finding water, immediately sensed the exceptional value of Ana de Jesús and determined to make her novice-mistress of the future convent of Salamanca.

The Mother Foundress and María del Sacramento arrived at Salamanca on All Saints eve, October 1570. All the furniture they brought was a bundle of straw, for 'where we have straw we have beds.'[2] A house had been allocated, but the tenants, a band of students, only left the place with loud protestations late in the evening. The two travellers went into it worn out, numb with cold, scared by the noise and din of a town where the fact that they were future doctors of the university did not prevent the students from behaving like hooligans. With fatigue added to everything else, María del Sacramento was seized with terror in this unfamiliar house which had been pillaged by its young inhabitants. In the darkness, broken only by the yellowish, tapering point of a candle flame, disturbing shadows flickered on the walls. The poor woman wandered tremblingly from room to room amid confusion and disorder like that of Judgement Day, making the sign of the cross at every step and sprinkling holy water while all the bells of the town tolled: it was the night of All Souls.

Mother Teresa long remembered this arrival. The thought of it made her laugh and she made her nuns in Ávila, Valladolid and in all her convents laugh over it too. They often begged her to tell the story once more:

> María del Sacramento could not forget that the students had been furious at leaving; she imagined they must be hiding in the lofts and dark corners to frighten us: it would have been easy, there was plenty of room. . . . We shut ourselves up in a room where I had thrown our bundle of straw and spent the night under two blankets someone had lent us.

[1] SEC, vol. V, p. 193, n. 1.   [2] Sb, F, c. xix-4.

When my companion saw that the door was fastened, she grew calmer as far as the students were concerned, although she kept on looking round anxiously. But the devil put into her mind ideas calculated to upset me in my turn. I am so weak that it doesn't take much. I said to her:

'What are you looking for now? No one can get in.'

'Mother, if I died suddenly, what would you do here all alone?'

She was so much in earnest that her terror communicated itself to me; I have always been afraid of dead bodies, even when there was someone else with me.

All this time the bells were tolling without interruption for, as I have said, it was the night of All Souls, and it was only too easy for the demon to scare us by childish fancies. . . .

Fortunately, I was dropping with sleep:

'Sister, if that should happen, I should have to think what to do. Just now, all I want to do is to sleep. . . .'

We had just spent two very bad nights and soon sleep remedied our fear. . . .[1]

Teresa needed all her gaiety to keep her going: this foundation at Salamanca was so beset with difficulties that years later the community was still looking for a suitable place to live; they could not succeed in extricating themselves from the tangle of litigation which one of the owners of the house, Don Pedro de la Banda, delighted in. The Foundress wrote to this quarrelsome man: 'May Our Lord give Your Grace a little calmness. . . .'[2] And in tactful words she reminded him of the shortness of this life: 'Anxiety about this world's goods should not turn our thoughts from thinking of our heavenly home. . . .'[3]

And yet it was there, in the midst of a thousand preoccupations, that she began to write the story of her foundations. God had commanded her to do so and the order was confirmed by her former confessor P. Ripalda, whom she met once more at Salamanca where he was Rector of the Jesuits. She began on 23rd August, 'feast of St Louis, King of France,' grieved by 'her want of talent, her clumsiness, the absence of peace and quietness in which to write, and her bad health. . . .'[4] 'My style is so heavy that I fear to weary others and myself as well. . . .'[5] To her objections Our Lord replied: 'Daughter, obedience brings strength.'[6]

And so she obeyed. In the meantime she had to go and found a convent at Alba de Tormes, under the patronage of Teresa de Layz, and under the invocation of Our Lady of the Annunciation. Every-

[1] Sb, F, c. xix-4, 5. [2] CTA, xlviii. [3] Idem, xlvii.
[4] SEC, vol. V, Prologo, 5. [5] Idem, 3. [6] Idem, 2.

thing there, however, went well, and she was able to work quickly. The foundation took barely a month at the beginning of 1571, and she was then able to return to Salamanca and sustain the courage of her nuns there.

The prioress of Salamanca was her cousin, Ana de Tapia, the daughter of her uncle Francisco; she had at last left the Mitigation and in the wake of Teresa had become Ana de la Encarnación. The sub-prioress, María de Cristo, María de San Francisco, Jerónima de Jesús, and two novices, Ana de Jesús who had at last arrived from Ávila, and Juana de Jesús, completed the initial nucleus of the community.

Teresa was always very fond of her novices. In motherly words she anxiously inquired about Juana's health, for she seemed to have 'such a tiny face.' [1] Ana de Jesús shared her cell, and Teresa watched her as she slept and traced little crosses on her forehead; she gave her her new cloak and kept the old one for herself.

One by one and by her own example she inculcated in them the great principles of Carmelite charity which bring so much gentle sweetness to the bedside of the sick, following Christ's counsel: 'The prioress who did not provide for the welfare of the sick would be behaving like Job's friends. God is trying them for the good of their souls, but she would be exposing them to the danger of losing their patience.' [2] Teresa ordered Ana de la Encarnación to eat meat, for she considered her overtired and in poor health.[3]

We can see her at the bedside of the dying 'caressing each one's face with her gentle hand, and encouraging them with loving words,' and no one had more sympathy than she for people's troubles and sufferings. She was the consoling angel of all her daughters, of all the people around her, and even of strangers whose complaints she listened to— she who never complained herself—'with supernatural pity.' [4] According to her view of things, the stronger we are the greater our obligation to stoop in tenderness towards those to whom a mere nothing often causes great suffering.

For her, each one of her nuns was a soul walking along the royal highway. There are no weights and measures in the Kingdom of the spirit and often a slight effort on the part of some is evidence of more virtue than great ecstasies on the part of others. She always refused to be considered holy because she had visions and raptures, constantly repeating: '*Yo que soy ruin* . . .' 'Vile as I am . . .' and gave continual proof of humility. She never failed to ask the opinion of the

---

[1] CTA, li.   [2] SEC, R, ix, p. 45.   [3] CTA, li.
[4] Cf. Sb, C, c. vii–5.

sisters and, what is more, she conformed to it. During her visits to the various convents she did not allow the nuns to come to her for things but sent them to their prioress, to whom she showed as much respect as if she herself had been her subject too. As far as the business of the Order and of the foundations, her correspondence, her charge of souls and bodies permitted, she took time, even if she had to take it from her sleep, to ply her distaff, to take her share like the others in providing for the needs of the community.

When, with her naturally quick tongue, she happened to hurt a sister by the way in which she reproached her, or by one of the ironical remarks that sometimes escaped her, she would prostrate herself at her feet and ask pardon. She did the same when she was at fault herself; the nuns at Malagón related that one day when she had made a mistake in reading an Office, she prostrated in the middle of the choir before their eyes: they were so touched that amid their tears they forgot to signal to her to rise again. And she signed her letters to the prioresses, those prioresses whom she had formed herself: 'Your Reverence's unworthy servant.'

That was her way of acting when she alone, the human personality called Teresa of Jesus, was in question. It was quite another matter when the Order was in question, and she required the same twofold manner of acting from her prioresses: she required that they should be exacting, firm, capable of severity and even hardness. The Mother Foundress's anger was short but terrible and of pitiless clarity; it never signified a loss of self-mastery, but an energetic intent to have things as they should be. Her letters are full of such expressions of displeasure, as sharp as her spoken words, since she never read over what she wrote; from one letter to the next her anger died down but the will which had prompted it persisted, made itself felt and triumphed. The fullness of her forgiveness blotted out every feeling of irritation or resentment, and she prayed particularly for those who might have reason to fear they had incurred her displeasure.[1]

She was a mixture of gentleness and of unswerving justice. Her skill in the art of dealing with human nature, and her understanding of the most complex characters were unparalleled. Her nuns at Salamanca never wearied of hearing her explain the deepest things of spirituality: they would spend the recreation listening to her. Without neglecting her spinning Teresa would go on talking and although she herself was no stranger to ecstasies, she warned them against the danger of seeking such a state, and denounced its false imitations.

[1] CTA, ccciv.

'I've known more than one, and persons of no small virtue, who spent seven or eight days in a state they thought was rapture: the most simple spiritual exercise affected them in such a way that they let themselves lose consciousness, convinced that they would otherwise be resisting Our Lord. . . .'

And the Foundress added, in that way she had of not mincing matters:

'In the end it's enough to kill them or send them mad if no remedy is applied. . . .' [1]

One sister asked how this condition of unconsciousness differed from rapture:

'The appearance is the same. But rapture, or union with God, is of short duration, its benefits are immense, it leaves the soul bathed in interior light, the understanding has no part in it, Our Lord acts on the will alone. In the other case everything is very different: the body is a prisoner but understanding and memory remain free; these faculties function in a disordered sort of way. . . .[2] In my opinion the soul has nothing to gain from such bodily weaknesses. . . .' [3]

And she advised the prioress 'to forbid such long fits of unconsciousness categorically,' [4] . . . and to forbid fasts and penances in the case of nuns whose prayer caused such bodily peculiarities, and to give them some office 'whose exercise would take their minds off the matter.' [5]

She was afraid lest some collective state of exalted but diseased imagination might occur in places like enclosed convents where women were eager to distinguish themselves in the eyes of God—if indeed their abnormal state was not due to the fact that they simply wanted to be important in the eyes of the community or in their own. Accordingly she never tired of repeating:

'The one who is humblest and most mortified among you is the most spiritual.' [6]

At that time melancholia was doing immense harm in all the convents of Spain. The doctors were powerless to cure these cases of what we should now call neurasthenia, the victims of which were subject to alternate fits of violence and depression, aggressiveness and self-pity, and all nuns were greatly afraid of this malady. Mother Teresa taught her prioresses how to recognize and reduce it as far as possible, and suggested remedies.

'Melancholia begins by overclouding one's reason. What limit is

[1] Sb, F c. vi–2.   [2] Idem, 4.   [3] Idem, 5.
[4] Idem, 5.   [5] Idem.   [6] Cf. R, iv, p. 26.

there to our passions when reason is not in control? Those who have this disease think they are quite well and consider the prioress more sick than they are. . . .'

For her descriptions Teresa could, unfortunately, find no lack of examples:

'Before all else they want their own way, say everything that comes into their heads, find in others faults which justify their own, and are content only when everything is to their liking. When passions are not mortified, what happens if there is no barrier by which to restrain them? . . . The prioress must then govern not only their interior but their external life and her mind must be as clear as that of the patient is clouded, she must force those who will not submit of their own free will, and not give way to pity, for to do that would be misplaced kindness. A single nun with melancholia can upset a whole convent.' [1]

Teresa who loved others so much showed that she also knew how to save a situation by severity, when it was necessary:

'This evil,' she wrote, 'is without remedy if passions are not controlled by every possible means: by punishments, if words are not enough; if punishments do not suffice, by severer penalties; if one month's imprisonment has no effect no hesitation must be shown in imposing four months: it would be doing the greatest possible good to these sick souls.'

Regretfully the Foundress admitted:

'Believe me: after having tried all sorts of remedies, I find no others than these. The prioress who through pity gave complete liberty to those suffering from melancholia would bring about an intolerable situation, and such nuns would have already done much harm to their sisters by the time we think about curing them. . . . It is a serious disease, it is sometimes necessary to purge the humours by medicines and the patient must then stay in the infirmary. A prioress must manage them without their being aware of it, and with a great deal of motherly compassion. . . .'

It was in things like this that Teresa of Jesus showed her skill in the guidance of souls and her knowledge of character:

It looks as though I'm contradicting myself for I've spoken of austerities. Such nuns must be made to feel that they will never get their own way, obedience must be imposed on them, they would be in grave danger if they thought they were free. But the prioress must avoid giving them orders which would provoke them to disobedience for they have not the strength of self-mastery. She must lead

[1] Sb, F, c. vii. The whole section concerning melancholia.

them without their knowing they are being led and with love. For them the best remedy is work and they must therefore be allowed only a short time for mental prayer: it's the imagination, which in most of them is very unstable, which does them the greatest harm. In the case of every disease, one either recovers or dies: one doesn't die of melancholia, but one gets cured of it only by a miracle. Those who suffer from it taste death a thousand times in the way of afflictions, imaginations, scruples, which they call temptations. If they refused to take themselves seriously they would obtain relief at once. In very truth I am terribly sorry for them. . . .

Teresa of Jesus, hidden away in her Carmel in about the year 1571, thus anticipated the future work of psychiatry. Deeply impressed, her daughters begged her to devote a chapter of her book of the *Foundations* to the treatment of those suffering from melancholia. They were thinking of the time when she would no longer be with them, their *Mujer Grande*, the woman with the mighty intellect and the big heart: whom would they find to understand them then, if the future retained no record of her intuitions and her genius? And they were proud of having been received in these convents where she would accept no one whom she considered mediocre:

'I won't have nuns who are ninnies,' [1] she said.

And about a prospective postulant whom she found too ready to give way to tears, she said:

'Perhaps I shall take this cry-baby. . . .' [2]

Gay herself, she liked others to be gay. All her nuns knew that 'foolish devotions,' 'gloomy saints' were not to her liking any more than she approved going on praying 'until one is exhausted.' [3] Her laughter was so infectious that when she laughed the whole convent laughed with her.

At Salamanca as in all her convents, when the bell rang for recreation, if the Foundress hurried away to her cell, the novices, her spoiled children, would bar the way :

'Mother . . . Isn't Your Reverence staying with us? . . .' [4]

While they got on with their spinning, they chatted and composed *coplas* which the young ones declaimed or sang very charmingly. Teresa improvised poems which her nuns memorized as she recited them; one can feel the rhythm of the music beating in that of the verse and sometimes even, in the exclamation which cuts a strophe, one can

---

[1] CTA, vi. [2] CTA, liv. [3] SEC, vol. VI, p. lii, n. 3.
[4] Quoted BRJ, p. 73.

Old engraving
of St. Teresa's
convent in Sala-
manca as it was
before its recent
restoration

The convent in Salamanca as it looks today

feel the *desplante*, the lunge forward which was a feature of the popular dances:

> *Vertiendo está sangre,*
> *¡Dominguillo, eh!*
> *Yo no sé porqué. . . .*[1]

The songs are illustrated by finely drawn illuminations in which the Virgin Mary appears as the daughter of a notable:

> *¿Es parienta del Alcalde,*
> *U quien es esta doncella?*
> *Ella es hija de Dios Padre,*
> *Relumbra como estrella. . . .*[2]

Ana de Jesús was professed at Salamanca. Such bridal feasts brought out all Teresa's warmth and fervour, and her love for the Child Jesus, whose statue Ana carried in her arms and called 'the Bridegroom', broke out into improvisations as fresh as the bouquet of a village bride:

> *Oh dichosa tal zagala*
> *Que hoy se ha dado a un tal zagal*
> *Que reina y ha de reinar.*
> *Ya yo, Gil, estoy medroso,*
> *No la osaré más mirar,*
> *Pues ha tomado marido*
> *Que reina y ha de reinar. . . .*[3]

For Teresa of Jesus tenderness and gaiety were such innocent manifestations of the love of one's neighbour and thus of the love of God that even at recreation fervour took possession of her and she became incapable of resisting the urge of the spirit. She would begin to dance, turning round and clapping her hands as King David danced before the ark, and as the girls of her country and those of her Carmels still dance to-day; the nuns accompanied her 'in a perfect transport of spiritual joy.'[4]

---

[1] Shedding this blood, Dominguillo, eh! I know not why (P, xv).

[2] Is she of the Mayor's kin?
Who can this maiden be?
She is daughter of God the Father
And bright as any star.

[3] How happy is this shepherdess
For she has to-day given herself to a shepherd
Who is royal and will continue to reign.
As to myself, Gil, I am afraid.
I shall never dare to cast eyes on her again
For she has taken a husband
Who is royal and will continue to reign.

[4] SEC, vol. II, p. li.

Years afterwards, when Ana de Jesús accompanied by Ana de San
Bartolomé came to France to found Carmelite convents there, the
French nuns, to their great astonishment, saw the venerable Mother
'more like a seraphim than a mortal creature executing a sacred dance
in the choir, singing and clapping her hands in the Spanish way, but
with so much dignity, sweetness and grace that, filled with holy
reverence, they felt themselves wholly moved by divine grace and
their hearts raised to God.' [1] These sacred dances were in the pure
tradition of Teresa of Jesus.

A new novice entered at Salamanca gifted with a voice as clear as
crystal and such a delightful inventive genius for music and verse that
Mother Teresa often asked her to sing. One Easter evening, when she
had been very sad all day, she asked Isabel de Jesús for a *cantarcillo* at
the after-dinner recreation.

With a voice like an angel's, she sang to the tune of a *villancico* [2]
the exquisite words:

> *Véante mis ojos*
> *Dulce Jesús bueno,*
> *Véante mis ojos*
> *Y muérame yo luego.*

> *Vea quien quisiere*
> *rosas y jasmines*
> *Que si yo te viere*
> *Veré mil jardines. . . .* [3]

The harmony of the words, the music, the nuns so pure and lovely
beneath their black veils, the novices with their coifs like dove's wings,
the beautiful April evening, a veritable apotheosis of the Resurrection,
all this moved Teresa of Jesus so profoundly that she felt her limbs
become icy and cold and fell into ecstasy—María de San Francisco
caught her in her arms.   They carried her to her cell unconscious.

When she recovered consciousness, 'in pain and with her hands as

---

[1] BM, vol. II, p. 313.   [2] Christmas carol.
[3] May my eyes behold thee,
Good and sweet Jesus,
May my eyes behold thee,
And then may I die.

Let him who will delight his gaze
With jasmine and with roses,
If I were to see thee,
A thousand gardens would lie before my eyes.

it were dislocated,' [1] she experienced in every bone an intense burning feeling which caused her to break out into impassioned verse.

It was to this we owe one of her finest poems: *I die of being unable to die. . . .*

> *Vivo sin vivir en mí*
> *Y de tal manera espero*
> *Que muero porque no muero. . . .* [2]

From that time onwards, when the Mother was rapt in God, her daughters surrounded her softly singing Isabel de Jesús' *cantarcillo*. For Teresa their voices were mingled with those of the angels.

[1] SEC, R, xv, pp. 97-8.
[2] I live without living in myself
And in like manner wait
For death because I cannot die.
(Cf. Peers: *Complete Works of St Teresa of Jesus*, Vol. III, p. 277 and n. 4—Tr.)

VIII

MANY DEVILS

'I FEAR a discontented nun more than I fear many devils. . .', [1] said Teresa of Jesus. An order from the Apostolic Delegate, the Dominican, P. Pedro Fernández, was to oblige her to confront one hundred and thirty discontented nuns.

One hundred and thirty nuns of her old convent of the Incarnation at Ávila. One hundred and thirty women of all ages, for the most part of noble birth, but poor, and dissatisfied at being poor. It is true that many among them were wise virgins, but the majority behaved like virgins—with a touch of foolishness. One hundred and thirty Carmelite nuns of Mitigated observance, very well satisfied with their laxity, and to whom the thing which they had been dreading ever since the foundation of the convent of St Joseph, had happened: somebody was coming to 'reform' them against their will. And it was their former companion, Doña Teresa de Ahumada, who was being forced on these hundred and thirty women obliged to live within the confines of a house too small for their number and with plenty of leisure to arouse one another to indignation.

'What grave fault have we committed that our right to elect our prioress by vote should be taken away?'

'They're giving us the only one whose reputation all over Spain is enough to make one tremble.'

No more visits, grilles everywhere, no more going out, an end of gossiping in each other's cells, a frightful fast, penances enough to make one shudder, the discipline till the blood comes through the broken skin, dry bread or the prison cell for the least disobedience, the slightest lateness in chapel, the least inattention, the smallest infraction of the Rule—that Rule that was originally made for hermits in the desert and not for poor girls many of whom would have preferred marriage to the convent, if so many young men had not gone overseas with Cortés, Pizarro, or Almagro. Why had not this Teresa de Ahumada been condemned to life imprisonment when her disobedient behaviour had so well deserved it a few years ago!

Newcomers questioned the older ones:

[1] CTA, clxxv.

'You knew her: what was she like?'

Some spoke of her gaiety, of her straightforwardness, of her compassion. Others spoke in the same breath of her love of God and of the gentlemen whom she received in the parlour. All declared that she saw Christ and Our Lady and that she fell into ecstasy or was raised above the ground.

'And that comes from God?'

'Great theologians have admitted that it doesn't come from the devil.'

In any case, she had found life at the Incarnation too pleasant and had gone off to found houses more like prisons than honest convents.

Even the youngest remembered the scandal of the foundation of the convent of St Joseph, the lawsuit which had lasted years, stirred up so much talk and finally made so much commotion that it had done more harm than good to the cause of religion.

Doña Teresa's present mission was to impose her yoke and her austerities upon the convent of the Incarnation.

Displeasure at having to accept the requirements of the primitive Rule was aggravated by the humiliation of the position, and the most fervent, even those who would one day be willing servants of the Reform and follow Teresa of Jesus, as so many of their sisters had already done, protested as angrily as the others.

As to Teresa, she did not hide the fact that she would have preferred to found four convents rather than reform even one. Particularly this one. The Rule of her convents was made for twenty-one nuns at the very outside. How could one make one hundred and thirty angry nuns live in silence? How could one form them to recollection and obedience? One might as well try to reform hell and its legions.

One hundred and thirty women! The Mother Foundress did not conceal the fact that she had a certain contempt for her own sex. How much tittle-tattle, foolish nonsense, exhibitionism, gossip, touchiness, how many lies small and great, how much over-sensitiveness, how many exaggerations would she not have to put up with before she had dominated all this by kindness! When she had occasion to praise a novice, it was for being 'far removed from the affected ways and childish behaviour of women, in no way inclined to scrupulosity, and very straightforward.' She was too familiar with the convent of the Incarnation not to know she would not find there the good, honest, 'ordinary' virtues she required of the Discalced Carmelites.

Appalled at the idea of finding herself 'in this Babylon' once more, she temporized and in spite of her resolute character, Teresa, whose

courage never failed her, wondered if there might not be some way of
escape. She had good reasons for not going immediately: P. Pedro
Fernández's order reached her right in the midst of a reorganization of
the convent of Medina del Campo. Was she to leave her nuns and the
work she was doing there, to impose herself where neither her presence,
nor fervour, good order nor peace was desired? She had logic on her
side.

But one day when she was begging God's help for her brother
Agustín, the most warlike of the handful of *conquistadores*, the one
who seemed to forget, as he made war against the Araucanians in
Chile, that he had to win heaven as well, she ventured to say:

'Lord, if I saw one of your brothers in such danger, what would
I not do to save him?'

To this imprudent entreaty, Our Lord replied:

'Oh, daughter! daughter! Those in the Incarnation are my sisters
and yet you delay! Take courage, and remember that I want it; it is
not as difficult as you suppose. Resist no longer for my power is
great!' [1]

Not only did Teresa hesitate no longer, but, in spite of the lateness
of the hour and the coldness of the weather, she decided to set out
immediately. How was she to find a means of transport? A water-
carrier agreed to lend her two mules and in this way she covered the
twenty leagues separating Medina del Campo from Ávila. [2]

While waiting to take up her functions at the convent of the
Incarnation, she installed herself at St Joseph's where she enjoyed a
delightful interval of peace. She took Ana de San Bartolomé, the little
lay-sister, into her cell and found great joy in talking about Our Lord
with this timid, simple girl who was yet so fervent and so intelligent.
In her naïve way Ana said to the sisters:

'You are like angels. But the Mother Foundress is a seraphim aflame
with the love of God and her neighbour.'

The Foundress, however, had chosen Ana de San Bartolomé to
share her cell for the same reason that she had taken Ana de Jesús at
Salamanca: both were heavy sleepers and Teresa was anxious that no
one should witness her raptures which were sometimes accompanied
by heavenly music.

On 6th October 1571 Mother Teresa of Jesus came to take up her
office as prioress at the Incarnation. The Provincial, P. Ángel de
Salazar, a Carmelite of the Mitigation, was to induct her.

[1] R. xx, p. 53.   [2] B, vol. I, p. 461.

Perhaps he was tactless: the matter would no doubt have gone off better if the Foundress had been left free to act with her customary discretion.

The reading of the letters patent was received with jeers: one hundred and thirty women jealous of their liberty—for the best of them it was a case of wanting to serve Our Lord in *their* way, and for the others the undisguised wish not to be deprived of the delights of the parlour, of going out, of wearing trumpery worldly jewellery over the habit—protested with a single voice and claimed their right to vote.

The Vicar Provincial grew exasperated:

'In short, you won't have Mother Teresa of Jesus?'

Amid the unanimous cries of 'no,' however, was heard the voice of Doña Catalina de Castro:

'We want her and we love her!'

This energetic affirmation afforded a slight respite which was sufficient to rally to the cause of Teresa a few timid souls who had not dared to swim against the stream; they, forcing their way through the barrier of rebels who continued to vociferate, tried to enter the choir in procession, preceded by the crucifix and the new prioress, as the ceremonial demanded. But the opposition, momentarily put out of countenance, now strengthened its defence, and P. Salazar gesticulated and harangued in vain. Finally those who stood up for Mother Teresa and those who, shouting for all they were worth, cursed and abused her, came to blows.

The tumult and scandal were such that you might have thought the whole convent was tumbling about your ears: the police were sent for with all urgency.

Teresa of Jesus, the occasion of the tumult, strove to mollify P. Salazar's anger and made excuses for the rebels:

'It is not surprising. . . . It is very hard to force anyone, no matter who it is. . . .'[1]

With the help of the constables, the party of those trying to sing the *Te Deum* increased in numbers, the Mother Prioress was finally able to enter the choir and everyone followed her.

Teresa had remained so calm on this veritable battlefield, clasping tightly in her arms the statue of her father St Joseph, which had accompanied her on all her foundations, and in her compassion had so completely dominated all violence and vexation that she was able to go to Communion next day without going to confession first. The

[1] FR, L. IV, c. i.

hundred and thirty who all had on their conscience ill words, ill-natured blows or at least unchristian thoughts, were amazed:

'Was it possible that Teresa was a saint after all?'

When the first chapter was held, on entering the room where for twenty-seven years she had been 'an insignificant little nun,' she absent-mindedly went and sat down in the seat she had formerly occupied. Her forgetfulness caused her infectious laugh to ring out; the whole convent relaxed in general hilarity. How natural she was! And how humble!—admitted her enemies. And many whispered:

'She really is holy!'

No, she would not impose herself on these poor nuns who really had the right to choose their prioress, nor would she take upon herself to reform them by force. She was not going to domineer from the prioress's stall and bring about the rule of fear in the spacious and delightful house which she had formerly left with regret. . . .

At this moment she left the choir for a few minutes to return carrying a statue of Our Lady which was very beautiful, more than three feet high and magnificently attired in embroidered and brocaded silk. She put Our Lady in her place in the prioress's stall. She then gave her the keys and sat down at her feet.

'Ladies, here is your prioress: Our Lady of Mercy. . . .'

She spoke with so much sincerity, good sense and kindness that the hardest hearts melted 'like wax in the sun.' [1]

She remembered that she was a daughter of this house and that she was suffering as much as her sisters from the imposition which made her prioress against their will. But was it not her duty, as it was that of all of them, to obey prelates?

'I am here only to serve you and to make things as pleasant as I can. I hope Our Lord will help me to do this. . . . As to the rest, any single one among you can help me to reform myself. Don't be afraid of my Rule for although it's true I've been living with the Discalced, I think I know, by the grace of God, how one should live among those who are not of that condition. My desire is that we should all serve Our Lord in sweetness. . . .' [2]

In this way she infused feminine charm into the application of one of her principles which rings out with the boldness of a statesman's maxim: 'Moderation in government is a great thing.' [3]

[1] MP quoted SEC, vol. II, p. 107.
[2] SEC, vol. II, p. 216.   [3] Sb, F, c. xviii-6.

IX

'A PRIORESS INDEED . . .'

MAY the Holy Spirit be with Your Grace, and may he show you as much charity as you displayed promptitude in bringing us Don Francisco's alms!'[1]

It was in these terms that Mother Teresa thanked the steward of Francisco de Salcedo, who had just sent her an important consignment of poultry. Sixty-two birds: 'But the poverty of this house is such, there are so many sick people that all that was very necessary.'[2]

The holy gentleman had constituted himself purveyor to the convent of the Incarnation as he was to St Joseph's: vegetables and chickens from his farm, bottles of *aloja*, the drink made of honey and spices which those suffering from fever appreciated so greatly, came to the two convents in abundance. The tiniest salad or basket of quinces filled Teresa of Jesus with joy and gratitude; the convent of the Incarnation was so wretchedly poor that the number of nuns and, still more, of secular persons had greatly diminished, for P. Rubeo, the Master General, had forbidden them to receive novices: they would have been in danger of dying of hunger there.

And so the new prioress began by transforming herself into a kind of quartermaster-sergeant: had not the first miracle of Our Lord Jesus Christ been to give wine to the guests at a wedding? Did he not give bread and fish to the multitudes who followed him on the mountain? Did he not put the petition for our daily bread before that for the forgiveness of our sins or for protection against all evil? Man does not feed 'on bread alone,' but it is right and proper that he should receive his just portion of it.

The Mother Foundress, who had established her Reform on a basis of nuns earning their daily bread and who scolded prioresses who contented themselves with merely making known the fact that they were in need, found herself constrained to appeal to charity to feed these hundred and thirty nuns who were too poor to provide for themselves and too aristocratic to work with their fingers. Before they could be reformed they must be fed: it was hunger that was largely responsible

---

[1] CTA, xli.   [2] Idem.

for the disorder in this miniature world of the convent of the Incarnation; it was in order to avoid starvation that the nuns often went off to their families for months at a time, or perhaps to stay with one or other of the convent's rich benefactors; the reason they flocked so eagerly to the parlours was because there was as much opportunity to stave off one's hunger there by munching the dainties brought by one's visitors, as there was to chatter.

The Duchess of Alba, Doña María de Mendoza, Doña Magdalena de Ulloa—who was known as God's almoner, for she had given more than five hundred silver ciboria to the churches of the Asturias and more than 16,000 ducats for the redemption of captives—played the rôle of Providence at regular intervals, but this did not deter Teresa from asking her sister Juana, whose resources were very modest, for a few reales for her own subsistence: from the convent stores she took only her bread and considered even that was taking too much.

Poor Juana boasted of the prosperity of her farm-yard that year! 'Send us some turkeys, since you have so many.'[1] Teresa scrutinized the accounts and signed the book of expenses daily; the strictly necessary must be considered fully sufficient, for the convent was in debt: it was essential to pay the debts, and they were paid and paid in full.

The Foundress sent for Isabel de la Cruz, formerly Isabel Arias, from Valladolid. Like herself, Isabel was a former member of the community of the Incarnation and knew the spirit of the convent. Assisted by her as sub-prioress, 'with a proper measure of diplomacy'[2] she set on foot the necessary reforms gradually and gently. She treated the nuns like restive fillies, pulled on the reins, but did not fail to offer a morsel of sugar hidden in the palm of her hand. To the poorest, those who had no inheritance—there were eighty of them—she gave one real each week; they were as much amazed at her tact as at her kindness: this small sum of money restored the dignity of those who were poor, and made them independent, far more than their past liberties had ever done.

For the era of anarchy was over. For Lent Teresa abolished all visits, not even making an exception for parents. In that house it was a revolution. But the habitual visitors to the parlour would not take no for an answer. One gentleman, tired of hearing the extern sister answer that the nun whose 'devout gentleman' he was would not receive him, took with him to the very door of the monastery a group of young riders to whom he swore that even if he had to confront the prioress

<hr/>

[1] CTA, xxxvi.   [2] FR.

herself, they should all be admitted in triumph to the parlour. Accordingly he summoned Teresa of Jesus to come and speak with him.

The Foundress settled herself behind the grille, with her spinning-wheel—for she never stopped spinning, unless the visitor was a prelate —and without a word of impatience allowed him to continue to pour out his flood of abuse and ill words until his eloquence dried up of its own accord.

Then she spoke—a few words but unanswerable ones:

'In future Your Grace will leave this convent in peace. If Your Grace persists, I shall appeal to the King.'

The blusterer left the convent abashed and his friends were so much surprised at the tone in which he said: 'There's no trifling with Mother Teresa of Jesus and we shall have to give up the parlour . . .', [1] that they forbore to laugh at his discomfiture.

The report of this incident soon spread round the City of Saints and the saints approved.

From the very beginning of Lent the mortifications which the nuns spontaneously practised in the refectory were 'worthy of all admiration' [2]—the youngest brought Teresa the worldly trifles to which they were still attached—a ring, a mirror, a fan; these hundred and thirty women who had really had their youth taken from them, and who tried to snatch what they could of it at recreation time by worldly dancing, delighting in the latest songs and music, gradually came to prefer to all that the conversation about God, the angels, or heaven which their prioress enlivened with as much wit as spirituality.

'All this goes on in great peace. We should praise Our Lord for the change which has taken place in them. It's those who were the most rebellious who are now the most pleased and who show their pleasure most. There really are great servants of God here and all make progress.' [3] They no longer say: 'A change is worse than death. . . .' [4]

Teresa was sad in spite of her success: she longed for her reformed convents where a round dozen of sisters in perfect recollection obeyed every stroke of the bell and lived in silence. Ávila's icy climate suited her so ill that she could not understand how she came to be born there. Moreover, the dignified simplicity of social relationships seemed to have disappeared in the City of the Knights as it had in the rest of Spain, the most insignificant *hidalgo* now insisted on being addressed

---

[1] Idem. [2] Idem.
[3] CTA, xxxiv. [4] CTA, xxxi.

as 'Don': 'In Ávila now, one finds nothing else than that and it is disgraceful. . . .'[1]

Now it is necessary to address as Illustrious those who were formerly called Magnificent. . . . It's almost necessary to erect a faculty where they teach us how to address the people to whom we write and how we should speak to them; in some cases the margin has to be placed on one side, in others on the other. . . . I've seen so many complete changes in these matters that I no longer know how to go on. . . . I pity spiritual persons who for the highest of reasons are obliged to live in the world: they have a heavy cross to bear. . . .[2]

The seething agitation at the convent of the Incarnation was more painful to her than the trouble of her foundations. She had to be ceaselessly on her guard and had no one in whom she could confide. She who was by nature so spontaneous, in this convent experienced nothing but tension and constraint. The whole time she was loved and honoured by some, suspected or decried by others. At that time it was hardly thought fitting for a woman to display so much energy. Quite recently the Dominican Provincial had asked P. Báñez:

'Who is this Teresa of Jesus of whom they tell me that she's very attached to you? It doesn't do to rely on the virtue of women. . . .'[3]

'Your Paternity is going to Toledo, there you will be able to see her and discover for yourself that it is with reason she is held in high esteem. . . .'

In Toledo, the Provincial, Juan de Salinas, saw her more or less continually throughout Lent and heard her confession nearly every day. He cleverly contrived not to eat his words by declaring to P. Báñez:

'You informed me wrongly when you told me that Mother Teresa was a woman; i' faith she's a man and one of those most worthy to wear a beard.'

This Father showed that he did not know much about women: for Teresa of Jesus was never other than womanly in all her struggles just as much as she was in the intense manifestations of her love of God. But at that time men were little disposed to admit that women had any capacity at all for strength or wisdom. It took both Teresa and her daughters to convince another Dominican, the appointed Apostolic Visitor of the Discalced Carmelites, P. Pedro Fernández, that they were capable of living in accordance with evangelical perfection.

[1] CTA, xciii. [2] Sb, V, c. xxxvii-10, 11.
[3] SST, vol. II, p. 505.

It was not one of the Mother Foundress's least merits that she proved by her example and that of the Carmelites she formed, that 'heroic deeds' are not incompatible with charm and graciousness.

When Teresa exclaimed in protest: 'From foolish devotions may the good Lord deliver us,' she did not attribute such things solely to women, any more than she assigned to them the exclusive prerogative of the 'childish nonsense,' superstition, scruples, pettiness for which she blamed them: in her eyes the 'most serious of men' were not free from such things. In men as in women she complained of unfaithfulness in little things, of self-complacency, blaming such matters all the more severely in those who in that age were the nation's warriors.

> In the case of insignificant little women like myself, weak and possessing but little courage, it seems to me that it is what one would expect that God should grant them to taste of his sweetness. . . . But when I see servants of God, men of weight, learned, intelligent, making a fuss because God does not give them devotion, I am, I must say, disappointed. If Our Lord grants it to them, of course, let them receive it and esteem it highly . . . but if they lack it, they must not be troubled and must understand that since His Majesty does not grant it to them, it is not necessary for them, and let them remain masters of themselves . . . many have begun but never persevere to the end; it is, I think, largely the fact of not embracing the cross from the beginning that makes them distressed for it seems to them that they do nothing. What His Majesty wants are our acts of will. But the afflictions for which we ourselves are responsible only disturb our souls; if such persons cannot make progress in one hour, four will make no difference to them. . . .[1]

Mother Teresa's spirit of determination, her courage in the face of reality, whether in the spiritual sphere or the material, was no masculine prerogative but that of a great mind and a fine character.

The Visitor, P. Fernández, esteemed the Foundress very highly, a fact which he concealed from her as much as he could. Grumbler as he was, he pleased Teresa of Jesus who liked those who treated her without indulgence: 'He keeps me alive, I do not think he is mistaken about me as others are, for God has made him see what a trifling thing I am; at each step, he catches me in some imperfection and this is a great consolation to me; and I do my best to let him know all of them.'[2]

Perhaps this great humility conquered the Apostolic Visitor's intransigence. Although when he spoke to her he did nothing but

[1] Sb, V, c. xi-14.   [2] CTA, xxx.

blame, he sang her praises when he had to argue about her with the Duchess of Alba, who wanted her at Alba de Tormes. 'The hundred and thirty nuns at the Incarnation all live together in as much peace and holiness as the ten or twelve in your convent. This has greatly surprised and pleased me. And it is solely due to the Foundress's presence. If she were missing for a single day, all that has been gained here would be lost. . . .'[1]

If Teresa had known about this letter, she would have replied in the same phrase as she used in writing to Doña María de Mendoza: 'It's my prioress who is working these wonders!'[2]

In point of fact Our Lady of Mercy had remained in the prioress's stall where Teresa had put her on the first day. Every evening it was to her she gave the keys of the convent. In the sub-prioress's place she had put St Joseph. The nuns accused this good saint of revealing all their small imperfections to the Foundress and so they christened his statue 'the chatterer' (*el parlero*) and alleged that St Joseph's mouth was always open. Our Lord began to bestow so many graces on this house that the Mother of God appeared there, in her prioress's stall, surrounded by her company of angels; she remained throughout the singing of the *Salve Regina*.

And then, so that the last might be first and her 'poor dears at the Incarnation' might have expert guidance along the royal road of mental prayer, Teresa gave them Fray John of the Cross as confessor.

She sent for him urgently from Pastrana, where he had been brought with haste from Alcalá to teach the Prince of Éboli's friars that moderation was a virtue. Wherever there was some great and difficult task to be done, Fray John was sent for urgently.

The friars of Pastrana 'seemed men of stone rather than flesh.' They spurred one another on and the church re-echoed with the sound of the blows with which they struck their breasts; when the spirit moved them or when they were inflamed with a kind of mad fervour, they could not restrain their cries, whether it was a matter of the public avowal of their sins or of a manifestation of their love of God. Some were so abundantly endowed by Our Lord with the gift of weeping that the flow of their continual tears carved deep furrows on their wrinkled and ascetic faces.

Mortifications, penances, disciplines were carried to the point of madness. Matters grew to such a pitch that the bare back of a novice was scourged as he knelt in front of a pile of unseasoned wood, in the expectation that fire from heaven would unfailingly come down if the

[1] Quoted SEC, vol. II, p. 247.　　　　　[2] CTA, xxxiv.

novice were very holy or very well beaten. Had that not happened in the case of the prophet Elias, father and model of all the Discalced?

Their feet were so tumefied by the cold and wounded by the stones 'that they were like egg plants. A newcomer, Fray Jerónimo de la Madre de Dios, discouraged, despite his zeal, by such violence and roughness, was on the point of giving up his vocation as a Carmelite.' [1]

Fray John of the Cross had been commissioned to restore some sense of measure and moderation to these fanatics. He displayed so much skill in turning this mad zeal to nobler ends that Mother Teresa judged that no one would be better able to excite fervour in lukewarm nuns than he would. This Father seemed to her to be the man who always struck the right chord.

[1] JGP, Dial. I, p. 21.

X

CHRIST'S BRIDE

'LADIES, I'm giving you as your confessor a Father who is a
saint!'[1]

It was in these terms that the prioress, Mother Teresa of
Jesus, introduced to the convent of the Incarnation, the little dark man
emaciated by penances: Fray John of the Cross. Although he was
thirty he seemed a very young man, so clear and pure was the look
in his dark eyes. 'His bearing was calm and extremely modest, his
mere presence was an invitation to composure. His countenance
reflected something regal that was not of this world, and he inspired
love and respect at the same time.'[2]

The Foundress had had a small hut built for him outside the
enclosure but in the immediate vicinity of the convent: he had no
time to lose in going to and fro; the work was considerable and urgent:
the confessions of one hundred and thirty nuns to be heard at least
once a fortnight besides their direction, ranging from the choice of
their reading to orientation in the ways of spirituality.

And they had to be led individually: the Foundress and Fray John
had the greatest respect for the liberty of souls: each one had her own
particular way. 'Our Lord gives each soul its own grace, in that I do
not interfere.'[3] No collective methods then, but detailed personal
direction, save for the indication of the great lines of mental prayer and
in the observance of the essential virtues, love, humility, obedience,
silence. 'A soul under constraint cannot serve God well, and it is
through that that the devil tempts them,'[4] said the Mother.

Fray John of the Cross echoed her words:

'It is better to leave expressions of love to develop naturally and
fully, in order that each one may profit by them in her own way and
according to the abundance of grace. . . .'[5]

The nuns of the Incarnation were thus called to a state of union
with God, but in perfect freedom: the Foundress showed them the
joys of this state and Fray John the difficulties. He wanted souls to
reach the very summit of spirituality even if everything collapsed or

[1] BRJ, p. 130.   [2] JJ, p. 786.   [3] Sb, V, c. xxii-8.
[4] CTA, cccli.   [5] JCC, Prologue.

crashed about their ears, even if events did not justify their expectations: to disturb oneself effects nothing. . . .[1]

He subdivided mental prayer into three parts:

1. An imaginative representation of the mysteries on which one is to meditate;

2. An intellectual consideration of the mysteries represented;

3. A loving rest in and attention to God. That was where one gathered the fruit, where the door of the mind opened to divine illumination. One passed from natural to supernatural knowledge when the soul put itself into this state of rest which was peaceful, loving and calm at the same time.[2]

Representation, consideration, illumination, love: the Foundress, in counterpoint, illustrated the theory of what he said by realistic images:

'I am sure that Our Lord is not displeased that we should find delight and consolation in contemplating his actions and meditating on his words, just as a king would be delighted to see a good little shepherd boy naïvely look at and admire his rich brocades and wonder what this can be and how that was made. . . .'[3]

Fray John insisted on strict control of the imagination, for contemplation must not be confused with the fantasies of the humours or melancholy. And in this matter, too, he was in agreement with Mother Teresa. He blamed all seeking for sensations, and affirmed that far from being a sign of perfection in mental prayer, the pleasures found therein are a sign of weakness. And if he spoke to them 'of the multitude of sweetness which God has hidden for those who fear him and of the torrents of delight which he will give them to drink,' it was in order that they might feel more surely 'the weight of glory to which the Bridegroom predestined you, on the particular day of eternity when he decided to create you. . . .'[4]

The weight of glory. . . . The Foundress was not exempt from the severities of the confessor of the convent of the Incarnation. She in no way sought to elude them but accepted them in all humility although to tease rather than to mortify her, Fray John one day said to her:

'When you make your confession, Mother, you have a fine way of excusing yourself. . . .'[5]

There is even reason to suppose that he was more severe for the prioress than for the most insignificant nun in the convent: was she

[1] JCS.   [2] JJ, p. 517.   [3] Sb, CAD, c. i–8.
[4] JCC, c. xxxviii.   [5] SST, vol. II, p. 390, n. 1.

not herself more severe towards those she loved most? When Office was over, the confessor ordered Mother Teresa to remain on her knees long hours in the chapel: she had to repent of experiencing too much delight in the love of Our Lord, those *gustos*, those pleasures that she was the first to proscribe. She bowed herself down in prayer and wept as much for the graces God showered upon her as for her sins. Yet what could she do about it? She in no way sought visions or other divine manifestations and did not solicit either the words she heard or the delights she experienced. God loved her, he had chosen her and drawn her to himself almost by force in this very convent more than twenty years ago, while she was still vacillating between heaven and earth; she was as little responsible for those raptures of the spirit as the water when the sun absorbs it and changes it into clouds.

What did Fray John think on Palm Sunday when Teresa, as she communicated, was seized with rapture to such an extent that she could not swallow the Host? When she recovered consciousness her mouth was full of blood which was running down her face—the very blood of Redemption—she experienced an overwhelming sweetness and Our Lord said to her: 'Daughter, I will that my blood be profitable to you. . . . I shed it for you in great pain, make your greatest delight of it. This is my way of returning the invitation which you have always made me on this day.' [1]

For more than thirty years it had been Teresa's custom to communicate on Palm Sunday to prepare her soul to give Jesus a place of sanctuary: 'the cruelty of the Jews towards him seemed to me so great, they had allowed him to go so far away to eat after having given him such a great welcome, that I prepared myself so that he might dwell with me.' [2] On that day she took no food until three o'clock in the afternoon and gave her portion to the poor.

Could Fray John be displeased with such simple tenderness? Despite the fact that her thirst was slaked with blood from the chalice, that she was fed with bread by the hands of Christ himself, drawn close to the Father who spoke 'very pleasant words' [3] to her, jealous, indeed, of Mary Magdalene but consoled by the Son of God: 'she was my friend while I was on earth; it is you I have chosen now I am in heaven' [4]—despite all this he whom the Foundress called 'my little Seneca' was none the less cautious: these emotions and visions seemed to him too earthy: for him 'the soul, unified and transformed by

[1] SEC, R, xxvi, pp. 56–7.   [2] Idem.
[3] SEC, R, xxv, p. 56.   [4] SEC, vol. II, p. 61, n. 1.

abundance of heavenly gifts and riches,'[1] must have 'subjected the passions and mortified the natural appetites.'

Fray John considered that Teresa was still too fond of these joys; and so, out of love, he let nothing pass which he judged to be an imperfection, just as a lapidary lets nothing pass in the diamond he cuts. And so he ended by drawing her away from the matrix-ore of these *gustos*, which too closely resembled this world's joys. And he caused the precious stone to sparkle with the fire that leaps up to meet the light which shines in the darkness and which man will never know until he is reborn of God alone.

One morning at the time of Communion, John of the Cross 'broke the host to give part to another sister,' said Teresa. 'I thought he did so to mortify me, not through want of hosts: I had told him how much I loved big hosts although I knew quite well that Our Lord was wholly present in the smallest particle. His Majesty said to me: "Fear nothing, daughter, nothing can separate you from me." He made me understand that that did not matter.'

Then he appeared to me in an imaginary vision, as he had done before, but in the very depths of my being. He gave me his right hand and said to me: 'Look at this nail: it is the sign that from to-day you are my bride. Until now you had not merited that; in future you will be jealous for my honour not only because I am your Creator and your King, but as my true bride. My honour is yours: your honour is mine.'

The action of this grace was so powerful that I remained out of my senses. I was as it were stupefied and asked Our Lord to enlarge my littleness or else not to give me such an immense favour, for my natural weakness could not bear it. I spent that day in a state of inebriation. Great benefits have come from it since, but also an increase of confusion and distress, for I do not serve as I ought to serve after having received such a great grace.[2]

Such was the mystical marriage of Teresa of Jesus. Her sisters, greatly moved by seeing such marvels in their convent, never again approached the Communion grille, 'blessed bridal couch of such espousals,'[3] otherwise than with awe.

Fray John had cut the slender but still solid thread which bound Teresa to her own will; free at last from the weight of dead matter, detached from herself, bound by no desires, she had accomplished her transfiguration.

[1] JCC, c. xi.   [2] SEC, R, xxv, pp. 63-4.
[3] SEC, vol. II, p. 111.

She gave expression to the ardent bonds of love of this mystical marriage in her *Conceptos del Amor de Dios*, or *Thoughts on the Love of God*.

Everything goes to prove that she wrote these clear, impassioned pages at Ávila.[1] It was at Ávila that Our Lord said to her: 'Do not fail to write down the teaching which I give you, so that you do not forget it. You greatly desire to have the teaching of men in writing: why do you think it is waste of time to write down that which I give you? A day will come when you will need it.' [2]

From the first pages of the *Conceptos* she emphasized her act of obedience to the divine command by answering Our Lord's question directly: 'I hold well employed the time which I shall devote to treating of a matter so divine that I do not deserve to hear it.' [3]

From the account of her visions and certain passages of the *Conceptos* there emerges a dialogue between bride and Bridegroom, and sometimes she likes to remind him of the most wonderful of his promises:

> *Christ:* My honour is yours, your honour is mine!
> *Teresa:* He will take charge of my affairs and I of his! [4]
> *God the Father:* I have given you my Son, the Holy Spirit and the blessed Virgin here. What can you give me? [5]
> *Teresa:* What can I do for my Bridegroom? What could anyone so clumsy as I do? Waste the graces you have given me. . . . [6]
> *Christ:* Do you imagine, daughter, that to be in a state of joy is meritorious? The only way to merit is to act, to suffer and to love.[7]
> *Teresa: Stay me up with flowers.* It does not seem to me that that is asking for death, but more to consecrate one's life to serve him to whom one owes so much. . . .[8] Let Bridegroom and bride be no longer two but one single will, not so much in words or desires but in acts.

Such was indeed the case. In future Teresa's sole delight would be to act for the Bridegroom and with him, in voluntary renouncement of pure contemplation:

[1] P. Silverio de Santa Teresa dates the *Conceptos* between 1571 and 1573 at Ávila, Salamanca or Medina del Campo. P. Bruno assigns to them the year 1574. But the likeness between this book and the spiritual notes made at Ávila during the time she was prioress at the Incarnation is too great for it to be possible not to admit that it stems directly from them. Moreover, is not this commentary on the *Canticle of Canticles* the very panegyric of the mystical marriage? She must have written it towards the end of her stay in Ávila and perhaps finished it at Segovia.

[2] SEC, R, xxviii, p. 58
[3] Sb, CAD, c. i–8.
[4] Sb, CAD, c. iv–8.
[5] SEC, R, xxv, p. 56.
[6] Sb, CAD, c. iv–11.
[7] SEC, R, xxxvi, p. 64.
[8] Sb, CAD, c. vii–1.

The soul asks that she may accomplish great things in the service of Our Lord and of her neighbour and for that she is more than content to forgo her pleasures. For although they fully understand all they will lose in this existence which is more active than contemplative, Martha and Mary never fail to act almost simultaneously when the soul is in this state. One's contemplative life expands into activities which seem exterior and when the works of the active life spring from this root they produce lovely and fragrant flowers: they spring from this tree of the love of God alone, for him alone, without anything of self-interest and the fragrance of these flowers spreads all around, for the good of many: it is a fragrance which does not evaporate quickly and it produces great effects.[1]

Contemplation was no longer to be an end in itself: it was becoming a force for action, in action.

And because Teresa of Jesus no longer sought for anything but the Kingdom of God, all the rest was added unto her: efficacious action and joy.

Despite the calm and peaceful tone which she forces herself to adopt in these *Thoughts on the Love of God*, a commentary on the *Canticle of Canticles* written for the nuns of the Incarnation—this much can be surmised from the precautions she takes not to discourage, by making too many demands, those who are not yet entirely detached from the world, and from the circumspection, delicate tact and discreet allusions to which she has recourse to detach them from it —her bridal love breaks out and is carried away on the tide of the Bridegroom's love:

... A sort of divine intoxication, oblivious of what it wants, what it says, what it demands. . . .[2] He wants to fill her to overflowing, to delight her still more, he changes her into himself, and like all those who faint away through excess of pleasure and joy, she remains as it were unconscious in the divine arms and on the divine breast. She no longer cares for anything except to abandon herself to joy, nourished by the divine milk. . . . This heavenly inebriation by which she is delighted and terrified at the same time . . . this holy madness. . . . *Thy breasts are better than wine . . .*[3] entirely saturated in the ineffable greatness of God. . . . My Bridegroom, a single drop of the precious wine which you give me makes me forget every created thing. . . . Let me gaze at my Beloved and he at me. . . . I beseech you, O God, by the blood of your Son, to give me this grace: *Kiss me with a kiss of your mouth!* [4] . . . And what can I do for my Bridegroom? [5]

[1] Sb, CAD, c. vii-3. [2] Sb, CAD., c. v.
[3] CC. [4] Idem. [5] Sb, CAD, c. v.

The younger nuns at the Incarnation badly needed to purify their idea of love in this way. At first they had irritated Teresa considerably by their tittering: they were mature in years but had never really grown up:

'I remember having heard a wonderful sermon on these delights of the bride in her intercourse with God; there was so much laughter and what the preacher said was so very much misunderstood, because he spoke of love, that I was appalled.'[1]

Teresa was like the woman of Samaria 'who so well understood Our Lord's words and took them to heart that she left Our Lord himself to go and bring the people of her village to him and as a reward for her great charity she merited to see the great good which he wrought in that place. The holy Samaritan woman inebriated with the wine of God, went through the streets crying aloud. At last they listened to her and the number of those who went to Our Lord was very great.'[2]

Teresa wrote the *Conceptos*, her expressions of love, at the order of her Bridegroom, Christ, but with the authorization of her confessor. Fray John of the Cross knew all about the work, discussed it with her, and his answer to this mysticism of love issuing in action was the arguments which he was later to develop on this same theme of the *Canticle of Canticles* in his *Cántico Espiritual*; but he gave pride of place to Mary rather than to Martha:

When the soul has reached this state of loving union, it is not fitting that she should busy herself with external actions even for God's service, for this may fetter her in this life of love in him. For a little of this pure love is more precious in his eyes and for the soul— even though it seems one is doing nothing—than all other actions put together. That is why Mary Magdalene hid herself in the desert for thirty years to give herself wholly to this love. . . . Consequently, when a soul has in herself a particle of this high state of solitary love, to occupy her in external or active things, however important, and even if only for a short time, would be to do her great harm.[3]

The spiritual marriage of Teresa of Jesus, the state of soul which resulted from it, to which she gave expression in the *Thoughts on the Love of God*, mark the difference between the mystical way followed by the prioress and that followed by her confessor. For her, to love was to act. For him, to love was to immerse oneself completely in contemplation.

The difference, however, in no way impaired their deep communion of thought. Teresa was fully aware that she owed much to the

[1] Sb, CAD, i-5.   [2] Sb, CAD, c. cvii—6.   [3] JCC, c. xxviii.

spirit and virtue which Our Lord had given Fray John,[1] ' people consider him a saint and in my opinion he is one and has been all his life.'
He was then and always the Father of her soul. As to him, it is touching
to see him turning gradually towards action after the Mother Foundress's death, as if he did not want to lose anything of that precious
heritage. The directives which he gave to prioresses were framed so
closely upon those of Mother Teresa that he even borrowed her homely
expressions: 'Watch carefully whom you accept in the beginning for
those who come afterwards will be like them. . . . Tell the sisters
that since Our Lord has chosen them as the first stones of the building
they must take care as to what sort of people they really are. . . . In a
beginning like this, let them set out anew along the way of perfection,
in all humility and detachment both within and without, not childishly,
but with a stout heart.'[2]

Mother Teresa would have smiled tenderly had she read her little
Seneca's letter to Ana de San Alberto, Prioress of Caravaca: 'I am in
Seville, busy with the removal of our sisters who have bought a very
suitable house; although it has cost 14,000 ducats, it is worth more than
20,000. They are installed there and the Cardinal will place the Blessed
Sacrament there with all solemnity on the feast of St Barnabas. I intend
to establish another house of friars here before I leave. . . . About the
feast of St John, I leave for Ecija where by the grace of God we shall
found another, then I go to Málaga and finally to the *junta*. . . .'

Thus Fray John also became a Father Founder.

Distinct both in temperament and in their ideas of the mystical life,
Teresa and John become identical when they are carried beyond themselves by the flight of the spirit.

In the little parlour of the Incarnation with its red-tiled floor,
prioress and confessor often spoke together. About the state of soul of
his spiritual daughters, Fray John could be as precise as the Foundress
usually was. On the subject of spiritual illuminations Teresa could be
as free from all earthly bonds as Fray John.

One day—it was the feast of the Holy Trinity—seated one each side
of the grille, he on a chair and she on her bench, they were speaking of
the essence of the Three Persons in One, 'this marvellous operation,'[3]
when Beatriz de Ocampo, who was looking for the prioress, saw her on
her bench indeed and Fray Juan in his chair, but both in ecstasy and
Fray John, borne upwards by the flight of the spirit, was touching the
ceiling.

[1] CTA, x.   [2] JC quoted SEC, vol. VI, p. 213.
[3] SEC, R, xxxiii, p. 62.

But both knew that perfection does not consist in such wonders.

'Humility, always humility,' said Teresa of Jesus. And John of the Cross echoed: 'Humility.'

The 'poor little nuns of the Incarnation' thus travelled along the path to heaven guided by one who was 'heavenly and divine,' Fray John. P. Pedro Fernández, taking advantage of this situation, did not let the Mother Foundress rest. He sent her to Alba de Tormes, recalled her to Ávila and finally sent her back to Salamanca to transfer the nuns to a new house. P. Antonio de Jesús was commissioned to accompany her, as well as a few nuns—quite a little escort—and naturally, Julian de Ávila. Once more in Ávila people would talk of nothing else but Teresa of Jesus and Julian! Teresa laughed heartily over it.

It was August and to avoid the heat they decided to start at nightfall.

Things began badly: first Antonio de Jesús, and then a servant girl, fell head foremost from their mounts.

And afterwards it was not much better. Julian de Ávila gave an amusing account of the journey to anyone who cared to listen:

It was very dark, the donkey which was carrying the money intended for Salamanca got lost and could not be found in the darkness; with all our searching and the falls we had in the pitch-black night, it was after midnight when we reached the inn. Next morning, a servant went out to look for the donkey we had lost and found her lying on the side of the path: her load was intact.

The next night we lost much more than the donkey, although she was said to be carrying five hundred ducats. . . .

What did he mean?—They lost Mother Teresa in person.

It was still dark and we were travelling in two groups: the one our holy Mother was with, and for the sake of their honour I won't say of whom it consisted, left her in the street of a little village, asking her to wait for us, and went off before the others; but when it came to finding the Foundress again, they couldn't remember where they had left her.

We kept on asking each other: 'Is the Mother with you?'

They replied: 'No!'

'She is with *you* then?'

'She was with us, but she isn't now. Where has she gone?'

We were thus in every kind of gloom and darkness, that of the night, which was thick, and that which was much darker still of finding ourselves without our Mother. We didn't know what to do: should we go forward or go back? We separated once more, some to look for her whom we had lost, others to call her with great cries in the hope that she would answer us from one point or another.

'Madre Teres–a–a–a–a–a!'

'Madre Teresa de Jes–ú–u–u–u–s!'

After a long time of suspense and anguish we saw our Mother coming with her companion and a peasant whom she had got out of his house and induced to set them on the right road by giving him four reales. He went back very pleased with his money and we still more so at having recovered all our riches, and merry at having these adventures to tell.

We stumbled upon an inn so overcrowded with muleteers that they were even sleeping on the ground, and it was impossible to take one step without treading on harness or on sleeping men. At last we found a small space for our holy Mother and the sisters we were bringing with us, although there were not six feet of empty space; to fit in at all they were obliged to stand up. Such inns had one good point about them, that we impatiently awaited the hour of our departure. . . .[1]

At Salamanca Mother Teresa was busy with the reconstruction of a house which was destined later to cause them a lot of trouble, but what did it matter? They had to provide for present necessities. More than twenty workmen erected 'more than two hundred yards of partitions,'[2] to make the cells and enclosures. The Mother Foundress directed operations and the workmen found, as she herself thought, 'that experience had given her a good knowledge of these matters.'[3]

She had the art of infusing any work with encouragement; Pedro Hernández, the head carpenter, told all his life afterwards how Mother Teresa would sometimes appear at the top of a skylight giving orders that all the workmen were to be brought something to drink. One day, he considered that her generosity was involving her in too much expense—a measure of wine cost a real and a half—so he sent only for a maravedi's worth and poured it out sparingly, but when he poured what he thought was the last drop, the jar was still full.[4]

Their thirst slaked with miraculous wine, how could workmen and masons be lacking in courage?

When this house was finished, there were fresh departures and fresh arrivals: Alba de Tormes, Medina del Campo, finally Ávila but for a very short time, for the turmoil over the foundations which had died down for the past three years was to begin again.

[1] JA quoted SEC, vol. VI, pp. 148–9. [2] CTA, xlvii.,
[3] Idem, 41. [4] SEC, vol. V p. 157, n. 2.

XI

THE SHADOW OF THE GRAND
INQUISITOR

MOTHER Teresa set out for Segovia carefree: all the indications for this foundation were good. The less attention she attracted, the better she felt on these journeys and this time she had with her only Fray John of the Cross, Julian de Avila, Isabel de Jesús—the nun who sang the *cantarcillo* at Salamanca—and a layman, Antonio Gaytán[1] : only four companions but very capable ones.

A widower and a man of some means, Antonio Gaytán had developed such a zeal for the reformed Carmel and Mother Teresa, that he had begged her to make use of him for whatever the Order needed: it was not necessary to use this sort of language twice to the Mother Foundress and from that moment Antonio Gaytán had no respite. He put a duenna at the head of his household, entrusting her with the upbringing of his daughters, and went off to accompany Teresa of Jesus.

As they went along the road he learnt principles of spirituality adapted to the needs of the daily life of a good layman: as Teresa saw things, just as in the world there are different climates, seasons and changes of weather, so the needs of each one's spiritual life vary according to temperament and occupation. She reassured him when he complained of the slow progress he made in prayer: 'Don't be in any way troubled about it, that is not your fault. . . .'[2] 'Don't tire yourself out by too much thinking, don't be distressed by your failures in meditation. The greatest grace God gives us is that of praising him without ceasing, and to do all we can that others may praise him. . . .'[3]

She had a dangerous mission for him: the secret removal—we might almost say abduction—of the fourteen nuns of the convent of Pastrana, victims of the extraordinary Ana de Mendoza y la Cerda, Princess of Eboli.

The Prince had died a year before. His wife had not been able to resign herself to being a widow like other widows: she took the Carmelite habit in Madrid—a habit which she had had patched

[1] Sb, F, c. xxi-4.   [2] CTA, lxvi.   [3] Idem.

beforehand—from the hands of the same priest who had given the Last Sacraments to her husband whom she loved to such an extent that she would have preferred not to survive him. Leaving in the lurch the pledges of this love, her ten children, she got into a completely closed cart, in imitation of the holy Mother Teresa, and, renouncing Satan, who did not, however, renounce her, she set off for Pastrana.

When the prioress, Isabel de Santo Domingo, was informed of her arrival in the middle of the night, she exclaimed:

'The Princess in the convent! This house is lost!' [1]

She did not come alone: like the widows of India who climbed on to the funeral pyre with all their suite, she brought a number of girls, her maids, and demanded that they should be admitted to the novitiate with her.

She demanded. All the woman knew was how to demand. A strange way for a Carmelite to talk. But this was only the beginning.

For Sister Ana de la Madre de Dios—such was the name she took in religion—neither rules, Constitutions nor bells existed and still less did she dream of obeying in the slightest degree. Her idea was to speak when she wanted to, receive visitors, go out; she had her cell made to communicate with the street. She insisted on being treated with all the honours due to her rank, ill-treated the prioress and openly snapped her fingers at chaplains, confessors and visitors:

'What have friars to do with *my* convent?'

In the end she caused so much scandal that they had to tell her it was too great an honour for a poor convent to have her among them and that the court alone was worthy of her: and this Isabel de Santo Domingo made her understand, politely, but firmly.

Ana de Mendoza, so-called of the Mother of God, did not fail to understand the meaning which lay behind these courteous words, exclaimed that they were turning her out and appealed to the King; she found herself put in her place once more, and this time with less regard for her feelings, in the world of sinful women who were only half repentant: Philip II, beside himself, now called her 'a notorious female.'

'Your first duty', he intimated to her, 'is to look after your children.'

Once back in her palace she sought for something to amuse her and found it: to persecute the poor Discalced nuns; the least of her cruelties was to suppress the revenue· which she had undertaken to give them, which was tantamount to imposing famine upon them, for nobody could help them in this isolated village.

[1] SEC, vol. V, p. 139, n. 4.

Mother Teresa with her sympathetic nature felt the sufferings of her nuns keenly and if she only took one sister for the Segovia foundation, it was because she intended to bring the Princess of Eboli's victims there.

Everything augured very well indeed for the new convent: a 'great servant of God,' Doña Ana de Jimena, had a house ready where the first Mass could be said immediately. The Mother arrived as usual *sin blanca*, but Providence would not fail to provide for the purchase of a suitable and permanent house: the good Lord had never failed them yet.

And so Teresa of Jesus was musing over these details, as one likes to do in a carriage bearing one swiftly towards an objective the fulfilment of which is already in sight, when Julian de Ávila came and asked her to let him see how the document in which the Bishop authorized her to found this convent was drawn up.

'A document? I haven't one. Isn't a Bishop's verbal authorization sufficient?'

The mules had difficulty in climbing the steep slopes of the Guadarrama, the cart jolted violently and, in addition, Julian de Ávila began to be sulky and scold:

'The Bishop is away. It only wants the Vicar-General to be the sort of man who's particular about papers. . . . Anyhow, don't let's think any more about it!'

At Segovia they got into the house at nightfall. Next morning they rang their bell, Julian de Ávila said the first Mass and installed the Blessed Sacrament: whatever happened, the convent of St Joseph of the Carmel of Segovia was founded. But what a fright followed! The worthy chaplain, without any false pride, told the story:

> The Vicar-General came in, and I never saw a man more angry. He shouted, wanting to know who had put the Blessed Sacrament there. The nuns had already withdrawn to the enclosure and as to myself, confronted with a rage like this, I took refuge under a staircase. The man happened to pick on Fray John of the Cross.
>
> 'Father, who has put *That* there? Take *That* away as quickly as possible, while I ask myself ought I to put you in prison or not?' [1]
>
> He didn't do so because it was a friar, but if he had noticed a poor little ecclesiastic like me, I'm sure he would have sent me there.

The Foundress remained unmoved by this scene: she scarcely worried at all once the first Mass was said: all her worries were 'before.' She stood up to the Vicar-General with as much boldness as

[1] JA quoted SEC, vol. VI, p. 194.

courtesy. He did not dare to suppress the convent, but in order that his prohibition of the saying of Mass should be observed, he left a constable there who frightened everybody considerably.

The storm was violent but quickly over: it was possible to prove to the Vicar-General the authenticity of the verbal authorization given by the Bishop and everything was then in order.

That is to say Julian and Antonio Gaytan were free to set off on their expedition to Pastrana. They took five carts with them.

The nuns were ready. On Mother Teresa's advice, for some time now the prioress had made a note each time of everything the Princess gave them, both in the way of ordinary things and sacred vessels and vestments. Isabel de Santo Domingo, who was as great an expert in legal niceties as if she had practised nothing else all her life, sent for the *Corregidor* and a notary public and, inventory in hand, gave back everything which did not form part of the convent's original possessions: what was left of the poor nuns' belongings amounted to very little.

The two rescuers, priest and layman, scaled the walls in great secrecy, and, very excited at playing such an important part in an adventure where it might be said that heaven was in conflict with the court, slipped silently into the convent. The first thing was to consume the sacred species, then, fortified with the Bread of the strong, the nuns followed their rescuers in single file, walking on tiptoe and with the utmost caution, invoking God, but in their hearts alone. The silence which preceded dawn seemed like the silence of an ambush: anything might be expected from such a powerful and vindictive enemy. Good Padre Julian admitted that to escape as they were doing took more courage than if they had been able to make a frontal attack on their enemy.

The carts were waiting a good way off in order not to attract attention in the village. At last the fourteen nuns got in, and the fugitives were able to get away from Pastrana amid a great clatter of galloping mules, cracking of whips and shouting of muleteers.

With the exception that they were all nearly drowned crossing the Tormes which Julian de Ávila compared to the sea, they arrived at Segovia safe and sound after several days' rapid travelling along roads as hilly and uneven as any in the world.

Teresa was overjoyed and showed it and she appointed Isabel de Santo Domingo, who had given such magnificent proof of wisdom, courage and wit in her dealings with Doña Ana de Mendoza, prioress of the convent at Segovia.

And it was thought that the matter was ended.

But if the Princess had not sent her myrmidons in pursuit of a few poor nuns, it was because she was holding in reserve a more sensational revenge.

How did she know, at the time of the foundation of the houses in Pastrana, that Mother Teresa had written an account of her life? Teresa of Jesus kept this autobiography, which was written solely at the command of her confessors and for them alone, secret; she had been on her guard against letting slip the slightest hint of it to the Princess, more than in the case of anyone else. And how did it leak out that the Foundress had brought a copy with her? The imprudence— for her ill intention is not proven—of an Augustinian nun whom Ana de Mendoza had forced the Foundress to accept and who was indeed promptly sent away, was to blame. This excitable lady was seized with so violent a curiosity over the book that she did all she possibly could to get hold of and read it. She tried to coax Teresa, but the Foundress was firm and persisted in her refusal. Feeling herself snubbed, Ana got excited, stormed and appealed to Ruy Gómez who begged Teresa to give permission for the sake of peace: finally Ana did not hesitate to swear that no one but she and her husband would read it. Besides, why should they mind her seeing it so much? Had not her aunt, Doña Luisa de la Cerda, had a copy in her house?

Teresa of Jesus had been forced to give way.

Persistent in all matters of spite or envy, the Princess was quite the contrary in the fulfilment of her pledged word: in Palencia the account of the *Life* of Mother Teresa lay about on the tables of the palace; the court and the servants had full leisure to derive edification from or to ridicule it: much amusement was derived from Teresa's visions and they were laughingly compared to the deceits in which the devil entangled Magdalena de la Cruz. The echo of all this ridicule even reached Madrid and the Princess did not fail to add her grain of spice; for an entire season one of the court's greatest amusements was to introduce this subject of conversation in which Ana de Mendoza's wit sparkled as did her spite.

So Mother Teresa thought she could tear her innocent nuns away from her, did she? The Princess of Éboli gloated over her denunciation of the *Autobiography* of Teresa of Jesus to the Inquisition and affirmed that the book contained 'visions, revelations and the setting forth of dangerous doctrine.' [1]

While this one-eyed lady was weaving her network of intrigue

[1] SEC, vol. I, p. cxxiii.

Teresa was enjoying the quietude of souls which are innocent and pure; she was very far from imagining to what lengths hatred and wounded vanity could go. She had just bought a good house for the Carmel of Segovia and had installed her nuns there with the usual ceremony for taking possession of a house: followed by the nuns singing *Laudate Dominum omnes gentes*, she went from room to room ringing a little bell and opening all the doors. They set up an altar in this place where in future no spirit would reign but that of Christ.

This convent was as humble and poor as she liked to have them, with low ceilings under the red roof-tiles, for 'thirteen poor little women, the least corner is sufficient. . . .'[1] The cells opened on to the patio. It was there that one day Fray John of the Cross was so transported with love at the sight of a picture of Christ falling under the weight of a cross in the form of a wine-press that he went totteringly to embrace the great dark cross which stood out against the white wall of the cloister and fell into ecstasy.

The Foundress could talk with the Father of her soul in peace and enjoy solitude in a cell at the top of the house where she frequently shut herself away. 'It is a long time since I've been able to isolate myself like this and I find it a great consolation.'[2] Her nuns surrounded her with an affection which, even if it was sometimes indiscreet was always sweet to her affectionate nature, so affectionate that the word 'love' was perhaps the one she uttered most frequently. 'I want to do nothing but love,' she said, 'there is no better remedy than love. . . .'[3] Because she herself loved so truly and sincerely, she found it natural that others should love her truly and sincerely too.

When Ana de la Santísima Trinidad who naïvely followed her everywhere discovered her praying in her cell at the top of the house Teresa scolded her with an indulgent smile:

'You little ferret! Won't you ever leave me alone?'[4]

These indiscretions had a happy consequence: Teresa of Jesus had brought to Segovia the little notebook containing the *Thoughts on the Love of God* and showed it to her confessor, P. Diego de Yanguas. This father was no less famous for his unpolished, sturdy virtues than he was for his commentaries on St Thomas. He read it and said:

'What's the good of using up your energy writing things like that? Throw it in the fire.'

Teresa did not answer, her face betrayed not the slightest emotion, a fire was lighted and she threw the sheets of paper into it.

[1] Sb, C, c. ii–9.   [2] CTA, lxx.
[3] SEC, R, v, p. 32.   [4] SEC, F, p. 178, n. 2.

P. Yanguas was 'animated with the zeal of St Paul who ordered women to be silent in the church of God: that is that they should not preach in the pulpit and must not write books.' [1] But that was not all: the Inquisition showed particular severity in everything touching on knowledge of the Scriptures. One of the accusations which had told heavily against the *Alumbrados* of Toledo had been that they met in groups, secretly, to comment on the Holy Scriptures 'in hidden corners'; they were even called 'disciples of secret doctrines and of hidden places. . . .' Teresa always took the greatest possible care to specify clearly that the Scriptures brought her great consolation when expounded to her by theologians whose holiness was equalled by their learning, but she made no allusion to any direct reading: yet the quotations she made from the Bible and her constant references to it prove that she knew it very thoroughly. She affirmed that the words of the Gospel made her more recollected than the most learned books, [2] and Our Lord himself said to her: 'All the evils of the world come from ignorance of the truths of Scripture in all their clarity, of which not one jot nor tittle shall fail. . . .' [3] But this did not prevent her interrupting a prospective postulant at Toledo whom she had just accepted, when the girl said she would bring her Bible with her:

'Child, stay where you are! We don't need you or your Bible! We are ignorant people who only know how to spin and to obey. . . .' [4]

In the heyday of the Grand Inquisitor Don Gaspar de Quiroga this was wise, and there was more prudence than narrow-mindedness in P. Yanguas' attitude. Fray Luis de León was shortly to be thrown into prison for having translated the *Canticle of Canticles* into Castilian at the request of one of his penitents: [5] he remained there four years.

One can imagine P. Diego's fear when confronted with Teresa of Jesus' vehement 'little notebook.' He defended himself against the charge of having behaved in an intransigent way by claiming to have spoken only in jest and to test the Mother's obedience: he never imagined that she would so eagerly throw into the flames such a wonderful little book 'which contained nothing against faith.' [6]

He little knew how the Foundress loved to obey or her total absence of literary vanity.

---

[1] SEC, vol. IV, pp. liv–lv. [2] Sb, C, c. xxi–4.
[3] Sb, V, c. xl–l. [4] SEC, vol. V, p. 129, n. 1.
[5] Largely because the penitent was indiscreet; the MS. was for her own eyes only—Tr.
[6] SEC, vol. IV, pp. liv–lv.

However, the text was saved: one of the 'ferrets' had copied the manuscript secretly. Teresa imagined that the whole thing was destroyed and thought no more about it. Each of her retreats on the threshold of a foundation contributed in increasing measure to detach her from all created things. From Segovia she wrote: 'I am freer, interiorly, day by day. . . .'[1]

At this time the Inquisition in Ávila was looking not only for her *Autobiography* but for all her other writings. P. Domingo Báñez, determined to support Mother Teresa with his weighty authority, took the book which had been denounced to the Inquisitors himself, after having made a few very slight emendations; he added a few pages of approval.

When Teresa learned what danger she was in, she was in no way troubled:

'God knows with what sincerity I have written what is true.'

Moreover, in all her books, great and small, did she not proclaim her fidelity to the Church, always and in every way? In the account of her *Life*: 'to tear the devils to pieces in defence of the very least of the teachings of the Church. . . .'[2] In the *Interior Castle*: 'If I said anything not in accordance with the truths of our holy, Catholic and Roman Church, it was through ignorance and not malice. . . .'[3] In the *Way of Perfection*: 'In everything I hold to the truths of our holy mother, the Roman Church.'[4] In her spiritual conversations with her confessors: 'I submit myself to the correction of the Church.'[5]

Submission for her was simply love.

What she felt more was the anxiety of her daughters and she reassured them by reminding them:

> Let nothing disturb thee,
> Let nothing affright thee,

or else she gently shrugged her shoulders:

'¿*Que más da*—?What if things are so?'

On leaving Segovia to return to Ávila, she stopped at the cave in which St Dominic had dwelt. She remained there prostrate in prayer for so long that her little escort grew impatient. With all her charm and graciousness she apologized: she had been kept by the holy Friar Preacher who had appeared to her. He had promised to help her in everything and especially in her foundations.

What had she to fear from anything or anybody, even from Inquisitors?

---

[1] CTA, lvi.   [2] Sb, V, c. xxv-12.   [3] M, Prologue.
[4] Sb, C, Prologue.   [5] SEC, R, i, p. 7.

XII

JERÓNIMO GRACIÁN DE LA MADRE
DE DIOS

ACROSS country that might be described as greyish-blue in colour, sharply delineated in the cold light, as with an etching-tool, the carts screeched their way as they clung to the sides of the Sierra Morena. At each turn of the wheel, stones from the side of the track loosened and rolled down into the void, rebounding from rock to rock, awakening in the depths to which they fell echoes which made ten valiant women shudder.

The seven convents of Carmelite nuns which Mother Teresa had founded so far had been situated 'in her part of the country' within about twenty or thirty leagues of Ávila in one direction or another; now, in February 1575, she was venturing further afield, to Beas, on the borders of Castile and Andalusia, in the province of Jaén. Dismayed by the distance and the prospect of travelling across high mountains, she had finally allowed herself to be persuaded by the persistent piety of the donors, the two Godínez sisters, ladies of noble birth, and by the attraction of a climate which was particularly mild and pleasant. She took with her the two most faithful among her loyal friends, Julian de Ávila and Antonio Gaytán and with them Gregorio Martínez who had known her at Medina del Campo and had followed her. Ana de Jesús, the beautiful Lobera girl known as 'Queen of the World,' was one of the party, as was also María de San José, formerly Doña Luisa de la Cerda's little waiting-maid. In addition there were Isabel de San Jerónimo, whom P. John of the Cross had cured of melancholy, Ana de San Alberto, María del Espíritu Santo, María de la Visitación, Isabel de San Francisco, who wrote so well that Teresa asked her to be Carmel's chronicler, tiny little Leonor de San Gabriel, so charming and affectionate that she was always *mi Gabrielita* to the Mother Foundress, and lastly Beatriz de San Miguel: when quite a child Beatriz had cut off her fair curls and brought them to her mother in a box:

'I'm leaving you this finery and I want to go to God.'

It was she who held the child Jesus in her arms, he went with her on all journeys.

For days the rickety, jolting carts jerked their way across the sierra. There was no end to the zigzags, steep ascents and abrupt falls. The mules went more and more slowly, less and less surely, and the drivers themselves seemed to have no lungs left as they shouted their *¡Ar–e–e–e–e!* to spur on their beasts.

The Mother, through a chink in the wooden planks which closed in her cart, saw a certain anxiety in the looks of the muleteers who were hesitating; a moment later they tackled a steep slope which might have been all right for goats, but was in no way intended for their wide, heavy carts. She scented danger.

Like the captain in a storm giving orders to reef the sails and lash the tiller, the Foundress ordered her nuns to suppress the fear they had good reason for feeling, and not to loose hold of their faith in God's protection:

'Those men no longer know where they're going. Let us betake ourselves to prayer, Sisters, let us ask Our Lord and our father St Joseph to guide us!' [1]

Then a voice rose from far away, from the very bottom of the ravine, the voice of an old shepherd who was used to making himself heard at an immense distance:—'Sto–o–op! sto–o–o–p! You will overturn and roll down the precipice if you go that w–a–a–y!'

Amid the clatter of wooden shoes, scraping over the stones, of men tugging frantically and brutally at the reins, of the jingling of harness, of screeching axles, of the clash of wheels, the carts made an abrupt halt whilst the shouts of the muleteers were echoed in the mountains around: 'Sto–o–o–p! *¡Par–e–e–en! ¡Par–e–e–e–e–n!*'

The panic of men and beasts lasted a few seconds, followed immediately by a great hubbub of questions, affirmations and exclamations: they were well and truly lost in the Sierra Morena! Actually, they were slipping down into an abyss! The voice coming up from the depths of the chasm had saved them. But how were they to get out of their present situation? How were they to turn round on the narrow path between the rock and the chasm? How were they to find the right road again?

With hand over mouth, trumpetwise, they shouted to the bottom of the precipice: 'Where can we pa–a–a–ss?'

And the bottom of the precipice answered:

'Go gently backwards, there's no danger in that. If you go back a hundred turns of the wheel, you will find the right track ag–a–a–i–i–n!'

[1] AJ, quoted SEC, vol. VI, p. 200 and the whole account of the journey.

The voice hovered in the silence and echo gave it back as a very clear mirror gives back a reflection.

A servant who went to reconnoitre came back declaring that the right track was indeed at the point indicated: it was concealed by a boulder which could be moved without great difficulty. While some of the men in the escort set to work to clear away the boulder the others tried to find their invisible rescuer. They shouted as loud as they could, peered into the depths of the chasm, one of them even tried to climb down it: all to no purpose. Where was this shepherd hiding? The air was so diaphanous that it was possible to distinguish the tiniest stone as far as the eye could see, and the sierra was so barren, the light so penetrated to every part of it that it seemed impossible to hide there.

Teresa's countenance was radiant with love amid her tears and confusion:

'I don't like letting them go on looking,' she said to her daughters: 'they will find nobody. But we can't tell them that the voice we heard is our father St Joseph's answer to our prayers.' They had still one day more of mountain travel, but from then onwards everything was so easy and the beasts moved so quickly that the muleteers grumbled and swore.

'Driving mules who fly is strange work.'

On the banks of the Guadalquivir the Carmelites were preparing to get down from their carts to cross the river, when they found themselves transported to the opposite bank: it was no longer possible to hide from anyone that heaven's angels were carrying the holy Mother in their arms. . . . [1]

The excitement this supernatural event caused was such that all the clergy of Beas in surplices, with all the inhabitants, children included, walking in procession with the cross at their head, came out to meet Teresa of Jesus; the party was preceded by horsemen who made their horses perform 'all the courtesies in the world.' [2] They escorted her to the church which she entered to the chanting of the *Te Deum*, in the midst of all the nobility of the place and all the notables in festive attire.

Such were the miracles which brought joy. But there was a miracle of a different sort: the new convent, which adjoined the parish church, was installed in what had been the assistant priest's house and the nuns were authorized to follow the Offices at the parish church through a small window. This authorization annoyed a certain Alonso

[1] Idem. [2] FR.

de Montalvo so much that he did not hesitate to go off to Madrid to
get it suppressed. He came back very proud of himself:

'The window will be closed up in three days or else my eyes will
be closed. . . .' [1]

Three days later his eyes were closed: he died suddenly. As the
psalmist says, it is thus that the just shall rejoice when he shall see the
retribution of the wicked.

The veneration and enthusiasm which Teresa inspired bordered
on delirium and the convent of St Joseph of our Saviour of Beas,
inaugurated on 24th February, became a nursery of saints.

The two Godínez sisters who had given the house and 6,000
ducats, took the veil there under the names of Catalina and María,
de Jesús.

Of the two it was Catalina who had the strong personality:
Catalina Godínez, or 'pride converted,' was the subject of a picturesque
story of the kind Teresa loved to write.

At fourteen she had been so proud of her beauty, her fortune and
her name, that she was annoyed at what she considered the lack of
ambition on the part of her parents when it came to the matter of her
marriage: they were contenting themselves with an heir, the eldest of
a great family, for her. She did not understand where she got so much
pride from but she found the thought of being tied to a man humiliating; she would have liked her lineage to begin from herself alone! [2]

God was going to make use of her pride to win her to himself.
One evening when she was thinking over her prospects of marriage,
raising her eyes her glance fell on the crucifix and in a flash she understood that God alone was a spouse worthy of her. She was a strong
character: she made a vow of chastity and poverty on the spot. The
devils, from whose clutches she was escaping, then made such a din
in the house that her father, awakened by the noise, came downstair
in night attire and sword in hand.

Her parents did not allow Catalina to enter a convent, and persisted in trying to force her to marry; to frighten off her suitors, she
secretly went to the farm buildings, wet her face and exposed it to the
sun to spoil her complexion, like Peau d'Âne. [3] All the time she could
snatch from her mother's strict supervision she spent in prayer and she
got up at night and groped in the dark to kiss the feet of the sleeping
servants: she asked their pardon for the fact that she was forced to let
herself be served by them.

---

[1] RD quoted SEC, vol. V, p. 192, n. 3.   [2] Sb, F, c. xxii-5.
[3] A character in one of Perrault's fairy tales.

She suffered from all sorts of diseases but was miraculously cured. The death of her father and mother left her free and she was at last able to obtain from Mother Teresa the foundation of a Carmelite convent at Beas of which she and her sister María would bear the cost.

She had learned of the existence of the reformed Carmel from an angel: she had seen herself in a great room of some convent, whose only light came from the candles which about fifteen nuns veiled in black were holding in their hands. When Catalina asked them to which Order they belonged, without breaking silence they raised their veils and she saw their radiant smiling faces. The day she took the habit she recognized in her new companions the faces she had seen in her dream.

But it was certainly not because there she lived in the Golden Legend atmosphere that Mother Teresa said afterwards that she had never been happier than at Beas: it was at Beas that she met Fray Jerónimo Gracián de la Madre de Dios.

'I shall never spend happier days than those I lived with my Paul. . . .'[1] That was her nickname for him, for it seemed to her that, like the apostle, he was alternatively 'on the mountain tops or in the depths of the sea,'[2] so easily did his enthusiasm turn to discouragement. She also called him 'my Eliseus'[3] because of his head which was 'large and bald.' She wrote to P. Rubeo, Superior General of the Order: 'Gracián is like an angel . . .';[4] and to the prioress of Medina del Campo:

O Mother, how I wish you had been with me just lately! Without exaggeration they have been the best days of my life. Gracián has just spent more than twenty days here. I tell you that I have not yet appreciated this man at his proper value. In my eyes he is perfect and for us better than anything we could ask God for. I hope Your Reverence and your daughters will pray His Majesty to give him to us for religious superior. I shall then be able to have someone else to refer to besides myself for the government of these houses; I've never seen so much perfection joined with so much meekness. . . . Julian de Ávila is mad about him and all here are the same. He preaches wonderfully.[5]

Teresa of Jesus was so excited that she almost seemed like Doña Teresa de Ahumada again. She declared that her soul only found peace in God or with the one person who understood her: 'All the rest is

[1] CTA, cxviii.   [2] Idem, cclvi.   [3] SEC, vol. VII, p. 189.
[4] CTA, lxxiv.   [5] Idem, lxxii.

such a heavy cross to me that I cannot bear it. . . .'[1] Although she was sixty she was full of enthusiasm. Given her generous nature and the constraint under which she had lived, this was not surprising. Even those who thought her visions and her voices wonderful found them a little awe-inspiring: P. John of the Cross judged that they were due to a feverish imagination and a result of too much clinging to the pleasures of divine love, and Teresa herself sometimes wondered if they were not a trap of the devil. To her it was as painful to be considered a saint as it was to be regarded as a sort of curiosity, and that was why among the novices she loved the gayest best; their affectionate familiarity gave her a sense of repose, relaxation and tenderness.

As to Gracián, when Teresa disclosed to him the secrets of her interior life, he was in no way surprised at her deep intimacy with Our Lord; as a man of learning, and with the support of Scripture for his opinion, he approved. This was an immense relief and consolation to the Foundress, to whom her very happiness was so often the cause of suffering: 'May he be blessed for ever!'[2]

Because he gave her a sense of security and peace, he meant much to her and soon became indispensable.

And then he was not 'dour': even in the first days of their acquaintance he made her laugh.

There had been quite a few clothings at Beas, among others that of Gregorio Ramírez who took the name of Gregorio Nacianceno. Julian de Ávila contented himself with asking P. Jerónimo Gracián if he would give him the scapular of the Order to which the good chaplain had devoted himself without counting the cost.

The Father Vicar grouped the novices in the choir behind the grille, made them sing the *Veni Creator* as was done at clothings and to all intents and purposes seemed to be going on with the ceremony. His sermon, on the beauties of monastic life, lasted an hour. Julian, poor fellow, was in despair: could they make a friar of him without his having asked for or wishing it? Were they going to force him to take a vow of poverty when he had several sisters to keep? But perhaps Mother Teresa had had a revelation about him, commanding that he too should discard his shoes and put on the coarse frieze? If that were so, how could he resist the command of Our Lord? 'He turned pale, went red, perspired, was much upset,'[3] but when the sermon was over P. Gracián merely gave him the scapular.

Julian de Ávila's account of his panic delighted the nuns, the

[1] Idem, ccclxvi.   [2] CTA, civ.
[3] JG quoted SEC, vol. VI, pp. 201–2.

Foundress laughed heartily over it, more pleased than ever with her Paul, her Eliseus, her Gracián.

With him she was able to take an easy tone and give rein to her vivacity, without feeling obliged to keep back some amusing retort or spontaneous expression of affection. To him she could write: 'You amused me very much and made me laugh. O Father! Your Reverence had no need to swear, not even like a saint and still less like a cart driver, for that's what I understood you to say. . . . I leave the matter, reminding Your Paternity that you have authorized me to judge and to think what I please. . . .' [1]

She loved him as a mother or a sister, as a saint who had reached such a degree of purity that on her lips the strongest expressions of love could not be misunderstood. If her soul had not been as clear as crystal, she would not have dared to use them: 'What a pleasure it would have been to give him a meal when he was hungry as he said he was!' [2] 'He is stout and in good health. Thanks be to God!' [3] When he signed one of his letters: 'Your dear son,' she was full of delight. 'You amused me so much when you wrote *Your dear son*! And I immediately said to myself that you were perfectly right!' [4]

She was concerned about him, his fatigue, his health, his clothes, his moods, and finally she rejoiced in the extreme goodness of the 'Master of the house' (*el casamentero*), Christ himself, who had linked them in so close a friendship that death would not separate them, they would be united to all eternity.[5] And the thought of P. Gracián helped her to praise God better.

If she begged him—not without a spark of innocent malice—not to fall off his donkey, if his failure to write frequently inspired her with the wonderful saying, 'where there is love, it doesn't sleep like that . . . ,' [6] if for certain prioresses—María de San José, for instance, with whom Gracián later formed a close friendship—she felt something very much akin to feminine jealousy, all this, which proves that Teresa of Jesus was human, in no way implied that her heart was not completely filled even to overflowing with a love which swallowed up all lesser affections: that of God and of her Order.

Had not P. Gracián the same ideas as herself, her tastes, her method of directing souls? 'Your Paternity is absolutely right as to what you consider necessary for the reform when you say that souls are not to be won by force of arms like bodies. May God keep you near me, for I like you very much!' [7]

---

[1] CTA, ccxxviii.   [2] Idem, cxl.   [3] Idem, clxxxi.   [4] Idem, cxlvii.
[5] CTA, clx.   [6] CTA, ccxc.   [7] CTA, clx.

The fact that such a strong expression of feelings escaped her caused her some uneasiness, but one day, after Communion, she was transported in spirit to a flowery meadow, so lovely that it reminded her of the images of the *Canticle of Canticles*: 'I saw my Eliseus there, not as he really is, a trifle too sallow, but beautiful in a way not of earth: he had on his head as it were a crown of large precious stones; numerous maidens walked before him with palms in their hands, singing canticles to the praise of God. I opened my eyes wide. . . . I thought I heard angels singing and also little birds which brought joy to the soul. And it was said to me: "This man is worthy to be among you."' [1]

Who then was this wonderful person to whom heaven itself gave letters of credence?

Aged thirty when he met the Mother Foundress at Beas, P. Jerónimo Gracián de la Madre de Dios was already Apostolic Visitor of the Discalced Carmelite friars and of the nuns of Mitigated observance in Andalusia. Very learned, gifted with persuasive eloquence, with childlike gaiety and austere as a desert father, he 'charmed' by his perfect manners, gentle and kindly ways, while his even temper made relations with him easy and pleasant.

He was preparing to enter the Society of Jesus when he got to know the Discalced Carmelite friars; to the habit of Ignatius Loyola's sons he preferred that of the sons of Our Lady and he took it at Pastrana.

He had always had a most tender devotion towards the Blessed Virgin and christened a statue of Mary which he frequently visited as a young man in one of the Madrid churches, *mi enamorada*, my sweetheart. It was this gift of pious gallantry that predestined him to be Teresa of Jesus' 'dear son.'

He was tender-hearted and had great delicacy and, although possessed of all the qualities which make for success in the world, was so little made for the world that nothing ever cured him of his ingenuousness. He was destined by his family to hold high office at court: the call of God was more peremptory than that of the King, more so even than the duty of helping his nineteen brothers and sisters to find means of livelihood. For although his father had been secretary to Charles V and his brothers Antonio and Tomás secretaries to Philip II and Luis secretary to the Queen-Regent of Sicily, the good graces of these sovereigns in regard to their important personnel were so capricious and so meagre that this family of high functionaries was as poor as it was honourable.

[1] SEC, R, xliv, p. 73.

Jerónimo Gracián was the man whom the Foundress needed: 'Although he was not one of the first, he came at the right moment: I should often have regretted having undertaken so much if I had not had such great confidence in God's mercy. I am referring to the monasteries of friars, who quickly fell away from perfection because they were not set up as an independent province and were governed by the Mitigated.' [1]

Whom had the Foundress to count on? The two 'first' friars of the Reform, Antonio de Jesús and John of the Cross, seem to be indicated. But P. Antonio lacked common-sense, he was touchy and given to romancing; as to P. John, the incomparable angel of the *Dark Night*, he still sought to escape the all-absorbing effort which foundations meant, with their worldly contacts, business and diplomacy: it was only much later that he adapted himself to all this. And then, Teresa could not manage him as she pleased: even the most intelligent saint cannot manage an archangel.

On the other hand she could manage P. Jerónimo Gracián.

Mother Teresa bent P. Jerónimo Gracián de la Madre de Dios to her will by the means all women employ, be they saints or sinners, geniuses or fools, to bring men under their domination: she vowed obedience to him, promised to do only what he commanded all her life long, unless it should be anything against God or the ecclesiastical superiors to whom she had duties. She likewise undertook to hide from him nothing of her interior life, or of her sins—in short, she put him 'both interiorly and exteriorly' [2] in the place of God.

After this, it only remained for P. Gracián to submit.

As quickly as possible the Foundress wrote to Philip II begging him to divide the Mitigated and Discalced Carmelite friars into separate provinces: she had at last found the man who could assume responsibility for the reformed Order: ' . . . A Discalced father named Gracián whom I've just seen. . . . Although quite young, he is of such a kind that I have greatly praised God for him; I think he has chosen him for the good of our Order.' [3]

Teresa was going to crush him whom she had chosen as her master under the weight of the work; she was pursuing one single aim: the autonomy of the Discalced in relation to the Calced, of her friars who had returned to the primitive Rule vis-à-vis the friars who were remaining under the Mitigation, of her fathers clad in frieze as against those who wore fine cloth. She had dedicated herself to this work

[1] Sb, F, c. xxiii–12.　　　　　　　　　　[2] SEC, R, xl, pp. 69–70.
[3] CTA, lxxvii.

until death. And of this work, P. Jerónimo Gracián was to be the instrument.

The Foundress revealed her inmost heart when she wrote to the prioress at Valladolid, her cousin María Bautista: 'It's a curious thing, I'm no more troubled about loving him so much than if he were not a person at all. . . .'[1] Indeed for Teresa, with her mind set on the realization of her plans, he was not a person, but more than a person: he was the best tool she had to carve her foundations out of the granite.

[1] CTA, lxxxvii.

PART FOUR

THE GREAT STORM

'I saw a great storm of trials and difficulties. . . .'
Relations, **xxxvii**.

I

THE ROAD TO THE SOUTH

THE Mother Foundress's one wish was to return to her Promised Land, Castile, but P. Gracián asked her to go and found a convent in Seville.[1] As she hesitated, he gave her a formal order to do this, with good reasons for his request: the support of the Archbishop Don Cristóbal de Rojas had been obtained, the new convent would be filled with novices with good dowries: the Sevillan girls seemed only to be waiting for Teresa of Jesus' arrival to take the Carmelite habit, and everything would be for the best in the richest city of all the Spains.

Such arguments did not quieten Teresa's apprehensions: Andalusia frightened her. She dreaded the climate, the customs, the inhabitants, the revolts—it was hardly five years since Don Juan of Austria had crushed the last Moorish insurrection with no little difficulty—and she feared the rabble of adventurers whom the ships leaving for the Indies attracted to its ports.

P. Gracián intoned his usual panegyric:

'Its wealth, its grandeur, its majesty are like the sun . . . it is the place of exchange, the gateway to and port of the Indies. . . . There is nothing in the world like what you see at Seville: when the galleons come into port, one hundred, nay two hundred carts, each drawn by two yoke of oxen, transport the ingots of gold and silver to the Royal House of Commerce for the Indies.' [2]

'All this gold is of no interest to us,' said Teresa.

Gracián described the rich dress of the inhabitants, the silks covered with thickly raised, padded and incrusted embroideries; wool was not used at all, but everything was of velvet, taffeta, damask and brocade.

And when the Foundress frowned slightly:

'It only depends on us, on Your Reverence, and the riches which are now used for so much vanity and frivolity will be given to the support of our Order.'

'Don't they say,' objected the Foundress, 'that the streets of Seville are less safe than the passes of the Sierra Morena? The folk there are

---

[1] CTA, xciii.   [2] Lope de Vega.

idle ruffians and quarrelsome. . . . Don't they call Seville "the
Babylon of the Great Sea"?'

She also knew that among this crowd of foreigners heretics would
insinuate themselves and get to work and that Lutheran propa-
ganda there was intense, the Inquisition more suspicious than in
Castile, repression more active even than at Valladolid and so cruel
that it was better not to have to prove one's innocence before the
tribunals.

But Teresa of Jesus had made a vow of obedience to P. Jerónimo
Gracián de la Madre de Dios. She was forced to yield and to quicken
her preparations for departure, for it was May and her health would
not have stood the journey in the great heat.

She left Ana de Jesús, whom a Provincial would one day dub
'captain of prioresses', in charge at Beas. John of the Cross considered
Ana de Jesús an angel of the highest order and Teresa herself declared:
'Ana does the work and I have the credit. . . .'

Sin blanca, as usual, Teresa borrowed a little money for the journey
from the convent of Malagón: she asked only for what was strictly
necessary, for P. Gracián declared that the generosity of the Andalusians
could be relied upon. She chose six nuns from the community at Beas:
Isabel de San Francisco, María del Espíritu Santo, Isabel de San Jerónimo, Leonor de San Gabriel, Ana de San Alberto and lastly the
future prioress, María de San José. Not only intelligent, but brilliant,
brought up in the best circles of Toledo, with Doña Luisa de la Cerda,
María belonged to an élite as much on account of her learning as of her
birth; she spoke Latin and made no secret of it, and she wrote to perfection in prose and verse and was only too willing to show people
what she had written. Teresa, who preferred a proverb in good
popular speech to a Latin quotation, teased her about her pedantry,
but after her own fashion which consisted in dressing the scratch with
a kind word: 'I wonder why I love you so much. . . .'[1]

Teresa of Jesus never took a nun away for a new foundation against
her will. María de San José, whose assignment on their departure from
Castile was to be prioress of Caravaca, was consulted:

'Would you give up Caravaca, where you're sure to be well lodged
and have sufficient money, to share the risks of this Seville foundation
with us?'

María de San José asked if she would be prioress of one or other
of these houses in any case: through humility she would have preferred to have no position of honour:

[1] CTA, clxxiii.

'Sister,' replied Teresa, 'you will be prioress, for when there are no thrushes we have to eat blackbirds. . . .'

'In that case I choose Seville.'

The Foundress broke into a triumphant laugh:

'You wanted it! Let come what will come!' [1]

The energy and staying power of a young prioress would be put to good use in an enterprise like this.

So now the carts were once more prepared for the journey, just as a ship is equipped for a long voyage. In each cart, which was covered over so that nobody could guess it was carrying nuns who were travelling the world over the better to renounce the world, the hourglass was hung up; it would remind them that conventual life was interrupted neither by mountains nor valleys; the little bell to announce the hours of prayer was put within reach of the Foundress's hand; lastly they piled up the provisions and the water-skins.

At dawn on 18th May, after Mass at which all communicated, the carts took the road to the south. Julian de Ávila, Antonio Gaytán, Gregorio Nacianceno followed on muleback. P. Jerónimo Gracián de la Madre de Dios had left for Madrid.

The sun beat down on them so fiercely that from the very first day the provisions went bad—although there was no meat among them—the very water was not fit to drink and everything had to be thrown away. What did it matter: the first halt in a flowery wood was so delightful that Teresa, who never felt the presence of God anywhere so much as when confronted with a beautiful landscape—she then forgot everything in praising her Creator—returned to her cart where the heat was suffocating with great reluctance.

A regular routine was observed on the journey. The Foundress rang her little bell at ordered intervals, and the rhythm of prayer kept pace with that of the mules to the accompaniment of the steady grind of the enormous cart-wheels right through the midst of the wood.

The little bell was also rung when it was time for silence. Then the *mozos de mulas*, the *arrieros*, the cart-drivers themselves kept silence: one word from Teresa had been sufficient for them to agree to abide by the convent discipline. The sounds along the road, the distant sheepbells only made the silence of the daughters of Carmel more perceptible. Precious silence: it is in silence that the soul embraces God and that God embraces and instructs the soul; just as Solomon's temple was built without any sound of axe or hammer, so Our Lord builds his dwelling-place in us in silence.

[1] MJ quoted SEC, vol. VI, p. 243.

A further ring of the bell and Teresa, still radiant from her prayer, offered the *arrieros* a wineskin filled with 'wine of the earth' to reward them for having kept silence so well. Then they began their songs again and also, in the innocence of their hearts, their oaths.

For their siesta the party halted under the shade of some eucalyptus trees or under a bridge; this was the moment for gaiety, even when it meant having to dislodge a drove of pigs from the little shade there was. Teresa had a most lively and picturesque way of speaking, and her sense of humour enlivened all the various vicissitudes of the journey and even their very worst misfortunes. Whether she was teasing Antonio Gaytán on his attachment to this world's goods—the good man was not very successful in concealing his anxiety as to how things were going at his house in Alba de Tormes—or Sister Leonor de San Gabriel on her small stature, she never hurt anyone's feelings and was always amusing. And when the conversation turned to more spiritual matters, she inflamed all her companions with the love of Our Lord. She improvised *coplas* which the nuns sang:

> Let us travel towards heaven,
> Nuns of Carmel . . .[1]

But along the steep uphill road to heaven, she never lost sight of the sharp stones by the wayside and saw to it that those whose souls were in her charge did not injure themselves on them.

The first night they slept in a hermitage on the stone floor, for, counting on the generosity of the Sevillans which P. Gracián had promised them, they had not even brought pallets. In the morning they unpacked the sacred vessels and the vestments, the only luggage they had of any value, and Julian de Ávila said Mass before they started on their way again.

As they advanced southwards, the sun beat down on them more and more fiercely, and the heat which had accumulated under the tarpaulins covering the carts was so appalling that the nuns could talk of nothing but the sufferings of hell and purgatory: to win heaven at the price of innumerable hardships was to earn the right to live for ever where it was cool. All six showed so much courage that Teresa was delighted.

'With nuns like you, I would not mind going to the land of the Turks!'

All they had to eat during this journey was a little bread, some beans and a few cherries, and that when they were not obliged by

[1] P, cx.

circumstances to go without anything at all. Thirst was their worst
suffering: the Andalusians sold their water at as high a price as their
wine. But Teresa only said:

'May God give us much to suffer for him, if only in the way of
fleas, wicked little boys and bad roads!' [1]

Whatever danger or unforeseen circumstances might arise, the
Mother Foundress maintained order by insisting on the observance of
the Rule and Constitutions. As they were crossing the Guadalquivir,
the force of the current swept away one of the ferry-boats which was
carrying two of the carts. The sisters pulled at the haulage ropes which
broke ; miraculously the ferry-boat drifted on to a sand-bank. The
travellers were now far away from any inhabited place, night was
falling and the guides no longer knew where they were. . . . 'O God,
we thank you for the bad roads!'—Teresa organized conventual life on
the banks of the river as if the circumstances were in no way unusual,
when all the goods and chattels of this convent now at the full mercy
of the elements consisted of a statuette of the Child Jesus, six flasks of
holy water and a few prayer books. They sang Compline and were
preparing to sleep under a rock when a riverside dweller came to their
assistance, not without uttering all sorts of abuse at both nuns and
friars. But he led them back to the right road again and they were able
to continue the journey as far as the halt they had planned.

Their worst terror was the inns, those *ventas*, noisy with the shouts
of drunken men, with the harsh twang of guitars, the click of castanets
and the thrumming of tambourines, or ringing with loud songs or
sacrilegious or obscene oaths.

In the midst of all this din and clatter Teresa caught fever and
became delirious and they had to find her a bed. The loft was so dirty—
'Thank you, dear Lord, for the fleas!'—the bed so hard, the sun darted
its burning shafts so fiercely through the slits in the tiles, the wet
bandages applied to the patient's forehead were so unrefreshing and the
din so terrifying, that she begged them to take her back to her cart:
she would suffer less there.

They continued their journey towards Córdoba where they arrived
in the early morning: the gipsies were already watering their horses
at the fountains while they pestered the girls who were filling their
jars with the aid of a long reed, with *piropos*.[2] From the bottom of
their closed carts, those who saw nothing of the external world caught
the sounds of a life quite different from that of Old and New Castile:
voluble, excited, restless, bustling, and all this was whirring around

[1] CTA, lvii.   [2] *I.e.* flattering compliments.

these lumbering carts which had come from beyond the sierras and were covered with dust and laden with mystery. Leaping up on the wheels in spite of the whips of the *arrieros*, some of the urchins managed to raise the tarpaulins; their laugh showed their sharp white teeth in swarthy faces.

The Foundress heard this noisy din going on all round her and could not contain her distress. Prepared even to forgo Mass, she would have liked to flee from this devilish town: Julian de Ávila disagreed, arguing on strictly theological grounds: all they had to do was to find a quiet church on the other bank of the Guadalquivir. But when the carts got to the bridge, the gates were still closed: the *Corregidor* kept the keys himself; when they ran to ask him for them he was still asleep, but they did not scruple to disturb his slumbers.

The excitement of the crowd, however, was growing greater; when access to the bridge was obtained it was found that the carts were too wide: the part that would not go across was accordingly sawn off. The amusement of the gaping crowd turned to frenzy: 'Thank you for the wicked little boys, dear Lord!'

The seven Carmelites and their escort of friars and laymen at last reached the church which Julian de Ávila had described as so quiet and peaceful! The feast of the Holy Spirit was being celebrated there, not only by a great procession but with dancing; the arrival of the nuns clad in frieze, with their white cloaks and black veils, was an unexpected attraction which proved such a sensation 'that if bulls had come into the place there wouldn't have been more commotion.'

All this upset cured the Foundress's fever. She could not get away from the place sufficiently quickly; the little band left as if in flight from their pursuers, in the full heat of the day. The siesta was spent under a bridge. At evening the hermitage of Écija seemed an oasis of prayer and amid the songs of the birds there Teresa, in the presence of Our Lord, renewed her vow of obedience to P. Jerónimo Gracián.

The respite was brief. In the *venta* at Albino, their only food a few sardines preserved in brine and not a drop of water to quench their thirst, the poor nuns thought themselves in the antechamber of the devil himself: certain 'devilish' individuals began to quarrel among themselves and, blaspheming for all they were worth, hurled themselves at each other weapon in hand: forty swords flew about, clashed, flashed like lightning in the sun, muskets were fired; in the middle of this cannonade the sisters rushed out of their cart and into Mother Teresa's to die by her side. She calmed them by laughing at their fright and proved right, for these furious madmen suddenly disappeared, no doubt in fear of the constables.

Teresa, God's knight errant, and her daughters arrived at Seville on 26th May, after eight days of a journey full of unexpected adventures which María de San José and Julian de Ávila vied with one another to recount. They all praised God who had provided them with wicked little boys, fleas and bad roads, giving them all kinds of mortifications for makeweight.

II

THE RICH CITY OF SEVILLE

PADRE AMBROSIO MARIANO ARAZO DE SAN BENITO was waiting for the Foundress and her nuns in the house he had rented for them: it was a tiny little hovel, very poor and very damp, situated in the Calle de las Armas, right in the centre of the town. The women who had been living in it gave it up for the nuns, but it did not seem to occur to anyone that the new-comers might be in need of some help in a strange town: nobody sent them a mouthful of bread or even a jar of fresh water.

They did, however, find there a few odd things for their use, of which María de San José has left us details:

'Firstly, half a dozen old wicker hurdles which P. Ambrosio Mariano had got from the monastery of Los Remedios; placed on the ground they served as beds; two or three straw mattresses, very thin and in bad condition, were kept for our Mother and the most delicate among us. There were neither sheets nor blankets, but we had two pillows which we had brought.'

So much for the bedding. As to the furniture and utensils:

'In the house we found a fibre mat, a small table, a frying-pan, one or two candlesticks, a mortar, and a pail for drawing water from the well. We were rejoicing over this initial help towards our household equipment, to which must be added a few plates and jugs, when the neighbours who had only lent their things for the day, came to take back, this one her candlestick and another her pail and table, so that we had absolutely nothing left, neither frying-pan nor mortar, and they even took away the rope for the well. . . .'[1]

The sudden and forced disappearance of the poor goods of this world seemed so comic an interlude to the travellers that they forgot their difficulties and laughed heartily over it.

Teresa of Jesus had compared the soul to a garden and the different forms of mental prayer to the different ways in which water irrigates, refreshes and fructifies the soil. With what exultant joy did she speak of abundant showers of rain! When August with its heat was wasting

[1] MJ quoted SEC, vol. VI, p. 241.

away her country of Castile, it was still possible to find an ice-cold spring in some high place or in the hollow of a rock. To her the love of God himself was refreshment: 'O living fountains of the wounds of my God!' [1] But 'the scorching heat of Seville' [2] burnt up and dried Teresa's very soul: 'We are burnt up here as if we were in hell. . . .' 'I have never been so cowardly and faint-hearted as I was then; I did not recognize myself. My confidence in Our Lord, indeed, never failed, but my character seemed to be so different that I understood that Our Lord was leaving me to depend on my own resources to show me clearly that if I had had courage hitherto, it was not to my own merits that I owed it.' [3] 'I am there, but I want you to know how small a thing you are without me. . . .'

From the moment she arrived she was blinded by the sun's reflection against the white walls; everything one touched was moist with heat, the least breath of air carried the smell of plants dying for lack of moisture or the heady perfume of jasmine which had lost its colour from the heat. She was distressed at the 'abominable sins' which stalked abroad in these lands where the very climate corrupts the soul: 'It seems as if the devils are better placed to lead us into temptation there.' [4] There was something about the place one could not explain—things seemed aggressive and the people evasive. 'The lies which are ordinary current coin here! It's enough to make one faint!' [5] 'I'm not made for the people of this country. . . .' [6] 'Seville either drives you away or swallows you up,' says the proverb. The Babylon of the Great Sea did not swallow up Teresa of Jesus.

P. Mariano himself was no longer the same as he had been in Castile. When the Foundress told him that it was necessary to say the first Mass and expose the Blessed Sacrament the very next day, he was evasive: it would be better to wait and see.

Worried for three days by the impatient Foundress, he finally admitted that the Archbishop, Don Cristóbal de Rojas, whose authorization they had taken for granted, now declared 'that it did not please him' [7] to give permission for this convent to be founded. He would willingly welcome Mother Teresa on condition that she dispersed her nuns among different convents in Andalusia which were in great need of someone to give them the example of a more recollected life. But foundations—certainly not: particularly without revenues.

Alas for the egoism of the rich! Was it possible 'that in such a

[1] Sb, E, ix-2. [2] CTA, lxxii. [3] Sb, F, c. xxv-1.
[4] Sb, F, c. xxv-1. [5] CTA, xciv.
[6] Idem, xciii. [7] Sb, F, c. xxiv-16.

wealthy town there were less facilities than anywhere else for a foundation'?[1] All the sounds Teresa heard were those of traffic or amusements. Who thought of God, indeed, in the excess of passion, the fever of adventure and intrigue, the confusion which made the great Mediterranean port a tower of Babel? They did not seem to have any thought of becoming Carmelites, these Sevillan girls with their bewitching chatter and fiery eyes, and were more anxious about their lovers than the salvation of their souls. Some of them did, indeed, come to see the Foundress, but after taking one look at them with their carefully adjusted circular gowns and high head-dresses, or showing only one eye under the shawl with which they were wrapped according to the custom of their country, she felt that they were not suitable birds for her dovecot.

She would have been only too glad to go back to Castile, but there was no money for the journey: she had only one solitary *blanca* left in her pocket and nothing to sell except the tarpaulins which closed in the carts; and in this city bursting with gold there was nobody to lend them a few ducats. With great difficulty P. Mariano managed to get enough money to enable Julian de Ávila and Antonio de Gaytán to go back. When she said good-bye to them, Teresa honoured Gaytán with the title of 'my good founder,' he had helped her so devotedly. He was fortunate in being able to go back to the waters of the Tormes, to his house at Alba, built of grey stone as became his rank, and to his small daughter whom the Foundress called 'my little pest,' and whom she loved so much.

By dint of insisting, in the end P. Mariano wrung permission from the Archbishop for Mass to be said in the Calle de las Armas, but he forbade the Blessed Sacrament to be exposed, the bell to be rung or the house to be given the external appearance of a convent: this was tantamount to condemning the nuns to feed on prayer alone, for who would know of their existence? Where were the munificent Andalusians, so much boasted of when Teresa and her nuns left Beas? Seville was either the most miserly of cities or the most neglectful of the affairs of God. One great lady, however, 'whose eyes followed the saints with longing and who opened her heart to the needy,'[2] gave to them generously, but she applied the laws of charity so thoroughly that, so that her left hand should not know what her right hand was distributing, she charged a *beata* to provide for the needs of the Discalced Carmelites anonymously: linen, crockery, pots and pans, money to buy oil and fish. This duenna had her favourite poor, her

[1] Sb, F, c. xxv–1.   [2] MJ, quoted SEC, vol. VI, p. 241.

prostitutes, whose souls seemed to her to be in greater danger than the nuns', and so Doña Leonor de Valera's alms went to the prostitutes.

All this time the sisters were sleeping very badly on their wicker hurdles, eating nothing but potatoes, and there were days when one small loaf fed the whole community as if by miracle.

Teresa could not shake off her sadness. She to whom Our Lord himself had revealed that poverty is a patent of nobility for entering his kingdom was nevertheless anxious and distressed. For she had come to Seville against the will of God: that was her secret and the reason for her discouragement. At Beas, Our Lord had commanded her to found a convent in Madrid; she had confided in P. Gracián who, setting aside the divine command, maintained his decision to send her to Andalusia.

'Obey your superior,' Christ had said to her, 'but he will have to bear the consequences.' [1]

That was why the Foundress was not at peace in Seville and why she said: 'No foundation cost me more hardships and my greatest sufferings were interior ones.' [2]

She felt the storm coming and was afraid.

The General Chapter of the Order had just opened in Italy and Teresa knew that Gracián would be criticized there; what there was human in her anxieties about him added to her trouble. She had warned her nuns against earthly attachments with a clearness of vision which allowed her to make no mistake: 'Our will is wholly occupied in hoping they won't die; if they have a headache we are upset; when they have trials to bear we are impatient; and so on with everything else. . . . What unhappy affection, and I do not speak here of guilty affections, from which God deliver us!' [3]

At Seville Teresa found herself under the influence of two affections that were intense: that for María de San José and that for Jerónimo Gracián. Gracián was absent and she knew he was in danger. Maria was with her, but elusive, reticent, too often presuming on her office as prioress to oppose her will to that of the Foundress. Already one could admire—or blame—in her an art of manoeuvring things, a talent for good administration which later earned her some of Teresa's famous 'terrible' letters; she called her a 'vixen' and said of her: 'In the Seville house I see a greed I cannot tolerate and the prioress is more clever than her office demands. I told her when I was there that she never acted towards me without malice. She has made me suffer very

[1] TC quoted SEC, vol. II, p. 324.   [2] Sb, F, c. xxvi-2.
[3] Sb, C, c. vii-2.

much.'¹ But all reproaches seemed useless: 'it was like running up
against steel.'² She did not spare her ratings and was afterwards ready
to beg her pardon, just as in her letters reproaches alternated with
praise and expressions of tenderness: 'I am unbearable with those I
love, for I should like you never to go wrong in the slightest degree
. . . and bad as you are, I should like to have many prioresses like
you.'³ In these reconciliations María remained distant: 'I treated you
as my dearest daughter and it hurt me not to find the same love and
simplicity in you.' The very faults of this favourite daughter were
faults only to be found in great prioresses and Teresa of Jesus exacted
much. Later the Foundress was to regret these differences, so cruelly
did she feel María de San José's absence; in the half playful tone which
enabled her to get many truths over to her correspondents, she wrote
to her that she would be very glad to make the journey in order to
quarrel with her as much as she wished. Perhaps she was more exacting
than María de San José was imperfect.

She was not at all satisfied with the Andalusian novices. She was
highly delighted with their skill as embroidresses, for she so much
liked a woman to be clever with her fingers, but her love of frankness
could not get on with their disposition to intrigue and duplicity.
There were not many of them, moreover; among those who, according to P. Gracián, were impatiently waiting for the Foundress's arrival
so that they could take the habit, only one had entered the day the
first Mass was said. Beatriz de la Madre de Dios was tiresome, but the
Apostolic Visitor and P. Mariano had promised to get her admitted
to Carmel. She had been persecuted and even tortured in childhood,
and this had left her with a thirst for revenge which she did not
succeed in mastering properly.

She was barely seven when one of her mother's sisters took a
liking to her and thought of leaving her her property. Her servants
who coveted this prize for themselves decided to eliminate her as a
rival and accused her of having ordered them to buy sublimate with
which to poison her aunt. Sent back to her parents, little Beatriz was
whipped every day for more than a year, and the least of the ill treatment to which she was subjected was to sleep on the bare ground.
God avenged her of those who calumniated her by permitting them
to catch rabies; seized with remorse, before they died they confessed
their lie. But their false swearing left something behind: on the first
occasion of her hand being asked in marriage, she told her father of her
desire to enter religion, but he thought she had committed some sin

¹ CTA, ccxc.   ² Idem.   ³ Idem, cccii.

which made her fear to accept a husband and he subjected her to such violent treatment, going as far as to hang her—and from this she escaped only by the grace of God—that she was in bed for three months unable to move. Her mother, said Teresa, was a good Christian.

The Seville Carmel refused more than one of these daughters of the south. One, however, was admitted as to whose name Carmelite charity has been silent. She was 'an important *beata* already considered as good as canonized by the whole town. . . .'[1]

The Foundress had hesitated:

'If she doesn't work miracles, sisters, we shan't come out of the affair without losing prestige. . . .'[2]

The unfortunate woman [relates María de San José] was holier still in her own eyes, and as she got no praise from us, the severity of the Rule being the touchstone which reveals the true value of all that shines in appearance only, she was soon dissatisfied with us and we were even more so with her. There was never any means of getting her to conform to the Constitutions; she was forty, very authoritative, and had a wonderful way of getting out of every difficulty: when she refused to eat the same food as we, she pleaded illness as an excuse, alleging that she was swelling and that we could read in Galen that those dishes were not good for her; on other occasions she pleaded that she was not used to it—nor to the great heat there is in these provinces. Our Mother told us we must put up with her and not annoy her, in the hope that time would correct all that; she even authorized her to go to confession and to talk with priests who were her friends. . . .[3]

Who would have thought that this wily person, who from the corner of her eye watched every movement and gesture of the Castilians, was effectively contributing to the creation of an atmosphere of hostility to them in Seville? For suspicion and opposition were daily more perceptible.

And that without any human hope of its coming to an end; after three months' stay in a city of wealth, no one had yet come forward to offer to help the Foundress in Our Lord's name.

Heaven sent her all she lacked by the hands of those who were most dear to her: her brothers Lorenzo and Pedro arrived from Ecuador. Lorenzo was as rich in gold from the Indies as he was in good dispositions.

In the parlour, behind the grille, one August day Teresa of Jesus lifted her veil as Carmelites are allowed to do in the case of close

[1] MJ quoted SEC, vol. VI, p. 243. [2] FR, L. III, c. vi.
[3] MJ quoted SEC, vol. VI, p. 243.

relatives: her brothers could look upon the face of the sister who, when they left her, was young and beautiful but torn between the world and God; they found her so radiant with inner light that the ravages of thirty years had left scarcely a trace upon her bodily appearance.

As to herself, her deep feeling did not prevent her from being amused at the gorgeousness of these Indians:[1] the serious-minded Lorenzo had acquired ostentatious habits in this country where his important position obliged him to live on a grand scale; how gorgeously he was dressed! Even the children, Lorencito and Francisco, the neck confined in starched ruffs, spread out fingers stiff with rings over their velvet clothes; Teresita, their little eight-year-old sister, was smothered in brocade and carried a fortune in emeralds on ears, chest and fingers. But since Teresa had received the finest precious stones of his kingdom from her heavenly Bridegroom, jewels of earth no longer impressed her. And she laughed: the contrast between these wealthy relatives and the wretched parlour in which she was receiving them was a perfect subject for merriment.

Teresita was surprised to hear a saint laugh: her father who was devout but not a saint, laughed but seldom. . . . The nephews were delighted: they had been a little afraid on their father's account, for his age and character inclined him to austerities, of the influence of this wonderful relative of theirs, the reformer of an Order already austere into one more austere still, and of whom people said that her cell in Ávila bore the trace of the blood of her disciplines. But this Reverend Mother spoke with more charm than anyone they knew and when she named God it was to praise him and say that he was good.

When the time came for them to go, Teresita did not want to leave the convent: they had to promise her that she should come and live with Aunt Teresa. And if Lorenzo rattled his doubloons a little noisily during the conversation, it was to declare that in future he would make himself responsible for the entire expenses of the convent and for the purchase of a house.

A few days later the nuns had beds, some utensils, and finally food to eat, while an awning stretched over the patio made the heat more bearable.

Teresita, in a frieze dress of suitable size, trotted about the convent 'like a friendly sprite' to the great joy of the sisters who at recreation never tired of hearing her tell 'stories of the sea and the Indians.'[2] A brief respite. . . .

---

[1] Spaniards who went to the Indies and returned were known as Indians—Tr.
[2] CTA, lxxix.

III

THE FULMINATIONS OF THE MASTER GENERAL

IN insisting that Mother Teresa of Jesus should go and found a convent in Seville, the reverend Apostolic Visitor, P. Jerónimo Gracián de la Madre de Dios, had disobeyed Our Lord. He had also disobeyed the Master General of the Carmelite Order, the Most Reverend Father Juan Bautista Rubeo.

It was not the first time that he had put the decisions of the Master General on one side, and yet one could not accuse him of rebellion for he found himself in a difficult position, caught between Scylla and Charybdis, *i.e.* between Philip II and the General of his Order. The persecutions of which Discalced friars and nuns were to be the butt for nearly five years can be attributed to no other cause, though it must always be remembered that the ill-will of the Calced friars made matters worse. This ill-will was to degenerate into hatred, as happens when there are differences between brethren. In an age when women were thought little of, the Mitigated friars could ill brook the striking success of Teresa of Jesus' Reform. The veneration with which she was surrounded, the general admiration which her sons and daughters aroused, were a perpetual stumbling block to the Mitigated friars and at the same time the example of the austerities of the Discalced was a thorn in their flesh: it was becoming far too obvious that the Mitigated were well clad, well shod, abundantly fed, comfortably lodged, and, above all, unmortified. They had been particularly upset at the return to the primitive Rule imposed on the convent of the Incarnation in Ávila: was this thirst for austerities going to spread to all their monasteries one by one? They were certainly in need of it: in Seville itself had not the police found 'two friars in a house of ill-fame' in broad daylight? 'They were taken to prison publicly, which was very bad; for,' added the Foundress who recounted the fact, 'weaknesses don't surprise me, but I could wish that some regard were had to honour.' [1]

When a Discalced friar, P. Gracián, was made Visitor of the

[1] CTA, lxxiv.

Mitigated there was panic and a state of war ensued. Barbarous excesses in penance, such as those of the Pastrana friars against which Teresa had protested and inveighed through the intermediary of John of the Cross, justified the Calced friars in their own eyes. When they decided to bring to nought the Foundress and her frenzied friars and ecstatic nuns, they were convinced that what they were striving for was for the good of the Order. The nomination of P. Gracián supplied them with a pretext which had every appearance of being an unanswerable argument.

It was the King, Philip II, who in his zeal for monastic austerity wanted to carry Teresa of Jesus' Reform into the very heart of the Mitigation: his zeal was so great that he considered P. Rubeo was moving too slowly. He got the Pope to agree that through the Nuncio, Ormaneto, he should appoint two Visitors, P. Pedro Fernández for the province of Castile and Fray Francisco de Vargas for Andalusia. Both were Dominicans.

Such Visitors were directly dependent on the crown and on the Holy See, which could give them orders directly contrary to those of the Carmelite Master General.

P. Fernández, who was extremely tactful, managed this delicate situation without any difficulties and succeeded in making himself acceptable to the Calced friars; he contented himself with placing a few Discalced among them, instructing the former to initiate them into a more austere way of life.

In Andalusia the matter was quite different. P. Vargas decided to found a considerable number of monasteries of Discalced friars who were to give an example of strict observance as practised by the disciples of Fray John of the Cross and Fray Antonio de Jesús. The Nuncio ordered these foundations, but the Most Reverend Master General of the Order, Rubeo, had not authorized them. Such was the situation P. Gracián found when the powers of Apostolic Visitor were delegated to him by P. Vargas.

To obey the Sovereign Pontiff, his Nuncio and the King, therefore, he had to act in formal opposition to the Superior General of his Order. To accept, he needed as much courage as he did coolness.

He left Pastrana with P. Mariano and set off for Andalusia: there, both received an imperious order from P. Ángel de Salazar, Provincial of the Mitigated or Calced Carmelites, and their Provincial also, for Calced and Discalced were not divided into separate provinces, instructing them to return to their monastery in Castile, under pain of being considered 'rebellious and contumacious.' One can understand why Mother Teresa made the separation of the two branches of the Order her essential objective.

Gracián set aside this command in virtue of his apostolic commission and continued his mission in Andalusia which the Nuncio confirmed.

If only P. Gracián and P. Mariano had deigned to follow Mother Teresa's advice when she begged them to inform the General, P. Rubeo, of the complicated situation in which they found themselves! She knew perfectly well that one could always count on a good reception from this worthy man if one went to him with frankness and confidence. But the Visitors, being young, thought they knew better than the old Foundress, they turned a deaf ear and the first P. Rubeo heard of their 'rebellion' was the violent protest of the Calced friars.

His anger was terrible. That was it then, was it? His most cherished sons, his beloved *figlia*, were setting themselves up against him? Against Gracián and Mariano he obtained a brief of recall, which he kept in reserve in order to hurl at them with more effect at the General Chapter of the Order which was about to take place at Piacenza in Italy.

Thus, the position of the convent at Seville was that it had been founded at the command of an Apostolic Visitor whom his superior was preparing to denounce; and because of this circumstance, Mother Teresa of Jesus appeared equally guilty.

She had no opportunity of clearing herself in time: if the letter in which she tried to defend herself and above all to defend Gracián had not reached the Master General with inexplicable delay, her spirited, sincere and skilful defence might perhaps have saved everything. All she could be blamed for was that she charged Ambrosio Mariano with errors of judgement for which Gracián was nevertheless partly responsible, but she did not become aware until much later of the blunders of her favourite. She said to P. Rubeo: 'We quarrelled, particularly Mariano and myself, for he is extremely impulsive, but Gracián is like an angel; if he had been alone, things would have turned out differently. . . .'[1]

We are surprised to find the Mother Foundress's perspicacity at fault. But no woman could bear entirely alone the crushing burden which had been hers for years. It was in 1574 that she wrote for the first time: ' . . . I am old and tired.'[2] Eight or nine months later 'she met Gracián and saw in him the man capable of supporting and succeeding her. He was far from having her intelligence, diplomacy and,

[1] CTA, lxxiv. [2] CTA, lx.

above all, her lights, but it was necessary that she should be convinced that someone else could accomplish what she could no longer undertake alone. Her work was slipping from her by its very extension. Which of us would not have done as she did in like circumstances?

In this letter to P. Rubeo, she repeated for the second time and in the self-same words: ' . . . I am old and tired . . . all this has meant for me an effort beyond my strength. . . .'[1] This admission—it cannot be called a complaint, for we are talking of a woman who never complained—was to become a kind of refrain which fell from her pen the whole time she was in Seville.

To her explanation of the facts, she added in her long missive to P. Rubeo loyal and warm expressions of her affection for him, but it was too late, too many slanders and misunderstandings had been accumulated for him to be touched by what she said: 'I would have Your Lordship know first of all, for the love of Our Lord, that all the Discalced put together are nothing to me in comparison with Your Lordship's very habit. That is a fact and I would give my eyes to save Your Lordship the slightest displeasure.'[2]

It is possible for an angry man, even if he is holy, to refuse to believe in the sincerity of such ardently expressed feelings. Moreover, the Chapter at Piacenza was drawing to a close and nobody could now prevent the fulminations from taking their full effect.

Such was the state of affairs.

We left Lorenzo de Cepeda trying to buy a house in which the convent of St Joseph might be installed. Since his arrival the fast of the Carmelites had been as prescribed by the Rule and not the result of their extreme indigence.

It was November 1575: P. Gracián had arrived in Seville and the orders of the King and the Nuncio Ormaneto were definite: he must visit all monasteries of the Calced Carmelites.

The return of her 'dear son' only caused Teresa further suffering: the Calced friars were in revolt against what they considered an intrusion, and 'a person of weight has told the Archbishop that they would go so far as to kill him.' Methods of violence were not infrequent at this period when God's law was not always successful in overcoming strong passions even in religious houses. The Foundress reassured herself when she remembered that some Franciscans who were dissatisfied with their Visitor had nevertheless not killed him. . . . But when P. Gracián presented the Nuncio's brief at the *Casa*

[1] CTA, lxxiv.   [2] Idem.

Grande of the Calced friars in Seville, he found them, said María de San José, prepared to defend themselves with arms. A scuffle broke out and such cries were heard behind the closed doors that they came to tell 'our Mother' who was at prayer with all her nuns, that P. Jerónimo Gracián had been assassinated. But she was not left to the mercy of false news. Our Lord calmed her panic:

'O, woman of little faith! Calm yourself, for all is well!'[1]

There was in point of fact more noise than real harm done, but Teresa was so frightened that for a long time afterwards she begged Gracián never to take his meals with the Calced friars, nor in their neighbourhood, lest they should poison him.

The nameless novice with the reputation for sanctity had left Carmel, furious when she realized that so many austerities were above her strength. Teresa of Jesus was glad she had gone and did not reflect that to mean souls revenge is sweet. Opportunity was not wanting. For although the Archbishop sometimes visited Mother Teresa, won by her charm which was made up of so much human graciousness of every kind subordinated to divine grace—he sent wheat and provisions to the convent—the Sevillans did not seem to have got over their suspicions. The folk around eyed with no goodwill this house where Mass was said without ever a bell ringing to call the neighbours to join in the prayers: there seemed something suspicious about it.

An event occurred which gave them their answer: one day, causing great excitement in the Calle de las Armas, the Inquisition and its train descended upon the 'foreigners.' Contrary to custom, everything was done with 'the most scandalous' publicity.[2] They came in great numbers. Judges and notaries entered the convent of St Joseph, while constables and servants stood about in groups in the street or mounted guard before the exits.

They searched the house and questioned Teresa of Jesus, who was always at her best under trials, whereas the nuns were in a panic. The heads of accusation bore visible trace of the calumnies of the proud *beata*, the novice as to whose name Carmel would be silent for all eternity, the one who preferred to defame the Carmelites rather than own herself defeated by their virtues.

The Foundress was suspected of nothing less than of following the shameful principles of the *Alumbrados*: that could have far-reaching consequences for a woman whose writings had been delated and whose ecstasies, which were supernatural manifestations, attracted dangerous attention.

[1] SEC, vol. II, p. 82, n. 4.   [2] LO, vol. VI, c. xxx, art. I.

Their very poverty was made a subject of complaint against the nuns: not having sufficient veils in which to present themselves at the parlour grille, they passed the few they had to each other and this was interpreted by the spy-novice as 'a ceremony.'

After receiving Holy Communion they turned to the wall to make their thanksgiving, for the communion grille was in a patio where the sun beat down fiercely: this was another suspicious rite.

It was alleged that the Foundress forced the nuns to confess their sins to her. . . . Teresa remembered the sly novice who walked about noiselessly and often pushed the door open seemingly inadvertently when she was talking with one of her nuns of spiritual matters, a practice they all loved. What were they *not* accused of? The reformed Carmelites—people said it was a certain fact—fastened themselves together with feet and wrists bound, and practised mutual scourging. . . . 'I hope to goodness they've said nothing else!' added María de San José. . . .

That day the Inquisitors went away as they had come, to the disappointment of the crowd who had hoped to see them take these nuns who had come down from the north away with them. But the situation remained just as serious. The suspension of the trial merely indicated a want of glaring proof: this tribunal always endeavoured to obtain such evidence and usually with success.

The threat restored all Teresa's courage. 'Not only did I experience no sense of trouble, but a joy so unusual that obviously it did not come from myself alone; what King David did when he went before the ark of the Lord does not surprise me, then, I would willingly have done the same. . . . Not to found any more convents, if it had not been for the displeasure of the Master General, would have been a great rest for me.' [1]

For the fulminations of P. Rubeo had just fallen on the Discalced; the decree of Piacenza ordered the dissolution of the monasteries founded without P. Rubeo's authorization, and the friars were condemned to leave within three days, under pain of the most serious penalties: in case of refusal recourse might be had to the secular arm.

As to the Mother Foundress, she was forbidden to proceed with further foundations, was to return to Castile immediately and never again to leave the convent where she chose to be confined. P. Salazar declared her 'apostate and excommunicated.'

Teresa would have liked to set out for Castile immediately: 'They

[1] Sb, F, c. xxvii–20.

think they're hurting me, but to me it's such a great good that I fear the day will never come. . . . It would be great happiness for me no longer to live among the bustle and disturbance of the Reformed. . . . I've often wanted to finish my life in peace: those who are endeavouring to procure this for me think they are causing me the greatest pain in the world, and other like "benefits." . . .' [1]

The Nuncio did not interpret the decree in this way and P. Gracián ordered her at least to finish the Seville foundation.

Never since the grave affair of St Joseph's in Ávila had Teresa of Jesus suffered so much. Her suffering was increased by her horror of Andalusia, she wavered and persisted in trying to honour P. Rubeo by obeying him in preference to anyone else.

María de San José produced an unanswerable argument:

'Your Reverence cannot go. What would happen if the Inquisition which is inquiring into the false testimony of this novice against us should come here to take you and not find you?'

María was right and the Foundress was amused about it:

'Sister, you have a strange way of comforting me in my great trouble: you assure me that the Inquisition is going to put me in prison!' [2]

She was able to laugh again: it was one of her ways of loving submission under the hand of Our Lord.

From this moment joy never left her. María de San José, who shared her cell at night, often heard her praising God in low tones or singing softly: *Magnificat anima mea Dominum.* . . .

She gave thanks for all that hurt, for all that would have slowly crushed another but which she turned into joy on the spiritual plane. Now she was sensitive only where others were concerned, over the grief of P. Rubeo whom unwillingly she had deeply hurt, over the danger with which her nuns and friars and 'the work she had begun were threatened. *No estamos para coplas,*[3] 'we're in no mood for songs,' she wrote to her niece María Bautista who sent her some verses. At this time Gracián, on whom troubles were falling 'like hail,' no longer found in her the sympathy he expected: when he told her all the evil people were saying of her, her joy was so great that she rubbed her hands together. . . . She was filled to overflowing with the graces Our Lord sent her as was shown by the two accounts of her spiritual life which she was asked to submit to P. Rodrigo Álvarez, the Inquisitor, together with other documents for her case. She was taught sublime truths by Our Lord himself. One day when she was afraid at

[1] Sb, F, c. xxvii-20.   [2] MJ.   [3] CTA, lxxxvii.

seeing so much majesty 'in a thing as base as my soul, I heard: "It is not base, daughter, for it is made in my image."' [1]

He made her understand how God is in all things: 'As an example he gave me that of a sponge which absorbs water into itself. . . .' [2]

Another time when she was thinking 'that this life which deprives us of the marvellous company of God is very hard' and when she said inwardly, 'Lord, help me to bear to go on living,' he said to her: 'Daughter, consider that when life has ended you will no longer be able to serve me as you do now, and eat for me, sleep for me, do all you do for me, as if it were no longer you who were living, but myself. . . .'

It was at Seville that she experienced the desire, 'not to die too soon,' [3] for she longed to serve, more than ever.

Though the world hunted her down, she could have danced like David. She did not even ask that justice should be done her, yet the nameless novice had entered another convent where they considered her mad. And the renown of Teresa of Jesus' sanctity began to spread in Seville.

She was none the less humble on that account. The most bitter mortification that P. Gracián could impose on her was a general confession, for the memory of her sins was torture to her, whereas the customary mortification of going to the refectory carrying a heavy cross seemed 'recreation and delight' to her.

Nevertheless, fervour in the convent ran to extremes. On feast-days the sisters represented the life and sufferings of the holy martyrs 'so vividly and with such fervour' [4] that Teresita, the little niece from America, was terrified on one occasion and had to be taken away. These nuns were fired with impatience for heavenly glory; they felt that persecution would afford them an opportunity of being dispatched straight to paradise by the executioner. The Foundress calmed them down. She knew now that it was more important to live, in order to serve.

The 'business' of the new house was going forward. Don Lorenzo de Cepeda indeed had had to use the right of sanctuary to escape imprisonment on account of disputes with an owner—but was anything else but trickery to be expected in a city which had more than forty courts of justice? The Franciscans were strongly opposed to

[1] SEC, R, liv and xlv.   [2] Idem.
[3] Idem, xlii.   [4] Idem, vol. VI, p. 309.

Carmelites settling in their immediate vicinity, but Teresa was not now to be frightened off by such a small difficulty: the nuns entered the house by night; a few of the more timid did take 'every shadow for a friar,'[1] but when confronted with the *fait accompli* 'the friars remained as silent as the dead.'[2]

The house was worth the risk. 'It is of such a kind that the sisters never cease to render thanks for it. All of them say that we have had it for nothing. . . .'[3] Teresa loved to describe it and to point to what was for her its principal attraction: 'The orchard is very delightful and the view extremely fine.' 'A house from which one can see the galleons is not to be despised. . . .'[4] In the distance they could see the Guadalquivir glittering in the sun.

'Covered with green boughs and white sails. . . .'[5]

In the long letter she wrote to P. Ambrosio Mariano Azaro giving him an account of the completion of this foundation, she passed from one idea to another with an astonishing buoyancy. It was not that she forgot the persecutions. 'I'm very much afraid of this business in Rome. . . . I should like to see our business about the Discalced settled—the separation of the Reformed and Mitigated into two provinces—for Our Lord will now no longer tolerate the behaviour of the Calced, and all these troubles will come to an end. . . .' But the feeling of triumph was dominant, together with a certain natural satisfaction at having overcome so many obstacles. It was in a playful tone that she addressed P. Mariano: 'God help us! What a fine state you are in, leading people into temptation! It must be very virtuous to write to you. . . . When I consider how entangled the situation in which Your Reverence left me was and how you ignore it all, I don't know what to think, except cursed be the man, etc. . . .'[6] The etc. cut short what might have been the lamentation of Jeremias, and Teresa gave free rein to her joy. Joy which was perhaps a little exuberant and which one would attribute to a sort of plenitude of physical well-being after a strain if we were not talking of a woman who was more or less a confirmed invalid. Her style is that of someone young and full of vigour. She is sixty-one, but her phrases are charged with enthusiasm, fervour, humour, feeling, they explain, describe, chide or bless without a tremor, and her enthusiasm is that of youth.

In María de San José she was to leave a great prioress at Seville. 'I marvel at her courage; she has much more than I have. . . .'

---

[1] Cf. Sb, F, c. xxv-7.   [2] CTA, xciv.   [3] Idem.
[4] CTA, cccxxvi.   [5] Lope de Vega.   [6] CTA, xciv.

Complaints were forgotten. Teresa contemplated her work and found that it was good.

It was of this joy that P. Gracián wanted to have some lasting souvenir. He took advantage of the presence of Fray Juan de la Miseria to get this former pupil of Sánchez Coello to paint the Foundress's portrait. She had to submit to 'moving neither head nor eyes,' and to holding her hands together at the height of her shoulders. These sittings she found extremely tiresome, and she declared: 'God forgive you, Fray Juan! You've made me ugly and blear-eyed! [1]

He also painted the portrait of Teresita which earned him nothing but praise.

The convent of St Joseph of Seville still had to be inaugurated.

> I should have liked them to bring the Blessed Sacrament there without anyone knowing, for I am opposed to causing people pain when it is possible to avoid it—we don't want to humiliate those responsible for the persecution. On the other hand a good deal of solemnity seemed indispensable if the convent were to be made known. The Archbishop gave orders to invite the clergy and decorate tne streets.
>
> Our cloister served as an entrance, the good Garciálvarez decorated it admirably as he did the church, too, he set up fine altars and was a very prodigy of inventiveness. Among other things there was a fountain perfumed with orange-flower which impressed us greatly. The magnificent way in which our festival was organized was a great satisfaction to all the nuns, as were the streets so gay with flags and so much music and so many minstrels; the saintly prior of Las Cuevas told me that nothing so fine had ever been seen at Seville. The Archbishop himself installed the Blessed Sacrament.
>
> So you see, sisters, the poor Discalced nuns are honoured by everybody; a short time before, however, you wouldn't have thought there was even water for them, although there's quite a lot in this river. . . .
>
> The congregation was an extremely large one. . . . [2]

What Teresa did not say was that after the procession she knelt before the Archbishop and asked him for his blessing which he gave her; she had hardly risen from her knees when, in front of this extremely large' congregation, the Archbishop of Seville, Don Cristóbal de Rojas, knelt down in his turn and asked Mother Teresa of Jesus, Foundress of the convents of the reformed Carmel, to bless him.

[1] JG, PA, D, xiii.   [2] Sb, F, c. xxv-12.

On her arrival in Andalusia, Teresa had been treated as an undesirable person, abused, threatened, dragged before the Inquisition. Now they recognized in her such a perfect portrait of perfection in all its forms that one of the highest dignitaries of the Catholic, Apostolic and Roman Church treated her as one only treats prelates and saints.

That happened on 3rd June 1576. That very night at two o'clock in the morning she who was now called *la santa Madre*, in Seville as in Castile, set out for her place of exile.

IV

EXILE

HER brothers, Don Lorenzo and Don Pedro de Cepeda, her nephews, Francisco and Lorencito, a few lay persons of whom Antonio Ruiz was one, and a few friars, among them Fray Diego who was 'a little angel,' accompanied Teresa of Jesus; her niece, Teresita, the little 'nun' of nine, made them all merry.

Don Lorenzo who even then was pious though still somewhat attached to gorgeous display, horrified at the account of the vicissitudes of the journey from Beas to Seville, was determined that the return should be speedy and not uncomfortable; at his own expense they travelled by good coaches and carried abundant food with them. When there was no room in the inns, they took their meals in the fields, and if the Foundress was frightened on one occasion, it all ended as happily as possible; she hastened to tell Gracián about it:

'We were having our mid-day meal in the threshing barn when a great lizard darted in between my tunic and my bare arm, it was by the mercy of God that he didn't crawl in anywhere else, I think I should have died, considering what I felt as it was. . . . My brother caught the lizard quickly but he threw it from him in such a way that it jumped into the mouth of Antonio Ruiz. . . .'[1]

After a halt at Malagón they reached Toledo by way of Almodóvar. At Toledo malicious tongues chuckled over the style in which the Carmelite was travelling: 'a light woman travelling along the roads with ladies and gallants. . . .'[2]

Don Lorenzo was insistent that his sister should follow him to Ávila immediately. He intended to settle there, and Teresa's plan was also to stay in Ávila, but she preferred to stop for a few days at Toledo: this stay was to last a year.

She loved this convent which she called 'my house of delight,' *mi quinta de recreo*, enjoying the pun: Toledo was the fifth of her foundations—*quinta* in Spanish—and 'house of delight' is rendered by *quinta de recreo*. . . .[3]

[1] CTA, xcv. [2] V quoted SEC, vol. VII, p. 240, n. 2.
[3] Y quoted LV, p. 131.

'I haven't been so well for years, I can fast like everyone else. . . .'[1] '. . . They've given me a cell apart like a hermitage, very cheerful and pleasant, looking on to the orchard. I am very little troubled by visits, and if I had fewer letters to write. . . .'[2]

If the Mother Foundress had fewer letters to write, she would find the inactivity terribly irksome. Already, when her instructions had not been closely followed out she would complain: 'Jesús! What it is to be far away when all these things are happening!'[3] 'If I were there, I should soon have given all that a shaking up.'[4]

For from this cell, day and night, she continued to direct all her convents and all the business of the Reform by correspondence. She entered into the smallest details, there was no gauze or frieze for the habits of the nuns in the most distant convents on which she did not decide, no choice of novice over which she did not give her opinion, in her way of seeming to advise rather than to command. Moreover she only remained in Toledo because the posts were better organized there than in Ávila. All that happened to herself and went on in the Order during the persecutions went into her letters.

Did her austerity come out in her correspondence? She had the art of treating serious subjects in few words and clearly and of taking up again at once the spontaneous tone which makes her smile, her laugh, the sound of her voice, whether tender or sharp, familiar to us.

All her letters bear traces of having been written under pressure or in haste; she wrote as people speak when they have both wit, heart, personality and style, and when they have at their disposal the very thing that Teresa of Jesus lacked—time. For her enormous correspondence was scribbled in the midst of other occupations: 'Don't trouble to re-read what you write to me,' she said to her brother Lorenzo, 'I never do. If I miss out a letter put it in yourself. . . . Since people understand what I mean, it would be to lose time to no purpose. . . .'[5]

The quarrels between Calced and Discalced seemed to be moving towards some sort of agreement and the Foundress was now less anxious than she was at Seville. The General, P. Rubeo, had sent a delegate to Spain, P. Tostado, who had failed to wrest from the Nuncio Ormaneto the desired permission to disturb the reformed convents: he left for Portugal, where it was hoped he might remain.

Gracián, who was still Apostolic Visitor, 'transforms enemies into friends'[6] so peacefully that the Foundress was amazed. In the chapter

[1] CTA, ci. [2] CTA, cxv. [3] CTA, xcviii.
[4] CTA, cxx. [5] CTA, clxiii. [6] CTA, cxl.

at Almodóvar which met in August and September, he displayed wonderful moderation and charity. It was decided to go on with the Reform, in spite of the opposition of the Calced friars.

To the Discalced, P. Jerónimo Gracián de la Madre de Dios said:

We are being submerged by a wave of opposition. It does not come from our enemies but from Fathers who are our friends; not from sinners but from good people; their intentions are not evil but very good; it is the most fearsome of contests for our position is weak, whereas our enemies' strength comes from the fact that they are our so-called friends and that they are good and well-intentioned. . . . They seek our ruin under the guise of friendship and unity. . . . They have only too much human power, whereas we lack it, although that of the great Philip who is on our side is mighty.

The divine Power, too, is on our side. It is this divine Power which has brought our primitive Rule once more into the light of day and given to Mother Teresa strength to do things for this Rule which the nations have never before seen. . . . Let us pray to God for our enemies as Christ commands us; let us suffer and be silent for patience is always triumphant in the end and the time will come when they will be the first to preach our observance, defend our institution and uphold our primitive Rule.[1]

The Reformed did not swerve from this attitude.

This is illustrated, among other episodes, by the story of Paterna, where three Discalced nuns were sent to reform a convent of Mitigated Carmelites. Things began so badly that the good Discalced nuns, threatened with death by a lot of seeming mad women, spent the night barricaded in a room, struggling to prevent them from coming in. In the end the counsels of Mother Teresa won over the rebels. She wrote to the nuns who were there to carry out the Reform: 'Don't be surprised that they're not like we are straightway, it would be folly to expect it; don't insist so strictly that they're not to speak among themselves or on other things which are not sins; people accustomed to another and utterly different kind of life might make them commit more sins than they cured them of. Time is necessary, and the action of God, otherwise one will only throw them into despair.'[2]

Nothing disconcerted her, and when they raised a false accusation against one of the three Discalced nuns of Paterna, saying that she was 'a virgin but with child,' she merely said that it was 'utter rubbish.'[3]

And she showed no greater concern at the calumnies which rained down on the sons and daughters of Our Lady. 'I have been very much displeased that our Father—Gracián—should contradict the things said

---

[1] JG, C, vol. I, p. 557.　　　[2] CTA, clxiv.　　　[3] CTA, clxvii.

against us, particularly when they are unjust to that extent. To my way of thinking we should laugh at them and let them say what they will.'[1] She went so far as to declare that 'it is a great imperfection on the part of this Father.'[2]

'It is curious that nothing which happens has power to trouble me, so deeply is the certainty that all will be well rooted in me.'[3]

Yet she unceasingly recommended Gracián to be prudent. 'With time Your Paternity will lose a little of your ingenuousness, though I know it is the ingenuousness of a saint. . . .'[4] She was putting him on his guard and added: 'How unkind I am! But it's all necessary in this life!'[5]

If we had not her correspondence we should have no knowledge of a delightful side of the Mother Foundress's character: a nun's gaiety of the kind that clearly proves that the greatest minds can without detriment keep a childlike spirit in the course of a life hidden in God. 'I've received the coconuts. They're something worth seeing. The sisters are delighted with them and so am I. Blessed be he who made them, for truly they're a wonderful sight. . . .'[6] And Gracián himself proceeded to the solemn opening of the curious fruit in the course of a little ceremony. . . .

It was María de San José who had sent these presents: 'You're no doubt dreaming that you're a queen. . . .'[7] Teresa of Jesus loved sweets made of pink sugar, 'sugar-corporals—how gallant they are,' but what she loved most was orange-flower water and the oil extracted from it, for it enabled her to give *en passant* some of the recipes in which she delighted: 'Orange-flower oil is excellent for heart trouble. . . .'[8] 'For the heart, you must inhale orange-flower water, not drink it. . . .'[9]

One can picture the great excitement of the young nuns at Toledo when these parcels arrived from Andalusia. The sisters there were so skilful at embroidery that Teresa asked them to make her a pall 'all in chain-stitch, small, with pearls and garnets.' Passing from trivial to serious matters, in the same letter she gives directions about a nun who has just died: 'The body of this little saint must be left where it is, in the choir, for we must be buried in the cloister and not in the church.'[10]

Persecutions and a code of names: lest her correspondence should go astray or be intercepted by the Calced friars, she agreed with

[1] CTA, clxxii.   [2] CTA, clxxii.   [3] CTA, cxl.
[4] CTA, cxxxiv.   [5] CTA, cxli.   [6] CTA, clxxxv.
[7] Idem.   [8] CTA, ccxxxiii.   [9] CTA, cccix.   [10] CTA, clxxx.

Gracián on pseudonyms for the principal people they were likely to
talk about. There was considerable humour in her choice of these
'war' names and also a sense of metaphor which suggests a slight
tinge of *culteranismo* [1] which is present neither in her prose nor her
poems. In this she was thirty years in advance of her time. The old
Nuncio, Ormaneto, was merely 'Matusalem,' but the Mitigated
friars were the 'cats' or 'owls,' because they lived in darkness;
the Mitigated nuns were 'crickets,' because of their chatter; the Discalced friars were 'eagles,' because they gazed at God in contemplation,
and she called her Discalced daughters 'the butterflies,' because of
their simplicity. The Inquisitors were 'the angels' and 'the mighty
Angel' the Grand Inquisitor-General, Cardinal Quiroga. This led to
phrases like the following: 'The mighty Angel is very pleased to have
a niece among the butterflies. . . .' [2] 'Matusalem has decided that our
vow of separation from the eagles shall be fulfilled. . . .' [3]

Another person is frequently mentioned in these letters, and he too
has his pseudonym: Joseph is the name for Our Lord during this period
of strife. . . . 'Joseph has told me. . . . Joseph has assured me. . . .'

Persecution and 'ointments,' 'bottles of rose water,' and confirmation of her unswerving objective: 'I shall devote my life to our
erection into a separate province for everything depends on that.' [4]
Purges, Persian syrup, and apposite lessons in feminine psychology:
'What you tell me about the habits seems all right. Once it is done it
will stay done, after a few days of querulous complaint: if a few are
punished the others will be quiet, for women are like that, timid for
the most part.' [5]

When P. Mariano tried to make her accept a novice whom she
did not want, she told him most energetically that he understood
nothing about women! 'Let Your Reverence not meddle with that
any more, for the love of God! The girl has a good dowry, she can
enter elsewhere and not in an Order where just because they are so
few, subjects must be very, very carefully selected. Your Reverence
amuses me when you say that you will very soon know her: we women
are not so easy to know through and through. You hear our confessions
for years and then one day you're surprised at having understood us
so little; for in the matter of owning up to their faults women don't
know themselves, and you judge them on what they tell you. . . .' [6]

[1] A literary movement somewhat, but not entirely, akin to euphuism in
England—Tr.

[2] CTA, cvi.   [3] Idem.   [4] CTA, cxlvii.
[5] Idem.   [6] CTA, cxxi.

She gave orders that novices 'who seem just made for us and who will help us to pay our way' [1] were to have preference. . . . There was Blanca de Jesús María, whom she quaintly called 'the one with the gold ingots.' [2] 'Don't take the daughter of the Portuguese if what she's to bring is not paid over, for I've learned that we shouldn't get a *blanca* of it, and we're not living in times when we can take subjects for nothing. . . .' [3] 'I am dismayed to learn that Beatriz's mother is only bringing one thousand five hundred ducats, although she's the sort of girl whom we should gain by accepting even without anything. As regards what you say about the payment of what is due, it is obvious that it would be a very good thing to lighten the charges. If with Bernarda's dowry you can make up 3,000 ducats. . . .' [4]

Was this the woman who was called *la Santa Madre*? All this calculation of dowries and revenues? If her daughters had 'abandoned themselves entirely into Our Lord's arms,' [5] as she did, she would have had no need to have recourse to human artifice. When the convents fell into debt or had not enough to eat, the Foundress was distressed at the sisters' want of faith: 'Your faith in God must be weak indeed if you don't think he's powerful enough to give those who serve him enough to eat. . . .' [6] Then she resigned herself to the task of administration. It was then that she gave such strict directives which she herself was the very first to break: 'As to this little slave, don't oppose her admission in any way. In the case of her sister it's more difficult, but take her too . . . and you will be putting an end to their great difficulties.' [7] 'Give us people who are really worth while and you'll see that we're indifferent to the dowry.' [8] 'She has only 200 ducats: I prefer her to a fool.' [9] 'Take that other novice too, since she is so good; we need many, because many die. They go to heaven, so don't be sad about it. . . .' [10]

Such was Teresa of Jesus' attitude over death, far removed from the pagan pomp and circumstance of everlasting regret. She was once exasperated at having to use a seal representing two crossed tibias beneath a skull: 'I do hope my seal arrives quickly, for I can't bear sealing my letters with this skull, I want to use the seal which I hope he will impress on my heart, I.H.S.' [11] For her, death meant resurrection and therefore joy. When Petronila de San Andrés died 'like an angel' Teresa saw His Majesty, his arms wide open at the head of her bed, and

[1] CTA, cxiii. [2] CTA, clxii. [3] CTA, cxiv.
[4] Idem. [5] Sb, V, c. xvii. [6] CTA, ccxx.
[7] CTA, clxxxiii. [8] CTA, cxxi. [9] CTA, vi.
[10] CTA, clxxxiii. [11] CTA, clviii.

the seraphim welcoming her into paradise [1]; she forbade funeral hymns and composed *coplas* of joy which the sisters sang as they danced round the coffin. Years before she had written about her sister María whom she had loved so much: 'I experienced great joy when I learned of her death. . . .' [2] She had known then that María was hardly a week in purgatory and Our Lord showed her to her as she entered into glory.

Many saints have sympathized, perhaps too much, with the grief of those who were left: Teresa consoled them with infinite sweetness and tact, but also reminded them how fleeting their own existence was: 'Your Grace should consider that you haven't a long life to live; it is all so brief that your solitude will only last a moment.' [3] And she sent the widower two melons 'although they're not as good as I should have liked. . . .'

Thus she softened with a gracious word or a gift whatever might appear hard in her detachment from created things. But, as leader, it was her duty to look to discipline. The discipline she imposed was sometimes severe. 'No sister may go out of her convent, be she prioress or ordinary sister, unless it be for a foundation.[4] Although I have authority to transfer to another convent a sister whom the climate does not suit, the effects of such changes are intolerable; it is better that some should die rather than that all should take harm.' [5] Can this be the same woman who, that very year, had written letter after letter about the illness of the prioress of Malagón, Brianda de San José, worrying about the slightest details. 'I am appalled at your being ordered to get up in this weather. For charity's sake, don't do so; it's enough to kill you, it's painful and difficult even for those who are fat and well. . . .' [6] She made the journey herself to go and fetch Mother Brianda and bring her to Toledo where the climate was milder. She none the less recommended María de San José a vigorous therapeutic to calm an outbreak of nerves: 'A few strokes with the whip will perhaps make her be quiet and won't do her any harm. . . .' [7]

The art of government, which she exercised in so masterly a way, would seem to be the art of contradicting oneself without unsaying what has been said and of yielding without being soft. She was strong enough to afford to be kind without people ever being able to accuse her of weakness. When she was angry it was with a promptitude and energy which left no room for doubt as to the firmness of her character.

[1] SEC, vol. V, p. 127. [2] Sb, V, c. xxxiv-19. [3] CTA, clvi.
[4] CTA, lxxxi. [5] Idem. [6] CTA, clii. [7] CTA, ccxxxiii.

After Brianda de San José's departure, there was trouble in the convent at Malagón over a question of precedence which had arisen between Ana de la Madre de Dios who was acting as temporary prioress and Beatriz de Jesús: this proved clearly that Teresa knew perfectly well what she was saying when she said that nuns should not be moved for any reason, except for the needs of new foundations: but when she infringed her own directives and applied the remedy with a strong hand, she knew equally well what she was doing. The chaplain at Malagón learned this forthwith:

'Your Grace's letters have caused me great distress; it is like death to me to think that in one of these houses things are going worse than with the Calced nuns in Andalusia. . . . I cannot do otherwise than blame Your Reverence for it. . . . Your Reverence will see where these quarrellers who cause me such worries end up. I beg you to tell this Beatriz so from me. My state of mind in regard to her is such that I do not even want her named in my hearing. . . .'[1] *This Beatriz* was her cousin-german, but she expected more of those who were her kin than of others.

She went into the details of the dispute and frankly took the chaplain to task: 'If Your Reverence does not undo what the devil has begun to weave, everything will go from bad to worse. I shall be sorry to lose you, but I see that you prefer your peace and quietness to rendering me service.'[2]

The letter was addressed to the 'Very Magnificent and Reverend Señor Villanueva, Licentiate,' a good many titles to give him on the occasion of his dismissal.

It must be admitted that he allowed his penitents to adopt strange customs: 'I've learnt that certain mortifications are practised at Malagón: that the prioress orders the sisters to slap each other when they least expect it; I also hear of pinches. . . . The devil seems to be teaching you the way to destroy souls. And I hear about this only now!'[3] There is every reason to think that if the Mother Foundress had been free to go about, she would have gone like lightning to Malagón.

No one had so much authority as she had for keeping in good order eleven convents of women and numerous monasteries of men, and no one had her tact and ability. To mingle severity and kindness in the right proportion, always to show the widest possible understanding, was what she set out to do and what she did. And so when she was at Toledo unable to move, she wrote very detailed instructions

[1] CTA, clxxxvii.   [2] Idem.   [3] CTA, cxxxi.

for the Visitors and in particular for P. Gracián. And if she apologized for doing so, it was to give greater force to her recommendations:

> It may seem troublesome for a prelate to investigate all the details he will find here, but it would be much more annoying for him to observe the absence of progress in his subjects if he ignored such details. However good they may be, all this is necessary. Women whom one intends to govern must understand that the person in authority will not give way for anything in the world, will insist on all the rules of the Order being obeyed and will punish their infraction; they must see that he looks to this point particularly and realize that not only will he visit them each year but that he knows what they are doing day by day. . . .[1]

In the convents of her Reform, there was nothing of what went on day by day that the Foundress did not know.

She took up a troublesome Visitor as sharply as she did the too easy-going chaplain.

'You now see the trouble caused by the Acts drawn up by Fray Juan de Jesús. Even to read them made me tired: what would it be if I had to observe them? That is just what my nuns fear: the coming of powerful prelates who overburden and crush them. Believe me, our Rule has no room for these ponderous people, it is already ponderous enough itself. . . .'[2] In Spanish these 'ponderous' prelates, 'ponderous' people, are described by the same term as is used for 'boring' people. The nuance appears in Teresa's letter.

She herself was not one of such boring people. Her laugh rang out, her wit was sparkling. Gracián had charged María de San José to see to it that all went well in the convent of Paterna. 'You must be proud of being "half Mother Provincial" . . . I laugh to see myself overwhelmed with correspondence, so much so that I begin to write impertinences. . . .'[3]

The memory of the misunderstandings with the prioress of Seville had been blotted out long ago, and her letters were now the best of recreations for Teresa. She was delighted at the multitude of details in them, and declared they were her very life, *con esto vivo*. . . .[4] It was with this same María that she playfully pretended to quarrel.

> It's all very fine to pretend that there's nobody like Teresita! I would have you know that my *Bela* [Isabel Dantisco, an eight years

[1] Sb, MVC, 36.   [2] CTA, cxxxiii.
[3] CTA, clxii.   [4] CTA, cxliv.

old novice, who was Teresa's joy at Toledo for she adored children]
is marvellously clever. With a few poor little shepherd boys, the
other young ones and a picture of Our Lady, she delights us on feast
days and at recreation by her inventiveness and the *coplas* she sings
to us. She causes me only one anxiety. I do not know how to correct
her mouth which is pursed; she laughs very coldly and she laughs all
the time. I make her shut and open her mouth and I stop her laughing. She says she can't do anything about it and that it's the fault of
her mouth. Don't repeat this to anyone but I should like you to see
me engaged in correcting her mouth. I tell you all this to make you
laugh. . . .[1] Ah! what a head your Foundress has![2]

It is true that this little Isabel, *la mia Bela,* was Gracián's young
sister. This family entranced Teresa. When she first met their mother,
Doña Juana Dantisco, she threw on to paper an impetuous letter to
this 'Paul,' 'Eliseus,' 'her dear son.'

I am crazy about her simplicity and clear intelligence, in that she
has the advantage over her son. . . . We were together as if we had
known each other all our lives. . . . Your Paternity amused me
when you authorized me to raise my veil for your mother: anyone
would think you didn't know me, I who wanted to open my heart
to her. I've been wondering which of us two Your Paternity loves
best, and I feel that Señora Doña Juana has a husband to love and
other children, whereas poor Lorencia [Teresa of Jesus gave herself
this name in some of her letters to Gracián] has only this Father in the
whole world. God grant that she may keep him for her consolation.[3]

Not many canonized saints have spoken so warmly and humanly.
A month later she wrote to him: 'Your Paternity must ask God to
make a true nun of Carmel of me, for better late than never. . . .'[4]

What is so remarkable is that in all her words, whether serious or
amusing, as for instance in the account of her *Life* or in the most
sublime pages of the *Interior Castle,* she speaks with deep humility of
her failures and faults and of the trouble the least progress towards
perfection causes her. She was not endowed by nature for sanctity,
but she has *become* a true nun of Carmel, she has become the great saint
of Ávila and one of the most influential minds in the world without
on that account ceasing to sparkle with gaiety, charm and often even
with mischief. For her the sign of the cross really is the *plus* sign; she
loses nothing of what she is and in addition there is the tremendous

---

[1] CTA, clxii. [2] CTA, clviii.
[3] CTA, cxi. [4] CTA, cxxiv.

working of the Spirit in her, and its extension in the world through her. Teresa de Ahumada + God = Saint Teresa of Jesus.

The most austere penance, the hardest and most exacting life of action, have never altered her womanliness. In her it is womanhood which is purified and sublimated.

And Teresa de Ahumada de Jesús has certainly formed more daughters of Eve for divine love than 'gloomy' woman saints have done.

V

DON LORENZO DE CEPEDA, INDIAN

FORMERLY she used to write: 'Señor. . . .' Now she begins her letters: 'May Jesus be with your Grace.' Formerly she ended: 'Your Grace's true servant.' Now she ends: 'I kiss Your Grace's hands more than once.' The 'Grace' is her brother, Lorenzo de Cepeda.

Already he had been her benefactor: now he was her disciple and her confidant as well. The missives she sent him from Toledo were interminable, for if she directed him in spiritual things, she was also his administrator in temporal affairs.

Don Lorenzo was Governor of the Municipal Council of Quito, Treasurer of the Royal Coffers, Mayor of the capital of Ecuador, and son-in-law of Don Francisco de Fuentes, one of the conquerors of Peru who took part in the capture of Atahualpa. He was a charming man—'my brother will cease to be charming when he ceases to live,' and both serious and devout—'he deserves the name of Carmelite,' said María de San José. He was rich, his lands in the Indies were worth 35,000 pesos, he had brought back to Spain 45,000 pesos in merchandise and saved 28,000 pesos in gold. He had now reached the mature age of fifty-seven but he was just like a small boy where his sister Teresa was concerned.

He dared not move one straw from its place without consulting her. Without her, his surroundings would be all wrong, he would be ill lodged, would throw away all his fortune like so much dust, would lose his soul by making a virtue of laziness and his boys would be very badly brought up.

'Let Your Grace not forget to take no special confessor for the moment, and the least number possible of people for your house: it is better to choose servants one by one than to have to send people away. . . .'[1]

He had rented a house in Ávila: 'Be careful, for I seem to remember hearing that one of the rooms in this house of Hernán Álvarez de Peralta is collapsing: take great care.'[2] Even after conquering the Indies one can let oneself be cheated by a not very high-principled landlord.

[1] CTA, ci.   [2] CTA, clviii.

He wanted to cut a good figure. The vainglory of the father is nothing in comparison with that of his sons. Accordingly his sister hastens to send him a 'memorandum' on the bringing up of Lorencito and Francisco.

> If someone does not take these children in hand immediately, I'm very much afraid that they will soon be just the same as all the other conceited boys of Ávila. Your Grace must send them to the Jesuits at once and make schoolboys of them.
> Your Grace thinks too much about the point of honour, mortify yourself in that. I would prefer that you didn't buy a mule for the present but only a nag to use for journeys and your daily needs. As to these children, they'll do well enough walking: let them get on with their studies.[1]

Teresa was typical of the old Spain, hard-working and serious, sober in its simple and patriarchal way of life; Don Lorenzo and his sons represented the new Spain, Spain beyond the seas, the Spain of easy money, of a life of luxury and idleness. Two epochs came into conflict in these two people who were so fond of each other. Naturally, it was Teresa who won, and the pity was that every *conquistador* on his return to Spain had not a sister Teresa by him, gifted with an equally clear instinct for economy: then the gold of the Indies would not have impoverished the realm.

Three miles away from Ávila, in the valley of the Adaja, Don Lorenzo bought a fine piece of wheat-growing and pasture land: 14,000 ducats.

Almost immediately he regretted it and complained: it would give him a great deal of work. . . . He would have done better to put out his money to interest; the sum properly invested would have given him a good income without any work. The rich man thought he was putting forward an unanswerable argument when he wrote to his Carmelite sister: ' I should then have more time for prayer.'

He was very much mistaken. She broke out:

> Don't let me hear any more of it. You should be praising God for this transaction. Don't imagine that if you had more time your prayer would be better. Undeceive yourself: time well spent in looking after the welfare of your children does not injure prayer. God often gives more in a moment than in long hours: his works are not measured by time. . . . Jacob who was busy with his flocks was none the less holy for that, nor Abraham, nor St Joachim. But we find everything tiring when we want to avoid work. . . .[2]

[1] CTA, ci.   [2] CTA, clviii.

Over there the *conquistador* had acquired the habit of living in grand style and of having slaves to do his work. That was why, rather than work himself he would have preferred to make money work in his stead, in order to provide him with leisure: this did not please Teresa at all, even though the leisure might be devoted to conversing with God: we must serve him 'as he wishes and not as we wish.'[1] 'God has given something better than wealth to your children, he has given them honour'[2]—the honour of these old Castilian families like the Cepeda y Ahumada, the honour of men like their father, Don Alonso Sánchez, who did not think it beneath him to carry out his duties as a country estate-owner. And the Carmelite quietly laughed at the Mayor of Quito: 'Don't you think that collecting your revenues would also give you a certain amount of work?'[3]

Don Lorenzo, the Indian, felt he had had his answer.

So now the sons would be at school and the father busy looking after his lands. Temporal affairs were settled, now for the spiritual.

She got him to read the *Way of Perfection*, particularly chapter XXX in which she comments on these few words from the *Pater noster*: 'Thy kingdom come,' and in this way tried to persuade him to surrender himself to Our Lord's will: this will for him was work. It was not unintentionally that in the Constitutions of Our Lady's Order the Foundress had written: 'Whoever wants to eat must work.'[4]

The disciple made very good progress. In the letters which Teresa wrote him, a fraternal exchange of confidences alternated with the most practical and sensible advice of any she gave:

I must tell you that for more than a week I have been in such a state that if it lasted I should find it more than difficult to attend to so much business. I have begun to have raptures again and this has been painful to me, for it has happened several times in public and at Matins. There is no way either of resisting or of concealing the fact. It causes me so much embarrassment that I should like to hide anywhere I could. I am begging God to spare me this in public; do you ask him, too, for it brings very awkward consequences, and it does not seem to me that prayer gains thereby. I am like one drunk. . . .

Let us thank the Lord for one another![5]

For Don Lorenzo told her about the great graces which Our Lord had granted him too. His sister spoke with her usual prudence: 'I don't know what to say to you, it's more than you can probably understand, and the beginning of many blessings if you don't lose them by your own fault. . . .'[6]

[1] Idem.   [2] Idem.   [3] Idem.
[4] CONS, 24.   [5] CTA, clxiii.   [6] Idem.

She tried however to define this state, using once more the delightfully halting accents of the account of her first ecstasies: 'It is a great suffering without pain, without reason, extremely delightful. . . . It is a wound which the love of God makes in the soul, one knows not where, nor how, nor if it be a wound, nor what it is; it is merely that one experiences a sweet pain, and one complains about it thus:

> Lord, You hurt without wounding,
> And without pain you destroy
> The love of creatures . . .

For when the soul is really touched by this love of God, the love for creatures fades away without any suffering.' [1]

It was in reply to a question her brother put to her when he was extremely troubled that Teresa touched on the very thorny point of the physical repercussions of mystical love; she did so with extraordinary delicacy or, to speak more accurately, with sublime indifference:

Of the disturbed feelings which follow, take no notice; that has never happened to me. God in his goodness has always spared me these passions, but I understand that the soul's keen delight causes a natural movement; if you don't pay any attention, that will wear off by God's grace. Several persons have spoken to me of it.

The tremblings will also disappear; for the soul, when confronted with what is absolutely new and strange to it, is frightened and it is enough to make it afraid. The more frequently these things happen, the more able the soul will become to receive these graces. Your Grace should resist such tremors as much as possible and every external manifestation, in order that such things may not become a habit; that does not help but rather hinders.

The heat you say you feel is of no importance; only it could be harmful to one's health if it were excessive; but it will disappear like the tremors. In my opinion, such things follow the humours and as Your Grace is sanguine, the great movement of the mind, with the natural heat which collects at the apex and reaches down to the heart, can cause them; but, as I say, that adds nothing to one's prayer.

I think I have already dealt with what you tell me: the fact that afterwards you find yourself as if nothing had happened. I think St Augustine speaks of this too: the spirit of God passes without leaving a trace, any more than the arrow leaves a trace in the air. I remember

---

[1] *Sin herir dolor haceis*
Y sin dolor deshaceis
El amor de las criaturas (CTA, clxiii).

now that I replied to you on this point, but I've received such a multitude of letters since those of Your Grace. . . .[1]

Thus Teresa of Jesus showed perfect balance, soaring far above what are called nowadays inhibitions and complexes, yet willingly conceding to nature the place which it will occupy with or without our permission. Better equilibrium could not be found.

And she dealt with such deep questions of the spiritual life, writing off-hand in the midst of an overwhelming correspondence concerning the most varied matters.

The rest of this long letter to Don Lorenzo included two receipts: the art of curing rheumatism and headache by burning sweet-smelling lozenges, and the art of wearing a hair shirt. . . .

'When you find it difficult to recollect yourself at the time of prayer, or when you want to do something for Our Lord, put on this hair shirt which I'm sending you; it excites love, provided you don't wear it on any account after you're dressed, or to sleep in.'

But she has misgivings about her brother's excessive zeal: 'I don't do this without fear. . . .'

'Write and tell me how you get on with this plaything. . . . And I'm laughing: for you send me preserved fruits, cakes and money, and I send you hair shirts. . . .' [2]

Kindhearted as always, the Foundress had her usual joke.

He wasn't very easy to direct, this Don Lorenzo, on account of his very zealousness. Did he not take it into his head to meditate on the horror it would be to be damned? Teresa led him gently back to paradise: 'I don't know why you should desire those fears and terrors, since God leads you by the way of love. The form of prayer which he gives you is incomparably higher than thinking about hell. . . .' [3]

He made a vow of perfection without consulting her. 'That's a fine way to show obedience!' [4] She set about changing his ideas on the subject. In the same way she succeeded in dissuading him from the idea of becoming a friar: 'My brother's monkishness went no further. . . .' [5]

He went so far in the ways of penance that he admitted to wearing the hair shirt for twenty-four hours. 'A new fashion, I don't think the Discalced nuns themselves display as much aptitude. . . .' [6] But she restrained this thirst for mortification: 'God prefers your health to your penances, and that you should obey. . . .' [7]

---

[1] CTA, clxiii.   [2] Idem.   [3] CTA, clviii.
[4] Idem.   [5] CTA, cxxxviii.
[6] CTA, clxxi.   [7] Idem.

He told her of the outbursts of fervour which seized him at night and made him get up to pray: 'It won't be a bad thing to sit on your bed a moment, always provided you have as much sleep as your head needs, for one can reach the point at which it is no longer possible to pray at all. . . .'[1]

She insisted: 'It is important not to go without sleep . . . six hours at least. . . . Good sleep is not one of God's lesser graces. . . . Don't be afraid to sleep. . . .' And she added: 'I have so much work this evening that I've been hindered from prayer. I have no scruple about it, only regret. . . .'[2]

If she considered that it was important for friars and nuns to avoid the occasions of scrupulosity, she took just as much care to save those living in the world from them, whether priests or laymen.

Among those who asked her for spiritual direction was a great prelate who was also a great temporal lord, Archbishop Don Teutonio de Braganza. Anxious over the continuance of a state of tepidity during a long period spent in travelling about, he wrote to Teresa of Jesus.

'There's nothing for Your Lordship to fear: the tiredness that comes from moving from one place to another and the want of regularity in the employment of one's time are the cause of it. When Your Lordship returns to your ordered life, the soul will find its peace.'[3]

One day he confided to her that he felt strongly inclined to give up mental prayer. The reply she made showed to what extent she understood the process of thought at the different levels of consciousness: 'Take absolutely no notice. Praise the Lord for the desire you have for prayer, believe that your will intends it thus and that it likes to be with God. When you feel that the tension is too great, make an effort to go where you can look at the sky, walk for a little, you won't waste your prayer time for that. Managing our weakness is an art and it doesn't do to oppress nature. All consists in the search for God and the means by which we can draw near him. The soul is led onwards by gentleness. . . .'[4]

It is obvious that nothing escapes her and that with her as guide not one jot or tittle of the life of perfection is lost.

She gave to each one only what he was capable of receiving and bearing: in the name of Christ she never failed in love. During the year she spent in Toledo, she had the grief of being disappointed by Don Francisco de Salcedo. The holy gentleman saw almost all his property swallowed up in a lawsuit and he did not display the courage his piety

[1] CTA, clviii.   [2] Idem.   [3] CTA, lviii.   [4] CTA, lix.

would have led one to expect. But she never thought of blaming him nor of trying to teach him a lesson when what he needed was friendship.

'Pray to God,' she wrote to her brother Lorenzo, 'for him to understand and cease to be worried. That's what happens when we're not entirely detached. But when God has given us this grace, we must realize that we shan't console those who are still in bondage by preaching to them, but rather by showing them that we really feel their grief.' [1]

To-day, when I was thinking that God distributes what is his according to his good pleasure, I was astonished that a man like Don Francisco, who has been serving him sincerely for years, should be so afflicted at losing a fortune which he distributed to the poor much more than he used it for himself. I told myself that in his place I should have cared very little about it, but then I remembered how anxious I was when I saw you in danger at Seville; we do not know ourselves. To flee from all for the sake of All is our best plan if we don't want to be slaves of such low and worthless things; but we should consider that all are not capable of it. . . . [2]

She knew 'that there is no soul such a giant that it does not often need to become a child again.' [3]

And so, seeing that her brother was very tense over his prayer, she made up her mind to give him a humorous lesson, even in the things of God. He asked her for subjects of meditation and the subject she gave him—a phrase she had heard—'Seek for Me in Thee,' had puzzled him so much that he asked the grave Francisco de Salcedo, the even graver P. John of the Cross, and the good Julian de Ávila, to set down what these words of Our Lord suggested to them, as he would do himself, and to send them all to Mother Teresa.

Overwhelmed with work as she was and almost crazy with headache, she sat up that night even later than usual and wrote out a reply to them in the style of the *Vejamen*, the satirical criticism delighted in by students. It was an exercise which formed the great delight of students when they wanted to poke fun at one another.

So that her light way of handling the matter should not annoy, she began by declaring 'that she loves them all very much for they have all helped her in her trials,' [4] and then she distributed some fine rebukes all round.

The holy gentleman was her first victim. Certain passages of his

[1] CTA, cxxix.   [2] CTA, cxxix.
[3] SB, V, c. xiii–16.   [4] SEC, vol. VI, p. 65.

commentary 'please her very much,' but 'I have not the least intention of praising what you have all said.' She criticized his comments appositely and in detail.

'What is worse, if he doesn't unsay it, is that I shall be obliged to denounce him to the Inquisition, which is not far away. For after having said all through his paper: this is of St Paul and of the Holy Spirit, he declares that he has set his signature to rubbish. He must make honourable amends quickly; if not, he will see. . . .'[1]

Julian de Avila 'begins well and ends badly; so he has no claim to credit at all.'

He seems to have understood his subject completely in the wrong way, 'but I forgive him his errors, for he has not written at such length as my P. John of the Cross. . . .'[2]

We can imagine P. John of the Cross letting himself be carried up to the heights, his answer not being a little beside the point but a thousand leagues above it: it was P. John of the Cross, holy and learned as he was, whom Teresa teased most merrily:

> This reply is very good doctrine for anyone making the exercises of the Society of Jesus, but not for us. It would cost us dear not to seek God until we were dead to the world, Mary Magdalene was not, when she found him, nor the woman of Samaria, nor the Canaanitess.
>
> . . . God preserve me from people who are so spiritual that, come what may, they want to turn everything into perfect contemplation. Once this has been made clear, we are grateful to him for having made us understand so clearly what we did not ask to know. That is why it is always good to speak of God, we shall derive the benefit we least expect.[3]
>
> It was the same with Señor Lorenzo de Cepeda whom we thank for his answer and his couplets. For if he says a good deal more about it than he can understand, the amusement he's caused us disposes us to pardon the want of humility with which he meddles in such high things, as he says himself. . . .
>
> . . . I hope they'll all correct themselves: I too will correct myself in order not to resemble my brother in lacking humility. . . .[4]

All accepted the merry 'sentence' merrily, except Don Lorenzo who was ill accustomed to being teased. He gave vent to a few complaints but his sister consoled him:

> . . . I knew you would be cross; but it wasn't possible to give a serious answer; if Your Grace reads the letter carefully, you will

---

[1] Idem, p. 66.   [2] Idem, pp. 66-7.   [3] Idem, p. 67   [4] Idem.

see that I have not failed to praise part of what you said; without lying, it was not possible for me to speak otherwise of Your Grace's answer. I can assure you that after a day overwhelmed with business and correspondence—it seems as if the devil piles it up sometimes —my head was so bad that I don't even know what I said, I had a bad night and the purge made me ill. It's a miracle that I didn't send a letter I wrote to P. Gracián's mother, to the Bishop of Cartagena; I made a mistake in writing the address, I can't thank God enough that it didn't happen.[1]

These detailed explanations calmed the Indian's wounded vanity.

Teresa ended her letter with a spice of mischief: 'God keep you and make you a saint. . . .'

While the Foundress was at Toledo in this year of grace 1577, a young Cretan arrived there, who was beginning to paint for the church of Santo Domingo el Antiguo saints such as people had never seen the like of before, so much spirituality was there radiating from their faces. His name, Domenico Theotocopouli, was so long to pronounce that the Toledans surnamed him *El Greco*.

[1] CTA, clxviii.

VI

AND THEN HE GAVE HIMSELF UP . . .

A T the beginning of the persecution Mother Teresa of Jesus
had said:
'If God grants the Pope, the King, the Nuncio and our
P. Gracián a year or two more of life, everything will work out very
well. But we're lost if one of them happens to be taken from us.'

But Ormaneto, the Nuncio, died. He had been the most powerful
defender of the reformed Carmel: his power came from his sanctity;
he died so poor that Philip II had to pay his funeral expenses. He was
scarcely in his grave when Tostado left Portugal and returned to
Madrid with all haste; he hung about the court, anxious to be on the
spot and only waiting for an opportunity to exercise his authority as
delegate of P. Rubeo, the Order's Superior-General. The King had
not yet authorized him to visit the monasteries of Discalced friars and
nuns, but he had influence, he was not above intrigue, what could he
not effect?

Teresa of Jesus' call to action took the form of a summons to
prayer in all her monasteries and convents: '. . . in order that whatever is for the greatest service of God may come to pass.'

Toledo set the example: in the patio, in the choir, in the cloisters,
the daughters of the Blessed Virgin walked in procession reciting
litanies of supplication, multiplied their penances and rivalled one
another in fervour:

'Leave no stone unturned,' said the Foundress, *no se descuiden.*

Her call to arms was always: 'Don't go to sleep! Don't go to
sleep!'

And she often added: 'But keep calm.'

For those around her were beginning to lose their heads. Gracián
was frankly nervous and P. Antonio de Jesús not much better. While
both were lodging at Cardinal Tavera's hospital in Toledo, one
evening at Compline time they saw a ghost appear behind one of the
chapel windows: a sort of monstrous octopus with many tails and
enormous tentacles. They hastened to tell Teresa about what they
considered an ill omen, but in their very faces 'she laughed heartily

at seeing the courage of her two squadron-leaders turning into cowardice.' [1]

It took more than a ghost to frighten Teresa of Jesus.

'Señor, we have no bread,' was what good Francisco de Salcedo wanted to write to the Bishop of Ávila in the name of the nuns of St Joseph's: Teresa would not consent. She would not complain, even if she were half-starved and persecuted. 'However great my trials have been in this life I do not remember having uttered words of complaint.' [2]

She had had to leave Toledo suddenly at the beginning of July 1577 and return to Avila to put St Joseph's under P. Gracián's jurisdiction. She found the first of her dovecots in a state of utmost destitution, but her view of famine was the same as of persecution and defamatory accusations: 'I didn't find it too hard to bear.' [3]

But she then received a shock which would have crushed anyone else but her or at least would have made them reel: two of her own side had played false. Two Discalced friars had betrayed P. Jerónimo Gracián de la Madre de Dios!

It was the beginning of a relentless conflict. The Mother Foundress was by turns indignant, sarcastic, demanding her rights, or magnanimous in her all-embracing forgiveness of injuries; but she never complained.

She wrote to the King and her tone was regal in its dignity.

The grace of the Holy Spirit be always with Your Majesty. *Amen.*
I have been informed of a memorandum which has been sent to Your Majesty against our Father, Master Gracián, of such a nature that I am horrified at the ruses of the devil and at those of the Calced Fathers; for, not content with defaming this servant of God—he is such in very truth and edifies us all, he doesn't visit a convent where they don't write to me that he has changed the spirit of the house for the better—they are now seeking to throw discredit on these monasteries where the Lord is so well served. To this end they have made use of two Discalced friars of whom one has often shown that he lacked judgement; of him and of other Discalced who are set against Gracián, the Calced friars have tried to make use, by obliging them to instance certain extravagances. If I did not fear the harm the devil can do, I should laugh at the accusations they are making against us Discalced nuns; but from the point of view of the Order it is monstrous.

[1] SEC, vol. VIII, p. 243, n. 2.
[2] *Ibid.*, R, iii, p. 18.   [3] CTA, cxciv.

For the love of God I beseech Your Majesty not to allow these infamous accusations to be brought before the courts. The world is such that even if the contrary were proved, a suspicion of evil might remain.

For the love of Our Lord, let Your Majesty consider this as touching your own honour and glory.[1]

Who were the traitors? Fray Miguel de la Columna, and in particular P. Baltasar de Jesús, whose habit Mother Teresa had sewn with her own hands when he had entered the Order at Pastrana. Turbulent, ambitious and harsh, he could not stand P. Gracián. Already, earlier, the rumour of certain intrigues engineered by him had much grieved Teresa 'as far as his soul was concerned.' [2] The very sight of Gracián was so hateful to him that to avoid him he went to hide himself away 'in his den.'

It was this hatred that those 'clad in fine cloth' had provoked and made use of. Mother Teresa, able to bear it no longer, added a post-script to her letter to Philip II in which she refuted the most dangerous of the calumnies against Gracián.

'If it is necessary, all we Discalced nuns will declare on oath that we've never heard him say or do anything which was not calculated to edify us; he is meticulous about observance to the point that even for chapters, when entering the enclosure would seem indispensable, he habitually stays behind the grille.' [3]

From this paragraph it seems that the Visitor was accused of culpable intimacy with his subjects. Gracián was simple, he did not see evil and still less imagined that anyone could invent evil where there was none. The Foundress who knew the world's wickedness put him on his guard, however: it was the duty of the Discalced friars, spied on by the Calced with extreme malevolence, to be more circumspect than ever.

Teresa of Jesus insisted on this point until she was tired:

. . . . If a friar has to stay in this convent, Your Paternity must tell him emphatically to see the nuns as little as possible. Father, this point must be watched very carefully. I should not even like the chaplain to see them frequently, for although he is excellent, from his very excellencies those who are ill-disposed can draw most unpleasant comments, particularly in small places, and indeed every-where.[4]

Will Your Reverence kindly believe that everything will go so much better if you see that your daughters have no particular friend-

---

[1] CTA, cxcv.   [2] CTA, lxxix.   [3] CTA. cxcv.   [4] CTA, clxxix

ships, even though the persons in question may be saints. I do not want you to forget this.

All these nuns are young. For greater security, they must not see the friars. There's nothing I fear so much as that for these convents.[1]

There's no reason for seeing a friar without a veil, whatever Order he belongs to, and still less for seeing our Discalced friars like that. One can discuss the things of the soul without lifting one's veil. . . .[2]

When P. Gracián was in Andalusia, Teresa was so much afraid that the Calced friars would poison him that she asked María de San José to serve his meals in the convent parlour, but there again every precaution had to be taken to cut short evil gossip:

'In order not to create a precedent, no one must ever eat in the parlour except P. Gracián, who is in a position of some difficulty; but this can be done without its being talked about. . . .'[3]

It did not take as much as this for the Mitigated friars to attack poor P. Gracián's reputation. They began to watch the penitents he had in the world as much as they did his Carmelite nuns: they then accused him of suspicious intimacy with the Marchioness of Elche and her grand-daughter: he had in fact spent an entire night at Évora 'speaking of spiritual things.'[4]

His ingenuousness played into the hands of his enemies.

A short time after this scandalous memorandum, P. Baltasar de Jesús and Fray Miguel de la Columna declared they had been forced by the Calced friars under threat of all sorts of ill-treatment to sign papers they had never read. Yet these infamous accusations were to pursue Gracián all his life.

As to Teresa, she took the 'fine goings-on' attributed to her and her nuns with her usual good humour.

'I am ashamed of what these gentlemen have said about us: they put us under the obligation of becoming what they depict us as being, in order not to show that they have lied. . . .'[5]

All this was only the beginning.

The new Nuncio, Felipe Sega, had arrived at Madrid. Prejudiced against the Discalced before he arrived, by Cardinal Boncompagni, protector of the Calced, he devoted himself wholeheartedly to the enemies of the Teresian Reform. The impudence of those whom Teresa called *los gatos*, the cats, knew no limits. Already P. Antonio de Jesús was obliged to remain in hiding in Toledo in a garret in the Tavera Hospital and even this did not prevent his being imprisoned.

---

[1] CTA, xcv.   [2] CTA, cccxxxv.   [3] CTA, xcvi.
[4] SEC, vol. VIII, p. 184, n. 2.   [5] MJR, ix.

He was promptly released but the great offensive of the Mitigated against the Reformed was launched.

Sega, the Nuncio, did not withdraw Gracián's mandate as Visitor, but he forbade him to visit even a single convent. The King and the Council of Castile expressed a contrary opinion, without making it abundantly clear that they supported Gracián. He withdrew to Alcalá and then to Pastrana, living as a hermit in austerity and penance, praying in an especial manner for his persecutors and bearing his trials with joy 'like a St Jerome.'[1]

It was the nuns of the Incarnation who provided the first pretext for violence through their attachment to the *Madre Fundadora*: the same nuns who six years before had rebelled against the Reformer, this time rebelled in her favour.

They were on the eve of the election of a new prioress and would have no one but Teresa of Jesus. Tostado had decided otherwise: he sent the Provincial of the Calced friars to preside over the election 'furnished with severe censures and excommunications' for those who gave the Foundress their vote.

Teresa related these facts with so much liveliness and vigour that, in spite of her suffering, woman of wit as she was she could not help laughing at the ridiculous anger of so grave a man:

> . . . Taking no notice, fifty-five nuns voted for me. Each time he was handed a vote the Provincial excommunicated and cursed; he crushed the voting papers with his fist, then stamped on them and burned them. The nuns have been excommunicated for a fortnight, they're not allowed to hear Mass or to go to choir, even when Divine Office is not going on; no one can speak to them, neither the confessors nor their own relatives.

> Best of all, the day after these forced elections, the Provincial returned and ordered them to begin all over again. They replied there was no reason to do so for they had already voted. Thereupon he excommunicated them again. He then called the others, to the number of forty-four, and made them elect another prioress. He appealed to Tostado for confirmation.

> There's nothing more to be said, the others are standing firm and claim that they will only obey this prioress as vicar.

> That, in short, is what has happened. All are horrified at such a serious wrong. As for me, I have no wish to find myself in that Babylon. . . .[2]

The new prioress imposed by the Calced friars was Doña Ana de Toledo.

[1] CTA, ccx.   [2] CTA, cxcviii.

The confessors to whom the excommunicated nuns had not the right to speak were P. John of the Cross and P. Germán de San Matías. They were shut up in the hut built by the Mother Foundress on the outskirts of the convent. John of the Cross kept Teresa informed of what was happening, succeeding in passing notes to her in which he begged her to intervene; in his opinion nothing was more dangerous for the souls of these poor nuns than the ambiguous position in which they found themselves.

The Foundress wrote letter after letter to Madrid and begged that action might be taken not only to get the excommunication lifted, but that the rebels should agree to obey Doña Ana.

All Teresa wanted was peace and it was of peace that she spoke to John of the Cross when he succeeded, 'hiding himself all the way along,' in cheating the vigilance of the Calced friars, and making a long détour to get to her. This brief interview was a great consolation to them both. Not that they had to seek in each other the courage which they derived from its source, the continual presence of God, but together they tasted 'of the delicious fruit of forgetfulness of self and of all things.' [1]

Through his intermediacy the Foundress was able to send her daughters at the Incarnation injunctions to show submission and pardon; yet the Calced accused P. John of the Cross of inciting his subjects to rebellion.

Rumours ran all round Ávila, that city of gossip.

'. . . The Calced have made an offer to P. John of the Cross for him to put aside the coarse frieze of the Reform and put on the cloth habit of the Mitigation. He has refused. . . .'

'. . . The Calced, who are furious, intend to seize P. John of the Cross and P. Germán by force. . . .'

For three days and nights the relatives and friends of the rebellious nuns and those of the confessors mounted an armed guard around the little wooden hut. The danger seemed averted and they went back home.

But in the night of 3rd-4th December, the prior of the Calced friars of Toledo, P. Maldonado, assisted by constables—the decrees of Piacenza authorized the Calced to have recourse to the secular arm against the Discalced—forced the door and took the two friars away. The Foundress had already said of this prior: 'He's better gifted than anyone for making martyrs. . . .' [2]

The whole of Ávila seethed with indignation:

---

[1] JC quoted SEC, vol. VI, p. 196   [2] CTA, cciv.

'. . . They've taken them off to prison as if they were male-
factors. . . .'

'. . . They've beaten them three times and the worst treatment
imaginable has been meted out to them. . . .'

'. . . . Maldonado has dragged P. Juan off to Toledo. . . .'

'. . . The prior of the Calced friars of Ávila has taken charge
of P. Germán, who was spitting blood; people saw him. . . .'

'. . . Both are saints. . . . [1]

'. . . P. Juan let himself be taken like a lamb. . . .'

'. . . In the morning he succeeded in escaping from them. . . .'

'In escaping from them? He's got away? He's saved.?'

The crowd of humble folk trembled with awe:

'He didn't flee to avoid martyrdom but he returned to his house
near the Incarnation to destroy papers about the Reform. He locked
himself in and while the Calced friars were wrestling with the door,
he ate the documents which he couldn't destroy otherwise.'

A single shudder of anguish ran right through the city:

'And then? . . .

'And then he gave himself up.' [2]

It was thus by comments passed from mouth to mouth that
Teresa learnt of the Calced friars' crime and the mortal danger in which
John of the Cross and Germán de San Matías were. She gave vent to
a cry of dismay. That very day she sent a letter of rather vehement
entreaties to the King:

> It is creating a scandal throughout the city. Everyone is wondering
> where they get the audacity from to act like that in a city so close to
> Your Majesty's residence; they seem to fear neither civic justice nor
> God.
>
> I am utterly crushed at knowing that our Fathers are in their
> hands; they've been wanting to get hold of them for several days; I
> should prefer to know that they were prisoners of the Moors, then one
> might expect more pity to be shown. This friar, this great servant of
> God is so weakened by what he has undergone that I fear for his life.
>
> For the love of Our Lord I beg Your Majesty to have him promptly
> set at liberty and to give orders so that those who wear the cloth
> cease to do so much harm to these poor Discalced: they say nothing
> and submit, it is therefore a benefit for their souls, but the scandal is
> all over the city. The Calced say they will put them to death, for
> Tostado has ordered them to do so.
>
> If Your Majesty does not remedy the situation, I don't know

¹ CTA, ccvii.   ² BJR, p. 163.

where we shall end, for on earth we have no one except Your Majesty. . . .[1]

On earth. But there is a higher Protector than a king. On 7th December she wrote: 'The persecution is of such a kind and so bad that our only hope is to have recourse to God.'[2]

And she prayed with all the abandonment she was capable of:

'. . . I go to the place where I pray and begin to speak to Our Lord whatever comes into my mind quite simply, for often I don't know what I'm saying; it is love which speaks and the soul is so much out of itself that I don't see the difference there is between it and God. Love knows who His Majesty is, but it forgets itself and thinks it is in him without any separation and it talks nonsense. . . .'[3]

O my Joy and my God! What shall *I* do to please you? My service is worthless, even if I were to render much service to God. For why must I remain in this wretched misery? Provided the Lord's will may be accomplished, my soul, what greater benefit can we desire! Hope, hope, you know neither the day nor the hour. Watch, all soon passes, although your desire makes that which is certain seem doubtful, and that which quickly passes, long. Know that the more you strive, the more you will show your love to your God and the more you will delight with your Beloved in joys and delights which will have no end.[4]

O my God, rest from every pain, how I wander![5]

O my soul! What a wonderful strife this pain is and how everything is fulfilled to the letter! *Thus, my beloved is mine and I am his.*[6] Who would dare to separate and extinguish two such ardent flames? It would be labour in vain for now they form only one. . . .[7]

Teresa of Jesus showed so serene a countenance that her niece Teresita was amazed: this was the effect of abandonment to God then? The majestic peace of a soul which divine love poises so high above events that it regards them untroubled and without letting itself be caught in their mesh is very great.[8]

When everything around her seemed to be crumbling away, the Foundress called on God for help. To those suffering persecution she counselled prayer far more than the seeking for human help. But her imperturbable common-sense added: 'Prayer, on condition that one doesn't take time from the sleep indispensable to the body.'

To Gracián who wrote her that he was taking time from his sleep

[1] CTA, cciv.   [2] CTA, ccv.   [3] Sb, V, c. xxxv-8.
[4] SEC, E, xv-3.   [5] SEC, E, xvi-2.   [6] CC.
[7] SEC, E, xvi-4.   [8] Sb, V, c. xx-25.

to think over possible solutions, she advised sleep and prayer, which would be worth far more to him than drawing up plans: 'The graces which Our Lord showers down then are immense, and I should not be surprised if the devil is not trying to deprive you of them. God doesn't give the grace of prayer just when we will it, and when he does give it us we ought to value it; in a second Our Lord will give you better means of serving him than any the understanding could discover. . . . If we go away from God when he wants us, we shall not find him when we want to. . . .' [1]

Teresa obtained peace and endurance in the midst of this 'storm of trials,' [2] for she sought God alone.

The days passed. What was the King doing? Was his aid, like all human aid, just dried rosemary?

Teresa was counting each hour as it passed: already more than a fortnight had gone by since the two Fathers had been taken away, she still did not know where they were or what was happening to them, or if Philip II had intervened. [3]

Fresh rumours reached her:

'. . . They've taken his coarse habit away from P. John of the Cross and forced him to put on the cloth the Calced wear. . . .'

'. . . A young muleteer, when they were taking P. John to Toledo, amazed by his gentleness under the ill-treatment his cruel captors were inflicting upon him, offered to help him escape. . . .'

'He escaped then?'

'No. He refused. He replied that he preferred this opportunity of suffering for Our Lord to liberty.' [4]

He had refused! The same questions over and over again: Where is Fray John? What are they doing with him? And the King. . .? Why does the King not answer? How is it he has not acted?

For the first time a letter from Madre Teresa de Jesús to the King of Spain remained without response.

Philip II was silent, but the devil was furiously busy.

It was Christmas night 1577. A blast from hell extinguished the lamp which Teresa was holding in her hand when she went down a staircase to go to the chapel, she missed her footing, fell and broke her left arm.

'The devil might have done much worse to me,' [5] she said.

She offered her pain for the safety of 'the little saint, Fray John.'

[1] CTA, ccix.   [2] SEC, R, xxxvii.   [3] CTA, ccviii.
[4] BR, p. 164.   [5] FR, L. IV, c. 17.

VII

NIGHT'S DARKEST HOUR

WAS the lamp she was carrying when she fell the one by whose light Teresa of Jesus worked in her cell when 'in the darkest hours of the night' she wrote the *Interior Castle* or the *Seven Mansions of the Soul*? It did not matter now: the book had been finished a month before.

The Foundress had been pleased with the account of her *Life*, but the *Mansions* caused her to give vent to a cry of joy: 'It is known for certain that this marvel—the *Life*—is in the hands of Don Gaspar de Quiroga, Grand Inquisitor and Archbishop of Toledo, and that he spends much time reading it; he says that he won't give it back until he's tired of it. If he came here, he would see another book, even better, for it treats of nothing but God; its chasing and enamel work are more delicate; the goldsmith was not so experienced when he produced the first work; the gold in this one is of a higher carat and the stones better set. Carried out to the instructions of the Master Glazier it looks very well from what they say. . . .' [1]

Was this the nun who held humility to be the essential virtue? The same person who at a word from her confessor had thrown the manuscript of the *Thoughts on Divine Love* in the fire at Segovia? The two are one and the same and her twofold attitude only makes her complete detachment stand out the more. Utter humility has nothing in common with the affectations of false modesty. Moreover in her *Mansions* Teresa proclaims: 'Humility means walking hand in hand with truth,' [2] *la humildad es andar en verdad*. It was not herself whom she was praising, but him who dwelt in and inspired her.

Speaking about prayer with P. Gracián in Toledo in 1577, she regretted not being able to express herself better.

'Oh, how well the matter was explained in the *Autobiography* which is with the Inquisition!'

Gracián had just made her draw up the *Method for the Visitation of Convents* and complete her history of the foundations as far as the lively account of the foundation at Seville; in his opinion, as in hers, 'the manner of visiting the Discalced nuns was in a sense taught of God,' [3]

[1] CTA, ccv.   [2] Sb, M, VI, c. x–7.   [3] Quoted SEC, vol. VI, p. 34.

and he had been delighted to find the *Foundations* 'very attractive.' [1]
Mother Teresa was overwhelmed with correspondence, business, cares,
anxious about her sons and him in particular. Excess of work forced
this woman of sixty-two to stay up until one or two o'clock in the
morning without ever claiming the right to get up later. What did it
matter: the Foundress had other difficult achievements to her credit.

However, she mentioned her headaches to Gracián:

'I do not spend a day without hearing much noise in the head and
writing makes me feel very ill,[2] for more than six months my head has
been in a bad way. . . .' [3]

The doctor had forbidden her to go on writing after midnight and
asked her to write as little as possible with her own hand; from then
onwards she dictated almost all her letters, but she could not dictate
a work of that kind.

'Many torrential rivers falling down into cataracts, many little
birds and sounds of whistling, . . .' [4] such was the bucolic but
deafening symphony which was rumbling unceasingly in Teresa of
Jesus' head when P. Gracián imposed on her the task of writing the
Interior Castle.

'Note down what you remember, add other ideas and make a new
book without naming the person in whom these things have taken
place.' [5]

After her wretched health, Teresa pleaded her incapacity, but,
being courageous, only laughed as she complained:

'How do they expect me to write? Let the theologians do it! They
have studied whereas I am only an ignorant woman. What is there
that I could say? I shall use the wrong words and there is a danger of
my doing harm. There are so many books on prayer already! For the
love of God, let me turn my spinning-wheel, go to choir and follow
the Rule like the other sisters: I am not made for writing, for that I've
neither health nor head. . . .' [6]

The Foundress was sincere. She knew no Latin in an age when
Latin was indispensable and she never quotes in Latin without making
mistakes; her horror of anything like pedantry constantly influenced
her in her rejection of technical terms and when she is obliged to use
them, she hesitates: '. . . What is called, I believe, mystical theology.
. . .' [7] '. . . I don't know why it's called illuminative: I suppose the
term is used of those who're making progress. . . .' She writes: 'One

[1] CTA, cxxiv.   [2] CTA, clxxviii.   [3] CTA, clxiv.
[4] Sb, M, IV, c. i–10.   [5] JG quoted SEC, vol. IV, p. ix.
[6] Idem, p. x.   [7] Sb, V, c. x–1.

who understands fountains,' instead of 'well-sinker,'[1] speaks of 'I
don't know what acts,' and does not hesitate to write, 'Here is a comparison which it seems to me I've heard or read somewhere. . . .'[2]

In those days women had no right to be learned and Teresa was
far from claiming any such right: even if her humility had not prevented it, her extreme womanliness would have been sufficient to
restrain her. 'Our Lord knows the confused state of mind in which I
write the greater part of these things. . . .'[3]

'I have been disturbed so many times while I've been writing
these three pages, which have taken me as many days, that I've forgotten what I'd begun to say. . . .'[4] This great mystical writer is what
the majority of women writers are: a woman, who writes; that is, the
work to be accomplished does not give her the right to live differently
from the way other women do. Life around her does not come to a
standstill because she is writing a book. She knew this only too well
and shrank from the overwhelming prospect.

She consulted her confessor who persuaded her with his entreaties:
Teresa was incapable of refusing anything that would give her friends
pleasure; she liked P. Velásquez very much and he was 'as pleased to
come and see her once a week as if he had been made Archbishop of
Toledo.'[5] Moreover he would later be rewarded for his faithfulness
by being made Bishop of Osma. Teresa gave way.

Once more, through obedience, with the sole objective, a practical and realist one, of explaining to others the way of access to the
marvels of the interior kingdom, she produced what was the work of
a writer of genius. Her style, brisk and homely as usual, was this time
adorned with the most scintillating phrases at her command as she
strove to express the wonders of spiritual glory.

It was from obedience that the old Foundress who slept scarcely
three hours a night derived her strength. Obedience also gave her
light, for nothing is more finely coloured with all the sparkling hues
of the prism than this account of the adventures of a soul which set
off in self-conquest through the seven mansions of the interior castle
until it attained union with God.

It is a question of one's inmost heart, that heart from which we
harshly eject ourselves when we say, under the stress of violent emotion
or anger: 'That has made me beside myself. . . .' This innermost
heart, these Mansions into which those who are farthest from any idea
of a divine presence in themselves nevertheless penetrate, for a few brief

[1] Sb, F, c. i-4.   [2] Sb, V, c. xi.   [3] Sb, C, c. xxxv-4.
[4] Sb, V, c. xxxix-17.   [5] CTA, civ.

moments when life forces them to reflect, to examine themselves in order to act afterwards with more wisdom or straightforwardness: 'I have entered into myself. . . .' they say.

This conquest of the soul comprises, in short, the exploration and domination of all the planes of consciousness. He who undertakes it rids himself of the weight of his worldly personality by obedience and humility, in order to obtain access to the highest regions of the spirit; just as the traveller who prefers air to railway travel has to leave his heavy luggage behind. But such a traveller, once his flight is over, finds himself a pedestrian again and this will occur more than once, whereas the soul which has experienced the metamorphosis of the spirit will never lose its wings again.

On 2nd June 1577, then, at Toledo, Teresa sat down in front of the blank paper 'like something completely stupid, not knowing what to say nor how to begin.'[1] 'I am, literally, like the birds who are taught to speak and don't know what it is they are taught to say: they repeat it often enough. If Our Lord wants me to say something more, His Majesty will make it known to me. . . . If I succeed in expressing it, it must be understood that that doesn't come from me; I am not gifted with very much intelligence and I should have no ability for such things at all if Our Lord in his mercy had not given it me. . . .'[2]

Our Lord did want her to say something more: the plan of the work was shown her in a vision: 'God showed her a very beautiful globe of crystal, in the likeness of a castle, with seven mansions and in the seventh, which was in the centre, the King of glory in immense splendour. . . .'[3]

Teresa did more than integrate all she knew and all His Majesty dictated to her into this theme: she was to put into it all she was, including the experience of her life of contemplation and action carried to the highest degree of conscious perfection. Like every other of her works, the *Interior Castle* is an act.

In writing of the effusions of divine love, her way of expression is the mystical language of the time fragrant with perfumes of the *Canticle of Canticles*, trembling with the caresses which the Sulamite exchanges with her Beloved; the setting, 'this delightful and beautiful castle,'[4] this fortress where the King dwells, these rooms where 'the men-at-arms' ready to fight against the enemy who threatens the walls

[1] SB, M, I, c. ii–7.
[2] Sb, M, prol., 2–4.
[3] Y quoted SEC, vol. II, p. 494.
[4] Sb, M, I, c. i–5.

pass to and fro, all remind us that Teresa of Jesus had been very fond of tales of chivalry.

The Mansions: Teresa then regards the soul 'as a castle cut from diamonds or from the clearest crystal'; [1] in this castle there are a great many rooms, 'just as in heaven there are many mansions.' [2]

'The senses are the people who live there. . . . Our faculties are the governors, major-domos and stewards. . . .' [3]

The entrance gate to the castle is prayer.

The soul who wanders about in the First Mansion is touched by grace, but so many 'venomous things, snakes, and vipers,' [4] are crawling around her that she does not see the light which is coming from the King's apartments. The devil takes advantage of this darkness to set his snares. The soul will only escape them by persistence in prayer, self-knowledge and confidence in the goodness of her King.

She will prepare herself to enter into the Second Mansion by disengaging herself from business which is not indispensable to her state of life: 'Without a beginning of this sort, I consider access to the principal apartments impossible.' [5]

The soul who penetrates into the Second Mansion is one who already practises prayer faithfully. God invites her so gently to go forward that the poor little thing is in despair at not being able to obey immediately 'and she is more troubled than before she heard the invitation. . . .' [6]

She is afraid and very cold, the light is still faint, temptations assail her like venomous snakes. She trains her will to obey God, begins to practise recollection not by forcing herself, [7] but in all gentleness. . . .

The enemy is at the doors of the Third Mansion, 'it is necessary to eat and sleep armed, in case he should succeed in forcing an entrance.' [8] . . . The soul avoids evil, likes to hear God praised and shows 'excellent dispositions' [9] for good, but love does not yet lift her above vainglory nor above the demands of her immediate temporal interest.

'She is impatient when she finds the door which leads to the apartments of the King, whose vassal she calls herself, closed, but consider the saints who have entered there and you will see the difference there is between them and us. . . .' [10] Get beyond your little

[1] Cf. Sb, M, I, c. i–3.   [2] Idem.   [3] Sb, M, I, c. ii–4.
[4] Sb, M, I, c. ii–14.   [5] Idem.   [6] Sb, M, II, c. i–2.
[7] Sb, M, II, c. i–10.   [8] Sb, M, III, c. i–2.
[9] Idem, c. i–5.   [10] Idem, c. i–6.

practices of piety, *obrillas*. . . . Your love must not be the product of your imagination but be proved by acts.' [1]

Detached from the world, masters over their passions, prompt to obey, concerned only with their own faults and taking care not to judge their neighbours, the guests of the Third Mansion live in silence and in hope. [2]

The great adventure begins in the Fourth Mansion. Here the King distributes his favours lavishly 'when he wills, as he wills, and to whom he wills.' [3] The soul must be ready to receive them, as the knight errant is ready to seize every fresh opportunity. Here, rampant or venomous creatures merely provide heroic occasions of victory.

'In this Mansion what is important is not much thinking but much love.' [4] If actions do not follow we have no reason to think that we're doing anything great.' [5] Here Teresa has the same thought as St Paul when he wrote: 'Knowledge puffeth up but charity edifieth.' [6]

Mansions of recollection and quietude; there the soul perceives greater lights, the invitation of the King is a gentle call but so penetrating that she forgets her past errors and thinks only of entering further into the mansions. [7]

When the soul enters the Fifth Mansion she is affianced to the King.

'. . . However clumsy the comparison may be, I find no other by which to make myself understood, but the sacrament of marriage. For although in what we are saying everything is of the spiritual order—there is an eternity of distance between the spiritual joys Our Lord gives and those of husband and wife—there all is love, love of such limpidity, of such delicacy and sweetness that it is impossible to describe.' [8]

It is the prayer of union in which the soul labours at its metamorphosis, as the silk-worm spins the cocoon in which it encloses itself in order to be reborn a butterfly.

'Such union is not yet that of spiritual marriage, but just as in this world, when marriage is in question it is desirable that both parties should know and love each other, here the Bridegroom is such that the soul has only to see him to become immediately more worthy to give him her hand. . . . She is so much in love that she does everything within her power so that nothing may occur which could break off these divine espousals. An inclination towards something other

---

[1] Idem, 7. [2] Idem, c. ii–13. [3] Sb, M, IV, c. i–2.
[4] Idem, c. i–77. [5] Idem, c. iii–9. [6] 1 Cor. viii–1.
[7] Sb, M, IV, c. iii–2. [8] Sb, M, V, c. iv–4.

than the Bridegroom alone would suffice to destroy everything, and
that is a loss more immense than it is possible to say. . . .'[1]

In this Fifth Mansion, delight is not all; 'love is never idle,'[2] 'Our
Lord wants works.'[3]

In the Sixth Mansion the soul lives in close intimacy with God, and
yet she never ceases to desire him. He speaks to her, she is rapt in
ecstasy and he raises and draws her to himself 'as amber attracts
straw,'[4] 'he wounds her with such a sweet wound that she wishes it
might never heal.'[5]

The King gives his bride gifts from his jewels, knowledge of the
greatness of God, perfect self-knowledge and perfect humility,
contempt for things of the earth unless it is to use them in the service
of such a great God.[6]

Teresa wanted to publish throughout the world the wonders 'of
the great God of Chivalry,'[7] it mattered little to her that people laughed
at her provided God was praised; 'what is to be will be!'[8]

'O Sisters, what folly, but what good folly!' She is no longer
afraid of hell, no longer worries about sufferings or glory, her only
interest is to love, 'mind and soul in her are one, as the sun and its
rays are one.'[9]

In the union described in the Fifth and Sixth Mansions, the soul
and God 'are like two wax tapers, so near to each other that wicks,
wax and lights form but a single whole, but it is possible to separate
them and find the two tapers again. . . .'[10]

In the Seventh Mansion the soul is in God and God is in the soul 'as
rain water falling into a river or fountain is only one water in which
the water of the river is inseparable from the rain water . . . or like
the light which enters into a room through two windows: although
divided when it enters, there is only one light.'[11]

Such is the intimate union wrought by spiritual marriage in the
secret chamber where His Majesty reigns. 'There the soul and God
enjoy each other in an immense silence.'[12]

The words which Our Lord speaks to the soul in this Mansion 'do
their work in us,'[13] they have the force of acts. For this high state of
prayer, that in which the silk-worm, now become a butterfly, has
finally achieved its metamorphosis, operates with one essential

---

[1] Idem.
[2] Idem, c. iv–10.
[3] Idem, c. iii–2.
[4] Idem, VI, c. v–2.
[5] Idem, c. ii–2.
[6] Idem, c. v–10.
[7] Idem, c. vi–3.
[8] Idem, c. i–4.
[9] Idem, c. v–9.
[10] Sb, M, VII, c. ii–4.
[11] Sb, M, VII, c. ii–4.
[12] Cf. Idem, c. iii–2.
[13] Idem, c. ii–7.

objective action: 'It is to that that the spiritual marriage tends: to produce works, works and again works!' [1]

The strength of the bride is increased tenfold, 'not for her own delight but to serve.' [2] Henceforward Martha and Mary are inseparable, for 'how could Mary, always at Our Lord's feet, give him to eat if her sister did not help her?' [3]

It needed the Mother Foundress, the Mother Prioress, the one who while she initiated her daughters at the Incarnation into the art of prayer, at the same time saw that they were fed properly, to translate into concrete terms the transcendent realizations of the mystical life.

When she reaches these heights of the Seventh Mansion, the soul, now both contemplative and active, is at last ready for combat. What could she have to fear? 'Death itself has no more terror for her than a gentle ecstasy. . . .' [4]

Teresa of Jesus had begun to write the *Interior Castle* at Toledo on 2nd June. In the middle of July her departure for Ávila interrupted it, she was only to resume it in September and she laid down her pen on 29th November.

Continually disturbed, harassed, with everything thrown into disorder, in the midst of the great storm of trials, it took her three months to put on paper in her neat handwriting 'whose rapidity was equal to that of a notary public,' [5] and with no erasures, one of the clearest treatises on mental prayer that exists.

In the silent hours of the night. But what nights!

One evening in Toledo, María del Nacimiento had a message to give her and entered her cell. The Foundress, sitting on the ground in front of her low table, her long pen in her hand, was beginning a new manuscript book.

She turned round towards María as she came in and took off her glasses to see her, for she was long-sighted, but before she had even lowered her hands she was caught up in ecstasy and remained so for a long time. María del Nacimiento, full of awe and wonder, remained in prayer beside her.

When Teresa of Jesus came to herself again, the white paper was entirely covered with her writing.

María broke into an exclamation of surprise, but the Foundress silenced her with her brisk and homely '¡Callate, boba! Be quiet, stupid'—and she threw the book into a drawer and turned the key.

[1] Idem, c. iv–6.   [2] Idem, 12.   [3] Idem.
[4] Idem, c. iii–7.   [5] JG quoted SEC.

VIII

RESTLESS GADABOUT

THREATS, calumnies, excommunication, imprisonment, sufferings caused by constant noises in the ears, rained down at the beginning of the year 1578 and seemed to prove that he whom the Foundress called 'whiskers'—*patilla*—*i.e.*, the devil, was launching his offensive against Discalced nuns and friars in full strength. This was indeed 'the mighty storm of trials' which Teresa of Jesus had already seen in vision: 'Just as the Egyptians persecuted the children of Israel, so shall we be persecuted; but God will make us pass through the waters as if they were dry land, and our enemies will be swallowed up by the waves.'[1]

Teresa suffered a great deal from her broken arm, but perhaps still more from being hampered in her activity: in future she could never dress herself without assistance; Ana de San Bartolomé became her inseparable companion, she accompanied her everywhere, wrote at her dictation, even helped her to put on her veil. For a woman whom neither sanctity nor age would ever cure of her quickness not only of wit but of movement, all this was a hard sacrifice. At night the good Ana would sometimes stay for hours kneeling outside the door of Teresa's cell, waiting for the moment when she would need her.

God tempered all these sufferings by what were really minor miracles, as on the day when, her mouth parched by fever, Teresa could take nothing but a little melon, if there should be any obtainable. Ana, who was also her infirmarian, was in despair; what chance was there of finding a melon in January? . . . There was a knock at the turn; someone had put in half a melon.

God also lavished spiritual consolations upon her: forced to keep her cell for more than a month, the Foundress could not receive Holy Communion. One of the sisters asked her:

'Isn't that the worst privation for Your Reverence?'

She answered:

'I consider it such a great privilege to have to submit to the will of God that I am just as happy as if I communicated as usual.'[2]

[1] SEC, R, xxxviii.　　　　　　　　[2] SEC, vol. II, p. 296.

Who, then, of those around her could have dared to fear, doubt or complain?

She never concealed either the danger or the calumnies which cast a slur on them when infamous accusations were made against any one of them. Kept well informed of what went on in the Order, she insisted that nothing of the excesses of the opposition should be kept back from her, or any of the 'fine goings-on' which were imputed to her in person.

When she received news of particularly offensive accusations, she rang the bell which summoned the community, smilingly apologized for having to repeat certain ill-sounding words which had been uttered in the Nuncio's presence by men with a high reputation and read:

'. . . The Calced allege that this old woman ought to be handed over to Whites and Blacks in order that she may have her fill of her evil conduct. For, under the pretext of making foundations, she takes young women off from town to town in order to give them the occasion . . .' [1]

She silenced the murmurs of the scandalized nuns:

'It seems also that we're preparing to leave for the Indies, a few poor little nuns on board a caravel, to found convents overseas. . . . Isn't it laughable? And these holy men are saying many other things about me which I can't repeat. . . .' [2]

The colour mounted on the forehead of the nun whom Teresa called 'the Fleming,' María de San Jerónimo went pale to the very lips, Ana de San Bartolomé and many others burst into sobs. The Foundress consoled them:

'They do me the greatest possible good, for if I am not guilty of what they accuse me of, I have offended God on so many other occasions that the one pays for the other. .. .' [3]

One day, news arrived from Rome itself: it was a matter of particular importance to the Calced that indignation against the Mother Foundress in the papal city should be considerable so that the Discalced should not be granted an independent province.

The Count of Tendilla, a nobleman very much attached to Teresa of Jesus, went to ask authorization for the foundation in Spain of two new convents of the reformed Carmel. The prelate who received him appeared shocked:

'I am surprised to hear Your Illustrious Lordship mention a nun who is as base as she is vile. It is well known that she is a bad character

---

[1] MJ quoted SEC, vol. VIII, p. 286, n. 1.
[2] CTA, cclii.   [3] MJE quoted SEC, vol. II, p. 295.

and has only adopted this pretext of founding convents in order that she may have free rein for her immorality.'

The Count of Tendilla, who was son of the Viceroy of Naples, feared no one; he did not hide the horror and disgust which such outrageous accusations caused him:

'Careful, Father! Don't say anything more, for chaste Castilian ears will not listen to remarks like that about a woman whose holiness is so undeniable that even while she's living Spain holds her for a saint. We Grandees and Lords of Spain bare our heads before her. Your Reverence shocks me and gives me offence.'

The Father sought to find an excuse:

'Your Lordship must forgive me, but I'm merely repeating what they write to me about her from Spain.'

From his correspondence he drew a letter which he handed to the count. It was written in a particular prelate's own hand:

> I have often written to Your Reverence about this impostor Teresa and the malice with which she uses the foundation of convents of Discalced nuns as an excuse for the liberty she abrogates to herself to lead an evil life. The justice of Our Lord has just denounced her in the eyes of all: a few days ago when she was pretending to go and found a convent in a certain city of these realms, the closed carriage in which she was travelling suddenly came to pieces right in the middle of the square at Medina del Campo, and the people who were there—a fairly large crowd—could see the said nun engaged in offending God with a certain friar. . . .[1]

Although all sorts of things were said about Mother Teresa, the one whose mission it was to inform her of these fresh lies was very embarrassed. She reassured him with a smile: what is humility worth if it cannot smile?

'Son, I should perhaps do much worse things than that if Our Lord didn't lead me by the hand. All that makes me sorry is to think of the dangers to which the man who says these things is exposing his soul. And I would be willing to put up with much greater insults and sufferings for his sins to be forgiven him.'[2]

Sega, the Nuncio, treated Teresa as a 'restless gadabout,'[3] he declared her disobedient, contumacious, accused her of inventing evil doctrines, of going out of her cloister in spite of the prohibition of the Council of Trent and of teaching, although St Paul had forbidden women to do so. He alleged that she had founded her convents without

[1] PP quoted SEC, vol. VI, pp. 383-4.
[2] Idem. [3] SEC, vol. V, p. 246, n. 2.

the authorization of the Pope or that of the General of the Order. Yet her letters to this same Nuncio, Sega, are written in all humility.

So much meekness astounded the sisters: their Mother's acts were greater even than her words. They saw that she was radiant with love and forgiveness and sometimes even a halo of heavenly light surrounded her. They went about repeating the saying of the Bishop of Ávila, Don Álvaro de Mendoza: 'Whoever wants to be treated as her best friend by Mother Teresa of Jesus has only to bear false witness against her. . . .'

She denied that she had any merit in this:

'I am so accustomed to it that it is not surprising that I do not feel these things. . . .[1] It's as though I had a block of wood inside me on which the blows rain down without touching my heart. . . .'[2]

The consequences of such calumnies, however, could be most serious; it was in the same year, 1578, that the scandal of the *Alumbrados* of Llerena had just come to light. The whole of Spain was appalled at what the trial revealed of the immorality and shamelessness of these heretics. The Calced were to try to identify Mother Teresa and her friars and nuns with these fanatics. The danger was so great that Teresa of Jesus had some difficulty in persuading her nuns to forgive injuries as she forgave them and to love their detractors as she loved them.

'Our Mother is a saint,' they said, 'and we are only poor insignificant nuns. . . .'

One day, she answered with almost girlish mischief sparkling in her eyes:

Sisters, you must understand that people have only spoken evil of me falsely three times:

The first was when I was young and they called me beautiful.

The second was when they took it into their heads to pretend I was gifted: a great lie, too. . . .

The third of these false judgements was to declare that I have some virtue. This is the most difficult of all for me to bear, for I am the only one who knows how many faults I have.[3]

The little sisters of St Joseph's added to themselves what the Foundress would have held to be a fourth false judgement. 'Our Mother is adorable.'

And indeed she was so, both in the human and the divine sense of

[1] CTA, ccv.   [2] FR, L. IV, cxvii.
[3] JG quoted SEC, vol. I, p. 260, n. 1.

the word. To concur in this opinion, it was enough to see her successively get angry, coax, act as a woman of feeling, a great diplomat and a soul truly angelic in an affair which added a great many small meannesses and quarrels to the weighty sufferings of the persecutions.

A Jesuit father, who was a very good friend of Teresa of Jesus, P. Gaspar de Salazar, had talked of leaving the Society to become a Discalced Carmelite. The Jesuits turned the matter into a tragedy. P. Salazar turned out to be two-faced; to prove his innocence he threw all the blame on the Carmelite friars and then and there turned against them in terms worthy of the worst detractors of the Reform: '. . . I wonder how people can say that I want to rule over people where there are more lice about than good rules of life. . . .'[1] For the Father alleged that the Discalced had tried to attract him by promising him honours, though the honours of an Order the best of whose subjects were defamed and hunted down could scarcely be considered an attractive offer.

There ensued between Mother Teresa and the Rector of the Jesuits at Ávila an exchange of letters in which the Foundress's style was more trenchant, more expressive than ever, but at the same time showed wonderful prudence. Gracián was the only one who knew how much the self-mastery cost her:

'The Provincial of the Society wrote me such an unpleasant letter about this matter that I should like to have replied to him more severely than I have done. I would like Your Paternity to know that their threats frighten me so little that I wonder at the liberty Our Lord grants me: I have therefore said to the Rector that when I can do him some service, the whole Society and indeed the whole world will not prevent me, but that I have had no hand or part in what has happened.'[2]

Finally, the whole matter died down; P. Gaspar de Salazar remained a Jesuit, absolved by his Rector, 'as if what he wanted to do had been heresy.'[3] It was important to be on good terms with the Society again but at the same time not to submit to injustice without a protest. Towards the calumniators the Foundress followed a line of conduct which was both dignified and prudent[4]; she felt it prejudicial to the Reform to let herself be attacked unless it were possible to seem to ignore the insults. She therefore concealed from her enemies as much as possible the fact that she knew all about their injurious accusations: but the Rector of the Jesuits had attacked her directly and

---

[1] SEC, vol. VIII, p. 156, n. 1.
CTA, ccxxxii.

[2] CTA, ccxiv.

[3] CTA, clxiv.

that being so, she would forgo nothing of her pride, the pride of one of Our Lady's daughters, while she meekly asked pardon for not having been wrong. With exquisite *finesse* she delicately worded her reply to Gonzalo Dávila, the Rector who had used her ill:

It's a long time since I have been so much mortified as I was to-day by what Your Grace wrote, for I am not humble to the point of wishing to be thought proud. . . . Never have I had a greater longing to tear up a letter coming from Your Grace. I assure you that you understand perfectly how to mortify one and to make me understand how worthless I am. Your Grace thinks that I claim to teach others: God preserve me from it! The fault lies in the affection which I bear you which makes me speak to you freely without taking account of what I say.

. . . I make the great mistake of pronouncing on these matters of prayer for myself, Your Grace therefore has not to take account of what I say, for God certainly gives you far greater talents than those of an insignificant little woman. . . .

After having informed P. Dávila about certain details of his inner life, she praised him charmingly, for what holy man is holy enough not to like praise? '. . . I should like my prelate to be like you. . . .'[1] and she admits the point in which she is at fault: '. . . I will correct myself in the matter of following my first impulses, since that costs me so dear. . . .'

This was erasing the memory of these unpleasant events with both good grace and magnanimity. Could the Society continue in its unfriendly attitude after this? One may well wonder, moreover, if it would have behaved so harshly if both Reform and reformer had been in greater favour with the authorities: 'How few friends one has in these difficult times!'[2] 'Trials and persecutions do not cease to rain down on this poor old woman.'[3] Even María Bautista herself, her cousin and the one who had given 'her inheritance' to help in the foundation of St Joseph's and who was now prioress of the convent of Valladolid, had allowed a Calced friar to give the habit to one of Gracián's sisters. 'I do not understand why this little prioress is so anxious to please these friars. . . .'[4] To give way to the persecutors was to betray the Reform.

Such defections were all the more bitter to the Mother Foundress in that she was only really hurt by the attacks of those she loved. Their perplexities, the infiltration of doubt in their minds, the blame

[1] CTA, ccxxxiv.   [2] CTA, cclii.
[3] CTA ccxiii.   [4] CTA, ccxxxi.

prompted by the best intentions, troubled her and caused her great suffering.

With those who were loyal to her, she exchanged innumerable letters, asking their help and advice. The correspondence had to be secret, for the slightest word from the pen of Teresa of Jesus would certainly have been interpreted by the Calced quite otherwise than as she intended. It was a correspondence carried out with haste. Peter, the servant who carried this correspondence, which was always urgent, to and fro, was no sooner back in Ávila than he had to leave again. The Mother was anxious about the risks he was running, his fatigue, and her compassion for him prevailed over the necessity of sending her messages with the utmost possible speed. One day when, without even taking his dinner, he was dashing off to take an envelope she had just given him, she stopped him:

'You won't go out from here until you've eaten two eggs which I've cooked myself. . . .'[1]

She was always ready to believe that she was mistaken and that her friends were right. The most courageous of those loyal to her then had to show her what solid ground she had for her words and actions and sustain her courage.

The most striking testimony came from Ana de Jesús. When the Provincial of the Mitigated friars announced his visit, the good-looking prioress of Beas replied:

> Mother Teresa could not clothe herself in camel's hair like Elias, I grant you; but she exchanged your fine cloth and your gauze for the roughest and coarsest frieze. And she imitates the prophet as far as she possibly can: fasting, withdrawal from the world, penance and prayer. I repeat it to Your Reverence, we would rather die a thousand deaths than separate from our trunk. In my opinion Your Paternity and all the Calced are separated from it: such brethren do not imitate their holy Father Elias, since they seek fine clothing, society instead of the desert, and instead of unceasing prayer, the latest news.[2]

Such uncompromising declarations gave Teresa confidence, and the sisters once more heard her say what she persistently repeated during these years of trouble and violence:

'You see all that is happening? Very well! It is for the best!'[3]

One of her loyal supporters was P. Yepes. He declared that it was God himself who gave her strength and courage. One day when he

[1] SEC, vol. VIII, p. 232, n. 4.   [2] AJ quoted BRJ, p. 195.
[3] MJE quoted SEC, vol. II, p. 295.

was discussing recent and serious events with her, all of a sudden he
saw that she had completely ceased to listen to the conversation; she
came out of this reverie as suddenly as she had fallen into it, and
remarked:

'We still have much to suffer, but the Order will not look back.' [1]

He took these words as a prophecy.

In the midst of all this Mother Teresa retained the presence of mind
to busy herself with even the smallest needs of her convents. Thus she
asked permission for her brother Lorenzo to enter the enclosure at
St Joseph's convent in Seville, to make a plan of a 'little oven which
the prioress had had made for cooking the meals, which will be a
treasure for both friars and nuns if it is as she says. . . .' [2]

The Foundress saw to the installation of this little oven herself and
two years later she did not fail to note that it had had to be demolished
although it cost 100 reales: it used more wood than they could afford. [3]

Like genius, the service of God is 'an unremitting attention to
details.' [4]

---

[1] Y quoted SEC, vol. II, p. 492.   [2] CTA, ccxxiv.
[3] CTA, cccxiv.   [4] Disraeli

THE SPELL CAST OVER FRAY JOHN

'I AM no worse than usual,' said Teresa of Jesus, 'trials are health and medicine to me.' [1] Her greatest suffering was the knowledge that her Discalced friars were being hunted, imprisoned and tortured, the Discalced whom she would have wished to be like beings from another world. . . . [2]

Fray Gregorio Nacianceno, prior of La Peñuela, as well as his companion Fray Juan de Santa Eufemia, and Fray Gabriel de la Asunción, were either in prison or had been so and only been able to obtain release with the greatest possible difficulty, like P. Germán de San Matías. P. Juan de Jesús Roca went to speak to the Nuncio, but Sega's only reply was to have him imprisoned in Madrid, in the monastery of the Calced friars.

For such violence Teresa endeavoured to make excuse: 'The Calced go too far, they are blinded by rage. . . . They wouldn't do what they're doing if they stopped to think. . . .' [3] But if they did not know what they were doing they were all the more to be feared. It was for this reason that Teresa of Jesus was so anxious about P. John of the Cross. She had been without news of him for months.

January: 'We don't know where they've taken him. . . .' [4]

March: The Foundress had a presentiment of P. John's sufferings, which were probably all the greater since P. Germán had escaped. 'He is all right, outside. . . . I am in anguish at the idea that the accusations against P. John may even take a turn for the worse. God has a terrible way of treating his friends and in truth he does them no wrong, since that was the way he treated his Son.' [5]

'. . . It's said that Fray John has been sent to Rome. . . .' [6]

April: 'We might remind the King how long our little saint, Fray John, has been in prison. . . .' [7]

May: Teresa made conjecture after conjecture over the complete silence which wrapped the disappearance of John of the Cross in

---

[1] CTA, ccxxviii. [2] Cf. CTA, cxx.
[3] CTA, ccxxiv. [4] CTA, ccx.
[5] CTA, ccxix. [6] CTA, ccxviii. [7] CTA, ccxxiv.

mystery and the 'spells' of the tales of chivalry came back to her mind: 'I am appalled about the spell which seems to have been cast over Fray John of the Cross and at the slowness of all these matters. . . .'[1]

August: Don't forget to see if it's possible to do something for Fray John of the Cross. . . .'[2]

'Remind the King. . . . Don't forget. . . .' Were they troubling so little about him? Although Doña Guiomar de Ulloa who was with Teresa at St Joseph's and wanted to take the habit wept over her Fray John of the Cross like all the sisters, 'by some trick of destiny or other, nobody ever thinks of this saint.'[3]

It was no trick of destiny: P. John had so well succeeded in living as he wished, 'wrapped in silence,'[4] that he passed unnoticed in the eyes of men and was effaced from their memory as he would have liked to be effaced from this world.

He was wont to say to the nuns:

'What we lack is neither writing nor speaking, for usually there is only too much of both, but to be silent and to act. For speaking distracts; silence and action concentrate our mind and give it strength. . . . To suffer, to act, to be silent, to withdraw from the senses by the practice and love of solitude in the forgetfulness of all creatures and all events, even if the world should crumble away.'[5]

Around Fray John of the Cross the world had crumbled away, he was buried in silence, 'a spell cast over him.' Henceforward he spoke to God alone in language understood by God alone, that of silent love.

But God knew where Fray John was: in the convent of the Calced friars at Toledo, imprisoned in a tiny dungeon, his only nourishment bread and water, scourged every day by all the friars in turn. His tunic stuck to the wounds on his shoulders. He endured it all with love and patience, the only thing that saddened him was the thought of the sufferings of Teresa of Jesus.

So pure a countenance and such a gentle look only exasperated his captors, as did the strength which this little man showed. He made them all mad with rage by his habit of remaining silent and perfectly still when the most eloquent of the Calced friars urged him to renounce the Reform and adopt their Mitigated rule. When promises proved themselves of no avail, they resorted to threats and then to blows and insults.

Fray John refused to break his silence.

---

[1] CTA, ccxxxii.   [2] CTA, ccxlii.   [3] CTA, ccxliii.
[4] JC quoted SEC, vol. VI, p. 210.   [5] Idem.

He spoke only to God, he complained only to him, in such accents that the words of this silent man ring through the centuries:

> *¿A dónde te escondiste,*
> *Amado, y me dejaste con gemido?*
> *Como el ciervo huiste,*
> *Habiendome herido. . . .*
>
> . . . .
>
> *Y todos más me llagan*
> *Y déjame muriendo*
> *Un no sé qué que quedan balbuciendo. . .*
>
> . . . .
>
> *¡Oh cristalina fuente,*
> *Si en esos tus semblantes plateados,*
> *Formases de repente*
> *Los ojos deseados,*
> *Que tengo en las entrañas dibujados! . . .*[1]

Was God hiding himself? 'Where there is no love, put love and you will find love.' Mother Teresa reduced this same axiom to three succinct words: *Amor saca amor*, 'Love calls forth love.'

Fray John *was* love but he found only hatred. Yet the severity around him was loosening. Perhaps the Calced were tired of flogging a frail man from whom they did not succeed in wresting a complaint. On two occasions they saw his dungeon lighted up, but when they rushed to see why, for he was forbidden to have any light at night, the supernatural light disappeared the moment they entered. After that they decided he must either be a saint or a sorcerer. Perhaps they

[1] JC quoted SEC, vol. VI, p. 197. The poem, *Canciones entre el alma y el Esposo*, was composed by St. John of the Cross in the prison at Toledo. The translation given below is by E. Allison Peers:

> Whither hast vanishèd,
> Beloved, and hast left me full of woe ?
> And like the hart hast sped,
> Wounding, ere thou didst go. . . .
>
> . . . .
>
> Each deals a deeper wound
> And something in their cry
> Leaves me so raptur'd that I fain would die.
>
> . . . .
>
> O crystal spring so fair,
> Might now within thy silvery depths appear,
> E'en as I linger there,
> Those features ever dear
> Which on my soul I carry graven clear ! . . .

decided that saint was the right word or perhaps they were afraid of making a martyr of this saint. They gave him a less brutal gaoler, a young brother named Juan de Santa María. He gave him writing materials and sometimes allowed him to get a little air in the room adjoining his dungeon. Better still: he loved his prisoner. By giving love, John of the Cross was beginning to obtain love.

He had no thought of escape: in his prison he had suffering, silence and that interior activity which is a tremendous adventure. It was Our Lady who prepared his escape and ordered him to flee.

One day during the Octave of the Assumption she showed him in spirit a window high up in a gallery overlooking the Tagus and told him she would help him to escape through it. She also showed him the way to unscrew his prison locks, both the lock of the dungeon itself and that of the room next door.

He took advantage of the quarter of an hour his warder allowed him to go 'to the humble office' while the friars were in the refectory, to go and identify the window which Our Lady had shown him, although he had to cross the entire convent to do so. That very evening he managed to unscrew the lock and release the padlock.

He waited till everyone was asleep; it was time to make the attempt. The first door yielded at his touch, but two visiting friars were sleeping in the room he had to cross. He hesitated, but could not resist the Mother of God; she ordered him to go straight on, assuring him of her help.

Accordingly he opened the door; as he was pulling it towards him one of the iron bars fell and the noise awoke the sleepers:

'Who's there?' one of them shouted.

The silence reassured them, the Blessed Virgin closed their eyes, stopped their ears, lulled their senses and John of the Cross stepped over their prone forms.

Out of his two old blankets and a strip of tunic he had made a rope which he attached to the window support—a bar of wood—towards which an interior voice had guided him. The voice then ordered him to let himself down into the void. He obeyed, slid down the length of his rope, and arrived at the end to find it was at least ten feet too short.

Hanging by a bare thread above the rocky bank of the Tagus, he wondered where he was going to fall. His confidence in Our Lady gave him the courage to jump.

He landed in a courtyard which he recognized as being part of the royal convent of the Immaculate Conception, belonging to the

Franciscan nuns, but outside the enclosure: only a wall was between him and the Zocodover.[1]

A voice coming from a belt of light said: 'Follow me,' and guided him to the foot of the wall. Fray John looked up; the wall was so high that he was leaning against it despairing of having the strength to scale it, when he felt himself lifted into the air and set down on the farther side, free.

It was still dark. In the market they were setting up the stalls; the vendors, mostly women, burst out laughing at this friar, whose blood-stained rags scarcely covered him and who seemed to have sprung from the walls of the Franciscan convent: less would have been sufficient to arouse their laughter. He escaped from them, darting in between the houses. The light which had guided him had disappeared but great confidence and a great interior light remained.

At five o'clock when the Angelus rang, he knocked at the door of the convent of St Joseph of Carmel.

When the extern sister, Leonor de Jesús, came and told the prioress that P. John of the Cross was there, and was asking her 'to come to his help and hide him, for if the Calced friars caught him again they would tear him to pieces,' Mother Ana de los Ángeles was at the bed-side of Sister Ana de la Madre de Dios, who was very ill but who nevertheless had a wonderful inspiration:

'Mother, I feel so ill that I cannot take my purge without going to confession first. . . .'

A friar could not enter the enclosure except to give absolution to a nun who was too ill to go to the confessional.

So the big door opened for Fray John and closed behind him. It was high time: the Calced friars, who could not understand how the slender rope made of strips of stuff could have borne the weight of a man, did not understand either how this man could have jumped from such a height without being killed; but they were forced to accept the evidence: their prisoner had escaped. At once they rushed to St Joseph's; with an escort of constables, they searched parlour, chapel and sacristy.

The whole convent throbbed with intense but silent emotion, the sisters mingling tears of joy with thanksgivings and prayers. There was none so proud as the infirmarian, Teresa de la Concepción, who had the honour of taking P. John of the Cross his meals. He took only a few pears cooked with cinnamon; the weariness, the joy, above all the emotion at being in the very convent which had been Mother Teresa of Jesus' prison, took away his appetite.

[1] *I.e.* market place.—Tr.

About ten o'clock when the doors of the church were bolted, they were able to shut him in there dressed in a priest's gown which the sisters declared suited him quite well. All wanted to see him and the community spent a very pleasant evening: the nuns took their spinning or needlework to the choir while P. John talked to them.[1]

He did not talk to them about his sufferings and dangers, but about God and about the Mitigated friars whom he considered his benefactors:

'They are free now from the faults which my wretchedness made them commit.'[2]

He also recited in a gentle, monotonous voice the poems he had composed in prison and a sister wrote them down.

Finally he talked to them at length about Our Lady who had set him free, and the delicious fruits of divine love which he had culled in his solitude:

'Blessed nothingness and blessed hiding place of the heart. . . .'[3]
'God's immense benefits fall only into empty and solitary hearts. . . .'[4]

As soon as night fell, one of the canons came at the instance of the prioress to fetch him in his carriage and put him out of the reach of danger in the hospital of Santa Cruz. As soon as he could he left for Ávila.

Fray John saw Mother Teresa of Jesus once again and Mother Teresa saw her 'little saint, Fray John.' He was still 'so wasted and disfigured that he seemed an image of death.'

He was not in the habit of complaining, any more than Teresa of Jesus was:

'As far as I am concerned, don't be in any way troubled, for I am not.'[5]

A cry of protest however escaped from the Foundress:

'I don't know how God permits such things!'[6]

She told Gracián about this meeting in disjointed phrases, scarcely able to speak for the beatings of her heart:

'Your Paternity doesn't yet know all. He's spent these nine months in a dungeon so small that there was scarcely room for him, tiny as he is; all this time he never changed his tunic, although he has been at death's door. Three days before his escape the Superior did give him a shirt of his own; nobody ever saw him.'[7]

---

[1] BRJ, c. xiii.   [2] JC quoted SEC, vol. VI, p. 196.
[3] JC quoted SEC, vol. VI, p. 213.   [4] Idem, p. 254.
[5] JC quoted SEC, vol. VI, p. 197.   [6] CTA, ccxlvi.   [7] Idem.

Alba de Tormes

Church of St. John of the Cross at Alba de Tormes,
the first one dedicated to the Saint

That was what Teresa of Jesus with her great love of cleanliness said. And she who as a child had wanted to die at the hands of the Turks declared:

'I envy him immensely. It is wonderful that Our Lord should have found him strong enough for a veritable martyrdom like that, and it is important that the matter should be known, in order that everyone may beware of these people.' [1]

She echoed Fray John's sentiments:

'May God deign to pardon them!' [2]

But she also cried out for justice for her sons: 'The Nuncio must be informed of what they've done with our saint Fray John, and without his having committed the least fault, for it is lamentable. Fray Germán must be told, he will see to it, he has a lot of courage for those things.' [3]

John of the Cross did not tell Mother Teresa that he had left his kind warder as a souvenir the only thing he clung to in the world: the little cross of precious wood she had given him when he took the habit and which he always wore under his scapular next to his heart. But he no more regretted parting with this treasure than he did having suffered so much: the ardour with which the Mother Foundress defended him, the warmth with which she begged him to take care of himself, caused him a joy he felt to be too human:

'Let us rather look at the riches gained in pure love on the road to eternal life. . . .' [4]

This moment of relaxation and plenitude was brief. Fray John had to go to the Congress at Almodóvar. Teresa was very displeased about it and complained to Gracián.

'I've been very much grieved to see how much he has suffered and I'm distressed that he is being allowed to go although he is so ill. God grant he does not die. I hope Your Paternity will see that he is well looked after at Almodóvar, and that he's sent no further. I beg of you, do not fail to see to this. See that you don't forget. I tell you that if he were to die, Your Paternity wouldn't have many like him left. . . .' [5]

For Gracián to think of John of the Cross, the Foundress had to remind him how useful he was.

Having thrown off his spell Fray John seemed to be back in it again and Teresa had to keep on saying: 'Don't forget Fray John. . . .'

The raptures of silent love are paid for by men's forgetfulness.

[1] Idem. [2] Idem. [3] Idem.
[4] JC quoted SEC, vol. VI, p. 209. [5] CTA, ccxlvii.

X

A FORETASTE OF THE LAST JUDGEMENT

A FEW days before the escape of Fray John of the Cross a
solemn delegation from the Nuncio Sega waited upon the
prioress of St Joseph of Ávila—thus ignoring the Mother
Foundress although she was there—with a counter-brief: it relieved
P. Gracián of his functions as Apostolic Visitor, and countermanding
all the measures taken by his predecessor, Sega took upon himself
the government of the houses of the reformed Carmel. All this was
conveyed in such a style that Teresa of Jesus, accustomed as she was
to the language of her enemies, could not believe her ears.

Seething with indignation, but at the same time thanking Our
Lord for leading her by the same path of humiliation which he had
followed himself, she snatched up her pen to inform the prioresses of
all the convents: '. . . To see all these outrages. . . . Perhaps the
Nuncio won't leave these wolves as free a hand as they expect. . . .',[1]
she summoned Julian de Ávila and sent him to Madrid forthwith to
acknowledge the Nuncio as her prelate, and to beg him not to hand
over the Discalced to the mercy of the Mitigated.

She kept a cool head and her consternation at this fresh disaster did
not prevent her from taking a broad view of the situation: 'I'm not
too greatly distressed; it's perhaps the way that will best lead to our
being erected into a separate province.'[2]

To Gracián, who had left her in ignorance as to his precise where-
abouts, she penned a letter which began by a deserved rebuke:

> Let Your Paternity tell me where you are for charity's sake and
> not play the fool when I have something to inform you of: I found
> myself in a false position over the cipher Your Paternity changed
> without telling me about it. . . . I fear they will try and lay hands
> on you; if this should be the case (God preserve you from it!) you
> would do better to go away. . . . I am writing to certain persons,
> to try and quell the Nuncio's anger in regard to you, letting him
> know that we should all obey him with the greatest pleasure, if it
> were not that Tostado is waiting to work our destruction. . . .

[1] CTA, cxxxix.   [2] CTA, ccxxxviii.

Anything which is not subjection to the friars clad in fine cloth seems to me acceptable.

'Fear nothing, Father. . . .'[1]

Over and over again she had to stand by and prop up Jerónimo Gracián. This Father was impetuous rather than courageous; he sometimes asked God for trials which he was not big enough to endure and let himself be crushed by the affairs of the Order which rested entirely on him since the Foundress was forbidden to take any action. But he had a wonderful way of getting himself forgiven: 'He's afraid like a man, but he writes like an angel. . . .'[2]

The Mother Foundress had the rare gift of allying the love of solitude and contemplation with the power of leaving such joys aside to 'negotiate' with the world, armed with lucidity, prudence and even astuteness. The success of her undertaking meant for her the realization of God's will upon earth. When she admitted 'I am old and tired, but my desires are not,'[3] she showed how strong was her love of action, under the banner 'of the captain of love, Jesus, our only good.'[4]

Yepes who had lived in her company said that for her difficulties were 'like the spark which falls into the sea only to be extinguished, like the wave which beats the rock only to be broken on it, like the blows which strike the diamond without dulling or injuring it.'[5] It might even be said that this diamond was cut out with many facets and made more precious and sparkling by such things.

One sorrow Teresa of Jesus did feel most deeply: the death of Padre Rubeo, the General who had authorized the foundation of the convents and helped her so much; affirming that she was doing as much for the Order as all the Carmelite friars in Spain, he had formerly enjoined upon her to found 'as many convents as she had hairs on her head.'[6] But it was this same P. Rubeo who afterwards disowned her, abandoning her to her persecutors. It was an injury to her sense of justice, her esteem and affection, but she never tired of trying to find means of showing him that her attitude towards him was unchanged. She had just asked Roque de la Huerta to act as intermediary:

Persuade him not to believe what is said about Teresa of Jesus; for truly she has never acted otherwise than as his most obedient daughter; he knows quite well that she wouldn't lie for anything in the world, he also knows what excitable people who do not know her

[1] CTA, ccxxxix.   [2] CTA, ccxvi.   [3] CTA, ccxxxi.
[4] Sb, C, c. vi-9.   [5] Y, L. III, c. xxviii.   [6] CTA, ccliii.

can say; let him be willing then to be informed of the truth of the matter, and in his office as pastor, let him not condemn without judgement or without hearing both sides. If he finds what you tell him valueless, let his Lordship punish her, but not leave her under his displeasure; she would prefer any punishment rather than to know he was angry; parents forgive even great faults in their children; how much more readily could he not do so when there was no fault, but only the great effort of founding these convents in the certainty of pleasing him. For besides the fact that he is her prelate, she has a deep affection for him. . . .[1]

P. Rubeo was not to know of this act of filial submission. The news of his death distressed Teresa considerably. She wrote to Gracián: 'The first day we wept our fill, being unable to do otherwise, in great sadness for all the troubles we had caused him, and which he certainly did not deserve. If we had taken him into our confidence over everything all would have been simple. God forgive those who have always prevented our doing so: I wanted to come to an understanding with Your Paternity on this point, and yet you were unwilling to believe me. . . .'[2]

The enmity of Calced for Discalced would never have degenerated into persecution if when the first misunderstanding arose an appeal had been made to the General's great kindness. The Foundress well knew that at that particular time Gracián was to blame; she had begged him enough then to write to P. Rubeo. But she preferred to find excuses for him rather than to own he was wrong and forgive him: such was true charity.

With P. Rubeo's death the last hope of conciliation disappeared. It was necessary to resign oneself to this insidious strife in which intrigue and machinations had as much share as violence, with the Nuncio and Tostado as enemies, while King Philip continued to keep silence. 'The Calced don't think now that they're going against God, for they have the prelates on their side. They don't worry about the King, who says nothing whatever they do. . . .'[3]

Teresa gave Gracián precise directives as to the steps he should take, the people he ought to see, what he should say, and reminded him each time of their essential objective: to obtain an independent province for the convents of the Reform. She flattered him: 'I see that at Madrid Your Paternity gets through a great deal in the day,' but however much he did it was not sufficient and she was forced to admit: 'It galls me not to be free to do what I want done myself.'

[1] CTA, ccli. [2] CTA, ccliii. [3] CTA, ccxxvi.

She told him quite clearly what she wanted said, with all the respect due to an ecclesiastical superior, in spite of a few little words of impatience here and there, and with a good deal of reserve: 'I see you are right, but. . . .'[1] There was always a 'but.' Gracián, the most supple of her instruments, was yet not a perfect one.

In this month of August when the persecutors' fury redoubled, the Nuncio Sega hurled an excommunication against him. This plunged poor 'Paul,' unhappy 'Eliseus,' into deep melancholy. Yet there it was, the trial he had been asking heaven for! He was obliged to go into hiding. Teresa secretly suffered at seeing her cherished son 'darting like a criminal in between the roof-tops. . . .'[2]

'Our Lord knew how to make me suffer by making the blows fall just where they hurt me most.' But her heroic nature suffered perhaps more when she saw he was afraid. He would drown in a glass of water; she found 'my Paul very silly, with his scruples,'[3] when he asked her if he was obliged to go to Mass: would not the Calced who were lying in wait for him be capable of taking him by surprise and carrying him off? Teresa asked the theologians: no, he is not obliged unless he can do so in complete security. She tried to cheer him up, this would all come right, 'for just as God wills that evil should come forth, so he causes good to come forth too.'[4] Nevertheless he continued to complain: 'If you are as sad as that when your life is not such a bad one, what would you have done had you been Fray John?'

That was indeed a telling comparison. Teresa let it sink in very gently, for her style was so conversational that it evoked the tones of her voice, which to Gracián were always affectionate even when her words were severe. Despite her partiality she was too perspicacious not to sum him up. When he leapt from despair to optimism but without taking any action, she grew irritated. 'Your Paternity really must answer me immediately, don't let's be satisfied with hopes any longer, for the love of God! All are dismayed to see that we have nobody who is working for us, and so the others do as they please,'[5] She announced the arrival of a friend of theirs: 'It seems to me that Your Paternity must see him, even if it tires you.'[6]

He was still the same Gracián whom an imaginary monster had frightened in the hospital at Toledo.

He was now shut up in the Calced monastery at Madrid. But he was treated reasonably well there. Yet he allowed himself to be tempted

---

[1] CTA, ccxxxii.　　　　　　[2] CTA, ccxlii.
[3] CTA, cclv.　　　　　　　　[4] Idem.
[5] CTA, ccl.　　　　　　　　[6] Idem.

by the suggestion that he should leave the Reform. With what pity and tact did Teresa not stoop to his weakness:

> . . . Stand firm in what is right, even if you find yourself in danger. Blessed be the suffering which, however great it is, does not prevail over justice. I am not astonished that those who love Your Paternity seek to remove the difficulties from you, but it would not be kind to abandon Our Lady in these difficult times. . . . God preserve us from doing so. . . . That would not be to escape trials, but to plunge into them, for these will end by the grace of God, whereas those of another order would perhaps last one's lifetime. Your Reverence should think about this.[1]

Yes: what would P. Gracián have done had he been P. John?

There was a rumour that he intended to pass over to the Augustinians. His mother, Doña Juana Dantisco, let him know that if he did so she would no longer regard him as her son. As to the Count of Tendilla, he went and sought Gracián out and with his hand on the hilt of his dagger said to him calmly: 'It appears you want to abandon the habit of Our Lady of Carmel. If that's the case, I've made a vow to thrust you through with my dagger.'[2]

Gracián affirmed that he had never thought of leaving the Reform and that there was nothing in the rumour but calumnies on the part of the Calced. He refused the Count's offer to help him to escape and took fresh courage. Teresa gently made fun of his moods. She herself was busy sending secret messengers to Rome, disguised in order to escape the police whom the Mitigated friars had at their disposal. It was no longer the period of the tales of chivalry, that of the picaresque novel had come into being. The mission her emissaries were entrusted with was to inform the papacy about this war between brethren and to make the Holy Father understand how necessary it was that those who were known as 'the Reformed,' although it was they who were the observers of the primitive Rule and the true heirs of the prophet Elias, should be independent of the Mitigated. She begged her convents to supply the money for this costly expedition. Hopes were high: the year 1578 seemed to be ending in a ray of sunshine.

On 24th December, in the morning, the door of St Joseph's convent had to be opened for the Nuncio's envoys who came to bring Mother Teresa of Jesus a decree. This decree, under threat of the severest penalties, put Discalced nuns and friars alike under the jurisdiction of

---

[1] CTA, cclv.   [2] SEC, vol. VIII, p. 274, n. 1.

the Provincial and of the superiors of the Mitigated friars of Castile and Andalusia.

This was the death-blow for the Reform. 'A foretaste of the Last Judgement,'[1] the Foundress said. 'All those who were present, the gentlemen of the law, the theologians, the great lords, were thunderstruck.' The terms of the decree were so violent that Teresa would have liked to stop her ears; but she did not dare either to move or speak.

Pedro, the servant who was on duty at the door when the delegates of Sega, the Nuncio, arrived, rushed out to tell Don Lorenzo de Cepeda, who hurried to the convent, accompanied by the *Corregidor*. What was the good? The Calced friars did not even respect the King; they had got accustomed to doing exactly as they wished and nobody stopped them.

While they read out the terms of the decree, Mother Teresa was looking at a paper one of the envoys was holding and expected that a sentence of excommunication would be hurled at her, but the Nuncio had contented himself with intimating that she was to be transferred to another convent for the rest of her days. 'If they mean a convent of the Mitigation, they will treat me a great deal worse than they did Fray John of the Cross! Although, to suffer as much as he did, I have not his merits.'[2]

She was forbidden to correspond with P. Gracián.

Teresa of Jesus had faced her triumphant enemies with her wonted dignity and calm; she was even seen to smile at the moment when her suffering was greatest; then she turned away from men to look only at God her Father, whose will it was that her work should thus be brought to naught. But when they had gone she suddenly left the grille without a word to Lorenzo; he saw her draw back into the shadow for the first time bowed down with grief; her daughters moved aside to allow her to pass; dismayed at her silence, they too were mute and had no consolation to offer; the Foundress admitted defeat.

Alone, locked in her cell, she opened the door to no one but Ana de San Bartolomé. Ana brought her something to eat, and, on her knees behind the door, she heard Teresa of Jesus praying in a voice interrupted by sighs and sobs. She was accusing herself of being the sole cause of all the trouble: if they threw her into the sea like Jonas, the storm would cease.[3]

When it was time for Office she came into chapel, walking as in a dream; she knelt down, stiffly; her face seemed turned to stone; and

[1] CTA, cclvii. [2] Idem. [3] Sb, F, c. xxviii-5.

from this ashen face tears were falling in such abundance that they made a pool on the ground.

In the evening, however, Ana ventured to go into her cell; they were going to sing the great Christmas Office and she begged the Mother to take something in order not to collapse with weakness. A light meal was ready for her in the refectory. . . .

Teresa shook her head, but leant on the kind little lay-sister's arm and agreed to go with her in order to please her.

For a long time she sat motionless before her plate; nothing seemed to distract her thoughts from the vision of her work in ruins. Ana de San Bartolomé did not dare to insist further. But suddenly she saw Our Lord Jesus Christ standing by the table, wearing a linen garment; he unfolded Teresa's serviette, broke her bread, and fed her himself as one feeds a child, mouthful by mouthful.

He said to her:

'Daughter, eat. I see how many sufferings you are enduring. . . . Take heart: it is nothing. . . .' [1]

Teresa ate her bread forthwith, although the wonder of it all might well have caused her throat to contract.

The spiritual marriage had been a splendid feast in heaven with a great concourse of angels and archangels, but now it was the everyday life of bride and Bridegroom. In the community room there was no one present but a little lay-sister.

They had now loved each other for so many years. For one another, with one another, they had striven and suffered so much! And despite these combats, nay in the very midst of combat they had experienced so many joys! Of their union magnificent things had sprung into being. Bride had never ceased to speak of Bridegroom except with trusting and sincere adoration: '. . . What seems good in his eyes seems good in mine, what he wills, I will. . . . I know not where this wondrous delight will end. . . .' [2]

The wondrous delight was leading her towards Love and Glory which would finally be 'for ever.'

[1] RD, vol. I, L. IV, c. xxxii.   [2] CTA, liv.

XI

THE CATHOLIC KING DON FELIPE

IT was a different woman who came into the chapel of St Joseph's while the bells of Ávila were ringing for midnight Mass. The Mother's face, whose ashen hue had so greatly frightened the nuns, was now tinged with the fire of the seven spirits of God. She sang the Gospel of St John in an angelic voice, though ordinarily her singing voice was neither clear nor true. All were amazed to see how quickly she had recovered her lost courage when the responsory of Matins rang out: 'To-day true peace has come down from heaven for us. To-day on the whole world the heavens have dropped down honey. To-day has dawned for us the bright day of the new redemption, the day when the original fault was done away, the day of eternal bliss. To-day . . .'

After this foretaste of 'the Day of Judgement' which had ended in glory, Teresa of Jesus' smiling calm never left her. As early as 28th December, she was writing to Don Roque de la Huerta, one of the Reform's most faithful supporters, a letter which rang with joy: '. . . May this Christmas week, this entering into the New Year be as happy for Your Grace as they are for me by reason of the good news you give me. The first two days I suffered much, but since the morning of St John's day we have all been much consoled.' [1]

Since P. Gracián had been shut up in a Calced monastery, the affairs of the Order at court were in the hands of a newcomer to the reformed Carmel, Fray Nicolás de Jesús María, whom only a year ago Teresa had still been addressing as *el Señor Nicolás Doria* for he belonged to the family of the Dorias of Genoa. A man with an infinite number of irons in the fire and extremely wealthy and powerful, eager for still more wealth and power, his love of banking and other financial transactions had brought him to Seville, which was the centre of commerce between the Mediterranean and the New World. He displayed so much skill in these operations that the Archbishop, Don Cristóbal de Rojas, begged him to put the treasury of the Archbishopric on a sound footing, for somewhat casual administration had made it precarious. He succeeded so well that Philip II hearing of the talents of this Genoese

---

[1] CTA, cclviii.

banker summoned him to court in order that the public finances might
in turn benefit from his good offices. But into this Ali-baba's cave
Our Lord, too, came like a thief, and to the astonishment of everyone,
the courtier, the man of ambition, the trafficker in gold and silver,
preferred the poverty of persecuted friars to a bishopric which the
King offered him: at thirty-seven he took the Carmelite habit, that
of the Discalced, from the hands of Jerónimo Gracián de la Madre de
Dios.

He put his talent for business and his skill in making a virtue of
necessity if needs be, at the service of the Order; in the eyes of the
Mitigated he came to pass for an eccentric whose wits the yoke of the
Reform had dulled, and when the Nuncio imprisoned those he considered most important among the Discalced friars, he left 'the good
Nicolás' severely alone and free for any business that offered. He
showed marvellous astuteness in living in the very monastery of the
Calced friars in Madrid and for this the Foundress never ceased to
praise him: 'we wrote to each other frequently and discussed whatever
was necessary. The whole time I was in a position to appreciate his
qualities and prudence. I have much affection for him in the Lord....' [1]

P. Nicolás Doria succeeded in concealing from the Mitigated friars
all his relations with the Spanish court and with Rome, and the fact
that he had the entrée to the King's person daily enabled him to set
things in motion on behalf of the Reform. And St Dominic, giving
his blessing to the ruse for the sake of the good cause, sent his hound,
his great black and white Dane, to accompany this cunning Italian to
the very doors of the great: when all danger was averted, the dog disappeared. St Dominic kept his promise to the Foundress that he would
help her, and signs of this sort were a consolation to the daughters of
Carmel.

For there was no lull in the violence of the persecution. It even
extended as far as Seville where María de San José was deposed,
forced under threat of excommunication to hand over the letters of
Teresa of Jesus, and the nuns called on to swear on the crucifix that
the false testimony against them, the Mother Foundress, P. Gracián,
the reformed convents, was the truth and nothing but the truth.

Their Foundress, who was their captain, dispatched an order of the
day that was both valiant and tender.

I would have you know that I have never loved you so much and
that you have never had such a marvellous opportunity of serving

[1] Sb, F, c. xxx-6.

Our Lord. To prayer, to prayer, Sisters! And let your obedience and
humility shine before men. What fine weather for gathering the fruit
of your decision to serve Our Lord! . . . Amid these persecutions
uphold the honour of Our Lady's daughters; if you do all you can
yourselves the good Jesus will help you; for although he sleeps at sea,
when the storm arises he commands the waves and they are silent. . . .[1]

Strive at all costs to be gay. . . . You are with your sisters and
not in Barbary. . . .[2]

The new prioress, the Beatriz de la Madre de Dios whose father
had wanted to hang her when she refused a husband (who was really
to be congratulated), had proved guilty of much intrigue and some
treason. Mother Teresa urged the victims to forgive:

Be not without fear, Sisters, for if the hand of God were removed
from us what evil should we not commit? Believe me: this sister
has neither intelligence nor talent in sufficient measure to be responsible for all the webs she weaves: the devil has been teaching her. . . .
May God be with her. Pray for her, pray for her, Sisters, for many
saints have returned to sanctity after a fall. . . . Do not show her
even the slightest hostility. . . . Believe me, this soul is in considerable distress. . . . Remember me to Sister Beatriz de la Madre
de Dios.

The very excesses to which the Calced, urged by their hatred, went
were finally to recoil on their own heads: the moment was coming
when 'our enemies will be swallowed up by the waves.'

Several Grandees, including the Count of Tendilla, went to the
King to tell him that they felt as a personal affront all the insults heaped
upon Mother Teresa of Jesus and the reformed Carmel, and the over-
prudent monarch had to put his reserve on one side. 'Our Catholic
King Don Felipe,' sent for Sega:

'I have heard about the war which the Calced are waging against
the Discalced Carmelite friars and nuns. I cannot do otherwise than
regard such attacks against people who have always practised the
greatest austerity and perfection, with the utmost misgiving. I have
been informed that you are not helping the Discalced in any way. In
future range yourself on the side of virtue.'[3]

The Papal Nuncio could not do otherwise than obey the Lord of all
the Spains.

By a brief dated 1st April 1579 he released the reformed Carmel
from obedience to Mitigated superiors and placed it under the juris-

[1] CTA, cclxiv.   [2] CTA, cclxxiv.
[3] Quoted SEC, vol. VIII, p. 134, n. 1.

diction of P. Ángel de Salazar who, although himself a Calced friar, was a great friend of Mother Teresa and of the Reform. The whole affair could now be regarded as virtually and happily finished and the Foundress could legitimately exclaim:

'When I consider the means Our Lord has used to turn the malice and cruelty of the enemies of Carmel solely to our advantage, I am speechless with wonder!'[1]

All that was wanting to crown this success was the erection of the Discalced friars and nuns into an independent province.

So now P. Ambrosio Mariano, P. Jerónimo Gracián, P. Antonio de Jesús, and all the other sons of Our Lady came out from hiding or from prison. P. John of the Cross, appointed rector of the College of Baeza, was able to leave Beas and its Calvario where he was answering the questions of the prioress, Ana de Jesús, of Beatriz de San Miguel or of Catalina de San Alberto, giving them what was really an anticipation of the *Dark Night* or of the *Spiritual Canticle*, the wonderful treatises on which he had been working since 1578.

Jerónimo Gracián was no sooner out of danger and worry than in his ingenuousness he once more experienced the thirst for trials. His view of matters did not coincide with Mother Teresa's.

'Leave us in peace for the love of God, for you would not be the only one to suffer them. Let us have a few days' rest. . . .'[2]

María de San José caused her the same kind of difficulty and she hastened to write to her:

'Daughter, let Your Reverence now leave foolish perfections aside, and stop refusing to be prioress once more. We all want you to accept this office again, we have made this clear and you are behaving childishly. This is not Your Reverence's business only, but that of the whole Order.'[3]

Accepting God's benefits with pleasure and gratitude is also submitting to his will.

Teresa did not think it right to take pleasures sadly; to her way of thinking, there was a time for trials and a time for rejoicing. And when the persecutions came to an end she declared: 'As to bodily health, I desire it; but I am satisfied with that of my soul.'[4]

Another thing she said was:

'When it comes to exercising government, I am no longer the same person that I was before: now it is all done through love. I don't

[1] CTA, cclxxviii.   [2] CTA, cclxxi
[3] CTA, cclxxxi.   [4] CTA, cclxxviii.

know whether this is because nobody now gives me cause to be angry or whether perhaps I've come to understand that that kind of action is more efficacious.' [1]

This joy and this progress in love were the fruits gathered by Teresa of Jesus from the tree of the cross. When born out of deep suffering, abundant meekness and gentleness are a remarkable sign of holiness; but for the Mother Foundress they only show their full value when issuing in action.

It was a message of organization and action which Our Lord ordered her to convey to the Discalced one day when she was raised with such force above the earth that in the suspension of her bodily powers she was admitted to the secret counsels of God:

> Tell the Discalced Fathers from me that they must strive to ob-serve four conditions; so long as these are kept, this Order will grow and flourish, but if they were to neglect them, it would become decadent:
> *Firstly*: Agreement among its superiors.
> *Secondly*: That there be only a few friars in each house.
> *Thirdly*: That they have as few dealings with seculars as possible and then solely for the good of their souls.
> *Fourthly* : That they teach by acts rather than by words.

Her Father and Bridegroom thus confirmed and glorified for future ages the work she had accomplished.

Teresa of Jesus had always taught by acts, but her testimony had never been more striking than it was during suffering. Not for one moment, during four whole years, were her acts found to be in con-tradiction to her words. Not for one moment did she through fear or weakness act otherwise than she advised others to do.

A clear summary, a pure epitome of her mystical works is to be found in her life, particularly during her latter years. Day by day she proved the efficaciousness of her teaching in *The Way of Perfection*, demonstrated that the castle of the soul had indeed Seven Mansions and that His Majesty is there awaiting man in the very depths of his being; it was great thoughts like these which engendered her great actions.

Rhythmic movements of the soul we might call them, attuned to the point of perfection by her continual song of praise to Our Lord and her goodwill towards all men.

Self-renunciation—without which the forgiveness of injuries would

[1] CTA, cclxxvi.

be difficult, to strive to overcome vainglory useless, and a fruitful surrender to the will of God impossible. When Teresa of Jesus said that
everything which is ephemeral and does not satisfy God is nothing,
less than nothing, and that she had enough dignity left to count
temporal things for very little,[1] she proved it by her deeds.

Liberty: in the security of her conscience, she was free: 'that is a
great thing.'[2]

Absence of all fear: because one cannot serve God in a state of
anxiety, she elected to live by hope.[3] She sought only the kingdom of
God and his justice, throwing all appearance of prudence to the winds,
and everything was indeed added unto her. It was perhaps in this total
and conscious abandonment of all human affairs into the hands of God
that she gave proof of the absolute harmony that existed in her between
intellectual and spiritual life. She went forward towards what was
most certain, 'for God knows what is best for us'; [4] 'he knows better
what he is doing than we know what we want.' [5]

She worked, she even schemed, she spared no effort, spent her
nights in writing letters and books, her days in ruling, maintaining,
encouraging, striving, but when all this was done, 'the most profitable
business is to keep silence and to speak with God.' [6] In short, to act as
energetically as if all depended on action and to pray as fervently as if
all depended on prayer. Always the two inseparables: Martha and
Mary.

'Sisters, to prayer, to prayer!' [7] 'And let every serious decision first
form the subject of prayer!' [8] 'Let us listen to God as we do to our
best friend. . . . When we set out to do his will we have nothing to
fear. . . .' [9] 'He takes everything in hand.' [10] 'Christ is a very good
friend, for we can look upon him as a man with his weaknesses and
sufferings, and he becomes our companion. When we have acquired
this habit, it is very easy for us to find him by our side. . . .' [11]

This good friend never left her. It was at the very moments when
reason seemed to forbid all hope that Mother Teresa was strongest:
friends disappeared or faltered, the King was silent, hatred against the
Reform redoubled in violence, there remained only God, but 'God
sufficeth.'

And the triumph was overwhelming. So true it is that 'when we
begin to place our confidence in human resources, divine help is with-

---

[1] Sb, F, c. xv-15.   [2] CTA, xciii.   [3] CTA, cdxxix.
[4] CTA, clviii.   [5] CTA, cccliv.   [6] CTA, clxxv.
[7] CTA, cclxiv.   [8] SEC, vol. II, p. 357. [9] CTA, clxxix.
[10] CTA, clxxv.   [11] Sb, V, c. xxii-10.

drawn.' [1] 'To do everything himself Our Lord only waits for our decision to abandon all to him.' [2]

What Teresa of Jesus taught by her actions after having affirmed it in words [3] was that in all trials there is no better remedy than love for Jesus, the good lover. Such love is proved in action and it was in the midst of temptations to disobey, to despair, to hate, to lie, to become proud of a success or to let herself be crushed by failure that Teresa as a faithful lover showed her obedience, her unwavering hope, her compassion and her humility.

In her, heaven and earth, palpable reality and the reality which was invisible, natural and supernatural were in perfect balance.

And when she spoke of 'the health of her soul,' the phrase was perfectly accurate.

[1] CTA, ciii.   [2] Sb F, c. xxviii-19.   [3] CTA, cccxvii.

XII

THE *BEATAS* OF VILLANUEVA
DE LA JARA

P ÁNGEL DE SALAZAR'S first gesture had been to restore to the Mother Foundress complete liberty of action: that is, she was once more free to show her obedience in other ways than by remaining shut up in one convent. What were they going to require of her? She wondered about this with some misgiving, and it was not long before she knew: this old woman, worn out by sickness, labour, struggle and penance, was commanded to resume once more the bustle and worry of her journeys and foundations; that and nothing less.

On 25th June 1579, accompanied by Ana de San Bartolomé and a small escort which included a surly friar, she said goodbye to her daughters in Ávila, her niece Teresita and her brother Lorenzo, and to the good and faithful Francisco de Salcedo and Doña Guiomar de Ulloa. Her heart was heavy but she braced herself against the tenderness of the farewells:

'Look at her, poor little old woman! Setting off for Medina del Campo, Valladolid, Malagón, Alba de Tormes, Salamanca![1] I tell you that makes me laugh for I feel I have the courage to do much more than that!'[1]

Mile after mile they went, under the scorching heat of Castile in summer, Teresa not even being able to enjoy the sight of the vast horizons she loved, for the carts were, as usual, closely covered.

Although she had insisted that they were not to make any fuss for her visits, her convents welcomed her triumphantly. She was very touched by her reception and repeated over and over again:

'What have I done to make them love me so much?'

She was delighted to find that these houses were flourishing, particularly considering the poverty of their beginnings.

At Valladolid she received good news: Don Felipe Sega, the Nuncio, had himself asked the King to separate Discalced and Mitigated into two independent provinces. She could now hope to see the fulfilment of her wish—for her, to wish for a thing meant to will it.

[1] CTA, cclxxvii.

But there was a shadow over her joy: she felt the threat of a war of succession between Spain and Portugal so keenly that she wrote to her friend Don Teutonio de Braganza, Archbishop of Évora, begging him to make the one claimant, his nephew the Duke of Braganza, understand that it was of paramount importance to avoid a conflict: '. . . If God were to allow things to come to this bad pass, I should long for death in order not to see it. . . . God grant that the truth be ascertained without having recourse to such a slaughter. For in times when there are so few Christians, it would be a great misfortune that they should kill each other. . . .'[1]

In this war there was no more question of 'truth' than there was in any other, but of those 'dark interests' which horrified Teresa of Jesus. The war broke out, and Philip II placed at the head of his armies his old friend the Duke of Alba. He brought him from prison where he was reading Teresa's *Autobiography* to put him at the head of an invading army of 35,000 infantry and 2,000 cavalry.

In the height of the summer, the Foundress was able to make a stay of some two months at Salamanca. There she came back to the same old struggles to get hold of a house. Of the prioress she said: 'Nobody helps me so much as Mother Ana de la Encarnación.'

The life of the nuns was so exemplary, their prayer bore such marvellous fruit, that she thanked the prioress:

'Ana, God will reward you for forming such good daughters for me.'[2]

There she found Isabel de Jesús once more; in her tender affection for her she was distressed to find her so thin and called her to her side:

'Come here, daughter. . . . Sing your *cantarcillo* for me. . . .'

And the good sister sang once more in her clear voice the verses to which Teresa owed one of her sweetest ecstasies:

> *Véante mis ojos,*
> *Dulce Jesús bueno.* . . .
> Let my eyes behold you,
> Good, sweet Jesus. . . .

In November there were fresh goodbyes and fresh departures. The Foundress arrived at Malagón on the 25th, exhausted by the long journey but radiant with joy: at last she would have the new buildings which Doña Luisa de la Cerda had delayed so long to give her. For the first time since she had been founding convent after convent, she found herself free to set one up where and as she wanted it.

[1] CTA, cclxxxv. [2] SEC, Vol. VIII, p. 328, n. 2.

Doña Luisa's steward accompanied her when she went up and down Malagón looking for a site:

'Not here: a monastery of Franciscan friars is going to be built here one day. . . .'

They were still wandering about all over the brick-red soil of Malagón to which the Mother Foundress paid less attention than she did to the sky, when by a dove that came and settled on the topmost branch of a leafy olive tree, Teresa recognized the site of her dovecot. . . .

She decided on the plans herself in collaboration with a good architect from Toledo and, together with Doña Luisa, put her signature to what would have been called nowadays an extremely detailed specification. This house was to demonstrate to future generations Teresa of Jesus' taste for simple materials—chalk and brick, beams of unplaned wood—her sense of proportion and arrangement. If the cells were small, the galleries were wide, the passages convenient, the offices practical. The smallest detail showed her talent for organization and that for her a certain regard for hygiene or a desire to facilitate the work which had to be done were by no means incompatible with penance. She installed a filter so that the water might be purer, and great porous jars to keep it cool, as well as a hand-grinder for crushing almonds—an excellent food for her nuns.

The Foundress got up at dawn and went immediately to the site; the contractors told her they thought the work would take six months to complete.

'We shall move in in a fortnight,' Teresa assured them.

And she took over the direction of operations herself. Sitting on a stone bench, despite the cold, she presided over everything; she went everywhere. Leaning on her stick which she was unable to do without since her fall at Ávila, she found the most expeditious solution for every problem as it arose, giving a word of encouragement and even lending a hand. She had no time to go and say her Hours until nearly midnight, but in these circumstances was not work a form of prayer?

And on 8th December, as she had foretold, the nuns made their solemn entry into the new convent which was completely and properly finished. They were so delighted at leaving their dark and miserable dwelling and being able to walk at ease in the light galleries that Teresa, who was as pleased as they were, said they were like little lizards darting in the sun.[1]

She had no wish to leave Malagón. All had not been smooth

[1] CTA, cccxx.

going in her recent journeyings. The persecution and campaign of calumny against the Discalced nuns and their Foundress had left a certain taint in the minds of some; in a small place in La Mancha the Foundress's entry into a church caused a disturbance which interrupted the Mass; when she was seen to go up to the altar people cried out it was sacrilege and the crowd was so hostile that she had to slip out quickly and take refuge in her carriage. She felt such violence now more than she had done formerly; she who loved so much to be loved was gladdened more than formerly by the least sign of affection and was touched by the friendly quarrel which broke out over her between the Duke of Alba and his wife, Doña María Enríquez: which of the two did Mother Teresa prefer? She could cast no vote: for God alone had all her preference.[1]

At Malagón she was surrounded with affection and there was peace.

She wrote to Gracían:

'Here there is no more question of Teresa of Jesus than if she did not exist. I am not therefore thinking of going away unless I am ordered to do so for I've often been in despair at all the foolish things I've heard. When people say about you, as they did over there, that you're a saint, it is very necessary to be one and that's not so easily done. Laugh if you like, but just try producing one: and see if it doesn't cost you more than the trouble of saying it. . . .'[2]

But rest was not to be her lot: P. Ángel de Salazar sent her orders to go and found a convent at Villanueva de la Jara. She must leave Malagón and move on once more.

'Remember me, all of you, before Our Lord, for I am tired out and very old. . . .'[3]

There were nine ladies of noble rank who for years had been living as recluses in the little town of Villanueva de la Jara, situated two-thirds of the way along the road from Toledo to Valencia. They never went out and it was only the two eldest who had the right to draw back the bolts of the heavy door when someone knocked. There was no prioress but each of the nine *beatas* assumed the responsibility of government in turn.

Nine ladies of noble birth, very simple and poor, attracted to the place by the reputation for sanctity of a very curious person, Doña Catalina de Cardona.

[1] SEC, vol. VIII, p. 394, n. 5.
[2] CTA. ccxvii.
[3] CTA, cccvii.

Daughter of the Duke of Cardona, Doña Catalina had been governess to Prince Don Carlos, son of Philip II, and to the famous natural son of the Emperor Charles V, Don Juan of Austria. When she was forty she left the court to live in the desert of La Roda, leading a life of such frightening penance and austerity that her bloodstained hair shirts and the discipline of chains which she took for whole hours on end caused as much consternation as they did admiration. In the cave where she dwelt continually, as if she were buried alive, the devils did not leave her alone: in their attacks they assumed the form of huge mastiffs or of serpents. One wonders if she had a calendar in her Thebaïd, for she was reputed to eat only on Sundays, Tuesdays and Thursdays.

When she decided to take a religious habit she chose the Carmelite one, but not that of the nuns: she insisted on wearing the friars' habit, for this penitent for all her hair shirts could not bear a coif upon her head. Her reputation for sanctity was so great that the Princess of Éboli, always on the look-out for celebrities, sent a carriage to her desert for her and brought her to court where she found her old friends once more.

One day the Nuncio learned of the scandal that was taking place in Madrid: a Discalced Carmelite friar was going about in a carriage with ladies of the aristocracy and leaning out of the window was blessing the crowd. He at once insisted that this friar should be brought to him to be punished for the bad example he was giving and also for his presumption. On arrival, the Discalced friar proved to be none other than Doña Catalina who, accustomed as she was to giving her blessing, blessed the Nuncio as she would have done anyone else. This by no means lessened his anger, but this daughter of the desert in disguise was too great a lady of the realm for him to be able to show much severity.

King Philip had, after all, personally invited her to spend a week at the Escorial with Princess Juana.

He tried to persuade her to enter a convent:

'I am not going to live among affected, sentimental, sugary nuns whose imagination makes our natural weaknesses worse. . . .' [1]

He let her go as she had come, in her friar's habit. On her way back to her solitude—from now onwards very busy with the crowd of pious persons who rushed to see her—she stopped a few days at the Carmel of Toledo; the sisters whose privilege it was to be near her affirmed to Mother Teresa that her very coarse and extremely dirty

[1] Quoted SST, vol. IV, c. iii.

habit exuded an odour of sanctity all the more remarkable 'since in view of the great heat one would have expected an unpleasant smell.'[1]

Doña Catalina Cardona had just died; the account given of the sufferings she inflicted upon herself in Our Lord's name awakened lively feelings of confusion mingled with admiration in Teresa of Jesus; she always reproached herself for being only a mediocre penitent. Fortunately God was watching over her. One day when she was distressing herself at not obtaining permission from her confessor to practise greater mortifications, to the extent of wondering if it would not be better for her to disobey him, Our Lord said to her:

'Daughter, as to that no! The way you are following is the best, for it is sure. You know all the penances she practised? I appreciate your obedience much more.'[2]

Thanks to this very clear order, Mother Teresa of Jesus remained the living example of common-sense spirituality.

Thus it was not without pain that she received the news that the nine poor but noble *beatas* of Villanueva de la Jara, Doña Catalina's fervent followers, wanted her to transform their hermitage into a Carmelite convent: was it going to be possible to make them submit to a rule which had some regard to reason? Up to the present they had been doing what they could: they were already wearing Our Lady's scapular and saying the Office as well as possible, which, in fact, was anything but well: it was their ignorance that was to blame and nothing more, for, not knowing how to read, they spent hours spelling out an Office letter by letter. They fasted seven months in the year not counting the days when they *had* nothing to eat, and plied the distaff to earn their scanty pittance and pay the messengers they sent to Mother Teresa of Jesus at the other side of Castile.

For they would not leave off worrying her. The matter was first broached at the time of her return from Seville in 1576; after that the poor *beatas* added prayers to the requests and negotiations: they made novena after novena, dragging themselves on their knees from the entrance to their hermitage to the altar in the church, the procession being headed by a little girl of five whom one of them, a widow, had been obliged to take into the solitude with her.

The Mother continued to hesitate, but the more she did so the more the *beatas* insisted, so much so that in the end their perseverance triumphed over her scruples. Moreover, during the persecutions, P. Antonio de Jesús had been in hiding with the Discalced friars of

[1] Sb, F, c. xxviii-32.   [2] SEC, R, xxiii, p. 54.

La Roda, quite near them, and he had given her information about them: touched by their good will and edified by their fervour, he persuaded the Mother Foundress to come and give them the habit herself.

Teresa decided to bring with her four nuns, chosen as much for their common-sense as for their great lights in prayer, to train the *beatas*; from Malagón she took one of the best nuns of Carmel, Ana de San Agustín, and Elvira de San Ángelo; P. Antonio de Jesús came to fetch them all. The Foundress was delighted to see him again and to find him looking plump and healthy; she declared that trials were certainly good for one's health for she herself had never been better.

They started off. Ana de San Bartolomé was naturally among the party, and it is from her we learn what a procession of triumph this twenty-eight league journey in the month of February 1580 was. They went through Toledo again to collect two other foundresses, Constanza de la Cruz and María de los Mártires.

At Robledo, the house of the duenna (who was known as 'lover of virtue') where the little company halted for dinner was stormed by a crowd of all the pious folk of the place. Two constables were installed to guard the doors, but those whose zeal outran their discretion jumped over the wall: several persons had to be taken off to prison before the *Santa Madre* could get a little rest.

The precaution she took of starting off again next day at three o'clock in the morning, before it was light, proved useless: people were waiting for her everywhere, and everywhere she was acclaimed. A rich farmer had taken up his position along the road and implored her to come to his house to take a collation specially prepared in her honour. From thirty leagues around he had sent for his children, grandchildren, sons-in-law, daughters-in-law, all his relations, all his serving men and women, for Teresa of Jesus to give them her blessing. He had also gathered together his flocks and the tinkling of sheep-bells mingled with the murmur of prayer that went up from this kneeling crowd dressed in their Sunday best. It was a goodly company, not unworthy of Biblical times or of the marriage feasts of Camacho,[1] with all these worthy peasants and the tables all prepared and loaded with meats, but without getting down from her carriage the Foundress blessed the good folk, both man and beast, and went on her way.

The friars of La Roda had arrived first: Teresa found them touching, 'with their bare feet and coarse habits,[2] and almost thought herself in the golden age of the holy Fathers of the Desert' : as an offering

---

[1] See *Don Quixote*—Tr.   [2] Sb, F, xxviii, 20.

they brought her two small but beautiful statues: one of the Blessed Virgin, smiling, and the other of the Holy Child. All the way from the monastery of Our Lady of Succour to Villanueva, it was nothing but streamers, branches of trees and decorated altars. All the people round joined the procession: Ana de San Agustín saw the statue of the Holy Child come to life and move from their Mother to the monstrance and back to the Mother again. . . . The countenance of Teresa of Jesus expressed no surprise. Ana de San Bartolomé who also saw what was happening kept silence. . . . And just as Ana de San Agustín was about to exclaim out loud, the Foundress cut her short with a categorical:

'Silly little child, be quiet!' [1]

Thus preceded by the Son of God, the *Fundadora* made her entry into Villanueva de la Jara amid a veritable whirl of enthusiasm, people shouting and singing and bells chiming, all honouring a few humble Discalced Carmelites for the love of Our Lord.

But she was eager to make the acquaintance of her new daughters, the nine *beatas*, both noble and poor. Behind the thick door of their hermitage the recluses were waiting for her, rather fearful: would she not go away again, appalled at their state of utter poverty? To think this was to misjudge the Mother Foundress. She took to them forthwith, although she could not help being aware of their dirt, as well as of their fervour. The pious creatures had been wearing the same garment —a lay dress but austere in form—ever since their entering upon the life of perfection and they thought they were proving to Our Lord their detachment from the world by scarcely ever washing. And so Teresa began by snatching up a broom and with her good arm she set to work with determination to put the house in order. The community followed her example.

She stayed a month at Villanueva de la Jara and spent it making the wretched house look something like a convent; anxious to make the place as pleasant as possible, she even planted a vine with her own hands.

P. Antonio de Jesús taught the new Carmelites how to say their Hours a little better than by just muttering them, and the sisters who had come from Malagón and Toledo taught them by their example the virtue of obedience and that other eminently Teresian virtue,

[1] I got this story from the oldest of the nuns of Villanueva de la Jara, who in her turn had received the tradition when she was young from the oldest then living. Madre María Margarita del Santísimo Sacramento also told me that when leaving this statue to her daughters Teresa of Jesus told them that in it they would always have 'a very prosperous farm'. . . .

moderation in all things, for only the love of God can be practised to an unlimited degree without danger.

When Mother Teresa went away again, in a convent that was poor indeed, but clean and polished in every corner, she left souls who were already travelling along the road to heaven.

Everything that was difficult or dangerous Teresa put into the hands of God and when action was not possible for her she then did her best to forget such matters. Accordingly she very seldom thought about her *Autobiography* which was still in the hands of the Inquisition. What could she do about it? Nothing. It was therefore useless for her to worry about it: and the business of the Order kept her attention occupied elsewhere.

After completing the foundation of Villanueva de la Jara, she remained in Toledo for some time and took advantage of her stay there to go and see Cardinal Don Gaspar de Quiroga, Archbishop of Toledo and Grand Inquisitor General. Gracián went with her for the purpose of the visit was to ask permission to found a convent of Discalced Carmelite nuns in Madrid, 'without mentioning the book.'

But the Cardinal, a man with a long nose and harsh mouth, whom El Greco has painted with his long white beard standing out against his scarlet robes and a look expressing weariness even more than severity, broached the subject right at the beginning of the interview:

> I am very glad to make your acquaintance for I have been greatly wanting to do so: look upon me as your chaplain, I will help you as much as ever is necessary. I want to tell you that a book of yours was presented to the Inquisition several years ago; its teaching was examined rigorously. I have read it all through and I maintain that its teaching is very safe, very true and very profitable. You can take it back again when you like: I give you the permission for which you ask and I beg you to pray to God for me always.[1]

That matter was thus happily ended.

[1] JG quoted SEC, vol. I, p. cxxvi.

XIII

OUR LADY'S ORDER—
AS I'VE WANTED IT

sixty-five, Teresa still retained her fresh complexion and
an astonishing youthfulness, but at Toledo she almost died
of an attack of the widespread influenza epidemic; after this
she was greatly changed, and when she got better had become thin
and old. She never completely recovered.

In 1580 this influenza epidemic made havoc all over Europe;
several of Teresa's friends died of it, among others the holy gentleman
Don Francisco de Salcedo, Don Cristóbal de Rojas, Archbishop of
Seville, and P. Baltasar Álvarez her former confessor whom she
greatly mourned. No one was more loyal in her affections than this
woman who was detached 'from all created things.' Ten years earlier
she had written to Don Francisco: 'God grant you life until I die, for
in order not to be without you, I should obtain from Our Lord that
he called you very quickly. . . .'[1] And yet after all he died first.

And in that same year she lost the dearest of them all, her brother
and spiritual son, Don Lorenzo de Cepeda. 'I am three years older
than he and yet I go on living. . . .'[2]

Teresa, a perpetual invalid, but endowed with amazing resistance,
was thus bereaved of her most tried and loyal friends. The hurt went
deep and she lamented:

'Why has God left me in the world to see so many of his servants
die?'[3] At Valladolid she had a relapse, her heart showed signs of giving
way, signs of paralysis of the tongue made them fear she might lose
her speech, and the pains in the head and noises in the ear were now
incessant. But, most serious symptom of all, she seemed to have lost
heart. It was pathetic to watch the woman who had wrestled triumphantly with Sega the Nuncio, with Tostado and with hundreds of
Mitigated friars, trying to struggle with herself. Her nuns had always
known their Foundress as a daring captain overthrowing the enemy
by swift counter-offensive, without stopping for skirmishes against
temptations and weakness. But at Valladolid her worn-out body was

[1] CTA, x.   [2] CTA, cccxxvi.   [3] CTA, cccxxxvi.

no longer capable of obeying the demands of the spirit, she recoiled, was afraid, wanted to give way.

She herself analysed what she termed her cowardice: 'To be ill and to suffer great pain is nothing if the soul is alert and praises God, taking everything as coming from his hand. But to suffer on the one hand and on the other to remain doing nothing is a terrible thing. . . .[1] In my weakness I had even lost the confidence that God in his goodness had given me of the necessity of undertaking these foundations. . . .'

Those around her put it down to her age. Was the Foundress too old? No, but she was 'bound by the devil or by disease,' a prey to panic, listless and with no will left.

She was reluctant to go and found the convents of Palencia and Burgos as P. Ángel de Salazar, with no compassion for her state of exhaustion, ordered her. And not only did no one succeed in restoring her courage, but all those around her, even the prioress María Bautista, began to waver.

Yet her listlessness was not such that she did not desire to know God's will. One day, after Communion, when she asked him about it, Our Lord said in a reproachful tone: 'What are you afraid of? When have I failed you? I am the same as I have always been. Do not fail to make these two foundations.' [2]

Teresa exclaimed:

'O God Almighty! How different are your words from these of men! They give me such courage and determination that the whole world would not stop me. . . .' [3]

Teresa of Jesus had uttered her great word: determination. The spirit of determination, the will, in her had acquired such power that from the moment of her decision the whole thing could be taken as accomplished: for 'the Lord helps those who are determined to serve and glorify him.'

She sent P. Gracián on to Palencia in advance; he found so many obstacles that he was quickly discouraged. Happily he also met a nobleman 'of cape and sword,' Suero de Vega, whose zeal was so ardent that he was not afraid to take a holy friar to task:

'He said so much to me of the excellence of a lively faith and of confidence in God, and in such a way, that I caught his fervour. . . .' [4]

That was one point gained. Canon Reinoso also undertook to help, as it proved, very effectively. He was a man 'well built, of fair complexion; his cheeks somewhat bright by reason of an inflammation

[1] Sb, F, c. xxix-3.   [2] Sb, F., c. xxix-6.   [3] Idem.
[4] JG quoted SEC, vol. V, p. 270, n. 2.

of the liver which made him more handsome still on account of the freckles which it caused. . . .' [1]

The second point gained happened as follows: From the depths of the sea P. Gracián rose upon the crests of the waves and let himself be carried ashore. In a town which claimed to be too poor to feed a few nuns it was absolutely essential to win over the most adamant of all: the *Corregidor*. Teresa of Jesus had charged P. Gracián to get from this man of flint an authorization which he had so far granted to no one.

'He received me very badly, flew into a rage and said to me in an angry tone: "Go, Father, and let what Mother Teresa of Jesus wants be done quickly. She must be hiding in her bosom a provision from God's own royal Council, for quite against our will and pleasure we have to do everything she wants." ' [2]

This account of the situation seemed so encouraging to Teresa that she decided upon an immediate departure. Once more the devil had raised difficulties which proved only apparent but which were all the more serious because they came from within herself. 'One knows perfectly well that he never succeeds in his purpose, but he makes one worried. . . .' [3] As always, the very clear and definite determination of Teresa of Jesus checkmated him.

And so once more the Mother Foundress journeyed up hill and down dale. Not in covered carts this time but on mule-back, in the winter's bitter cold, through so thick a fog that the riders could scarcely see each other. She reached Palencia in a state of collapse, but next morning, 29th December 1580, the first Mass was said and the convent founded. There, as elsewhere, she had difficulties in bringing off the purchase of a house, and against the opinion of the whole town, she finally installed the Carmelites hard by a certain hermitage known as Nuestra Señora de la Calle—Our Lady of the Street—where such extremely unedifying happenings were going on that Our Lord willed the presence of the Carmelites there to end the scandal.

According to the Foundress it was the prioress, Inés de Jesús, who did everything to bring about this foundation :

'I no longer serve any useful purpose, except perhaps for the stir the name Teresa of Jesus makes.' [4]

St. Joseph's convent of Our Lady of the Street at Palencia was barely founded when she set off to found a convent at Soria in response to the appeal of Doña Beatriz de Beamonte y Navarra—*Beamonte*

---

[1] Quoted SEC, vol. V, p. 271, n. 5.   [2] Idem.
[3] Sb, F, c. xxix-9.   [4] CTA, cccxliv.

being a Spanish form of Beaumont—a descendant of the Kings of
Navarre, who placed at her disposal her palace and a revenue of
500 ducats.

Quite a lot of the route from Palencia to Soria lies in the plain, it is
extremely well watered, and Teresa just loved it:

'It was a tremendous pleasure for me. . . . I often found companionship in the very sight of the rivers. . . .'[1] For her the spirit
of God moved above the face of the waters. One incident in the
journey amused her: the Bishop of Osma, who was her old confessor
P. Velázquez, sent his bailiff to meet and accompany her, carrying his
standard; the crowd flocked up and imagined the nuns were being
taken to the dungeons of the Inquisition. Both her humility and her
sense of humour derived the greatest amount of pleasure from this
mistake.

At Soria as in other places she attended to the organization of the
convent down to the last detail, in particular to the strictness of the
enclosure.

>   . . . Behind the parlour grille, there shall be added, set back a
> little way, a wooden grating made of very thin bars but so close
> together that the tiniest hand cannot pass through; over this a
> thick veil is to be nailed. This grating shall only be opened for
> near relatives and the Mother Prioress will keep the key.
>   . . . The communion grille shall likewise be bolted. The
> Prioress alone shall have the right to open it.
>   . . . A private window will allow Doña Beatriz de Beamonte
> to talk with the nuns, but a veil shall be drawn if any of her suite
> accompany her.[2]

Mother Teresa insisted that Doña Elvira, a niece of Doña Beatriz,
should come but seldom, 'for she is a young married woman and is
dressed according to her station. . . .' It was important that the nuns
should not get a longing for worldly attire.

Grilles at the windows looking out on the orchard, grilles in the
choir, grilles at even the smallest opening on the world.

But the Foundress was as keen about the health of her daughters as
she was about their absolute separation from the world—they were not
to live in cells recently built until the walls were perfectly dry!—and
their safety: 'When coming out from Matins they should light a little
lamp which would last on until morning, for it is dangerous to sleep
without a light; so many things might happen! It would be very

[1] CTA, ccclxxviii.   [2] SEC, vol. VI, pp. 357-8.

dangerous if one of the sisters had an accident and there was no light. A candle with a little twisted wick doesn't cost much.'[1]

The choice of the prioress for Soria astonished P. Gracián:

'Heavens, Mother! Do you know that Catalina de Cristo cannot write and can scarcely read? She knows nothing about administration and will be incapable of governing.'

'Be quiet, Father!'—for if necessary Gracián, too, was silenced like the others—'Catalina knows a great deal about the art of loving God and she is very intelligent: no more is needed to know how to govern and she will be just as good a prioress as anyone else would have been.'[2]

Catalina de Cristo, who was a relative of the Foundress, was a tall woman with a severe face worn thin by excessive mortifications. She had begun by finding the discipline too easy, the straw pallet on her bed too soft, the prayers too short, and the spare diet on fast days too plentiful and too palatable. Her father, most fanatical of men, was haunted by fear of the *Alumbrados*. To protect his daughter from clandestine heretical books and pamphlets, he had discovered a method that was foolproof: not even to show her the letters of the alphabet. Cloistered, as it were, in her father's house, only allowed to go to Mass very early in the morning, she left the church before the sermon, in case the preacher were contaminated by the accursed sect. Catalina de Balmaseda thus grew up without seeing a living soul; far from finding her solitude displeasing, she grew so accustomed to it that she even spent nine months in a cellar and finally obtained leave to enter Carmel.

Mother Teresa loved her all the more because she had had a lot of difficulty to make her see that austerity must be tempered by a little common sense and a great deal of gentleness in regard to one's neighbour; she succeeded, however, and did not hesitate to impose upon her the searching test of governing her sisters and setting the tone of a new convent. And from Soria she was able to write to P. Gracián: 'The prioress is very satisfactory.'[3]

Thus, one by one, often trusting much more to what her intuition told her about the qualities of her daughters than to appearances, Mother Teresa of Jesus formed a circle of great prioresses.

The law of God, the Rule and Constitutions

Point by point, during twenty years of daily observation recorded down to the last detail, attentive to every reaction however slight, to

[1] Idem. Such little twisted wicks are still in use in certain Spanish Carmels.
[2] SEC, vol. V, p. 290, n. 2. [3] CTA, ccclxx.

the most insignificant details as much as to the most important gener-
alities, modifying one thing, taking into account another, appealing
to experience against tradition and to tradition against some over-
venturesome innovation, Teresa of Jesus achieved in 1581 the final
form of the Rule and Constitutions of the reformed Order of Our
Lady of Mount Carmel.

During the few months she spent at Palencia, this preoccupation
never left the Mother Foundress: the Discalced, met in chapter at
Alcalá de Henares, were to adopt the Constitutions permanently. Up
to the last minute, sending message after message to P. Gracián, she
never ceased putting retouches and amendments.

In the first place she begged them to avoid anything which might
give the timorous a pretext for scruples:

> About the stockings of hemp or frieze, I hope that Your Paternity
> will see that nothing definite is laid down: let it just be said that they
> can wear stockings, otherwise they will make endless scruples. . . .
> Where it says 'hempen cap' just say cloth. And see if you can remove
> the clause which forbids them to eat eggs, and bread at collation: in
> that matter it is sufficient to observe what the Church imposes with-
> out adding anything more. To do so would make them scrupulous
> and so do them harm.[1]

Will men ever understand nuances like these? The undesirable
results of excessive zeal are beyond them and the Mother had no small
amount of trouble to protect her daughters even against P. Jerónimo
Gracián. And she blamed him for it, too, with no hesitation: 'Antonia
has told us so many things ordered by Your Paternity that we're all
scandalized over it. Believe me, Father, these houses are going on very
well, and there's no need to overload them with observances. For
charity's sake, don't let Your Paternity forget this. Just watch very
closely to see that the Constitutions are observed, without expecting
anything more; if they keep them well, they will be doing a good
deal.' [2]

Again, 'for charity's sake,' she begged him not to forget everything prescribed about the wearing of the black veil before the face.

And 'for the love of God,' [3] she begged him to stipulate that beds
and table linen must always be spotlessly clean. She wanted to put
cleanliness in the Constitutions, she loved it so much and considered
it so indispensable, and the friars—not her daughters, happily—
esteemed it so lightly.

[1] CTA, cccli.   [2] CTA, ccxxxii.   [3] CTA, ccci.

She who was called 'mystical doctor' while still alive—a circumstance which was to displease her greatly—made them stipulate that prioresses should be put at the head of the list for sweeping, 'so that they may give good example in everything.' [1] And they were to 'make themselves loved in order to be obeyed.' [2]

A single sentence of the Constitutions showed clearly both her knowledge of the human heart and her sense of justice: 'Never punish until your anger has died down.' [3] And her ever-watchful compassion tempered the rigours of the penalty for those who were undergoing punishment for a 'graver fault.' The culprit must indeed receive the discipline, confined in a cell, 'deprived of the company of the angels,' but, added the Foundress, 'Let the Mother Prioress show compassion and send a sister who can comfort her, and if there is any humility of heart in her, let her good intentions be taken into consideration.' [4]

As to her beloved poverty, she inscribed it in the Rule in terms that were unforgettable: 'Let poverty, ever present, shed its fragrance over everything. . . .' [5]

How deeply these Constitutions bear the imprint of Teresa of Jesus. They start from earth, mindful of the stones along the road, rising progressively, yet surely, step by step, to heaven.

In novices she insisted on 'good health and common-sense,' explaining to someone who expressed surprise at this:

'Our Lord will give them devotion here: we shall teach them prayer. But common-sense? We can't do anything to inculcate that into them.[6] And the devil knows only too well how to take advantage of their want of intelligence. . . .' [7]

On the thorny question of dowries Teresa of Jesus added: 'When the person is satisfactory from our point of view, she should be accepted, even if she can give no alms to the house, as has been done up to the present.'

Eventually, 'the law of God, the Rule and Constitutions of the Order' were adopted at the chapter of Alcalá de Henares. All the Mother Foundress had to do now was to wait 'for them to be printed, so that nobody can change anything.'[8] At the year's close she had the joy of having the book in her hands.

It was at Palencia, too, that she learned that Discalced and Calced had at last been erected into independent provinces by Pope

[1] SEC, CONS, p. 11.   [2] Idem. p. 15.   [3] Idem, p. 18.
[4] Idem, p. 22.   [5] Idem, p. 10.
[6] FR, L. IV, c. xxiv.   [7] CTA, cclxxiv.   [8] CTA, cccli.

Gregory VII. This bull, given under the form of a brief, set the crown on the Foundress's work. P. Jerónimo Gracián de la Madre de Dios was elected Provincial of the new Province which comprised 'all the monasteries in these realms founded up to the present and all those which shall be founded in the future, whether of friars or nuns, which observe the primitive Rule. . . .'

Teresa of Jesus saw the Reform not only accomplished and achieved but given permanence and perpetuity. 'That was one of the greatest joys I could have in this life. Now we are all at peace. Calced and Discalced, no one will hinder us any more from serving Our Lord.'[1]

Twenty-two monasteries and convents, three hundred friars, two hundred nuns, details the Holy Father's bull, will in future be free, before men as before God, because they will all be subject to one austere unchanging Rule, by means of which they will be born again of God alone.

When the bell wakes the sisters at Palencia, at five o'clock in the morning, Mother Teresa now follows in thought what is taking place in her twelve other dovecots: at Ávila, Medina del Campo, Malagón, Valladolid, Toledo, Salamanca, Alba de Tormes, Segovia, Beas, Seville, Caravaca, Villanueva de la Jara. Our Lady's doves, black veils or white, are going to renew their plumage in the lustral water of prayer and resume their plaintive notes for Christ Jesus.

For Christ, and for those whom he has preferred to all others: sinners, the sick, the desperate, the dying, those who are contending against difficulties, those who are suffering hardships, those who fight, those who want peace, those who seek love and those who find tears.

The Foundress sees columns of light rising to heaven like Jacob's ladder: prayers are rising up to meet the angels, everywhere, and at the same time.

Bells—for work. Bells—for recreation to the hum of the spinning-wheel. Bells for Office, bells for the discipline, bells for penance. Bells for examination of conscience. Wherever she is, whatever she is doing, in every Carmel at the same moment, each Carmelite kneels down and purifies the transparent crystal of her soul, the beauty of which Teresa of Jesus has described, and two hundred souls of crystal purity reflect the countenance of their King.

Only one occupation has no fixed time: the meal. 'The time for eating cannot be arranged, for this depends on what Our Lord sends us. In winter at half past eleven when there is anything to eat. . . .'[2]

---

[1] Sb, F, c. xxix–32.   [2] SEC. CONS, p. 12.

And at eight o'clock in the evening the bell will ring in the silence: until Prime on the following morning no word will be spoken except to Christ or to the hosts of heaven. And in this silence the rhythmic movement of adoration will be so great that it will refresh the ever feverish world more than morning dew.

The Foundress sees this white guard of love gaining the whole world and, across the ages, thousands of souls who are active in prayer peopling the convents of Carmel.

'God has sufficed' to the Mother Foundress.

She remembers the beginnings, *sin blanca*; the praise, adoration, inebriation with God, would raise her to the clouds if she did not stoop towards the earth, to ponder over the work accomplished. And she wrote to María de San José:

'At last, I can re-echo Simeon's words, for I have come to see Our Lady's Order as I desired it. I beg you then not to ask God for me to live, but that he grant me to go and rest: for the future I am no longer necessary to you.'

Ana de San Bartolomé came into her cell unnoticed; she saw Teresa of Jesus put down her pen every two or three words; she heard her utter deep sighs. From her countenance came such dazzling rays of light that the little sister could scarcely bear their brilliance.' [1]

[1] FR, L. III, c. x.

PART FIVE

'BELOVED, IT IS TIME. . .'

I

ÁVILA, 1581

'YOU'LL see what this poor little old woman is ordered to do. . . .'[1]

Scarcely had she returned from Soria when Mother Teresa of Jesus was elected prioress of the convent of St Joseph, at Ávila.

She protested very gracefully, and found abundant reasons why they should choose a more worthy prioress. But Jerónimo Gracían, now Father Provincial, ordered her to show her humility merely by kissing the ground, and while she was thus prostrate he intoned the *Te Deum*.

The Foundress's distaste was sincere: she was overwhelmed by years, her ill-health, the responsibility of all the foundations past and to come. 'They have made me prioress because they're starving. . . . How can I with my age and all I have to do, make a success of it ?'[2]

It was not a spiritual famine, but one of their daily bread. She wrote to her other convents: 'All of you, ask God to give these nuns something to eat.'[3] Once more the Foundress began by straining every nerve to find food for her subjects, convinced as she was that it was useless to deal properly with the souls of poor girls 'who have very little indeed for dinner and nothing for supper.'[1] In this year 1581, it wanted the saints of the city to turn its stones into bread.

For ten years the situation in Spain had been growing steadily worse. The destitution of the convent of the Incarnation in 1571 will be recalled; from the account books kept that year by Teresa at Medina del Campo, we learn that in the course of a week the sisters earned only 11 reales by their work, whilst the expenses in bread, oil, eggs, fish, honey, rice, vegetables and a little mutton for the farm servant amounted to 79 reales. Alms amounted to about 30 reales, not including the gifts in kind which pious people left in the turn.

In 1581 the nuns' work brought in just as little—they were not to fix the prices themselves, but to take what was given them—and the cost of living was five times higher; during Teresa's last journey, Ana de San Bartolomé offered four reales for two eggs and could not get

[1] CTA, cclxxviii.   [2] CTA, ccclxxxv.   [3] CTA, ccclxxxv

them. Provisions were scarce in Castile: at Toledo the Foundress was distressed at the extreme poverty of the place and if it had not been for the parcels María de San José sent from Seville—even to fish kept fresh inside a loaf during the long journey—the Carmelites would have often fasted quite apart from the Rule. Teresa remarked that one could not find woollen material in this city of materials of all sorts, but, on the other hand, ells of gold brocade: Spain's economy had become unbalanced. Alms to convents were becoming scantier and scantier as well as rarer, for to reduce their expenses without lessening their reputation the *hidalgos* spent as much time as possible on their estates which were so badly cultivated that they brought in very little money, and did not bother about giving to convents.

The curse of gold is a fact: the conquest turned Spain into a new, wealthy kingdom, which had lost the liking for work and acquired that for ostentation. Osuna in the Fourth and Fifth *Abecedarios* paints a lively picture of the times and unmasks laziness as enemy No. 1: 'See these nobles who have fallen from their high condition: they live on in idleness amid hardships. In public they are seen with their long sleeves and every appearance of luxury; at home, they fast on many days of the year, not from devotion but because they have nothing to eat. You tell them, "Take service then with some great Lord, or work." They answer: "God forbid!" '

Spain's second enemy was pride: 'For many *hidalgos* a horse and two grooms would suffice, but in their ambition they want to have two palfreys and a mule in their stable, plus three or four grooms to look after them. And the result? In this noble household nobody eats his fill. . . .'

And Osuna writes again: '. . . A page in sumptuous livery whose hands, ceremoniously raised, bear two dishes of silver placed one upon the other. Preceding this page and his cumbrous burden of silver dishes, walks a major-domo in full dress and staff of office in hand. But if by chance you ask: "Gentlemen, what are you carrying on those dishes?" they will answer you: "A radish!"'

'The squire's aim is to be equal to the nobleman, poor folk dress in Courtrai cloth whereas they ought to content themselves with simple frieze.'

It was at this time that the sorry gentlemen who, in their fine clothes of which the cloak hid the threadbare condition, would use the toothpick with much ostentation whereas they had not dined, were first heard of. The Lazarillos and Rinconetes were replacing the Amadis and Olivantes.

Mistaking wealth for power, Charles V and Philip II had made gold the instrument of their policy of expansion; mercenaries proved even more expensive than spies. As to the nobles, who were fighting only for glory and maintained their regiments with their own money, they ruined themselves to follow the Emperor. In such devotion pride, too, had its share: 'The Duke of Bejar, having learnt that the Emperor willed to go and fight against the Turk, passing through the gate of Salamanca journeyed until he came up with the Emperor in Spires, with such a great display of arms, and such a show of men and riches that the foreign princes could not help but notice the Spaniard and marvel, but his household and descendants have felt the effects of it down to this day. . . .'

Throughout the whole country people chose to dream rather than pay attention to keeping accounts: like those who when they are expecting ten pounds make projects that would cost twenty and get thirty pounds into debt. Montezuma's treasure which Cortés brought back was not sufficient to pay for a single one of Charles V's journeys.

Wars without ceasing, a ruined fleet, an idle and extravagant nobility, too many functionaries, the abuse of pensions and perquisites, in short every Spaniard expected that a little of the royal gold should find its way into his purse, while the King expected the galleons to pour the gold of the Indies into his coffers; often, however, the English, French or Dutch corsairs helped themselves first.

If the Grandees managed to live on loans and mortgages, the state of the people was wretched. Already 'the merchants are leagued together and organize monopolies. In time of famine, speculators buy up all the corn which arrives in the ports and sell it again very dear. The wealthy landowners of Burgos centralize all the wool of Castile and send it away to France or England. As a consequence, whole families are deprived of their means of livelihood and all the spinners and weavers are thrown out of work. . . .'[1]

Mother Teresa, who could keep accounts as well as dream, estimated at 300,000 maravedis the income necessary for a convent to subsist, *i.e.* so that thirteen nuns—or twenty-one at most—accustomed to fasting, should not die of hunger.

Of the fourteen convents of Discalced nuns which remained out of the fifteen founded by Teresa of Jesus in nineteen years, those where the nuns did not lack essentials were rare. Such happy exceptions were due to the fact that the people round happened to be extremely

[1] RO, O, p. 26.

charitable—as, for instance, at Palencia, or to unusual gifts for administration and managing money which a prioress happened to possess—
such was the case at Valladolid, thanks to María Bautista. Mother
Teresa however teased her on the tendency she had to 'hoard,' [1] to
'provide for her small house without considering the good of all.'
At Caravaca, Alba, Beas, even at Seville which the imprudent management of Beatriz de la Madre de Dios had put into debt, the Carmelites
knew something of what famine meant. But the Ávila convents
remained the poorest; at the Incarnation the last elections had passed
off very quietly, 'for famine has turned these nuns into lambs. . . .'
But want does not always have this sedative effect and Teresa was
determined to take every possible step to feed this first of her dovecots.

She considered good management so important that she passed
naturally from the spiritual to the temporal, as in the instructions given
to P. Gracián.

It is desirable to examine the account books with care and attention and not to pass such things over lightly. The houses provided
with revenues must regulate their expenses in accordance with such
revenues, and be satisfied therewith whether it pleases them or not:
otherwise they will get into debt; prelates find it inhuman not to
allow their families to provide for the nuns: I would rather see a
convent dissolved than come to that. That is why I said that temporal
evils can engender great spiritual evils; this matter is thus of extreme
importance.[2]

The convents without revenues must take care not to contract
debts; if the expenditure is reasonable, if the sisters have faith and
serve God well, they will want for nothing. It is essential to know
how much food and what sort of treatment to give to them and also
to the sick, and to see that all have what is necessary; experience has
proved that Our Lord always grants this when the prioress is
courageous and diligent.[3]

Look at the work accomplished, work out what each one has
earned with her hands; that brings a double advantage: it encourages
and thanks those who have done much and serves as a model of
imitation for other convents; for in addition to the temporal benefit,
it is a great advantage all round to keep a strict account of work.[4]

See that there is no excess in anything. . . .[5] Don't agree to the
houses being large nor that they should get into debt through building work or enlargement, except in case of urgency. This must not
be considered as a small detail which can't do great harm, it must be

[1] CTA, cclxxviii.   [2] Sb, MVC, 10.
[3] Idem, 11.   [4] Idem, 12.   [5] Idem, 13.

clearly understood that it is better to put up with the inconveniences of a house which is too small than to be crushed with debts or suffer from the want of food.[1]

As regards money, the Foundress had the same broadness of mind as in everything else; for her it was a means which she utilized without contempt but without being attached to it; she was a slave neither to poverty nor to abundance. If a talented and virtuous novice was admitted to Carmel without a dowry, Teresa gave thanks for it. 'Glory be to God!' But she would say with equal freedom: 'I am delighted at the entering of this nun who is very rich. Everything works out well. Glory be to God!'[2]

The fact that even girls vowed to poverty had chosen it because they hoped not only to grow perfect in the love of God under her direction, but also to get slightly better food, did not scandalize her. She immediately set her hand to the task, crushed under the 'rubble' of letters and business, and continued to work part of the night helped by two secretaries, Ana de San Pedro, the Flemish girl, whose fine handwriting she esteemed, and Ana de San Bartolomé.

And firmly yet with great sweetness, after having put aside loyal Julian de Ávila whose age had seriously weakened his authority— 'God preserve us from confessors who are too old'[3]—she again took in hand the guidance of her nuns.

With love, but without enthusiasm. She could not succeed in overcoming the sadness she felt each time she returned to her native city: she suffered, not from being alone there, for solitude was a delight to her, but from being isolated: particularly since the death of Lorenzo de Cepeda and of Don Francisco de Salcedo. And even more than she felt their absence, she felt the desertion of those who remained: her love for perfection increased but in a world which seemed to be renouncing it.

And since her battle cry: 'Do not sleep!' seemed to be heard only from Carmel to Carmel, she undertook to found one more convent, at Burgos, the burial place of the Cid, city of Kings and former capital of Old Castile.

When her lifelong friend, Juana Suárez, who had remained at the convent of the Incarnation said to her affectionately: 'You have founded enough of these dovecots. . . . It is time for you to rest. . . .' she doubtless thought, 'God preserve us from advisers who are too old.'

[1] Idem, 14.   [2] CTA, cxvii.   [3] CTA, ccclxxxii.

P. John of the Cross

At this juncture Fray John arrived at Ávila with all the mules and baggage necessary to take Mother Teresa of Jesus with him to found the convent of Discalced nuns at Granada. But she had promised to go to Burgos.

Teresa only mentions this meeting briefly: the indifference she showed we may put down to haste. She wrote to a preacher whom she greatly admired, Don Pedro Castro y Nero: '. . . I want to tire you as little as possible. . . . I am tired, this evening, through a Father of the Order, although he's saved my sending a messenger to the Marchioness, for he will be going through Escalona. . . .'[1] Next day she wrote to Gracián: 'The nuns left to-day, which has caused me great pain and left me very much alone. They do not seem to mind, especially María de Cristo who has done everything to get away.' Antonia del Espíritu Santo, who also came with Fray John, was one of the first four nuns of St Joseph's, and one of the Foundress's most loyal companions. Of little Fray John of the Cross, the saint, not a word. Yes: 'Fray John of the Cross would very much have liked to send Your Reverence a little money, he hoped to do so if he had been able to take something from what he has for the journey, but he has not been able. I think he will strive to the utmost to get some to Your Reverence.'[2]

Gracián needed money to defray the expenses of printing the Constitutions: for the Foundress that was now the principal objective. She forgot all the rest, she forgot the person of Fray Juan. Women of action—like men of the same type, moreover—are subject to such eclipses of feeling with regard to what their heart holds dear when obsessed by the idea that is uppermost in their minds. At her first leisure moment Teresa was full of tenderness for her *Santico* and wrote him letters full of spiritual illumination.

Meanwhile John of the Cross returned with the mules and carriages he had prepared for 'her.' He went back singing: it was his habit to sing when he was suffering. . . .

Witnesses are silent as to the feelings of Mother Teresa, and the grief of Fray John: but one has only to know him whom the Foundress called 'my little Seneca' to realize that if he mistrusted bursts of feeling it was because his own heart was too sensitive. He was bursting with joy when he went to fetch her and his disappointment was intensely bitter: he loved her more than he had ever said.

He did say it once, or rather moaned it out, a few months before this incident convinced him that his isolation would be without

[1] CTA, cccxc.   [2] CTA, cccxciii.

relief, in a letter sent at random, like a bottle dropped in the sea, to Catalina de Jesús:

> To Sister Catalina de Jesús, Discalced Carmelite, wherever she may be. . . .
> Jesus be with your soul, Catalina my daughter. Although I don't know where you are, I want to write you these lines, feeling sure that our Mother will send them on to you if you are not with her; if such is your case, console yourself by thinking that here I am more of an exile than you, and more alone. For since this whale swallowed me and cast me up again on this foreign shore [he was at Baeza, in Andalusia, and he did not like 'these people' any more than Teresa did] I have never deserved to have the good fortune to see her again, neither her nor the holy people who are there with her. God's name be praised, for affliction is like a file, and we are storing up great joys for ourselves by suffering in darkness. God grant that we do not remain there. What a lot of things I should like to say to you. But I write in the dark, not believing that you will receive this. That is why I break off without finishing. Recommend me to God. From here, I will not say anything more to you because I have no heart to do so. . . .

No tengo gana. . . . A sigh of infinite weariness, a cry from the very heart of the little man from heaven, of whom, when he was chaplain at the Incarnation the Foundress said:
'There's no way of talking of God with P. John of the Cross because he immediately falls into ecstasy and you with him.' [1]
They were made both to understand and not to understand each other. Their psychological make-up was too distinct in character. The strength of refusal of John of the Cross, his despairing sweetness, made Teresa, in her relations with him, more virile than her character was in reality and perhaps even a little brusque. One day a great Spaniard would call Teresa of Jesus *Padraza,* 'the great Father,' and John of the Cross, *Madrecito,* 'the little Mother. . . .' [2] without this transposition of rôles appearing unfair.

Without thoroughly understanding it, John of the Cross admired Teresa of Jesus' astonishing adaptability to all circumstances, her talent for worldly business, the way she was at home in joy as in trials, her natural energy in action; Teresa of Jesus esteemed at its super-terrestrial value 'this soul to whom God communicates his spirit' [3]; the way she introduced him to the nuns of Beas was:

---

[1] Quoted BRE, p. 176.   [2] M. de Unamuno.   [3] CTA, ccc.

He is a man really heavenly and divine; since he went away, I have
found nobody like him in all Castile; no one guides me so well in
the ways of heaven. His absence leaves me in a solitude past believing.
In this saint you have a great treasure, open your souls to him. You
will see how much profit you get from so doing and how much you
will advance in spirit and in the way of perfection; for in such matters Our Lord has endowed him with a singular grace. . . . Padre
John of the Cross is truly the Father of my soul, and one of those in
whom I have confided with the greatest benefit.[1]

Yet the refusal to be happy even in God with which Fray John of
the Cross opposed the unsought delights which Mother Teresa found
in divine love, created a supreme want of understanding between
them. Visions and voices were not to his taste. He admitted to María
de Jesús that at Toledo he had known the deepest recesses of the Dark
Night, complete desolation: 'I asked him if he received the consolations of God in prison: he told me that that was rare; and I think he
said that he had never experienced them, that everything in him
suffered, both body and soul.'

John of the Cross was a tortured mind, and Teresa of Jesus a happy
nature. There is nothing more ardent nor more painful than the love
mingled with envy which such minds experience for natures like hers.

The Foundress had never concealed from John of the Cross the fact
that his demands frightened her. We have only to recall the *Vejamen*
game, where it is true she was jesting, but the liveliness with which
she conducted the contest betrays a kind of relief; each argument is too
closely in conformity with Teresa of Jesus' profound realism not to be
sincere.

She loved him greatly; her despair when he was 'under a spell,'
her efforts to free him from it, her joy when she saw him again, all
prove this, but, admiring him immensely as she did, she would have
liked to love him still more. As to him, loving her more than he
allowed himself to love a human being, he would have liked to admire
her less, for he did not wholly approve her. More than once he found
himself writing that he would not develop some point of prayer, for
'. . . the blessed Teresa of Jesus, our Mother, has written wonderful
things on these spiritual matters. . . .'[2] but he chiefly admired her for
reasons which were instinctive and of this world: as a child hampered
by its timidity admires the natural ease and grace of another child.

When the Mother Foundress had sent for him to come to the
convent of the Incarnation, he had left everything to hurry to her.

[1] CTA, cclxi.   [2] JCC, 1, 3.

This time it was he who needed her and came to seek her out: she did not go back with him.

Not a single one of Teresa's letters to John of the Cross remains. One day he suddenly said to one of his brethren that there was still one thing to which he was attached. From a sack he brought out paper after paper covered with firm, graceful handwriting, and burned them: they were the letters of Teresa of Jesus.

II

THE CITY OF KINGS

EVERYTHING was ready for the Burgos foundation. A rich widow, Doña Catalina de Tolosa, who already had two daughters in Carmel, had obtained the authorization of the city; the new convent could be inaugurated in her own house; the grilles and turn were installed there and the enclosure set up for the first nuns. The Archbishop had formally promised his authorization and extolled the perfection of these Discalced nuns. Besides, was not his name Don Cristóbal Vela? Was he not the son of the Don Blasco Núñez Vela, first Viceroy of Peru, for whom and with whom the Ahumada y Cepeda brothers had fought at Iñaquito? Had not his uncle, Don Francisco Vela y Núñez, stood godfather to little Téresa de Ahumada? Were not the houses of the two families at Ávila next door to each other? Both issuing from good Ávila stock, the Mother Foundress and the Archbishop of Burgos were related, and, better still, were linked together by memories and affinities.

After the mishap at Segovia, Teresa hesitated to set out to found a convent without written authorization, but in the present case what had she to fear? Nothing except the rains which that year were torrential, the January cold, the tracks which were sunken and under water, and her deplorable health. She was so ill that she thought of delegating the prioress of Palencia, Inés de Jesús, to go in her place. Her divine Counsellor reproved her:

'Do not trouble yourself about the cold, for I am the true warmth. The demon is using all his strength against this foundation, use yours in my name to bring it about and do not fail to go there in person: that will be very profitable.' [1]

The Provincial, P. Jerónimo Gracián de la Madre de Dios, and Tomasina Bautista, the future prioress, had just arrived from Alba de Tormes; the Foundress had had to impress upon the Provincial that they must not travel together: in his ingenuousness, P. Gracián would never imagine that a friar and nun seen together in the inns and along the roads might cause evil talk. She never tired of giving him motherly advice and spoke very kindly of him:

[1] Sb, F, c. xxxi–11.

'How good it is of him to be willing to undertake this journey to look after a sick old woman?' 'They seem to be anxious for me to go on living. . . .'[1]

Thus the principal persons in this expedition were the Mother Foundress, P. Gracián, Fray Pedro de la Purificación who had come from Granada, Tomasina Bautista, Inés de la Cruz, Catalina de Jesús to whom P. John of the Cross wrote his pathetic letter, a lay-sister, a lay-brother, Ana de San Bartolomé and the Mother's niece Teresita, together with a complete world in miniature of muleteers, servants and men to form the escort.

The carts left Ávila at dawn on January 2nd 1582. They had to stop at Valladolid to pick up one more nun: Catalina de la Asunción, one of Doña Catalina de Tolosa's daughters. Her sisters and María Bautista the prioress loved her so much that they did not want to let her go. The Foundress, with her 'astuteness from heaven', then spoke of taking away a nun who was indispensable to the community, and Catalina de la Asunción was hers.[2]

From Ávila to Medina del Campo it stopped raining only to snow; from Medina del Campo to Valladolid, sky and earth seemed fused in one unending stream; Teresa arrived there with incipient paralysis which made her shake from head to foot and affected her speech; a raw wound in her throat caused her to spit blood and prevented her from taking anything other than liquids to compensate for the fatigues of the long journey. The doctors declared that if she did not set off again immediately it would be impossible to move her later.

It was not the moment to think of her health: she left Valladolid in veritable whirlpools of water.

On her arrival at Palencia she found the streets decorated with streamers and garlands: this town revered her and received her triumphantly. The crowd before the convent where they were waiting for her was so dense that she had great difficulty in getting out of her carriage to reach the cloister; the chanting and lighted shrines seemed to her like paradise itself.

But any earthly paradise is of brief duration: and in this particular one, moreover, the Foundress was very ill, a fact which did not prevent her from plunging into the deluge again after two days' halt.

To set off in such weather was audacity beyond belief: a servant sent on ahead to reconnoitre came back and reported that the roads were impassable. This information did not weaken Teresa of Jesus'

[1] Sb, F, c. xxxi-16.   [2] SEC, vol. IX, p. 158, n. 3.

determination for she was determined to obey His Majesty and him alone, be the circumstances what they might. Had not Our Lord said to her when she was hesitating to go and found this convent at Burgos: 'What is there to be afraid of ?' [1]

Nobody in those parts could remember such floods. Along the Carrión and the Arlanzón the muleteers, aided by the friars, succeeded with the utmost difficulty in pulling out the carts which were sunk deep in the mire, while the Carmelites waded through the puddles in their sandals. At the top of a slope which went sheer down to the river Mother Teresa saw one of the carriages in front staggering over into the void; one of the servants, with God's help, succeeded in pulling it back by throwing himself on to the wheels: human strength alone would have been inadequate, and those who thus escaped blessed him as 'an angel rather than a man.' [2]

After this incident Teresa insisted on going first so that she alone might be exposed to whatever danger there was.

That evening, when they were hoping to rest after their fright and weariness, the pioneers of Carmel found nothing but an inn so poor that there was no bed.

Next day the Arlanzón had to be crossed. The bridges had been carried away by the flood and there were only makeshift footbridges. The horrified innkeeper begged Teresa—most obstinate of saints— to wait a few days until the crossing should be feasible, but she was determined to go on and all the worthy man could do was to guide them as best he could. He led them to the least dangerous spot.

When the party reached what they thought was the river bank, all they saw was an enormous sheet of water, so large that it was difficult to find the pontoons; these were so narrow that at the slightest deviation or movement of the current, vehicles, mules, friars, nuns, servants and Foundress would have rolled back into the torrent. But were they not to 'live without fear either of death or of the events of life'? The Discalced nuns, however, asked the friars for absolution and their mother for her blessing. She gave it to them in all cheerfulness:

'Well, daughters! What better thing can you want than to die as martyrs for the love of the Lord?' [3]

Her carriage moved forward first and she made all her companions promise to return to the inn should she be drowned.

[1] Sb, F, c. xxxi-4.
[2] AB quoted SEC, vol. II, p. 234.
[3] Idem.

God had said to her: 'When have I failed thee?' [1] He did not fail her in the midst of these perils.

Those who were on the bank saw her carriage swerve and stop as it hung over the torrent: the Foundress jumped out into water which came half way up her legs, she was not very agile and hurt herself. As always, her cry was a calling upon God: this time she complained:

'Lord, amid so many ills this comes on top of all the rest!'

The Voice answered her:

'Teresa, that is how I treat my friends.'

'Ah my God! That is why you have so few of them!' [2]

Had she had time for reflection, she would have used the same words that the imprisonment of P. John of the Cross inspired her with: 'The way God treats his friends is terrible, but in so doing he does them no wrong, for that is how he treated his Son. . . .' [3] Such was indeed the substance of her thought, and Our Lord who had bestowed upon his daughter the gift of a ready answer could not be displeased at this slight variation on the theme. He extricated her; her cart and those of the escort in which seven Carmelites were shouting the Credo as loudly as they could, reached the bank unharmed, if not without fear.

The whole company was happy, 'for once the danger was passed, to talk of it was recreation.' [4]

On 26th January, twenty-four days after they had left Ávila, they reached Burgos at nightfall; after a halt at the church of the Augustinian friars to pray before the miraculous crucifix [5] which was an object of P. Gracián's veneration, the little company went forward through the streets which had become veritable rivers. Anxious to avoid arousing too much curiosity among the good folk of the Huerta del Rey, the eight Carmelites managed to make their entry into Doña Catalina de Tolosa's house unperceived. Worn out and wet through, they were at last able to dry themselves in front of a good log fire.

The Father Provincial, Jerónimo Gracián, and the friars went to lodge with the great theologian and preacher, Canon Manso. The Foundress would have liked Gracián to go to the Archbishop forthwith to ask for permission to expose the Blessed Sacrament and say Mass on the very next morning, but the storm broke out afresh with redoubled fury and prevented him.

That evening Teresa had a syncope and her vomitings which had

[1] Sb, F, c. xxxi-4.   [2] Quoted LV, p. 449.   [3] CTA, ccxix.
[4] Sb, F, c. xxxi-17.   [5] This crucifix is still in Burgos cathedral.

begun again with increased force finally set up inflammation in her throat; after a night of suffering, she was unable to move, so much so that she could not even raise her head, and she received the people with whom she was obliged to speak lying down behind the grille and covered with a black veil.

There was much that had to be said, and to be done, too:

His Illustrious Lordship Don Cristóbal Vela, Archbishop of Burgos, had intimated to P. Jerónimo Gracián de la Madre de Dios that he had asked Mother Teresa of Jesus to come and 'treat' with him of the matter of the foundation, not to come and found: still less to bring nuns with her. This kind of negotiation had to be conducted slowly and prudently. There was no question of allowing Mass to be said in a private house. Moreover, what need had Burgos of reformers? The nuns there were perfectly reformed already and Mother Teresa of Jesus would do just as well to go back where she came from!

'Along these roads and in this weather!' [1]

The Father Provincial, more like Paul than ever, and for the moment in the clouds, brought back the news without any trace of emotion. But the Foundress could keep her feet on the ground when something had to be carried out: in her opinion the devil was beginning his tricks.

Negotiations went on for three months.

His Illustrious Lordship kept changing his mind, first saying a thing and then unsaying it, while time slipped by; he promised the licence and then withdrew his promise. The Foundress would not precipitate matters, saying they should avoid worrying him too often, and when Gracián once more crossed the threshold of the archiepiscopal palace, which was situated below the immense cathedral, Don Cristóbal Vela feigned surprise:

'What! You are still here? I thought you had gone back again!' [2]

One day he refused through over-solicitude for them:

'The house is damp and I cannot bear the idea of the privations which these poor women will have to undergo in a convent without revenues.'

The next day, taking advantage of these kindly feelings, they begged him to allow Mass to be said in the house:

'They are so distressed at having to come out into the world to go to Mass, that the people cry out because they see the pavement wet with their tears. . . .' [3]

[1] Sb, F, c. xxxi-21.   [2] Cf. AB quoted SEC, vol. II, p. 235.
[3] Idem.

But that morning the Illustrious Archbishop's mood was severe:
'Very well! In that way they are giving an edifying example!'

What had he against the Discalced nuns? The Foundress wondered:
'Such opposition on the part of the Archbishop. . . . And yet I
am certain he wants this foundation. There's a mystery somewhere. . . .'[1]

And she tried to get to the bottom of the mystery:
'He says he well remembers the agitation which the foundation
of the first convent caused in Ávila. . . .'[2]

But she told no one whom she suspected of refreshing his memory.

It was time to take the matter in hand herself. She took advantage
of a day when she was not feeling quite so ill to go and see him,
trusting in the ability which God usually gave her for 'negotiating':
she had always found her strength adequate to the task.

Don Cristóbal Vela chatted with her for several hours in the most
friendly way in the world, as was fitting among good friends and old
neighbours: they recalled the Plazuela Santo Domingo, so many relations in common, so many tragic events which linked the two families,
the death of Teresa's brother Antonio when he was fighting under the
flag of the Archbishop's father, the assassination in Peru of his uncle,
Don Francisco, who was the Carmelite's godfather.

The Foundress, like a clever diplomat, managed to plead her cause
in between two reminiscences without appearing to insist too
greatly:

'My poor nuns are so anxious that I should obtain this authorization from Your Lordship that they have promised God to take the
discipline for as long as our conversation lasts. They are actually striking
themselves at this very moment. . . .'

He seemed very glad of it:
'Let them continue then, for I shall not reverse my decision!'[3]

His Illustrious Lordship rose: he regarded the interview as concluded.

Yet this frigid man had considerable admiration for his country-
woman: 'I thought I was listening to St Paul himself speaking,'[4] he
said to those around him.

The impatience with which the Mother Foundress's return was
awaited at Doña Catalina's may be guessed. She had much difficulty in
calming those whom the Archbishop's attitude annoyed but she would
not allow them to blame him in her presence:

[1] CTA, ccclxxiv. [2] CTA, ccclxxiv.
[3] AB quoted SEC, vol. II, p. 236. [4] VH, p. 144.

'He is a saint. He must have good reasons.'[1]

And Fray Pedro de la Purificación admired her even more for 'her divine gift of patience '[2] than for her high state of prayer, her visions, ecstasies or raptures.

He was astonished to find a kind of youthful freshness in a woman who had accomplished such great things. And yet Dr. Manso declared that he would rather argue with all the theologians in Spain than with this nun who knew no Latin. Deprived of Communion by the same Dr. Manso, who prided himself on not being taken in by her reputation for sanctity and wanted to test her, she none the less asked Fray Pedro to hear her confession almost daily: the sacraments were her very life. Fray Pedro protested:

'Heavens, Mother! Leave it alone! You don't commit any sins. We should have to go back to the grimaces you made when you were a child to find matter for absolution. I won't hear your confession!'

She answered in all seriousness:

'Don't be stingy with other people's riches. By giving us graces Your Reverend Lordships are deprived of nothing: it is God who gives us his special graces in the sacraments of which you are the ministers. . . .'

Fray Pedro de la Purificación loved to recount his conversations with Teresa of Jesus just as they happened:

One day a young bride came to visit her, a beautiful girl and very richly dressed; among other things she was wearing very fine pearls, and two or three valuable diamonds placed to advantage set off her charms.

When she had gone the Mother asked me:
'Tell me, Fray Pedro, did you see Doña So and So?'
'Yes, Mother. Why do you ask?'
'Don't you think she's beautiful and has fine jewels?.'
'I didn't notice particularly; but everyone says she is beautiful and well dressed.'

She said to me smiling:
'Those diamonds would be much more in keeping on the child Jesus, for to me all worldly things seem very ugly.'

She took hold of my cloak, led me into a corridor and began to say a thousand and one things to me about God, among others:

'Believe me, Father, since Our Lord Jesus Christ has done me the favour of coming to me, with the Eternal Father and the Holy Spirit, under such a divine aspect with so much splendour and beauty, he is so vividly present to the eyes of my soul that nothing here below

[1] Ab quoted SEC, vol. II, p. 236.   [2] PP quoted SEC, vol. VI, p. 383.

satisfies me; to me it all seems ugliness, and dross, the only thing that gives me any satisfaction is to see souls adorned with Christ's gifts. That's why I said to you that I did not find this servant of God beautiful. . . .'[1] '

Woman, but a saint too; jewels, finery, heaven; and affectionate spontaneity of gesture, graciousness and warmth in speech; that was what she was like.

In the midst of these great troubles or lesser conflicts and conversations with confessors and doctors, the kindness and affection of Doña Catalina's children—Lesmes, Beatriz, and Elena, whom she called 'my little roly-poly,' *mi gordilla*—helped to take her thoughts off the difficulties. She found Tomasina Bautista, the future prioress, a woman of excellent health and stolid temperament, a pattern in the ways of prayer and penance, who overworked herself and would have been quite willing to overwork others, too, had Teresa not intervened.

The Mother Foundress's heaviest burden proved to be her best-loved son, Jerónimo Gracián. From optimism founded on a lack of judgement, he fell, through want of courage, almost into despair.

Finally the Archbishop promised authorization under two conditions:

Firstly: the convent must be installed in a house which belonged to the nuns;

Secondly: it must be provided with revenues sufficient for their maintenance.

Gracián continued to grumble, all the same: where were they to find a house for sale in Burgos? Even should such a house exist, how were they to pay for it? And where would the revenues come from? The Archbishop was really being more difficult than ever, for he was imposing conditions which he knew were prohibitive. The Provincial talked of leaving it all alone and bringing the Foundress and her nuns back to Ávila.

Teresa of Jesus to go away again? The Mother Foundress to give in? It would have been the first time. The Voice whispered to her: 'Now stand firm!' [2]

She managed to persuade P. Gracián to go away: alone she would be in a stronger position, and have her hands more free for the contest.

For there was a great struggle to be faced. That was just as it should be. And now it was necessary for them to leave Doña Catalina's house, for her confessors were threatening to refuse her absolution if she kept the Carmelites with her.

[1] PP quoted SEC, vol. VI, pp. 380–1.   [2] Sb, F, c. xxxi–26.

Where were they to live in this hostile city?

Only with some difficulty did they manage to find two small attics on the top floor of the Concepción hospital: and they only obtained these because they had the reputation of being haunted by all the ghosts of Burgos; even so, there were clauses in the agreement which Teresa found lamentable:

'Anyone would think the Confraternity was afraid of our taking the hospital away: it isn't very likely. . . .' [1]

One consolation: they could follow the Mass said for the sick from the top of a gallery without going through the streets. . . .

But who was it in Burgos who was stealthily trying to stir up opposition against eight poor Discalced nuns? Was it perhaps known that two of Doña Catalina's daughters had decided to pay with their own money for the house the Archbishop was insisting on? Or again, was it because it was no longer a secret that the generous widow, who was already treating the Carmelites as her own children, was intending to endow the future convent with revenues? Now before there was any question of this foundation, Doña Catalina de Tolosa had left all her fortune by will to the Jesuit College in Burgos. Not that the Society of Jesus was hostile to the reformed Carmel: Mother Teresa herself was never tired of saying how much she owed to it. But perhaps her work as Foundress was assuming dimensions which threatened to rival certain ambitions. The quarrel about P. de Salazar's vocation to Carmel may have left some slight feeling of resentment. However this may be, at Burgos Teresa felt 'avowed hostility':' And for all this the "sinister" interests are to blame.' [2] 'They're afraid people will say that their Order and ours are one and the same. . . .' [3] And she added: ¡Qué raza! as one might say: 'What an idea!' 'That doesn't hold water!'

But she had only one policy: peace. That was why, in order that her opponents might have no cause whatever for complaint, she did not hesitate to leave good Catalina's pleasant house and, having collected her nuns and their clothes and belongings, went to perch under the hospital rooftops in the bitter cold, despite her rheumatism and her heart trouble.

Elenita de Tolosa went with her. When the Foundress was ready to go, she asked her:

'Will you come with us?'

'Little roly-poly' ran to get her cloak: she was ready.

'Is that the way girls leave their home?' her mother asked.

[1] Sb, F, c. xxxi-27.   [2] CTA, cdxx.   [3] CTA, cdvii.

'Our Mother Foundress calls me, I cannot do other than obey.'

She said she had thought she heard Our Lord's call to his apostles and so left her mother as happy as she herself was, and in great peace. That was Elenita de Tolosa's entry into Carmel.

At the Concepción hospital, Teresa of Jesus, who was so compassionate to all in trouble, found herself in the midst of plenty of suffering. It became impossible to get her to show the slightest consideration in her own regard or even to feed herself properly: she used to escape from Ana de San Bartolomé who would find her in the wards amid all the stench, distributing the oranges she had hidden in her sleeves. Sufferers from gangrene, cancer, those with infected sores, all those who suffered tortures from horrible wounds, ceased to moan when she was near; and they asked their nurses to go and fetch this holy woman, the very sight of whom eased their pain.

Every day, whatever the weather, Catalina de Tolosa came to see Teresa and brought her the best she could find. This continued until the day when her Jesuit confessors forbade her all contact with the Discalced Carmelites.

'They are afraid she may catch our prayer. . . .' [1]

As if it had been an infectious disease. Hell was one of the least of the punishments with which Doña Catalina was threatened but she stood firm. All the same she was in a state of great confusion: they drove her nearly mad with one scruple or another, telling her in the same breath that she was doing her children an injustice and that her will made all further dispositions void. Mother Teresa, who was Our Lady's advocate and as clever in such matters as the Archangel Gabriel, soon reassured her and the widow whose testamentary dispositions were arousing so much cupidity came back from the Concepción hospital ready to face anything. Such was doubtless the 'prayer' whose infection the Fathers of the Society feared so much for their penitent.

Having come to the end of their arguments, they invoked the early arrival in Spain of the General of the Order who, as events afterwards proved, was not even thinking of setting sail. In short, if it was not war, it was guerrilla tactics.

Teresa neutralized the bitterness of such spiteful behaviour by refusing to take offence.

'I see clearly that the devil has had a hand in these intrigues. . . . For it is sad to see people with such high purpose indulge in such childishness. . . .' [2]

An apology was made: the Burgos Jesuits informed Teresa that

[1] CTA, cdxx.   [2] Idem.

they would visit her when she was installed in a house that had been purchased in due form and order, in which the convent should be founded as His Lordship required.

A house? Impossible to find one. The Confraternity in charge of the hospital had fixed a limited time for the Carmelites' stay there and the date was getting near.

At the very last moment a house was offered and so suitable that it seemed as if God himself had reserved it for Carmel. It had a delightful orchard, a fine view, water in abundance. The Foundress was enthusiastic.

'I like it so much that if they were asking twice as much for it I should consider it was being sold cheap. . . .'[1]

But she had the interests of the Order at heart and hesitated all the same. Our Lord was displeased:

'You are letting money be an obstacle?'[2]

In answer to the prayers of the community, the transaction was concluded for the feast of St Joseph.

The Foundress and her daughters were thus at last in their own house, provided with what they needed by Doña Catalina who had deprived herself of everything so that they should go short of nothing. The Archbishop was charming, came to visit the house and deigned to find it to his liking; he asked for a glass of water, and Teresa of Jesus while she poured out the contents of a jar of ice-cold water seized the opportunity to offer him a small present, 'a thing which he would not have permitted anyone other than Mother Teresa to do.'[3] And he allowed her to hope that the authorization might be forthcoming by Easter Sunday.

Meanwhile, the daughters of Our Lady of Carmel were still forced to go to Mass in the town, as they had been doing, and in those days prayer was not the only purpose for which the churches were used: on Holy Thursday Teresa was thrown down and kicked by men who thought she did not move out of the way to let them pass quickly enough. She only laughed at this and nicknamed the people of this rowdy quarter *chamarilleros*, which may be roughly rendered 'rag and bone men.' The name has stuck to them.

Instead of complaining of the Archbishop, she pitied him:

'When we hear him say so kindly that he'd like to give us permission for Mass to be said in the house, what more could we expect? He can doubtless do nothing. . . .'[4]

[1] Sb, F, c. xxxi–35.   [2] Idem, 36.
[3] SEC, vol. V, p. 314, n. 4.   [4] CTA, cdxi.

In the very end, after much diplomacy and displays of anger ranging from mild indignation to wrathfulness, his Illustrious Lordship gave way, apparently without any more reason than he had had for refusing during the past three months. The man who brought the news set the bells ringing at full speed: actually only religious houses had the right to peal their bells in that way and often to let people know she had founded a new convent, the Foundress would say: 'I have had the bells rung . . . .' [1]

It was high time: that day the sisters were more discouraged than ever. Poor Elenita de Tolosa was so disconsolate that there was no means of cheering her.

As to Teresa, she wrote to María de San José that very morning:

'After my death, and even while I am alive—with all my heart, I should like them to choose you for Foundress, if my opinion counts for anything; for you know more about it than I do and you are better. To say this is the truth. I have a little more experience than you, but in future I must be left out of account: if you could see me you would be frightened to find me so old and good for so little. . . .' [2]

Next day, 18th April, Canon Manso said the first Mass in the presence of the Archbishop who was all contentment, of Doña Catalina de Tolosa now triumphant, and of a crowd of people, amid a great noise of minstrels who had hastened upon the scene uninvited.

The Foundress was old and good for nothing, was she? Success, like fighting, gave her strength: to this woman everything gave strength. Hardly was the affair concluded when, three days after the foundation of the convent of the glorious St Joseph of St Anne of Burgos, she wrote to Toledo to get persons to see Cardinal Quiroga on her behalf, for she was eager to get on with the foundation of a convent in Madrid. All possible steps should be taken, let them even entreat the King on her behalf. . . .

And yet she was happy at Burgos, cloistered once more behind her grilles and veils and overwhelmed with graces by Our Lord.

Ana de San Bartolomé was a heavy sleeper, but this did not prevent her being awakened one night by the sound of exquisite harmonies. She realized that the angels were gladdening their sister, Teresa of Jesus, with heavenly music.

In the morning, she could not hold her tongue:

'Mother! What an excellent night you've had!'

Companionship with the seraphim did not deprive Teresa of Jesus of the gift of repartee:

[1] CTA, cccxlvii.   [2] CTA, cdx.

'Well, daughter, if you heard it, *your* night could not have been a bad one!'[1]

All Burgos now revered the Foundress and her Carmelites. Wisely, she effaced the quarrels with the Jesuit Fathers from her memory and she heaped all the little favours she could upon them. She did not forget to tell the prioress:

'Don't fail to go to confession to the Rector from time to time, and ask him for sermons. . . .'[2]

One last thing she had to do was to save the convent from a flood.

On Ascension day the Arlanzón overflowed its banks, carrying away whole houses and disinterring the dead from the cemetery. But Teresa did not recoil before the elements any more than she recoiled before human beings; she refused to evacuate the convent:

'They've seen enough of us at Burgos!'[3] she said.

She had the Blessed Sacrament exposed in an upper room—the Mansinos' former ballroom—and, with her nuns around her, ceaselessly called upon God: 'Seek ye first the Kingdom. . . .'

The terrified neighbours thought they ought to run and tell the Archbishop about the danger to which the holy women were exposing themselves of their own accord:

'Leave them, leave them alone,' replied Don Cristóbal.[4] 'Teresa of Jesus has a safe-conduct which enables her to succeed in everything she undertakes. . . .'

From six o'clock in the morning until the middle of the night the convent of St Joseph of Burgos was in danger—a little islet of prayer encircled and lashed on all sides by the waters. The Foundress was worn out with fatigue and a sister had to go through the water to get her a little food.

Finally the Arlanzón subsided: once more Teresa of Jesus had been right.

The Archbishop was the first to proclaim that the Santa Madre had not only saved her convent but Burgos itself.

He was still unaware that, anxious about the trouble which might arise for Doña Catalina because of her deed of gift to the Discalced nuns, she had made her cancel her testamentary dispositions in a document which had been kept secret. Thus, whether he liked it or not, Don Cristóbal had a convent of nuns without revenues at Burgos. And, what made it worse, as they were not thought to be necessitous, people gave them no alms. The Foundress did not worry: God would

---

[1] Quoted SEC, vol. VII, p. 452.   [2] CTA, cdxxxiii.
[3] CTA, cdx.   [4] Idem.

provide as he had done for all the rest. Of this convent dedicated to St Joseph and also to St Anne, she could say what she said at the monastery of Palencia: 'The mercy of God is so great that he will not fail to favour the house of his glorious grandmother. . . .' Teresa had a fine family sense both as regards earth and heaven.

She could now ask him who had sent her amid so many dangers to hold her own against so many mighty ones and to overcome so many obstacles:

'Lord, are you satisfied?'

The Lord answered her:

'Go. You must now suffer things greater still!' [1]

She left Burgos on 26th July 1582 with Teresita and Ana de San Bartolomé.

[1] AB quoted SEC, vol. II, p. 238.

III

FAMILY AFFAIRS

'I HAVE been so pestered with relations since my brother's death that I wish I had not to contend with them any more.'[1]

Such was the degree of discouragement at which Mother Teresa had arrived over her family, always ready to take advantage of her. Unfortunately, not all the Cepeda y Ahumada were beyond reproach: arbitrarily to include her in a uniform series of miniature saints would be to detract from Teresa of Jesus' greatness. Those among her relatives who had embarked upon the quest for a more perfect life were led, sometimes even somewhat forcibly, by her. All she owed to them was her valour and her fighting blood.

Her sister María, long since dead, had profited by her teaching; Lorenzo, always a charitable man, had launched out into the ways of penance somewhat tardily; Juana, the wife of Juan de Ovalle, bore the humiliation of being poor, and the burden of an indolent, rather frivolous husband and badly brought up children, with a patience as much due to apathy as to submission to the will of God.

Agustín was a perfect example of the adventurer whose deeds were gilded over with the fair name of *conquistador* in order to embellish to the full a fascinating legend. Whereas Lorenzo in his prudence had turned his attention as soon as possible to making a good marriage and amassing a solid fortune, Agustín with his wild ideas had preferred to go on fighting. Having conquered the Araucanians in Chile seventeen times, he had lately been made governor of an important place in Peru, but did not seem as if he could settle down quietly. Teresa had cause to be anxious about his soul. 'I am extremely sorry to see him still concerned about these things. . . .'[2]

What things? One of those expeditions of which he gave an account himself in a letter to the Viceroy, Martín Enríquez:

'. . . An expedition to the richest land in men and gold that has ever been seen; according to what people say, it's El Dorado. . . . I've decided upon this not so much through my eager desire for the place as on account of the certainty that God and His Majesty will thus be well served.'[3]

[1] CTA, ccclxxxv   [2] CTA, cccxcviii.   [3] PO. p. 72.

Men with such daring and extravagant temperaments never
became rich; when at the beginning of 1582 Agustín contemplated
returning to Spain, his sister for all her joy was anxious:

'. . . If he doesn't bring back enough to keep himself he will
have a lot of trouble, for nobody will be able to pay for his keep, and
it will be a great trouble for me not to be in a position to help him.' [1]
Agustín was relying on the King's gratitude; Teresa was less naïve:
'It is distressing,' said Teresa, 'to see him undertake such a perilous
voyage for money at his age, when we shouldn't be thinking of anything else but preparing ourselves for heaven. . . .' [2]

Pedro's experience was warning enough: living as best he could—
and a poor best it was—on the hospitality of some and the alms of
others, he trailed the bitterness of his failure as a *conquistador* all over
Spain; the royal treasure passed this good henchman by, and the ruin
of his ambitions was simultaneous with the passing of Charles V's
empire into the hands of Philip II.

It was Ahumadas and Cepedas like these, with their legitimate
children and their natural daughters, who overwhelmed the Carmelite
with their problems and demands. The constant trouble they caused
her was doubtless not unconnected with the attention she gave in the
Constitutions of the Order to the matter of the nuns' contact with their
near relatives:

'As far as possible let them avoid much contact with their relatives;
for besides taking their interests to heart, it will be difficult not to speak
of worldly things with them.' [3]

'Let them be very cautious about conversations with people from
outside, even when they are close relatives; and when the visitors don't
like talking about spiritual things, let the meetings be brief and at
infrequent intervals.'

After two warnings, a relapse into such conversations without any
apparent spiritual fruit might entail the penalty of nine days in prison,
with discipline in the refectory on the third day: 'For this matter is of
great importance for the Order.' [4]

Poor Mother Teresa! Her brothers and sisters, not to mention
nieces and families-in-law, plunged her into unexpected troubles and
difficulties. True, she was in no danger of incurring nine days of imprisonment after talking to them; concern for their souls never left her,
and she spent much time and trouble with the sole purpose of preventing their foolishness impeding their salvation. And then, how could

[1] CTA, cccxcviii.   [2] Idem.
[3] CONS, p. 9.   [4] Idem.

she have disinterested herself from the affairs of her family? They were closely linked with the affairs of the Order.

This was particularly the case since the death of Lorenzo who had lent considerable sums of money to the convent in Seville. 'The loss of such a good brother was nothing in comparison with the trouble that the relations who are still left give me. . . .'[1]

Having left Burgos, *en route*—as she thought—for Ávila, she stopped at Valladolid: it was only to find herself back once more among the intrigues from which the foundation of a convent in the royal city had momentarily turned her attention; the most entangled intrigue of all had been woven around Don Lorenzo de Cepeda's inheritance. He had left a very detailed will and therefore one calculated to lead to much trouble, and had made Teresa his sole executrix.

The intervention of third parties unleashed the storm: Francisco, the eldest of Lorenzo's sons, the one to whom he left his property in Spain, leaving the remunerative offices he had held at Quito to the younger one, had suddenly got married, after imagining, like his father, that he had a vocation to religious life which led to his clandestine but brief appearance among the Discalced friars. His aunt Teresa announced the marriage in these terms:

> The bride is Doña Orofrisia. She is not fifteen but she is a beautiful girl and has common sense. I mean Doña Orofrisia de Mendoza y Castilla. Her mother is a cousin of the Duke of Alburquerque and niece of the Duke El Infantazgo and of a great number of other titled lords. She has therefore connections in Ávila, with the Marquis of Las Navas and with the Marquis of Velada. . . . I see only one drawback: Don Francisco's small fortune: his property is so heavily mortgaged that if they did not send him what is due to him from America I don't know how he would live. May God, who has showered so many honours upon them, not allow them to go short of the means of subsistence. . . .[2]

Perhaps after all it was not God who was the author of all these vanities, as indeed Teresa insinuates between the lines, for the household soon got through what little it possessed: pride of birth, the love of luxury and the carelessness of youth took little heed as to whether the galleons from Ecuador laden with gold arrived late, having suffered damage, or not at all. Such was indeed often the case with those who had been in the Indies. They returned to the home country with extravagant tastes, 'eating into a great deal of money,'[3] so accustomed to carving up new continents that they were no longer capable of working

¹ CTA, cdvi.   ² CTA, cccxcii.   ³ CTA, cclxxxix.

the old lands, so accustomed to having servants for every need that they had lost the art of managing their affairs.

Now when fortune has deserted a couple athirst for vainglory, where is it to be looked for if not among those who already possess it? The devil who came to tempt them borrowed the physical appearance of Doña Orofrisia's mother, the most exalted cousin of so many dukes and marquises, Doña Beatriz de Mendoza y Castilla. This unscrupulous person whispered to the young couple:

'Don Lorenzo left money to build a chapel in the convent of St Joseph at Ávila. . . . Teresita is to have a part of the inheritance for her dowry on entering Carmel. . . . If the chapel were never built. . . . . If Teresita did not enter Carmel. . . . If. . . .'

Don Francisco threatened to dispute his father's will, although, according to learned men, this was a mortal sin.

Teresa saw the great danger all these souls were in, she trembled, too, for Teresita and no longer dared to travel without her for she feared she would be taken in by specious lies or even carried away by the intriguers.

When she arrived at Valladolid with this novice of fifteen, she found Doña Beatriz de Mendoza y Castilla in the midst of all the intrigues litigation could provide. And the prioress, her beloved niece María Bautista, had been lending her sharp tongue in the service of the wrong cause.

Behind her small forehead she who was formerly María de Ocampo had a narrow mind.[1] This was a certain advantage for her 'little house,' for she administered it with incomparable prudence and with a skill for which the Foundress praised her when opportunity offered. It was she who had hunted out a silver chalice for Don Lorenzo: 'I could not have hoped to find one at such a reasonable price, and of such a good shape, had it not been for this little ferret of a prioress, who arranged it all with one of her friends. . . . God must be praised for the way in which she runs this house and the talent she shows. . . .'[2]

We can picture a woman quick to take advantage of an opportunity and to get what she could from people. But Teresa did not want to see skilful management turning into sharp practice, organization into egoism, the spirit of initiative into excessive independence and self-confidence into vanity. And she did not fail to intimate this to María Bautista:

Her first words were tender: 'It is strange that almost all letters

[1] María Bautista's skull is in the refectory at Valladolid.
[2] CTA, cclxxxix.

but yours weary me. . . .' Detailed reproaches follow: '. . . It's a big thing to think one knows everything as you do; and yet you say you're humble! I would have you know that I'm not pleased that you should think that nobody does things better than you. . . . In future Your Reverence must not be so sharp: you must be satisfied with knowing the affairs of your own house. . . . I know for a certainty that you no longer speak to me freely and frankly. . . .' [1]

During this visit to Valladolid, María Bautista treated Teresa of Jesus as an enemy.

Insulted by the lawyers, deceived by some and threatened by others, the Foundress at this time suffered more from her friends than she had done from her worst enemies during the persecutions. All this was nauseating to her to such an extent that she declared she was 'rotten' [2] with it.

Teresita's loyalty might perhaps have comforted her, but she could read her very soul and saw her sometimes hesitate and waver despite her kind words.

As to her niece Beatriz de Ovalle, Juana's daughter, a scandal had arisen over her, the gossip about which had not died down. A gentleman of rank in Alba de Tormes, a friend of Juan de Ovalle who used to go riding and hunting with him, was a frequent and regular visitor to the house. The gentleman was married and there was Beatriz, a girl of twenty with all the Ahumada y Cepeda charm. The gentleman's wife took umbrage and spread such shameful calumnies about her husband and Beatriz that her very relatives decided to punish her by killing her with their own hands: 'To take away life from her who was exposing their honour seemed to them a lesser wrong than the harm her accusations were causing: but the relatives of the Santa Madre were opposed to this assassination.' [3]

Nobody suspected Beatriz's virtue, then, but was it seemly that there should be so much uproar about a girl's good name? Teresa tried, all to no purpose, to persuade Juana to take her daughter away from Alba until the matter had blown over: she offered to pay for the mules for the journey and for lodging; but Juana would not make up her mind to go. Teresa was indignant at so much casualness on the part of the mother and unconcern on that of the daughter; she tackled the father who did not seem any more inclined to bestir himself than the others, and finally implored them all: 'In one way or another for the love of God finish with it. Kill me if you like!' [4]

---

[1] CTA, ii, ap.   [2] CTA, cdxxxiv.
[3] SEC, vol. IX, p. 52, n. 1.   [4] CTA, ccclxxxi.

With her love of absolute and unswerving justice, Teresa did not consider Beatriz entirely innocent; to give cause for scandal was to be at fault. She wrote 'terrible things' to Alba and showed this careless family what risks they were running with regard to both God and the world. She confided her trouble to P. Gracián:

'As to the loss of honour, I would pass over that, however much it cost me, but I don't want souls to be lost and I find them all so devoid of common-sense that I don't know what the remedy is. . . . May God deign to provide one!' [1]

But Beatriz proved herself courageous: the gentleman having become a widower—his wife died of rage without its being necessary for anyone to help her to do so—asked for the hand of the girl he had compromised. To the great disappointment of her people, for he was very rich, the proud girl refused, thus proving she had nothing either to fear or atone for and begged her aunt to accept her for Carmel. This put the Mother Foundress in a difficult position, despite the joy a vocation for which she had prayed so much caused her: could she impose upon Carmel such a near relation of her own who had no dowry to offer? The Ovalle drama was complicated by the growing poverty and wretchedness of the Spanish nobility.

'What a lot of trouble all these relatives cause me! I'm fleeing from them!' [2]

Could she flee far enough away to avoid poor Don Pedro, her brother, that ruined remnant of a *conquistador*, still bitter, nursing a grievance, continually up against it, so ill suited to his parasite existence which he made unbearable for himself? She put up with all of them because she loved them. All of them. Even to the natural daughters of Jerónimo and Agustín, over whose satisfactory marriages she was delighted.

It was the little illegitimate daughter whom Lorenzo, son of Lorenzo, left in Spain when he returned to the Indies to make a rich marriage, who gave her one of the last joys of her life. She began to love her with the same affection she bestowed on all the rest of her unsatisfactory relatives and wrote to her nephew:

'I find I do love you, although the offence before God is a heavy burden for me to bear; but when I see how very closely the child resembles you I cannot help keeping her near me and loving her a great deal. Baby though she is, she already has the patience of Teresita. . . .' [3]

Teresa's affectionate nature did not stop at words of tenderness;

[1] CTA, ccclxxv. [2] CTA, ccclxxxv. [3] CTA, cccxcviii.

she took all necessary steps for this innocent girl to be brought up so that she should one day become 'a good servant of God . . . for that is not her fault. . . .' [1]

It took angelic purity like hers to welcome a love-child unconditionally and with such tender charm.

And then she never refused an opportunity of showing love: even if it were a Cepeda or an Ahumada.

And yet, how often had she been disappointed in human affections! Each time she had been moved by special love for a creature, it had come to nothing. P. Gracián himself had not turned out as she had hoped. She would have liked him to remain near her in order to finish the task of putting the convents in Castile in order, not to mention her personal need of his presence: no confessor brought as much peace to her soul as he did. But he had left for Andalusia in order to arrange the studies there and exhort the friars not to hear the confessions of *beatas*: all this, she maintained, could have been done by letter. She felt his absence at such a time so keenly that she even lost the wish to write to him and could not bring herself to do so. Her imperious but affectionate nature which, forty-seven years before, had renounced the world and its ineffectual love to satisfy to the full her thirst for the absolute, had not changed. When she did write to Gracián, she said:

'Up to the present, we had not told Teresita that you were not coming. She has been very much upset! In one way I am glad of it, for she will thus understand how little reliance must be placed on all that is not God alone. As to myself, no harm has been done. . . .' [2] It is sometimes a good thing to have an opportunity of realizing more deeply the vanity of every attachment.

The knowledge that Gracián was in Andalusia made her uneasy, for she knew he was weak and too much inclined to be heedless. He was simple and unsuspecting, and this often led him to make concessions for which those who ever sought to find fault with him blamed him. Teresa was not without misgivings about the state of exaltation into which his preaching success in Seville plunged him, though she was glad of the success itself: 'What the old women say about our Father has greatly amused us and I give thanks to God for the good he does by his sermons and his holiness. . . .' [3] All the same, she urges him to be doubly careful: 'In your preaching I beg of you to pay great attention to what you say. . . . Don't give credence to what the

---

[1] Idem.   [2] CTA, cdxxxiv.   [3] CTA, cccxlvi.

nuns tell you, I can assure you when they're set on a thing, they'll make you believe anything. . . .'[1]

Such were the typical reactions of a good Castilian to the imaginary visions of the South. And she added: 'Don't act the Andalusian, you have no gifts for that. . . .'[2]

If P. Gracián had followed her advice, he would not have fallen into the traps that were set for him. He had many enemies: the signal protection of the Mother Foundress aroused violent jealousy; it was only with difficulty that she succeeded in preventing him whom she supported with her full authority from giving way on his weak points.

This authority was perhaps beginning to weigh heavily upon the young members of the Order, including Gracián. Did they not realize that the old Foundress had more lucidity than all of them put together? But 'old and young cannot go along together. . . .'[3] Ana de Jesús, whom only recently she had been calling 'my daughter and my crown,'[4] had deliberately infringed her instructions for the Granada foundation, and the convent was so much the worse for it. Yet this created a precedent which prioresses could take advantage of to grant themselves privileges. So Mother Teresa armed herself with the thunders of the Lord:

> If we are going to stir up disobedience as you do, it would be better not to found anything at all; for it is not in the existence of numerous convents that good consists, but in the sanctity of the people who dwell in them. . . . In everything which concerns the Discalced nuns, I have the powers of the Father Provincial. In virtue of these powers, I say and command that the nuns you have brought from Beas are to return there, except the prioress, Ana de Jesús. . . . By this His Majesty will be well served, especially as it will be a greater sacrifice for you. Remember that this foundation will be the first in the kingdom of Granada, and that there you must conduct yourselves like valiant men, not like weak women. . . . Either trials have made you stupid, or the devil is introducing the principles of hell into this Order.[5]

As to Ana de la Encarnación, the prioress of Salamanca, her excessive longing for a house did her so much harm spiritually that when she found one, at a price out of the question for poor Discalced Carmelites, she began not only to disobey but to be deceitful. 'The desire she has for this wretched house is making her lose her head.'[6]

---

[1] CTA, cdxxxiv.   [2] Idem.
[3] CTA, cclxii.   [4] CTA, cclxii.
[5] CTA, cdxxi.   [6] CTA cdxxxiv.

'They must not do anything more in the matter until I go there. . . .'

The Mother Foundress was not yet giving up the reins.

These defections weighed heavily upon a woman who had already borne so many responsibilities. She would have liked not to have to reprimand severely any more. Moreover she had been forced to give up one of the essential principles of her Reform: to agree that the convents should have revenues, for towns and villages were becoming increasingly poorer. It was all the more important then that God should be well served in these convents.

It seemed there was nothing else but laxity. The suggestions for the Constitutions made a few months earlier by the different convents showed such a marked tendency to softness that the Foundress exclaimed: 'What a life is this!'[1] Even her eldest daughters, those of St Joseph of Avila, were suggesting that they should be permitted to eat meat. Were they only waiting for her death to fall back into the errors of the Mitigated Rule?

At Valladolid then, faithful to her principle: 'All things turn out as they have begun,'[2] she did not forget the convent at Burgos. Although at a distance she saw to it that the beginnings were good and she impressed upon the prioress, Tomasina Bautista, in an unusually solemn way:

'Although you have the advantage over me in virtue, I have the advantage of you in experience. I hope you will never forget certain of the things I tell you. . . . I tell you these things as if I were speaking to my own soul. I want you to understand that I do not do so without a reason. . . .'[3]

And she reminded her:

'. . . Charity towards the sick. . . .'[4]

'. . . See that you do not overwhelm the novices with work while you do not know in which direction their mind is turning. . . .'[5]

Never forget. . . . With these troubles added to her other sufferings, the Foundress knew quite well that she had not much time left to repeat what she had stressed so many times.

Her farewell to the Valladolid Carmelites was a final call to high things: '. . . Do not perform your religious exercises mechanically, but let each one of them be an heroic act.'[6]

---

[1] CTA, cclii.   [2] CTA, xcv.
[3] CTA, cdxxxiii.   [4] CTA, cdxxx.
[5] CTA, cdxxxiii.   [6] SEC, vol. II, p. 244.

Such had been every action, every thought, every consent or refusal of her who was a sister of *conquistadores*.

Mother Teresa of Jesus stayed more than a month in Valladolid. On the day of her departure, María Bautista accompanied her to the door and said to her by way of good wishes for the journey:

'Go! And don't come back here again!' [1]

[1] AB.

IV

GREAT ADVENTURES ARE OF THE
SPIRITUAL ORDER

'THESE trifles that we call offences, these wisps of self-love of which we build castles like those which children make of wisps of straw. . . .'
The conflicts at Valladolid had touched Teresa of Jesus in appearance only. She was now invulnerable, at the summit of the castle of the soul, free, in the kingdom which her heroic acts had conquered.

She lived the reality of God's omnipresence, in so close an intimacy with Christ that she had no closer counsellor, no more efficacious consoler, no more tender friend. God in everything, God in everyone. Was it for her to judge people? She could only love and act for her Lord. For the steward who acts on behalf of an all-powerful master takes no account of his own interests: zealous but without feverishness or cupidity, he reprimands without hate and rewards impartially, 'buys as one not possessing, uses things as though not using them.' And he is without anxiety. About every convent founded her thought was as it had been about the first: 'Lord, this house is not mine; it has been made for you; it is for you to take care of it. . . .' [1]

She gave up trying to describe her inner peace; [2] what she experienced was inconceivable for anyone who had no experience of the world of mystical graces. She had lived the greatest of all adventures, for great adventures are of the spiritual order. United to God and with eyes for him alone, poverty and wretchedness had no power to make her sad any more than her reputation for sanctity had to give her satisfaction. 'All is nothing.'

Henceforward Teresa was free from every earthly attachment or anxiety. What about Gracián? The rebellious prioresses? Teresita? Her relatives? It was not the first time she smiled to think how mistaken were those who took care not to offend, or who did not care if they did offend, a heart they thought was their own possession. She no longer loved them according to the flesh—they no longer had power to separate her from the presence of God which was infused into her soul— but in the spirit, she loved them so deeply that they were constantly present to her, in that light; and to save any one of them she would gladly have given her share of eternity.

[1] Sb, V, c. xxxiv. 14.   [2] SEC, vol. II, R, VI, p. 39.

Any one of them, or indeed any least member of the human race. For she was even detached from the desire for heavenly glory: she served God 'for nothing, as the Grandees serve the King.'[1] Her one passion was to love God and make others love him.

'I should rejoice if I saw others in greater glory than myself in heaven, but I could not bear for anyone to love God more than myself.'[2]

To have some part in the awakening of a soul to divine love seemed to her henceforward more important than winning paradise. She grew to mortify her body less with fasts and penance, to take more care of her health which was so necessary to her for the work to be accomplished.

She took the weight of the world upon herself as Christ upon the cross had taken upon himself the weight of original sin, and she carried the world to God. It is through the sign of the cross that the creature undertakes to work with the Creator to perfect his creation. 'I fill up in my flesh what is wanting to the Passion of Christ for his body which is the Church.'[3]

Busy as she was day and night in organizing, administering, constructing, directing both souls and affairs, getting things done, controlling characters and events, breaking down obstacles, suffering shocks, she none the less lived in a state of continual prayer. 'I have in my soul this presence of the Three Persons. . . .'[4] The presence of Christ burned within her with a flame which took away her desire for life, while at the same time the habitual vision of the Holy Trinity set her on fire with charity. The most detailed occupations could not distract her from this presence.

'All is nothing': the fact made her all the stronger for action. She had thrown everything into her heroic adventure and had gained all, having counted all as lost.

Through the close union in her of Martha and Mary, she reached the point at which contemplation and action are no longer divided but inseparable: His Majesty is adored and served at the same time.

The union between her soul and God was so complete now that she had scarcely any of those external manifestations, ecstasies, raptures which had so often proved mortifying to her humility: at least she had no more of them in public. The sudden invasion of divine love did not now disturb a body in which it dwelt continually. But, wrote her niece, Teresita, she showed a smiling and calm simplicity which

[1] CTA, cdiii.
[2] TC quoted SEC, vol. II, p. 307.
[3] Colossians i. 24.
[4] SEC, vol. II, R, xviii, p. 51.

reminded one of a candid child or of the innocence of man and woman before the twofold concept of good and evil separated them from the All in One.

Never did she lie, never did she misjudge anyone. Firm when the interests of the Order were at stake, she was so humble where she alone was concerned that she obeyed her own subjects. She said:

'I don't know why they call me Foundress, since it's God who has founded these houses.' [1]

Although old and ill, she did not fail, whenever possible, to cook, sweep and spin to contribute to the support of all by the work of her hands.

As far as possible she concealed the great favours which Our Lord granted her, took care not to assume pious attitudes, but on the contrary behaved so naturally and was so pleasant and courteous, 'gay with the gay and sad with the sad,' [2] that people were astonished that she should be the one who was considered a saint.

At length the praise of God came to be in her an expansion of her nature, overflowing so abundantly that the verses of King David seemed to come spontaneously to her lips; there was no beautiful thing in the world from a river like the Guadalquivir to the tiniest flower of the field which did not make her cry out: 'Blessed be he who created thee!' [3]

Before going to sleep, even when she had been dealing with her correspondence or working at one of the books her confessors ordered her to write even in the last years of her life, she would say her rosary, pronouncing each word, as she taught her daughters to do, slowly, lovingly, with the full awareness that sprang from her saintliness. She found special joy in reciting the *Credo* in this way and in reiterating her faith in eternal life.

Her sleep was one long ecstasy.

Ana de San Bartolomé came one morning into her cell at Valladolid, having instructions to awake her earlier than usual. Teresa was still sleeping and her face was shining like the sun. Ana took care not to wake her and began to say her prayers at the bedside, praising God for the exquisitely sweet perfume which filled the room with fragrance.

When she awoke, Mother Teresa of Jesus asked her in astonishment what she was doing there on her knees at the side of her bed. But the good little lay-sister kept silence about what she had seen in order not to cause her embarrassment.

[1] TC quoted SEC, vol. II, p. 307.
[2] SEC, A, 9.   [3] TC quoted SEC, vol. VI, p. 334.

V

ANTONIO DE JESÚS, VICAR PROVINCIAL

THE Mother Foundress would not admit that she was unwell; in actual fact she was a dying woman.

When Christ, her Beloved, said to her in Burgos: 'All is finished here, you can go away,' it was because the last adventure of God's knight errant, her encounter with death, was to be victorious on condition that she fought one fight more.

After the troubles at Valladolid time was short; she had to hasten to snatch a little rest at Medina, hasten to reach Ávila, hasten to give the veil to Teresita de Cepeda, hasten to put the difficulties at Granada in order—tendencies to independence on the part of Ana de Jesús—and the house in Salamanca and the new foundation in Madrid, and to overcome the obstinacy of Cardinal Quiroga in the same way as she had already won many prelates over to her side. A little more time remained in which she made haste to act and to suffer, without sparing the worn-out scabbard which sheathed her ardent soul.

She suffered with her head, her throat, in all her bones. Since Burgos the taste of blood was always on her lips and the vomitings were continual. Never had she felt the need of a respite so much, and from the remotest recesses of her mind she smiled with pity upon the poor old woman whose head twitched with nervous trembling. And so she let Ana de San Bartolomé look after her for a few days while she gathered her strength together again to achieve the end in view: Ávila, Madrid.

The convent of Medina del Campo had retained its rural aspect. When the Foundress got back there, she found the patio from which she had directed the work on the ruined house, her cell and the little gallery which led to it, as she had left them; there, too, there was the heavy swish of gowns of frieze: the nuns hid to catch a glimpse of her, although she had forbidden it; but does not love always win the day, even among women vowed to obedience? The prioress, Alberta Bautista, pretended not to notice anything, though she was by no means easy-going.

At the beginning of her novitiate, the Carmelite Rule had seemed so mild to this sister in her eagerness for austerities that she had wanted to leave in order to have freedom to practise unbridled mortifications. The Foundress had applied her usual method when dealing with souls difficult to manage: a sweetness which was inexorable. One day when the Foundress was presiding over the games and songs, Alberta Bautista grumbled that they would do better to spend the time in contemplation. She was sent to this occupation forthwith:

'Go, daughter. Go and contemplate in your cell while your sisters and I make merry with the good Lord here!' [1]

And it was Alberta Bautista who, in her unsatiable longing for the Eucharistic Bread, obtained from a soft-hearted confessor permission for daily Communion, against the Constitutions which granted permission to communicate only on Sundays and feastdays: she persuaded the good man that she would die if she were deprived of the privilege. This revolution in 'holiness' threatened to spread to the whole convent, already a lay-sister was making the same demands under threat of dying. The matter seemed to be serious and Mother Teresa was informed. She made the journey to Medina on purpose:

'What's all this, daughter? Do you suppose that your sisters and I don't feel the same desires?'

Since every appeal to reason proved futile, the Foundress preached by example, faithful to her principle: deeds, not words:

'I will therefore impose upon myself the deprivation of Communion,[2] like you. If we all three die, what better thing can Carmelites hope for, since they desire only heaven?'

For the first few days, the two sisters seemed as if they were going to die; but the Foundress remained inflexible, time had its effect and things returned to order. Mother Teresa had shown Alberta Bautista that it is more meritorious to bend oneself to obedience than to let oneself be carried away by outbursts of piety against the Rule, or to give oneself up to austerities on one's own authority. Rewarded for her submission by high graces in prayer, her character none the less remained difficult, prompt to criticize and ready with a retort. She had been elected prioress some years before, although the nuns of Medina del Campo had had misgivings about her excessive liking for penance. She would have been quite capable of imitating the nun who demanded of her subjects that they should take the discipline throughout the recitation of the seven penitential psalms and a few additional prayers, a thing which the Mother Foundress hastened to forbid.

The Foundress appreciated this generous and rather harsh woman;

[1] RD, L. IV, c. xx.   [2] Sb, F, c. vi, 9–10 ff.

in her she found the most useful thing for perfection: someone who would not flatter her.

That was why, when she arrived at Medina, hoping for rest as a sick person has the right to do after a difficult journey, and Alberta Bautista, without even offering her the necessary refreshment after a journey, curtly told her that the Vicar Provincial was asking for her in the parlour, Teresa of Jesus did not complain of not being received properly by this daughter of hers, but went to obey the summons of her superior.

She said to Ana de San Bartolomé who came to the parlour with her:

'We have had more than one quarrel, P. Antonio de Jesús and I. But this good Father cannot deny that he likes me, since old as he is he has come to see me. . . .'[1]

Massive in height and breadth, grey-haired, with the hollow temples of an ascetic and the sulky lips of a touchy child, this was what P. Antonio de Heredia had become. That was how P. Antonio de Jesús, Vicar Provincial, appeared at the age of seventy-two. As he grew older it was more and more irksome to him to bow submissively to the authority of the Foundress—he despised women—as well as to accept the slight favour of chaff with which she seasoned her contact with him. This had gone on since the day when setting out to install the first monastery of Discalced friars at Duruelo, in his zeal he had provided himself with five clocks but forgotten the straw pallets. Teresa had then been seized with one of her fits of laughter[2] and when she laughed, everybody laughed. He was not disposed to admit that she usually liked to tease those she loved best.

Yet she treated him affectionately, calling him 'this blessed old man, the first of all the Discalced friars,'[3] and only grew weary of writing to him because she received no replies. 'Remember me especially to Fray Antonio de Jesús and if he has made a vow not to answer me, let him say so. . . .'[4] In spite of this she knew him to be so touchy that she said to Gracián: 'Remember me to Fray Antonio; I don't write to him because he never replies but try and prevent his knowing how often I write to you, as much as possible.'[5] In the end it was she who broke the silence: 'His way of doing things distresses me so much that I have decided to write to him. . . .'[6] It was impossible to be more patient with an obstinate old man. Finally she announced

---

[1] CTA, cccxiii.   [2] FR.   [3] CTA, cciv.
[4] CTA, cli.   [5] CTA, clix.   [6] CTA, cdxi.

with delight: 'I have a letter from him. . . . He is becoming my friend again. . . .' [1]

Padre Fray Antonio was perfectly well aware that Mother Teresa had discovered the point of vanity which he allowed to come to the surface despite his austerities: she had let him understand this when she had forbidden him to go barefoot, enjoining the use of sandals upon him as upon the others. He blamed her for her great liking for the 'talented' and 'scholars' and for having said to him: 'For these monasteries I hope for men of talent and too many austerities might frighten them away.' [2] Yet he himself was a man of learning but he did not possess the one quality which Teresa of Jesus appreciated in the highest possible degree: common-sense.

On the other hand the Foundress had blamed him for the 'pusillanimity' which he had shown as Prior of Los Remedios and, worse still, 'for not carrying out his office properly,' [3] and had been 'amused' at his fits of authority. Did she take him for a weakling or a chatterer? She did not condescend to keep him informed of the affairs of the Order, he said. The Foundress admitted he was right and apologized. His cavilling disposition was nonplussed with a woman like Teresa: before her simplicity and humility, there was no recourse left to him but to take refuge in systematic bad temper. This was what Fray Antonio did. He raked up grievances from ten years before: he still bore Teresa of Jesus a grudge for having frowned when she read the letter he wrote to the Duchess of Alba on the occasion of the Princess of Éboli's tantrums at Pastrana: 'As to the news of our novice, the Princess, here she is, five months pregnant, installed in the convent, imposing herself as prioress, demanding of the nuns that they serve her on their knees and observe the rules of court etiquette. . . .' Mother Teresa had not appreciated the gossipy tone of this highly coloured sketch, intended to amuse the Most Illustrious and Excellent Duchess. But he who in the world had been Antonio de Heredia remained a courtier and flattered himself on being one of the intimate friends of the Duke and Duchess.

He knew perfectly well that the Foundress had advised against his election as Provincial of the Order: the casting vote in favour of P. Jerónimo Gracián de la Madre de Dios and against him had been her doing. Gracián! That greenhorn! Charmer of the devout old women of Andalusia!

But in the absence of the said Provincial, it was to him, Antonio de Jesús, his Vicar, that the Mother Foundress owed obedience.

[1] CTA, cdxxxiv.   [2] CTA, cxlviii.   [3] CTA, cxliv.

The dying woman's face which he saw behind the parlour grille at Medina del Campo awakened no sympathy in him. But he dared not look Teresa of Jesus in the face as he gave her orders to start next day for Alba de Tormes, where the Duchess of Alba, Doña Maria Enríquez, was demanding her: to aid her daughter-in-law in her confinement, nothing less than the prayers of the woman whom Spain held to be a saint would do.

The Foundress was utterly overwhelmed.

'Never,' said Ana de San Bartolomé, 'have I seen her suffer from an order given by a superior so much as she did from this one.'

Teresa saw through Antonio de Jesús. If only fifteen years before she had kept to her first impression. If only she had then sifted to the bottom the significance of the uneasiness she had felt in this very convent when he had given her his confidence about his ardent desire to be the first of the Discalced Carmelite friars. A soul on fire with enthusiasm, beyond a doubt. But he was so pleased with his own importance, this prior of St Anne's. The choice had not been hers, for she was then only 'a poor Discalced nun, loaded with briefs and good will but without means of action,' [1] without a farthing, without a friar. And he had gone off to found the monastery of Duruelo with Fray John of the Cross.

From Duruelo, John of the Cross had taken his flight to the mystic heights of Mount Carmel and P. Antonio de Jesús had gently come down again to the attachments of earth. He who claimed to be the first Discalced friar had wanted the first place in the Order; the importance of Gracián had made him first jealous, then bitter and finally aggressive. The Foundress had had to speak out in her Paul's defence: 'Nothing special in the matter of Fray Antonio except that I cannot bear that he should annoy you even in the smallest way.' [2] His bitterness went so far as to create small groups of dissidents. Teresa had put her foot down at this. 'We all belong to the faction of Christ crucified!'[3] Finally she had intervened so that he could not attain the highest place in the Order, but at the same time she arranged that he should have the second place, that of Vicar Provincial, 'in order that he may die in peace, since that is what makes him melancholy; and these small factions will come to an end and, having a superior over him,[4] he will be able to do no harm.' Being herself a great superior she summed him up, and she loved him well.

But that evening she saw what was only too clear: the Vicar Provincial was nursing the grievances of Antonio de Jesús.

[1] Sb, F, c. ii-6.   [2] CTA, cxxxi.   [3] CTA, clxxix.   [4] CTA, cccv.

It would have been interesting to see how he would have gone
about forcing the Mother Foundress, had she refused: her state of
health would have justified her in taking care. The idea did not enter
her head. Had she not written recently: 'Out of obedience, I would
go to the end of the world'?[1] The Bridegroom had asked her to fight
for him, to suffer, to be considered crazy in men's eyes: she had always
obeyed. And now that he was bidding her, through the mouth of one
of his prelates, to turn aside from her last earthly attachment—Ávila,
the cradle both of her body and of her foundations—to journey towards
a strange tomb in a rickety old carriage that was most unsuitable for
her old bones, was she to draw back?

It was quite lawful for her to complain humbly to the Father Vicar
of such a cruel demand: she did not do so. She complained only to Our
Lord of the extreme helplessness of her soul, the prisoner of a body
which was sick, worn out or cowardly.

She was not going to show weakness before the hard prioress,
Alberta Bautista, whom formerly she had herself formed to obedience.
This was a reminder to her that she was nothing: should she not daily
learn again from her daughters the very virtues she had taught them?
She merely said:

'I shall obey Your Reverence.'

Teresa of Jesus went back to her cell supperless: the prioress had not
invited her to come to the refectory. She accepted hunger, solitude,
departure at dawn next morning without any secret reluctance,
silencing all resentment: after the prioress of Valladolid, were not
Antonio de Jesús and Alberta Bautista to be the occasion of her
greatest victory? Now she was with Christ in the Garden of Olives.

Even before entering Carmel, she had preferred this scene of the
Passion to all others, for, persuaded as she was of her unworthiness, she
dared not keep company with Jesus, except when she saw him
abandoned and betrayed. 'I used to think of the sweat, the distress he
had suffered. I wanted to wipe away this painful sweat; I remember
that I dared not, thinking of the gravity of my sins. For many years
before going to sleep, when I recommended myself to God, I always
spent a short time thinking about the scene in the Garden of Olives.
It was in this way that I began to practise mental prayer without
knowing that it was mental prayer. I acquired the habit of it, as I did
that of never omitting to make the sign of the cross.'[2]

[1] CTA, cclxxviii   [2] Sb, V, c. ix-4.

That night, when fever and pain prevented her from sleeping, she drained to the dregs the chalice of abandonment at the hands of those belonging to her: but was it not a new favour to be thus called by her Master to share his solitude? Jesus was there with her in her solitude as she had kept him company in the Garden.

Teresa set out after Prime. P. Antonio, her niece and Ana de San Bartolomé went with her.[1]

The Duchess of Alba had sent her carriage, if a cumbersome piece of machinery, on four wheels, badly sprung, can be so called. At the first jolts Teresa felt so ill that she feared she would cause her companions and the Duchess's men trouble by dying on the way. Her sufferings were such that only her extreme weakness and the abating of the fever made them bearable. Having eaten nothing since the night before, she made an effort, in order to keep up her strength a little, to eat a few figs, but she could not digest them; towards the day's end her heart began to fail and the beating of her pulse was practically imperceptible. Although the taking of food was as repugnant to her as it was to give trouble, she begged Ana de San Bartolomé:

'Daughter, if you can get hold of something, no matter what, cook it for me, I can do no more.'

Ana gave a servant four reales to buy two eggs and wept when he returned without having found any. The Mother's face was that of a dying woman and yet it was she who comforted the lay-sister:

'Don't weep: it is God's will it should be like that. . . .'[2]

She had a seizure. And in this isolated place there was nothing to give her relief. Teresita was indeed affectionate but did not know how to deal with the situation. P. Antonio bustled about uselessly. The Duchess's men were indignant: 'The people in Peñaranda have killed the saint!'

After a night spent in a bad inn where all that could be obtained for the sick woman was a few herbs cooked with a great deal of onion, they were able to start off again. Ana de San Bartolomé did not take her anxious eyes off the Mother's face, as she shuddered with pain at every jolt. Teresa was perhaps more grateful to Ana for her loyalty than for her care.

They were approaching Alba when a cloud of dust came to a standstill at their carriage door, with the noise of a galloping horse pulled up with a jerk: it was a courier from the Duke of Huescar bringing the news of the happy birth of the heir of the house of Alba. The young Duchess and her child were both doing very well.

[1] CTA, ccclxxxv.   [2] CH, L. ii.

When the interests of the Order were at stake, the Mother Foundress had always stood out against the whims of the Grandees, but now her own life had been the stake of such a whim. And yet the Duchess, Doña Maria Enríquez, loved her. It was not Doña María Teresa had in mind when she asked God to preserve her from all powerful lords and ladies because they were curiously apt to contradict themselves. She found the strength to say humorously:

'God be praised. Now they will no longer need the saint![1]

[1] CTA, ccclxxx, quoted H, p. 221.

VI

FACE TO FACE

ALBA was aflame with the glory of the setting sun, the Tormes rippled with golden light. Teresa of Jesus entered the convent of the Annunciation of Our Lady of Carmel to the singing of the *Te Deum*: in all her convents her daughters expressed their joy at her coming in this way. That evening her fatigue was so obvious that the hymn of joy died away to a whisper. She admitted that she was a broken woman:

'I haven't got one sound bone left. . . .'[1]

But she made the effort and smiled and consented to bless her nuns, though usually she refused this gesture which seemed to her contrary to humility; she did so 'with much elegance and grace.'[2]

The prioress of Alba de Tormes was one of the nuns from the convent of the Incarnation at Ávila who had left the Mitigation to join Mother Teresa. Juana del Espíritu Santo was so gentle that when she scolded a nun she ended by throwing herself at her feet and asking pardon; the only thing Teresa had to reproach her for was her excessive fasts.

Taking advantage of the fact that the Mother Foundress claimed to be one of the prioress's subjects and nothing more, the latter begged her to rest and led her to her cell. Ana de San Bartolomé brought white bed-linen: only the sick had the right to this and the little lay-sister was happy at being thus able to satisfy her patient's liking for extreme cleanliness. And indeed, when she found herself wearing fresh linen down to the coif and sleeves, in a spotless white bed, she smiled happily:

'It's more than twenty years since I went to bed so early. . . .'[3]

But in the convent the excitement which an unexpected event aroused among women who lived apart from the world was soon replaced by consternation. Had the Foundress come to Alba to die? Was this what the supernatural signs which had been noticed in the convent since the beginning of the year signified? In the choir the sudden appearance of lights had frightened all those whom the occurrence had not plunged into a state of deep prayer. Recently, when the community were at their prayers, the nuns had heard three

[1] AB quoted SEC, vol. II, p. 239.   [2] JGM.   [3] CH.

very faint and gentle moans which they now said were like the sighs of a hind at the point of death.

But next morning Teresa of Jesus was at Mass and received communion: she was not accustomed to give way to the weaknesses of the body. For some days they saw her go backwards and forwards leaning on her stick, going upstairs to enjoy from the topmost rooms the view of the Tormes she loved so much, inspecting the convent with her usual thoroughness, anxious about the smallest details. Despite illness and her years her looks retained an indefinable something of pride and victory, which perseverance in obedience and humility, and the many labours and persecutions she had sustained had not worn down.

The Foundress had work to do at Alba: in the first place it was necessary to put right the benefactress, Doña Teresa de Layz, who gave the sisters a regular allowance but tormented the good nuns.

It was a long time since the day when this lady had had a vision of this very house, with its green patio planted with white flowers so beautiful that it was impossible to describe them, and its well near which St Andrew stood in the form of a fine old man. To the woman who wanted children for the glory of her name he had said:

'Your children will not be those you ask for. . . .'[1]

From this revelation the convent of Alba de Tormes had come into being, but the pious patroness had become a shrewish mother to the daughters of Carmel.

The Foundress chided her.

'You will never keep a prioress long, they all flee from you. You should reflect that this house is yours and that people who are worried can't serve God. All this is only childish nonsense and attachment to oneself. Ah, madam! How different things are where the spirit truly reigns.'[2]

Doña Teresa de Layz had been won over. For wherever Teresa went, she re-established order and introduced peace.

Two or three days later, the Rector of the College of Discalced friars in Salamanca made the journey to Alba de Tormes to talk to her about 'this devil's intrigue,'[3] this sad story of a house. The discussion went on the whole afternoon. Her indignation against the prioress would have done honour to a person in the best of health. Ana de la Encarnación, who was her cousin Ana de Tapia, and one of the oldest Discalced nuns, had just ignored the Foundress's prohibitions and bought the house, with which indeed she was infatuated.

[1] Sb, F, c. xx-7.   [2] CTA, cdxxix.   [3] CTA, cdxxxiv.

The Rector defended the culprit: if she had done wrong it was out of despair at having wandered from hovel to hovel for twelve years; and he added:

'After all, it's done now, the papers are signed, the deposit paid. What is the use of fighting against an accomplished fact? Let Your Reverence forgive your daughter and console her, now you have made her wretched.'

The Foundress protested:

'An accomplished fact, my son? It is not an accomplished fact and never will be.[1] Never will the Discalced nuns of Salamanca set foot in this house, because such is not the will of God and because this house is not suitable for them.'

For her the will of God meant perfection.

It was the last battle she fought in the interests of the Order: she won it as she had done before, and once more she was glad to think that she knew everything going on in these houses of God, and that in them she had even become 'a haggler and a busybody,'[2] she who detested money and business. Was it not essential to see that things were properly run?

As she had foretold, the purchase of the house at Salamanca fell through.

In the midst of all this, the thought of the wretchedness of the little convent of St Joseph's at Ávila was constantly on her mind, and she told Teresita and Ana de San Bartolomé of her anxiety about it:

'Where are these poor girls going to find money to buy bread with?'[3]

For where the Foundress was, the Carmelites had not only the Lord's peace, but good bread. She even said to Ana:

'Daughter, do something to please me: as soon as you see me a little better, get me an ordinary carriage; you will install me in it as best you can, and we will all three set out for Ávila.'[4]

Not that she was attached to her native soil any more than she was to any other earthly thing, but because of the intrigues of Francisco de Cepeda, it was important that Teresita should take the habit as soon as possible.

Now, at the end of September, Teresa of Jesus' marvellous courage failed her for the first time; she was vomiting blood, and at times her tongue seemed paralysed.

On the morning of Michaelmas day, after the Mass at which she

---

[1] CTA, cdxxxiv quoted SEC, vol. IX, p. 320, n. 3.   [2] CTA, xix.
[3] TC quoted SEC, vol. II, p. 367.   [4] Idem.

communicated she had a haemorrhage and had to be carried up to her bed. The doctor found her cell too cold and she was moved to a more sheltered room, a sort of alcove with a passage in front. A window looked on to the cloister.

The day before one of the nuns had seen this window lit up with a light whiter and more sparkling than crystal: after this, nobody doubted that the Foundress would die there.

She herself knew this better than anyone else. As early as 1577 in Salamanca she had said to the doctor who was enjoining upon her to rest: 'For the four years I have to live, it is useless to take so much care. . . .' She had waited for her hour, always peacefully and always at her task.

Now her hour was come.

Formerly she had been afraid of death. Then, in love with God to the extent of being, so far as this world was concerned, 'like one sold into a strange land,'[1] she had worn herself out with macerations, dying of being unable to die. For where shoul Life be found except in death? This world's life she had found in activity.

After having founded her first convent, when her desire for solitude and prayer was satisfied to the full and when she was raised by Christ to the heights of love in the blessed house of St Joseph of Ávila, she begged the Lord either to take her to himself, or to give her the means to serve him.

He then ordered her to found seventeen convents of nuns besides the houses of friars, to revolutionize the religious life of her time, to infuse the work with the virtues of the highest contemplation and to make of contemplation a work that should be efficacious, to do away with all social differences by a love which should be the same towards all, to put the law of God above human precepts. And lastly, poor,. detached from all things and in particular from herself, a humble and weak woman, in times when women enjoyed no prestige and had still less resources, she had to finance, organize, administer these houses of Our Lady, to feed and govern some hundreds of subjects with the same broadness of vision and yet the same careful attention to detail, as if she had been rich, ambitious and covetous. To 'muffle oneself up'[2] in prayer would not do. 'The Lord wants deeds, he wants works! If you see a sick person whom you can comfort, do not hesitate to sacrifice your devotion, and attend to her; you should feel her pains as if they were your own; fast, if necessary, to procure food for her. Such is true union with God.'[3]

[1] Sb, V, c. xxi–6.　　　[2] Sb, MVC, iii–11.　　　[3] Idem.

From that time onwards, for Teresa of Jesus divine love was no longer a matter of dying in order not to die, but of understanding, suffering, renouncing and serving.

Until she had finished her Father's work. Now it was at last to be given to her to go back to him.

For her this was as simple as it would be for a child.

But for her alone. For as with the birth of a King's son, the death of a daughter of God who even in her lifetime was considered a saint could not take place without witnesses. There was a numerous assembly in the cell of Mother Teresa of Jesus. It was a cell just like all the others in the convent of Alba de Tormes and in all the convents of Carmel: a great cross of rough wood on the limewashed walls, the brown frieze against the whiteness of the sheets, the blue sky of Castile to be seen through the window.

Catalina de la Concepción and Catalina Bautista helped Ana de San Bartolomé to look after the dying woman. Her patience, her endurance, her distress at the trouble she was giving them, made them praise God for her virtues.

Doña María Enríquez came to see her: Teresa apologized, fearing that the smell of a medicine which had been spilt by accident might be troublesome to her. But, not only was the smell of medicine imperceptible, but a marvellous fragrance scented the room; everything Teresa touched was impregnated with it.

Teresita remained with her, as did Doña Teresa de Layz, P. Antonio de Jesús, the prioress, Juana del Espíritu Santo, and María de San Francisco who had caught her in her arms at Salamanca on the day when Isabel de Jesús' sweet song made her fall into ecstasy. There was also Teresa de San Andrés who went about loaded with hair-shirts and steel bracelets, but who was so beautiful and concealed her austerities with such humility that Teresa, kissing her, had one day called her 'the honour of penance.'

'I will come to fetch you when your turn comes,' [1] she said to her as she thanked her for assisting her on her death-bed.

In a corner of the room could be seen the anxious face of Antonio Gaytán's daughter, Mariana de Jesús, whom Teresa used to call 'my little pest' and whom she now called 'the little angel,' for this novice was not yet fifteen. Teresa guessed at her secret anxiety: after the death of her protectress, would she be allowed to take the veil in this house, for she had no dowry? She reassured her:

'Don't fret, child: you will be professed here.' [2]

[1] CP, vol. iii, p. 479.   [2] CP, vol. iii.

It seemed as if she were not concerned about her death, to such an extent did she appear to be solely occupied in blessing and consoling others: love's miracle was completing the metamorphosis.

All this took place amid a profound silence. Catalina de la Concepción who was near the window was accordingly annoyed at hearing all of a sudden the sound of a gay crowd; she was about to leave the room to stop the noise when she saw a great company of ladies and gentlemen in shining garments crossing the cloister and entering the saint's room: the ten thousand martyrs had come to bid Teresa of Jesus welcome to the eternal marriage feast.

On 2nd October the Foundress told Ana de San Bartolomé that her death was near. She asked for the Holy Eucharist. The Reverend Father Antonio de Jesús, Vicar Provincial, knelt by her to hear her confession. Then he implored her:

'Mother, ask Our Lord not to take you away. Don't leave us so quickly. . . .'

She was heard to answer:

'Father, be quiet! Can it be you speaking like that? I am no longer necessary in this world.'[1]

Now that her work was finished, she allowed her soul to be flooded with the love of God and the desire she had to be united with him.

Her recommendations to her daughters were brief:

'My daughters and ladies, for the love of God I ask you to observe the Rule and Constitutions well; if you keep them strictly, no further miracle will be necessary for your canonization. Don't imitate the bad example which this bad nun has given you, and forgive me.'[2]

Was not this tantamount to a recommendation of her favourite virtues: love, humility, obedience, work?

She repeated several times clearly and majestically: 'Lord, I am a daughter of the Church.'[3]

She was so ill that it took two nuns to move her in her bed. But when she saw the Blessed Sacrament entering the room, she sprang up suddenly and got on to her knees; her face was on fire with joy and love.

Her last Communion brought from her lips the final expression of love: 'My Bridegroom and my Saviour! The longed-for hour has come. It is time for our meeting, my Beloved, my Saviour. It is time for me to set out. Let us go, it is time. . . .'[4]

---

[1] MF quoted SEC, vol. II, p. 242.   [2] Idem.   [3] Idem.   [4] Idem.

When P. Antonio de Jesús asked her if she wanted them to take her body to Ávila, a smile played about her lips which had spoken in praise of joy as much as they had preached renouncement:

'Jesús! Is that a question one should ask, Father? Have I anything whatsoever of my own? Won't they give me the charity of a little earth here?' [1]

All through the night, which she passed in ecstatic bliss, she repeated over and over again the verse of a psalm; she who had so often declared that she did not want any 'Latin' nuns, said it in her own Castilian tongue: 'A sacrifice to God is an afflicted spirit. . . . A humble and contrite heart, O God, thou wilt not despise!' [2]

She repeatedly dwelt on the words 'contrite heart' and seemed to find pleasure in accentuating them.

At dawn on the following day, which was the feast of St Francis, she lay on her side 'in the position usually assigned to Mary Magdalene'; her sisters could thus see her; the wrinkles caused by age and sickness had disappeared; her face, transfigured, was so calm and radiant 'that it seemed like the moon at the full.' [3]

Those who had seen her in ecstasy said that she was in the presence of God.

Only once did her glance turn back towards the world; P. Antonio de Jesús had just ordered Ana de San Bartolomé to go and get something to eat—for several days the poor woman had had neither food nor sleep. The Mother opened her eyes anxiously and tried to turn her head as if looking for someone. Teresita understood and ran to call the little sister of the white veil. When she saw her come in the Foundress was at peace again, took hold of her hands and, with a smile which never left her, laid her head on her arms.

It was in this way, supported by a peasant woman of Castile, that she waited to be borne away beyond the Seventh Mansions by 'the impetuous eagle of God's Majesty.' [4]

Her body gave forth a wonderful fragrance.

She expired with three very faint and gentle moans.

The countenance of St Teresa of Jesus remained so beautiful and resplendent in death 'that it seemed like a radiant sun.' [5]

The Duchess of Alba had the body of her who had chosen to spend her life clad in frieze, covered with cloth of gold.

[1] Idem, p. 243.   [2] MF quoted SEC, vol. II, p. 243.   [3] Idem.
[4] SEC, E, xiv.   [5] MF quoted SEC, vol. II, p. 243.

EPILOGUE

ST TERESA OF JESUS

Her incorruptible body

AMONG the various accounts of the burial of Mother Teresa of Jesus, let us quote the few lines left by Ana de San Bartolomé:

> The day after her death, she was buried with full solemnity. Her body was put into a coffin: but such a heap of stones, bricks and chalk were put on top of it that the coffin gave way under the weight and all this rubble fell in. It was by the orders of the lady who endowed the house, Teresa de Layz, that the rubble was put there: nobody could prevent her, it seemed to her that by acting thus she was making all the more certain that no one would take Teresa's body away.[1]

But so delightful a fragrance was found to issue from Teresa of Jesus' tomb that the nuns longed to see the body of their Mother once more. They seized the opportunity of one of Gracián's visits to express their wish. Francisco de Ribera's account says:

> He approved and they began to remove the stones very secretly: there were so many that it took him and his companion four days. . . . The coffin was opened on 4th July 1583, nine months after the interment; they found the coffin lid smashed, half rotten and full of mildew, the smell of damp was very pungent. . . . The clothes had also fallen to pieces. . . . The holy body was covered with the earth which had penetrated into the coffin and so was all damp too, but as fresh and whole as if it had only been buried the day before.[2]

Here P. Grácian has added a note to P. Ribera's account:

> She was in such a perfect state of preservation that my companion, P. Cristóbal de San Alberto, and I retired while they undressed her; they called me back again when they had covered her with a sheet; uncovering her breasts, I was surprised to see how full and firm they were.[3]

---

[1] Quoted SEC, vol. II, p. 240.   [2] FR quoted SEC, Vol. II, p. 260.
[3] Quoted SEC, vol. II, p. 260, n. 5.

R. Ribera continues:

They undressed her almost entirely—for she had been buried in her habit—they washed the earth away, and there spread through the whole house a wonderful penetrating fragrance which lasted some days. . . . They put her into a new habit, wrapped her in a sheet and put her back into the same coffin. But before doing this, P. Provincial removed her left hand. . . . [1]

Here Gracián added a further note to P. Ribera's text:

I took the hand away wrapped in a coif and in an outer wrapping of paper; oil came from it. . . . I left it at Ávila in a sealed casket. . . . When I severed the hand, I also severed a little finger which I carry about on my person. . . . When I was captured the Turks took it from me, but I bought it back for some twenty reales and some gold rings. . . . [2]

But Ávila refused to be dispossessed of the body of such an illustrious citizen. Accordingly it was decreed at the chapter of Discalced friars that the body of Mother Teresa should be exhumed and taken to her native city: in order to prevent the Duke of Alba from raising obstacles, this was done secretly.

Canon Don Juan Carrillo, chancellor of the cathedral at Ávila, has left us an account of the proceedings, in which he took part:

P. Julian de Ávila and I set out very early on Friday, the 23rd of this month of November, 1585. The next day, Saturday, we arrived (at Alba) very early, as P. Gregorio Nacianceno had said we were to do. Before entering the city, I informed him of our arrival and he sent me word that we must enter the town secretly and with the greatest prudence and that I was to go and see him at seven in the evening at the inn where he was staying. I went and found him alone. P. Jerónimo Gracián who had arrived that day from Salamanca arrived shortly afterwards. We spoke of the way Our Lord had arranged everything, so that the translation of the holy Mother's body should take place at this particular time, and of the singular means he had used to remove from Alba all those likely to prevent it: not for years had the town been so deserted, the Duchess herself had left the day before. We decided to meet again the next day, Sunday, at the same place and time, and not to show ourselves till then. And so it was done.

That day . . . P. Gregorio, who was anxious to get the business done and was less timid than P. Gracián, came to the convent with him. The nuns begged to be allowed to see the holy body. At nightfall the two friars took it out of the coffin where it lay; they found

[1] FR, quoted SEC, vol. II, p. 260.　　[2] Idem, p. 261, nn. 1-2.

the habit and the linen which covered it in a very bad state. They took the holy body and put it where the sisters could see it, and all looked upon it with intense joy and satisfaction. When they had gone to recite Compline and Vigil—which, in their haste to get back again, they did so quickly that it was necessary to order them to say Matins in the choir upstairs, the Fathers remained alone with the prioress and sub-prioress and Juana del Espíritu Santo; and, since this seemed to them the time to do so, they notified all three of them of the letter from the chapter, decreeing that the holy body should be translated to St. Joseph of Ávila. This caused them very great distress and sorrow. The Fathers removed an arm. . . .[1]

P. Gregorio Nacianceno undertook to carry out the amputation. The following is P. Ribera's account of the operation:

> . . . with extreme repugnance—he has since told me that it was the greatest sacrifice he ever made for Our Lord—in fulfilment of his vow of obedience, he drew a knife which he was carrying in his belt . . . and inserted it under the left arm which was the one from which the hand was missing and which had been dislocated when the devil threw the holy Mother downstairs. Wonderful to relate: without using any more effort than in cutting a melon or a little fresh cheese, as he said, he severed the arm at the joints as easily as if he had spent some time beforehand trying to ascertain their exact position. And the body remained on one side, and the arm on the other.[2]

The body would not go into the trunk which the friars had brought. '. . . they therefore put the clothes on again and wrapped it in a covering of frieze. P. Gregorio took it up in his arms, and deposited it in a room opposite the convent.' P. Gracián followed. Julian de Ávila was waiting for them.

> . . . When they had deposited the holy body on the bed, P. Gracián uncovered it and we saw it just as it was when it was buried, not one hair missing, well covered with flesh from head to foot, the stomach and breasts as if they were not a corruptible substance, so much so that when one touched the flesh with the hand, it felt as flesh does when the death is recent, although lighter than it would have been in that case. The colour of the body was like that of the bladder-skins in which beef fat is put. The face was somewhat flattened, obviously the result of the large quantity of chalk, bricks and stones thrown upon the coffin when she was buried, but not at all broken. The odour coming from this holy body when one came quite close was extremely good and pleasant; it was not so strong as one moved farther away, but was the same odour. Nobody could

---

[1] Idem, p. 249   [2] Idem, p. 262.

say what it resembled. If it reminded one of anything at all, it was of clover, but very slightly. When we had seen this holy body and were completely satisfied with everything as I have related, we wrapped it, thus clothed, in a sheet and then in a covering of frieze, and after having well sewn and bound it up, we carried it over to the inn. . . .[1]

Gregorio Nacianceno and Julian de Avila spent the night 'in this great and holy company, and the perfume was such that when the body was placed on a mule between two bundles of straw for the return journey, the fragrance lingered in the room where it had been.'[2]

And so God's knight errant was once more journeying up hill and down dale, escorted by those who had been the faithful companions of her foundations. This was in November 1585, three years after her death.

We left Alba on the Monday, at four o'clock in the morning and the night . . . was as calm and warm as if it had been June. The weather was like that throughout our journey, until we got back to Ávila, about six o'clock in the evening.[3] The precious relic was handed to the sisters of St. Joseph's, who were just as overjoyed at having it as the nuns at Alba were distressed at losing it. . . .

Mother Teresa's body was laid reverently in a place where all the nuns could have the joy of coming close up to it. It was first of all in the chapter-house, wrapped in draperies very well arranged; then they made a long casket in the shape of a coffin, lined inside with black taffetas with trimmings of silk and of silver, covered on the outside with black velvet with trimmings of silk and gold, and with gilded studs, as well as gilded locks, bolts and keys; they put in two gold and silver shields, one with the coat of arms of the Order, the other with the most holy Name of Jesus. On this tomb was an inscription embroidered in gold and silver: 'Madre Teresa de Jesús.'[4]

The Bishop, Don Pedro Fernández de Temiño, was informed 'of the treasure he had in his city,' and he announced his intention of visiting the convent forthwith.

At nine o'clock, the Bishop, accompanied by about twenty people, including the judges, two doctors, P. Diego de Yepes and Julian de Ávila, came into the entrance porch; the door leading to the street was closed and Teresa of Jesus was laid on a carpet. The holy body was uncovered in the light of torches, and all kneeling, and bareheaded 'gazed at it with reverent awe and many tears.'[5]

---

[1] Idem, p. 250. [2] Idem. [3] Idem.
[4] FR quoted SEC, vol. II, pp. 262-3. [5] Idem, p. 263.

The doctors examined the body and decided that it was impossible that its condition could have a natural explanation, but that it was truly miraculous . . . . for after three years, without having been opened or embalmed, it was in such a perfect state of preservation that nothing was wanting to it in any way, and a wonderful odour issued from it.[1]

The Bishop forbade all those present to speak of the matter, under threat of excommunication. 'But they said: "Oh, what great marvels we have seen." These people had such a strong wish to describe what they had seen that the Bishop had to lift his excommunication and the facts were published all over the town.' [2]

When the news of the secret removal of St Teresa's body came to the ears of the Duke of Alba, he was exceedingly angry. He began by threatening the Carmelite nuns of Alba de Tormes with the gravest reprisals if they allowed the arm which had been left them as a consolation to be removed, and opened negotiations with Rome. He was powerful, and it was the destiny of the Mother Foundress that she must continue her journeys. His Holiness gave orders that her body was to be returned to the convent at Alba. It was removed once more 'in great secrecy' from the little convent of St Joseph's, transported clandestinely and brought back to Alba de Tormes.

It was in vain that P. Provincial stipulated 'that it was only a loan,' the holy remains of Mother Teresa of Jesus never came back to her native town. . . .

They were to be identified and exhibited many times yet. . . .

Ribera saw the body in 1588:

It is straight, although a little bent forward, as old people walk, and it is easy to see that she was of good stature. When one raises the body up, it is sufficient to support it with a hand behind the back for it to remain upright; one can dress and undress it as if it were living. . . . It is of the colour of dates. . . . The eyes are dry, but whole. The hairs are still on the moles she had on her face. . . . The feet are pretty, well proportioned. . . .

And good Ribera added:

It was such a great consolation for me to see this hidden treasure that I do not think I have spent a more wonderful day in all my life. . . . My only regret is to think that one day this body will be dismembered, at the entreaty of important personages or at the request of her convents. . . .[3]

---

[1] Idem.   [2] Idem, p. 264.   [3] FR quoted SEC, vol. II, pp. 266–7.

And so it was indeed.

The body of Mother Teresa of Jesus was dismembered and the parts sent to different places. The right foot and a piece of the upper jaw are in Rome, the left hand in Lisbon, the right hand, the left eye, fingers, fragments of flesh, scattered all over Spain and indeed over all christendom.

Her right arm and heart are in reliquaries at Alba de Tormes, with what remains of this perfect and incorruptible body.

Beatification and Canonization of Teresa of Jesus

As early as 1602, requests for the beatification of Teresa of Jesus began to pour in at Rome. In 1614, seventy galleons left Genoa under the command of the High Admiral of the Fleet, Don Carlos Doria: they were bringing the news of the Foundress's beatification, to Spain.

In 1622, Blessed Teresa became Saint Teresa of Jesus. During the canonization ceremony, doves and a multitude of other small birds were let loose in St Peter's.

In 1926, the Cortes nominated St Teresa patron of all the Spains. But Spain already had a patron in St James, and his clients caused the decree to be revoked. But if St Teresa has not this official glory, at least she retains the prestige non-officially.

In 1915, King Alfonso XIII, in a circular from the Ministry of War, declared St Teresa patron of the regiments and troops of the military commissariat. This was justly deserved recognition of the talent for administration of her whom the University of Salamanca had already christened the mystical doctor and on whom the Holy Father had conferred 'the honours of the Church.'

Housewives might also well take her as their patron, and so might the women of action of our twentieth century, all those who build, work, create; all those who hold friendship dear; all those who continue to hope, feeling the odds are against them.

For it is not one of St Teresa of Jesus' least merits to have shown that a personality which is to be sublime must be complete in every sense and that great saints are in no wise contemptuous of small virtues.

ANA DE JESÚS

It is to Ana de Jesús that we owe the *Spiritual Canticle* of St John of the Cross. He composed it at her request and dedicated it to her. In 1586, with him, she founded the convent of Discalced Carmelite nuns in Madrid.

She it was who collected the manuscripts of her whom Carmelites call 'the Holy Mother' for publication and gave them to Fray Luis de León. Accordingly the beautiful letter which prefaces the first edition of 1588 is addressed: 'Fray Luis de León, to the Mother Prioress Ana de Jesús and the Discalced Carmelite nuns of the convent of Madrid.'

Ana de Jesús was unmistakably an Egeria: it was at her request that Fray Luis wrote his *Commentary on the Book of Job*.

In 1591 she suffered the penalty of three years' confinement for having valiantly taken the part of P. Gracián who was attacked by Nicolás Doria.

In 1604, her superiors chose her as the most fitting person to go to France to introduce the Teresian spirit in the Carmelite convents which Mme Acarie was proposing to found. Bérulle came to fetch her. She founded the Carmels of Paris and Dijon, then, in 1607, went to the Low Countries where she founded the convent of Brussels.

There she found P. Gracián again and worked with him to get St Teresa's *Book of the Foundations* printed. It had not been possible to publish this at the same time as her other works.

Ana died at Brussels in 1621. Her cause for beatification was introduced in 1876.

ANA DE SAN BARTOLOMÉ

The faithful little lay-sister was likewise destined to go away and found Carmels in France. When she was obliged to accept the office of Foundress and prioress of the Pontoise Carmel, she had to consent, out of obedience, to take the black veil of the choir nuns.

She died at Antwerp on 7th June 1626 and was beatified on 6th May 1917.

ANTONIO DE JESÚS

P. Antonio de Jesús survived the Mother Foundress nineteen years. He died at Vélez Málaga, aged ninety-one.

THE PRINCESS OF ÉBOLI

The Princess of Éboli was arrested, on 28th July 1579, on the charge of complicity with Antonio Pérez, secretary to Philip II, in the assassination of Escobedo, secretary to Don Juan of Austria. She was imprisoned in the Pinto tower.

After a term of imprisonment in the castle of Santorcaz, she was finally imprisoned in her own home, at Pastrana, until her death in 1592.

Thus ended up Ana de Mendoza, at the age of fifty-two, the victim of her own intrigues. More than once, Teresa of Jesus told P. Jerónimo Gracián to go and see, comfort and cheer the woman who had done everything to ruin her.

JERÓNIMO GRACIÁN DE LA MADRE DE DIOS

The attacks against P. Gracián began with Teresa of Jesus' death. He was then Provincial of the Order, and, still naïve, still lacking in perspicacity, he sent Nicolás Doria to Rome. The latter took advantage of this to get himself appointed Pontifical agent, and, armed with this title, he immediately set up opposition against Gracián and his project of extending the Order to Africa. He did not hesitate to formulate such accusations against him that some demanded that the Provincial should be deposed.

This did not prevent Gracián himself from proposing to the chapter of 1585 P. Nicolás Doria de Jesús María's election as Provincial. There is no doubt about it, Gracián was a saint. . . . He was named Vicar Provincial in Portugal: this was to remove him from the scene of events and leave the field open to his enemies. P. Nicolás Doria did not hesitate to scheme until he was governing the Carmels of Spain in a way exactly opposite to Gracián's government and the Teresian tradition. That was why Teresa's most dearly loved daughters, like Ana de Jesús and María de San José, who were loyal to the Mother Foundress, were persecuted too.

The campaign of defamation, to which P. Jerónimo de la Madre de Dios' only answer was an angelic patience, led to his expulsion from the Order in 1591: they took Our Lady's habit away from him.

In secular clothes he left for Rome, where his efforts to overcome the hostility stirred up by Doria met with failure. He embarked for Naples, fell into the hands of the Turks, was taken to Tunis as a captive of the Pasha, loaded with chains and tattooed with crosses on the soles of his feet. For all this he did not cease his apostolate, 'converting Moors and renegades.' Ransomed in 1595, on his return to Rome Pope Clement VIII reinstated him in the Order of Carmel.

He lived in Belgium until his death in 1614. He invoked the name of Teresa of Jesus with his last breath, clasping her relics. (Based on: Fray Jerónimo Gracián de la Madre de Dios, *Discurso leido ante la Real Academia de España*, por el Excmo Señor Marqués de San Juan de Piedras Albas.)

SAINT JOHN OF THE CROSS

It was not until after the death of Teresa of Jesus that John of the Cross finished the greater part of his works on mysticism which had been begun in 1578: *Ascent of Mount Carmel, The Dark Night of the Soul, The Spiritual Canticle*. Prior of the monastery of Discalced Carmelite friars of Granada, he remained there more or less permanently until 1588, at which time he was appointed prior at Segovia.

He supported Gracián strongly against Doria's innovations and he suffered for it cruelly. Deprived of all offices and dignities at the beginning of 1591, he was ordered to retire to the desert of Peñuela.

He spent the last weeks of his life at Úbeda and died there on 14th December 1591, after great suffering, both physical and moral.

John of the Cross was canonized in 1726, and proclaimed a doctor of the Church by Pius XI in 1926.

His tomb is at Segovia.

MARÍA DE SAN JOSÉ

María de San José was sent to Portugal to found, in 1585, the Discalced Carmelite convent at Lisbon. For her loyalty to P. Gracián, in the conflict between him and Doria, she too reaped defamation, persecution, and the spending of nine months in prison. She was marked out to be one of the foundresses of the French Carmels, as being one of the most faithful continuers of the Teresian tradition, when she died at Cuerva, in the province of Toledo, in 1603.

CHRONOLOGY

1515 Birth of Teresa de Ahumada y Cepeda.

1519 Birth of Lorenzo.

1520 Birth of Antonio.

1521 Birth of Pedro.

1522 Teresa's flight with Rodrigo.

1527 Birth of Agustín.

1528 Birth of Juana. Death of Doña Beatriz de Ahumada.

1531 Teresa enters the convent of Our Lady of Grace as a boarder.

1532 Fernando sets sail overseas. Teresa ill, returns home.

1515 Wolsey made a Cardinal. Henry VIII appoints him Lord Chancellor.

1516 Accession of Charles V.

1519 Luther breaks with Rome. Charles V Emperor of Germany.

1519-21 Conquest of Mexico by Cortés.

1520 Field of the Cloth of Gold. *Comuneros'* rising.

1521 Excommunication of Luther. Discovery of the Philippine Islands.

1522 Capture of Rhodes by the Turks. Cortés, Captain General of New Spain. Return to Spain of Magellan's expedition. Conquest of Milan.

1523 Clement VII (Julian de Medici) elected Pope.

1524 Pizarro with the Incas. Alonso de Madrid's *Arte de servir a Dios*.

1527 Birth of Philip II. Sack of Rome by Imperial troops. The Pope prisoner at Sant' Angelo.

1527-54 Osuna's *Abecedario Espiritual*.

1527 Erasmus' doctrine examined by the council of Valladolid.

1528 Famine in Castile.

1529 Beginning of Henry's 'Royal Divorce,' Fall of Wolsey. Sir Thomas More Chancellor.

1530 Francisco Pizarro in Madrid to ask the favour of continuing the conquest of Peru. Intellectual Spain divided between Erasmites and anti-Erasmites. Renewal of the measures against the *Alumbrados*.

1531 Philip II at Ávila.

1531-41 Conquest of Peru and Chile.

1532 Pizarro crosses the Andes and takes Atahualpa prisoner.

1533 Henry VIII 'marries' Anne Boleyn.

1534 Charles V in Ávila. Paul III (Alexander Farnese) elected Pope.

1534 Acts of Succession and Supremacy. Henry declared head of English Church. Break with Rome.

1535 Rodrigo leaves for overseas.

1535 B. de Laredo's *Subida del Monte Sion.*

1535 The Carthusians, St John Fisher and St Thomas More suffer martyrdom.

1536 Teresa enters the Convent of the Incarnation, taking the habit on 2nd November.

1536 End of the Conquest of Peru.

1536 First suppression of monasteries in England, and Pilgrimage of Grace.

1537 Teresa professed on 3rd November. She falls seriously ill.

1538 Departure for Castellanos de la Cañada and the treatment at Becedas. She is believed dead.

1538 Excommunication of Henry VIII.

1539 Death of Empress Isabella. Conversion of St Francis Borgia. Mercator's map of the world. The Jesuits organized.

1539 Final Dissolution of the monasteries in England.

1540 Lorenzo, Jerónimo and Pedro embark for Peru. Teresa's cure.

1540 St John of God founds the Brothers of Charity.

1541 Philip II invested with the government of all the Spains. Barbarossa crushes the Spaniards.

1542 Birth of St John of the Cross. Copernicus: *De Revolutionibus.*

1543 Death of Don Alonso de Cepeda.

1543 Garcilaso de la Vega's *Eglogas.*

1545 Opening of the Council of Trent.

1546 Antonio's death at Iñaquito.

1546 Trial of Magdalena de la Cruz.

1547 Death of Henry VIII. Accession of Edward VI.
Birth of Cervantes.

1549 Charles V separates the Low Countries from the Empire.

1549 First Act of Uniformity and Book of Common Prayer.

1552 Second Act of Uniformity and Book of Common Prayer.

1553 St Teresa's re-conversion.

1553 Death of Edward VI and accession of Mary Tudor.

1554 Meeting of St Teresa and St Francis Borgia.

1554 England reconciled to Holy See by Cardinal Pole. Marriage of Philip II and Mary Tudor.

1554 Jesuits in Ávila. Fray Luis de Granada's *Libro de oración y meditación*.

1555 Abdication of Charles V and retirement to Yuste.

1556 Marcel II Pope, then Paul V. Accession of Philip II. Fr. Luis de Granada's *Guía de Pecadores*. Death of Ignatius Loyola.

1557 Rodrigo's death in Chile.

1557 War with France. Battle of St Quentin.

1558 Meeting of St Teresa and St Peter of Alcántara.

1558 Destruction of Spanish protestantism. Archbishop of Toledo tried by the Inquisition. Death of Charles V.

1558 Death of Mary Tudor. Accession of Elizabeth.

1559 Spaniards forbidden to study in foreign universities. Auto-dafé in Valladolid. Pius IV Pope. Acts of Supremacy and Uniformity in England.

1560 St Teresa and her friends decide to found a Carmelite convent in conformity with the primitive Rule of the Order.

1560 Marriage of Philip II with Elizabeth of Valois. Philip II moves his court to Madrid.
The Inquisition at Toledo and Seville.

1561 Work for the future convent put in hand.

1561 Birth of Góngora. Fr. Luis de Granada's *Memorial de la vida cristiana*.

1562 St Teresa at Toledo with Doña Luisa de la Cerda. June—she finishes the first draft of the *Autiobography*. July—she returns to Ávila. August 24th—foundation of the convent of St Joseph, immediate return to the convent of the Incarnation.

1562 Death of St Peter of Alcántara. Birth of Lope de Vega.

1563 St Teresa finally leaves the Incarnation, for St Joseph's.

1563 Close of the Council of Trent. Rise of the Low Countries against Spain.

1565 Fernando's death in Colombia.

1565 Birth of Mme Acarie.

1567 P. Rubeo arrives in Ávila. He gives St Teresa patents to found houses of friars and nuns. August 15th, foundation of the

1567 Spanish terror in the Low Countries.

convent of Medina del Campo. First meeting with St John of the Cross.

1568 Drawing up of the Constitutions of the Discalced Carmelites. April 11th, foundation of the convent of Malagón. August 15th, foundation of the convent of Valladolid. November 28th, foundation by St John of the Cross of the first convent of Discalced friars at Duruelo.

1569 May 14th, foundation of the convent of Toledo. June 28th, foundation at Pastrana of the convent of Discalced Carmelite nuns; July 13th, foundation of the monastery of Discalced friars there.

1570 Foundation of the convent of Salamanca on Michaelmas day.

1571 January 25th, foundation of convent of Alba de Tormes. St Teresa prioress of convent of Medina del Campo. October 6th, she is imposed as prioress at the Incarnation.

1572 St John of the Cross chaplain to the convent of the Incarnation. St Teresa begins to compose the *Conceptos del Amor de Dios.*

1573 St Teresa signs and attests as correct the copy of the *Camino de Perfección.* Gracián professed at Pastrana. Princess of Eboli enters the convent of Pastrana as a nun. St Teresa begins the *Foundations.*

1574 March 19th, foundation of the convent of Segovia.

1575 February 24th, foundation of Beas. First meeting with Gracián. Beginning of struggle between Discalced and Calced. Opening of General Chapter of the Order at Piacenza. May 29th, foundation of convent of

1568-70 Revolt of the Moriscos in Andalusia; its repression by Don John of Austria.

1568 Mary, Queen of Scots, flees to England and is held prisoner by Elizabeth until 1587.

1569 Northern rebellion in England.

1570 Alliance of the Pope, Spain and Venice, against the Turks. Pius V excommunicates Elizabeth.

1571 Moriscos crushed and dispersed to all parts of Spain. Victory of Lepanto.

1571 Laws against Catholics in England made more severe.

1572 Gregory VII Pope. Fray Luis de León a prisoner of the Inquisition.

1573 Don John of Austria seizes Bizerta.

Seville. P. Á. de Salazar notifies St Teresa of the General's decision: she must retire to one convent and make no more foundations.

1576 Foundation of the convent of Caravaca by Ana de San Alberto. June 4th, St Teresa leaves Seville for the convent of Toledo. Continues the *Foundations*, writes *Modo de visitar los Conventos*. The persecution becomes more intense.

1577 June 2nd, St Teresa begins to write the *Interior Castle*. At the end of July she arrives in Ávila. Excommunication of fifty nuns of the convent of the Incarnation. November 5th, St Teresa finishes the *Interior Castle*. Night of December 3rd–4th, capture of St John of the Cross. December 24th, St Teresa falls and breaks her arm.

1578 Death of P. Rubeo, Carmelite Master General. A decree of Sega, the Nuncio, puts the Discalced under the authority of the Calced. The most troubled year for the Reform.

1579 Sega withdraws from the provincials of the Mitigation their power over the Discalced. End of the persecutions.

1580 February 2nd, foundation of the convent of Villanueva de la Jara. St Teresa seriously ill in Toledo and in Valladolid. Death of Lorenzo de Cepeda. December 29th, foundation of the convent of Palencia.

1581 Philip II gives the necessary instructions for the execution of the brief of erection of Discalced and Mitigated into separate provinces. The chapter of Alcalá confirms the Constitutions of the convents of Discalced. June

1576 El Greco comes to Toledo. Don John of Austria, governor of the Low Countries.

1577 Pope Gregory XIII puts in hand the revision of plain-chant.
1577 Cuthbert Mayne, first martyr of the seminary priests, is executed at Launceston.

1578 Assassination of Escobedo by Antonio Pérez. Death of Don John of Austria.

1579 Arrest and imprisonment of Antonio Pérez and the Princess of Eboli.

1580 Philip II is recognized as King of Portugal.
1580 First Jesuits, Edmund Campion and others, arrive in England. Beginning of active and violent persecution of Catholics that continued to the end of the reign.

14th, foundation of the convent
of Soria. St Teresa elected prioress of St Joseph's at Ávila. The
Constitutions printed.

1582 April 19th, inauguration of the   1582 Gregory XIII reforms the calen-
convent of Burgos. October   dar.
4th, at 9 o'clock in the evening,
death of St Teresa at Alba de
Tormes.

[This chronology, established by the author from two sources:
  1. That included by the Paris Carmelites in their translation of the
     Works of St Teresa of Jesus (some dates revised after P. Silverio);
  2. *Chronologie des Civilisations*, by Jean Delorme;
has been adapted for English readers. Some events, *e.g.* those of special
interest to France, have been omitted and important happenings in
England added—Tr.]

When we look at the events of the period, we see that the actions
and writings of St Teresa of Jesus are in perfect harmony with the times
in which she lived.

She has carried over to the spiritual plane the great conquests of
the time. She found the passage joining contemplation and action, as
Magellan found the strait joining two oceans. She drew up the chart
of the spiritual universe as Mercator did that of the globe.

St Teresa of Jesus loved music although she sang out of tune,
and although she established the use in her Carmels of the recitative
for Office. But both she and her daughters made up for this at recreation: the tradition has remained and both music and poetry are a
normal accompaniment of recreation in the Carmels of Spain. I
therefore asked M. Roland-Manuel to be kind enough to give me
the few essential dates of importance for music in Spain at the time of
St Teresa. The notes which he has sent me are so interesting that I do
not hesitate, with his permission, to publish them in full. I am deeply
grateful to him for this.

When St Teresa entered the Incarnation convent, she would
probably know and must have heard the worldly music of the
vihuelistas. The *vihuela* is the Spanish lute, an instrument which
filled the rôle the piano fills to-day. It was both a solo instrument
and used to accompany *canciónes, villancicos* and *ensaladas*. Albums of
music by Luis Milán of Valencia, Narváez, Mudarra and Fuenllana
begin to appear from about 1536; but these are albums probably well
known. (Luis Milán, 1536; Narváez, 1538; Mudarra, 1546; Fuenllana, 1554.)

At this time, too, our Doña Teresa de Ahumada would probably hear the organ pieces of Antonio de Cabezón, the Spanish Bach, who is obviously her contemporary (1510-1556).

For directly religious music, our saint would know the great masters of vocal polyphony of Spain and the Christian world. Escobedo, who lived at Segovia, was born in 1500. The great Morales who demanded of music that it should give to life 'nobility and austerity' was almost a contemporary: 1512-1553. Guerrero, the gentle lover of baroque, was born in 1528 and died in 1600. And we should not forget the great theoretical and practical musician, Salinas (1512-1590), who inspired Fray Luis de León with the famous ode:

Música que es la fuente y la primera. . . .

Finally, Tomé Luis de Victoria was her fellow-citizen. Born between 1535 and 1540, he died in Madrid in 1611.

Sentimental historians would always like it to be true that these great minds met. They cannot make such a meeting likely, however. Victoria left for Rome about 1565. At that time he was quite unknown and had published nothing. He only returned to Spain a year after the saint's death, in 1583.

To excite our imagination there remains the fact that this man, of whom one knows almost nothing, came from a family which lived in the parish of San Juan in Ávila, the same parish as our saint.

There also remains chapter xxix of the *Foundations*:

' . . . An ecclesiastic who accompanied us, named Porras, a great servant of God, said Mass, and another friend of the Valladolid nuns, Agustín de Vitoria, who had lent me money to get what was necessary for the house, and had been very kind to us on the way. . . .'

The brother of our Victoria was called Agustín and was a priest: were they the same?

ROLAND-MANUEL

The first time that the Foundress mentions this Agustín de Vitoria is in 1577, in a letter to Maria Bautista, prioress of Valladolid. The name of the musician is frequently spelt Vitoria, and he used to put after it, as if it were a title to fame, 'of Ávila.'

It is probable that St Teresa of Ávila and Tomé Luis Victoria, of Ávila, never met, but all the same it is touching to think that they were both baptized in the baptistery of San Juan, and that in his compositions the musician expressed that longing for the divine which the Mother Foundress of Carmel extolled in her writings and lived to the full in her deeds.

BIBLIOGRAPHY

THERE is no fact in this work which is not in strict conformity with historical truth. There is not a word attributed to St Teresa which she did not in fact either write or utter. Thus, if I were to quote all my sources as they came, every page would be overloaded with references: this would give the book a forbidding appearance, little to the taste of her whom it is my chief wish to please: St Teresa of Jesus herself. She valued pedantry so little that she declared she did not want any 'Latin nuns' in her convents. Thus instead of emphasizing the considerable work of documentation which has been carried out, I have rather striven to remove the traces of it, in order that the account may appear as supple and, I hope, lively and pleasant, as possible.

Thus, only references to quoted passages are given, to permit of reference to the Spanish text. As I have re-translated all the extracts myself, such references are those of the works and letters of St Teresa in Spanish (editions of P. Silverio de Santa Teresa, Burgos):

Shorter edition, in one volume.

Critical edition of the *Complete Works*, in nine volumes.

I have chosen the Shorter edition wherever possible, its numbered paragraphs facilitating research.

As is permissible when incorporating a quotation in a text, I have sometimes changed the tense of the verb, or made a few very slight modifications which do not alter the meaning of the sentence or falsify the personality of its author.

I group my sources below under classifications numbered I to IV, according to their importance for my documentation.

I. SOURCES

The complete works of St Teresa of Jesus in the two editions indicated above.

II. WRITINGS AND DECLARATIONS OF ST TERESA'S CONTEMPORARIES

María de San José: *El libro de recreaciones. El ramillete de mirra.*

Jerónimo Gracián de la Madre de Dios: *Obras completas.*

Diego de Yepes: *Vida, virtudes y milagros de la Bienaventurada Virgen Teresa de Jesús. Relación de la vida y libros de la Madre Teresa que el P. Diego de Yepes remitió al P. Fr. Luis de León.*

V. M. Ana de San Bartolomé: *Autobiografía.*

P. Crisóstomo Henríquez: *Vie de la Vénérable Mère Anne de Saint-Barthélémy.*

Julian de Ávila: *Vida de Santa Teresa de Jesús.*

Francisco de Ribera: *La vida de la Madre Teresa.*

Fr. Luis de León: *Vida, muerte, virtudes y milagros de la Santa Madre Teresa de Jesús.*

Procesos de beatificación y canonización de Santa Teresa de Jesús (Editorial Monte Carmelo, Burgos).

And all the documents and accounts published by P. Silverio de Santa Teresa in the notes and appendices of his critical edition.

III. WORKS OF PRIMARY IMPORTANCE

P. Silverio de Santa Teresa: *Vida de Santa Teresa* (5 vols.)

Fr. Gabriel de Jesús: *La Santa de la Raza* (4 vols.)

Historia del Carmel (Ed. Monte Carmelo, Burgos), tomos 1-2-3-4.

D. Manuel María Polit: *La familia de Santa Teresa en América.*

Anonymous: *Les Parents de Ste Thérèse, Alfonso Sánchez de Cepeda et Beatriz de Ahumada* (Ed. Carmel of Mongalose).

Paris Carmelites: *Notes et appendices de la traduction française des œuvres completes.*

IV. WORKS CONSULTED

Read by St Teresa herself, or writings of contemporary mystics.

Osuna: *Abecedario.*

Bernardino de Laredo: *Subida del Monte Sion.*

Alonso de Madrid: *Arte de servir a Dios.*

S. Pedro de Alcántara: *Tratado de la oración y meditación.*

Ignatius of Loyola: *Ejercicios espirituales.*

Antonio de Guevara: *Oratorio de religiosos y ejercicios virtuosos.*

Alonso de Orozco: *Obras.*

A. de Cabrera: *Sermones.*

Fr. Luis de Granada: *Libro de la oración y meditación.*

San Juan de la Cruz: *Obras completas.*

Works entirely devoted to St Teresa.

History of St Teresa, after the Bollandists.

R. P. Léon (Van Hove), *La joie chez Sainte Thérèse.*

L'Espagne thérèsienne ou le pélérinage d'un Flamand à toutes les fondations de Sainte Thérèse (album of pictures).

R. Hoornaert: *Sainte Thérèse écrivain, son milieu, ses facultés, son œuvre.*

E. Allison Peers: *Works of St Teresa of Jesus. Letters of St Teresa of Jesus.*

Sánchez Moguel: *El lenguaje de Santa Teresa de Jesús.*

G. Etchegoyen: *L'amour divin, essai sur les sources de Sainte Thérèse.*

A. Lepée: *Sainte Thérèse et le réalisme chrétien.*

P. Lafond: *Quelques portraits de familiers de Sainte Thérèse.*

M. Legendre: *Sainte Thérèse d'Ávila.*

F. M. de T.: *La Mujer grande.*

E. Marquina: *Pasos y trabajos de Santa Teresa de Jesús.*

Works not entirely devoted to St Teresa, but important.

J. Baruzi: *Saint Jean de la Croix et le problème de l'expérience mystique.*

P. Bruno de J. M.: *Saint Jean de la Croix. Madame Acarie. L'Espagne mystique.*

Études Carmelitaines: *Amour et Violence* (the struggle between Gracián and Doria).

E. Allison Peers: *Spanish Mysticism.*

F. de Ros: *Francisco de Osuna. Bernardino de Laredo.*

P. Emeterio de J. M.: *Ensayo sobre la lírica carmelitana. Mística y novela.*

Hermano Timóteo Garcia: *Santuario y monasterio de N. S. de la Calle.*

P. Vicente B. de Heredia: *Dominicos de Castilla.*

La Puente: *Vida del P. Baltasar Alvarez.*

Jerónimo de San José: *El don que tuvo San Juan de la Cruz para llevar las almas a Dios.*

Marqués de San Juan de Piedras Albas: *Fr. Jerónimo Gracián de la Madre de Dios.*

J. Turmel: *Histoire du Diable.*

R. Picard: *Notes et Matériaux pour l'étude du Socratisme chrétien chez Sainte Thérèse et les spirituels espagnols.*

R. Menéndez Pidal: *La Lengua de Cristóbal Colón.*

Bergson: *Les deux sources de la morale et de la religion.*

Arvède Barine: *Portraits de femmes.*

Condesa de Pardo Bazán: *Cuadros religiosos.*

Barbey d'Aurévilly: *L'internelle consolation.*

Huysmans: *En route. L'oblat.*

V. HISTORICAL WORKS

Menéndez Pelayo: *Historia de los heterodoxos españoles.*

M. Bataillon: *Érasme et l'Espagne. Introduction au 'Roman picaresque'.*

Llorente: *Historia crítica de la Inquisición de España.*

M. de la Pinta: *Carceles inquisitoriales.*

R. Altamira: *Historia de España y civilización española.*

H. Ch. Lea: *A History of the Inquisition in Spain.*

Melgares Marin: *Procedimientos de la Inquisición.*

Sabatini: *Torquemada.*

Prescott: *The Incas and the Conquest of Peru.*

M. Legendre: *Nouvelle Histoire d'Espagne.*

A. Mousset: *Histoire d'Espagne.*

C. Cardo: *Histoire spirituelle des Espagnes.*

A. de Brunel: *Voyage en Espagne.*

Ranke: *Spain under Charles V, Philip II and Philip III.*

Pfandl: *Philippe II.*

F. de los Rios: *Religión y estado en la España del Siglo XVI.*

R. Schneider: *Philippe II.*

Gregorio Marañón: *Antonio Pérez.*

A. Marichalar: *Las Cadenas del Duque de Alba.*

F. Rodriguez Marín, T. IX and X of the *nueva edición crítica* of *El Ingenioso hidalgo don Quijote de la Mancha.*

Ticknor: *Spanish Literature.*

J. Hurtado, J. de la Seriña, A. González Palencia: *Historia de la literatura española.*

J. M. Quadrado: *España* (vol. 'Salamanca, Ávila, Segovia').

P. Sandoval: *Vida y hechos del Emperador Carlos Quinto.*

E. Ballesteros: *Estudio histórico de Ávila y su territorio.*

B. García Arias: *Recuerdos históricos de Ávila.*

M. Foronda: *Carlos Quinto en Ávila.*

T. Dudon: *Saint Ignace de Loyola.*

VI. CUSTOMS OF THE SIXTEENTH CENTURY

F. Antonio de Guevara: *Epistolas familiares.*

Diego Hermosilla: *Diálogo de pajes.*

A. Valbuena Prat: *La vida española en la edad de oro.*

Fr. Luis de León: *La perfecta casada.*

Malón de Chaide: *La conversión de la Magdalena.*

Baltasar Gracián: *El Criticón.*

The facts which I have used to write this account of the life of St Teresa have all been taken from sources I and II.

INDEX

Lightning Source UK Ltd.
Milton Keynes UK
UKOW05f0101180714

235324UK00001B/82/P